THE BACKGROUND AND CONTENT
OF PAUL'S CULTIC
ATONEMENT METAPHORS

Society of Biblical Literature

Academia Biblica

Saul M. Olyan,
Hebrew Bible/Old Testament Editor

Mark Allan Powell,
New Testament Editor

Number 19

THE BACKGROUND AND CONTENT
OF PAUL'S CULTIC
ATONEMENT METAPHORS

THE BACKGROUND AND CONTENT OF PAUL'S CULTIC ATONEMENT METAPHORS

Stephen Finlan

Society of Biblical Literature
Atlanta

THE BACKGROUND AND CONTENT OF PAUL'S CULTIC ATONEMENT METAPHORS

Copyright © 2004 by the Society of Biblical Literature

All rights reserved. No part of this work may be reproduced or transmitted in any form or by any means, electronic or mechanical, including photocopying and recording, or by means of any information storage or retrieval system, except as may be expressly permitted by the 1976 Copyright Act or in writing from the publisher. Requests for permission should be addressed in writing to the Rights and Permissions Office, Society of Biblical Literature, 825 Houston Mill Road, Atlanta, GA 30329, USA.

Library of Congress Cataloging-in-Publication Data

Finlan, Stephen.
  The background and content of Paul's cultic atonement metaphors / by Stephen Finlan.
    p. cm. — (Academia Biblica ; no. 19)
  Includes bibliographical references and index.
  ISBN 1-58983-152-7 (paper binding : alk. paper)
  1. Bible. N.T. Epistles of Paul—Theology. 2. Atonement—History of doctrines—Early church, ca. 30-600. 3. Bible. N.T. Epistles of Paul—Language, Style. 4. Metaphor in the Bible. I. Title. II. Series: Academia Biblica (Series) (Society of Biblical Literature) ; no. 19.

BS2655.A7F56 2004
227'.06—dc22
                                          2004020653

Printed in the United States of America
on acid-free paper

To

my patient advisor

at the University of Durham,

Dr. Stephen C. Barton,

and to

Prof. James Dunn.

Also to Prof. Markus Bockmuehl

at the University of Cambridge.

Table of Contents

Abbreviations xi
Standards xii

Introduction: Cultic Metaphors in Paul 1
    Keys to Paul 2
    Conflation of Metaphors 5
    Spiritualization 6
    Material for Soteriological Metaphors 8
    The Scope of This Study 9

1. The Logic of Sacrifice 11
    1.1 Theories of Sacrifice 12
        1.1.1 Tylor: Sacrifice as Gift 12
        1.1.2 Smith—Sacrifice and Tribal Identity 15
        1.1.3 Hubert and Mauss 16
        1.1.4 Bloch's Theory 19
        1.1.5 Douglas on Impurity 21
        1.1.6 Sacred Violence: Girard and Hamerton-Kelly 23
        1.1.7 Assessment and Theory 27
    1.2 Hebrew Sacrifice 29
        1.2.1 Temple Purification 31
        1.2.2 The Meanings of כפר 36
        1.2.3 The Logic of Kipper 40
        1.2.4 An Intercultural Theory of Sacrifice 44
    1.3 Spiritualization 47
        1.3.1 Levels of Spiritualization 47
            1.3.1.1 The First Four Levels 47
            1.3.1.2 Rejection of Sacrifice 51
            1.3.1.3 Spiritualization as Transformation 60
        1.3.2 The Meanings of Spiritualization 61
        1.3.3 Spiritualization of Rites 64
        1.3.4 A Spiritualized Theory of Sacrifice 66
        1.3.5 Typology 68
    1.4 Paul's Sacrificial Typology 70

2. Curse Transmission Rituals and Paul's Imagery 73
  2.1 The Ritual Practice 75
    2.1.1 Curse Transmission in the OT 75
    2.1.2 Gentile Expulsion Rituals 77
    2.1.3 Purification and Separation 80
  2.2 Analyzing Expulsion Ritual 81
    2.2.1 Distinguishing Expulsion Ritual From Sacrifice 81
    2.2.2 Allegations of Sin-bearing in Sacrifice 84
    2.2.3 The Different Laying-on of Hands Gestures 86
    2.2.4 Blended Concepts of Atonement 93
  2.3 Paul's Usage 96
    2.3.1 The Insistence on One Model 96
    2.3.2 Gentile Expulsion Terms in 1 Corinthians 4:13 97
    2.3.3 The Scapegoat Image in 2 Corinthians 5:21 98
    2.3.4 Galatians 3:13 101
      2.3.4.1 McLean on Curse-Transfer 102
      2.3.4.2 Explanatory Limitations of the Deuteronomic Curse ... 103
      2.3.4.3 The Incorporative Messiah's Death 107
      2.3.4.4 Elliott: Curses in Galatia; Paul's Dual Audience 108
      2.3.4.5 Summary 110
    2.3.5 The Body of Sin 111
    2.3.6 Romans 8:3 114
    2.3.7 Participation and Atonement 116
  2.4 Post-Pauline Usages 119
  2.5 Conclusion 120

3. The Sacrificial Metaphor in Romans 3:25 123
  3.1 Meanings of ἱλαστήριον in the Literature 124
    3.1.1 The Mercy Seat 125
    3.1.2 Two Different Meanings 126
    3.1.3 Pagan Usage 129
    3.1.4 A Jewish Hellenistic Usage 131
    3.1.5 Anarthrous Occurrence of ἱλαστήριον 132
    3.1.6 ἱλαστήριον in Ezekiel and Amos 133
  3.2 Linguistic Relatives of ἱλαστήριον 135
    3.2.1 Dodd's Argument for Expiation 136
    3.2.2 Critics of Dodd's Position 138
  3.3 The Meaning of ἱλαστήριον in Context in Romans 3 140
    3.3.1 Translation Choices 141
    3.3.2 The Implied Ritual Action 142
    3.3.3 A ἱλαστήριον of Faith? 145
    3.3.4 Bailey on Christ as Center of a New Sanctuary 149
    3.3.5 Revelation at the Shrine 153
    3.3.6 The Place of Synecdoche 155

3.4 Justification in the Sequence of Salvation 157
3.5 The Place of Cultic Formulas 160

4. Redemption and Substitution 163
    4.1 The Usage of ἀπολύτρωσις in Romans 3 164
        4.1.1 Lexical Background 164
        4.1.2 Paul's Usage 166
    4.2 New Identity in Sonship 169
    4.3 Substitution and Aqedah Themes in Romans 5-8 170
    4.4 Notions of Representation and Substitution in Isaiah 53 174
    4.5 Kinds of Redemption 178
    4.6 Correcting the Atonement: Inclusive Place-Taking 179
    4.7 Paul's Attitude Toward Cult 185
    4.8 Spiritualizing Strategies 187
    4.9 Conclusion 190

5. Martyrology and Metaphor 193
    5.1 Martyrological Soteriology 193
        5.1.1 The "Dying Formula" 194
        5.1.2 The Effective Death Motif in Maccabean Literature 197
        5.1.3 The Usage of ἱλαστήριον in *Fourth Maccabees* 200
        5.1.4 Paul's Martyrology 204
        5.1.5 A Standardized Martyrological Formula in Romans? 205
        5.1.6 Williams: The Dominance of *Fourth Maccabees* 207
    5.2 Six Soteriological Metaphors and A Literal Model 211
    5.3 Cultic Thinking 213
        5.3.1 Primacy of the Cultic Metaphor 213
        5.3.2 Is Paul's Thinking "Fundamentally Cultic"? 216
    5.4 Formulas of Salvation 221

Conclusion 225

Bibliography 231

Index of Modern Authors 251

Index of Ancient Texts 255

Abbreviations

AB	Anchor Bible
ABD	*Anchor Bible Dictionary*
ACCS	Ancient Christian Commentary on Scripture
AGJU	Arbeiten zur Geschichte des antiken Judentums und des Urchristentums
ANE	Ancient Near East
Ant.	*Antiquities of the Jews* (Josephus)
ANRW	*Aufstieg und Niedergang der Römischen Welt*
ATR	*Anglican Theological Review*
BAGD	*A Greek-English Lexicon of the New Testament and Other Early Christian Literature*, eds. W. Bauer, Arndt, Gingrich, and Danker
B.C.E.	Before Common Era
BJS	Brown Judaic Studies
BTB	*Biblical Theology Bulletin*
CBQ	*Catholic Biblical Quarterly*
C.E.	Common Era
CH	*Corpus Hermeticum*
CTQ	*Concordia Theological Quarterly*
DSS	Dead Sea Scrolls
ETL	*Ephemerides theologicae lovanienses*
EvQ	*Evangelical Quarterly*
ExpT	*Expository Times*
GRBS	*Greek, Roman, and Byzantine Studies*
HB	Hebrew Bible
HR	*History of Religions*
HTR	*Harvard Theological Review*
HUCA	*Hebrew Union College Annual*
ICC	International Critical Commentary
JBL	*Journal of Biblical Literature*
JJS	*Journal of Jewish Studies*
JRS	*Journal of Roman Studies*
JSJ	*Journal for the Study of Judaism*
JSJ Sup	*Journal for the Study of Judaism*, Supplement Series
JSNT	*Journal for the Study of the New Testament*
JSNT Sup	*Journal for the Study of the New Testament*, Supplement Series
JSOT Sup	*Journal for the Study of the Old Testament*, Supplement Series
JSS	*Journal of Semitic Studies*

JTS	*Journal of Theological Studies*
J.W.	*The Jewish War* (Josephus)
KJV	King James Version
LCL	Loeb Classical Library
LSJ	*A Greek-English Lexicon*, eds. H. G. Liddell and R. Scott, rev. H. S. Jones, 1940
MT	Masoretic Text
n.s.	new series
NAB	New American Bible
NASB	New American Standard Bible
NIV	New International Version
NJB	New Jerusalem Bible
NovTSup	*Novum Testamentum*, Supplement Series
NRSV	New Revised Standard Version
NTS	*New Testament Studies*
o.s.	old series
OTP	*The Old Testament Pseudepigrapha*, ed. James Charlesworth
PRSt	*Perspectives in Religious Studies*
RSV	Revised Standard Version
SBLDS	Society of Biblical Literature Dissertation Series
SBLSP	*Society of Biblical Literature Seminar Papers*
SJLA	Studies in Judaism in Late Antiquity
SJT	*Scottish Journal of Theology*
SR	*Studies in Religion/Sciences Religieuses*
SNTSMS	Society for New Testament Studies Monograph Series
TDNT	*Theological Dictionary of the New Testament*
TDOT	*Theological Dictionary of the Old Testament*
TNIV	Today's New International Version
VT	*Vetus Testamentum*
WBC	Word Biblical Commentary
WMANT	Wissenschaftliche Monographien zum Alten und Neuen Testament
WUNT	Wissenschaftliche Untersuchungen zum Neuen Testament
ZAW	*Zeitschrift für die Alttestamentliche Wissenschaft*
ZNW	*Zeitschrift für die Neutestamentliche Wissenschaft*

Standards

Except where indicated, NRSV is the translation of the Bible used throughout.

The formatting guidelines in *SBL Handbook of Style* (Peabody, Mass.: Hendrickson, 1999) are followed.

Passages quoted from German and French authors are my translations, if the title in the footnote is in German or French. If the title given in the footnote is in English, then I have used that published English translation.

Introduction:
Cultic Metaphors in Paul

Paul makes use of cultic and social metaphors to describe the soteriological significance of the death of Christ. The cultic metaphors picture the death of Christ as either a sacrifice or an expulsion ritual that eliminates or carries away sin. The social metaphors describe the beneficial aftereffects, for believers, of this saving event. The social images (redemption, reconciliation, adoption, justification) make metaphorical use of transactions that move people from a negative social or interpersonal condition to a positive one: from slavery to freedom, from alienated to reconciled, from stranger to son, from condemned to acquitted. These metaphors that involve a change of social status or interpersonal standing, promise rich possibilities for sociological analysis. This dissertation, however, will pay more attention to the theological implications—that is, the *concepts of God*—wrapped up in the cultic metaphors, as well as in the redemption metaphor, which is also used to describe the death of Christ. The redemption[1] metaphor can be used both to describe the saving event and its beneficial aftereffects.

My main interest is to comprehend the background and content of Paul's soteriological metaphors, and explicate the attitudes of God implied in this teaching.

Paul's soteriological reasoning is by no means clear to modern (or postmodern) interpreters. The death of Jesus has cultic or social effectiveness, according to the metaphors Paul deploys, but exactly *how* these transactions are understood to work, still needs explication. This has too often been undertaken without sufficient attention to the metaphysical logic of Paul's metaphors, especially the implied logic of the rituals he uses metaphorically. Therefore

---

[1] The key term, ἀπολύτρωσις (Rom 3:24), usually refers to the manumission or purchase of slaves (David Hill, *Greek Words and Hebrew Meanings: Studies in the Semantics of Soteriological Terms* [Cambridge: Cambridge University Press, 1967], 76).

I investigate cultic background, and also the ideology and interpretation of cult through the ages, primarily, but not exclusively, by Jewish interpreters.

Once it is established that Paul expresses his soteriology by means of sacrificial, scapegoat, redemption, reconciliation, and justification metaphors, we may ask what these metaphors are saying about God. Clues can be found in the ways that Paul conflates them, and subordinates one to another. Paul spends more time on the social metaphors (especially justification) than on the cultic ones, but the cultic metaphors are foundational, often expressing the last soteriological word in an extended argument. What concept of God is Paul communicating by describing salvation as either a cultic event or a ransom payment? Cultic language is used even when he is not crafting a soteriological metaphor, so to what extent can we say that Paul's thinking is "fundamentally cultic"?[2]

Christian concepts of atonement are partly based on understandings of the Jewish sacrificial and scapegoat rituals. There is some danger in using the broad English term "atonement." Throughout the ANE, cleansing of impurity was carried out through sacrificial cults, and with expulsion rituals like the scapegoat rite. The English word *atonement* tends to emphasize forgiveness and reconciliation, and is often used without any connection to cultic activities, but we should not forget that biblical atonement terms (כָּפַר, ἱλάσκομαι) originate within a cultic arena. By Paul's time, the understanding and interpretation of cult was being spiritualized, that is, discussed in moral and philosophic categories, but the atonement concept still had this cultic basis, and this is quite evident in Paul's usage.

Examination of Paul's use of cultic metaphors heightens one's appreciation of his subtle continuity *and* discontinuity with the tradition in which he grew up. Using time-honored cultic practices as metaphors for salvation suggests a certain continuity with tradition, and intimates that God still operates in ways similar to the way he operated through the law of Moses. But precisely the same metaphors suggest an obsolescence of the old and outward practice, now that its real and hidden significance has been revealed: "what once had glory has lost its glory because of the greater glory" (2 Cor 3:10).

Keys to Paul

Paul's question, "Is God the God of Jews only? Is he not the God of Gentiles also?" (Rom 3:29) is not incidental, but central, to his concerns. This verse is the underpinning of the one that precedes it, where he asserts salvation by faith, not by works of the law. The universal sovereignty of God underlies

---

[2] As asserted by David A. Renwick, *Paul, the Temple, and the Presence of God* (Atlanta: Scholars Press, 1991), 74.

both the universal availability of salvation and the fact that the faith-approach to God is the same for Jew and Gentile alike.

Three different foci contend for central attention in descriptions of Paul's gospel: the spiritual focus of faith and reconciliation, the doctrinal or transactional focus of the atoning death of Christ, and the social focus of the extension of salvation to the Gentiles. Some scholars speak of a theocentric, a christocentric, or an ecclesiocentric focus to Paul's gospel, usually with an awareness of the danger of pitting these foci against each other, since these aspects are in fact intimately linked. Hays has effectively argued that much of Paul's typological use of scripture is ecclesiocentric. When Paul says that the Israelites during the exodus were "baptized into Moses" (1 Cor 10:2), and that "the spiritual rock that followed them ... was Christ" (v. 4), he is arguing that the church was foreshadowed there. These events happened as "τύποι ἡμῶν (10.6) ... [which] means 'types of us', prefigurations of the *ekklesia*."[3]

On the other hand, inasmuch as it is God who is worshipped, who is all-powerful, who raised Jesus from the dead, and who thus provided the means of salvation, Paul's gospel can be called theocentric.[4] Yet it is also obvious that the central role of Christ would be apparent to anyone hearing Paul preach; Christ is "the fulcrum point of Paul's theology."[5] The salvific role of Christ's death and resurrection utterly distinguishes his gospel from other manifestations of Judaism, even from other Christian forms where the death of Christ is not made the central saving event (e.g., *The Gospel of Thomas*).

Is there a key that links these three foci and enables us to keep them all in sight when analyzing Paul? Perhaps Paul's own hermeneutical approach to the scriptures provides the key. But, again, that can be expressed in three different ways: either Paul uses a universalizing hermeneutic that is linked with the goal of drawing in the Gentiles (Boyarin sees Paul this way); or Paul's is a monotheistic hermeneutic that focuses on the saving acts of God (many scholars); or Paul has a spiritualizing hermeneutic that speaks metaphorically of the death of Christ as a cultic or economic transaction that accomplishes human salvation (the emphasis in this dissertation). The latter approach involves examining Paul's depictions of salvation issuing from a cultic event or from a purchasing of freedom, and resulting in a favorable legal standing: justification.

---

[3] Richard B. Hays, "The Conversion of the Imagination: Scripture and Eschatology in 1 Corinthians," *NTS* 45 (1999): 400–1.

[4] John L. White speaks of "Paul's root idea of God as creator" (*The Apostle of God: Paul and the Promise of Abraham* [Peabody, Mass.: Hendrickson, 1999], 14).

[5] James D. G. Dunn, *The Theology of Paul the Apostle* (Grand Rapids: Eerdmans, 1998), 722.

The cultic metaphors picture *how* the death of Jesus accomplishes salvation, and they underlie the social metaphors. The death of Christ had to come first, enabling justification before God, and participation in Christ.

Paul describes Christ as a purification sacrifice, the Paschal sacrifice, or a scapegoat—Christ "becoming a curse" or being "made sin"[6] for us. Paul's metaphors imply that God chose to *recognize* the crucifixion as an effective ritual and to respond to it. The crucifixion corresponds to the ritual act, the resurrection corresponds to God's response to the ritual, and reconciliation or justification is the transformed status that ritual participants receive.

The same logic underlies the cultic metaphor and the cultic practice, whether Greek or Hebrew: what is *done* in ritual evokes a desired response from the god, and the person for whom the ritual is performed experiences an improved status before the god. Paul does not argue that Christ's death changed God's mind, in fact he explicitly states that God initiated this saving event (Rom 5:8), but the logic of appeasement is evident in the next verse: God's wrath is averted *because* of the spilt blood: "now that we have been have been justified by his blood, will we be saved through him from the wrath of God" (Rom 5:9). Sacrificial thinking seems to entail manipulation. Chapters One, Two, Four, and Five will test this assertion.

Paul probably did not initiate the sacrificial interpretation of the death of Christ,[7] but he did formulate a sacrificial theology. In so doing, he took up and transmitted a primitive current in religious thinking, but spiritualized it with an emphasis on the generosity of God, and with ideas of "noble death" (a major theme in Hellenic, Hellenistic, and finally Maccabean literature). His emphasis on the outgoing love of God stands in some tension with the transactions pictured in the soteriological metaphors. But Paul never asserts a division in God's nature between justice and mercy. God is both just and merciful; he will punish sin . . . or overlook it, if a person has connected himself to the Messiah. God has provided a way out from under sin: "if anyone is in Christ, there is a new creation" (2 Cor 5:17).

For Paul, Christ is the sacrificial gateway from God-alienated status to justified and reconciled status. But Paul also brings in ideas that are not implicit in sacrifice; especially important is new creation: Christ as the source of new life for humanity. Since he was given life by God, Christ has the power to give

---

[6] Rom 8:3; 1 Cor 5:7; Gal 3:13; 2 Cor 5:21.

[7] His use of "cultic imagery . . . is beholden to tradition," (Ralph Martin, *Second Corinthians*. WBC 40 [Dallas: Word, 1986], 157). Cf. Rudolf Bultmann, *Theology of the New Testament* (New York: Charles Scribner's Sons, 1951), 1:46; John Reumann, "The Gospel of the Righteousness of God: Pauline Interpretation in Romans 3:21–31," *Interpretation* 20 (1966): 436, 449.

it to others, putting life in place of death-like slavery to sin and the elemental spirits.

Conflation of Metaphors

Paul indicates that salvation is not free: "you were bought with a price" (1 Cor 6:20; 7:23). Here, the Christian gets a new owner: Christ. The death of Jesus functioned as legal tender to make this purchase. In Rom 3:24–25 we have justification, redemption, and place of atonement—a conflation of judicial, economic, and sacrificial imagery. Paul will move from one metaphor to the other, but always there is a transaction by which salvation is purchased, arranged, or ritually obtained for us.

The main metaphors and models that Paul uses to describe the death of Christ as a saving transaction are:

- **sacrifice** (περὶ ἁμαρτίας, τὸ πάσχα, other terms)—Christ dying as a sin/purification sacrifice, the Passover sacrifice, a new covenant sacrifice; or functioning as the ἱλαστήριον, which is not a sacrifice but the place where sacrificial blood is sprinkled on Yom Kippur;

- **curse transmission ritual**[8]—an exchange of status, with Christ being "made" sin or "becoming a curse for us" (2 Cor 5:21; Gal 3:13), so that believers might take on Christ's righteousness or innocence;

- **redemption** (ἀπολύτρωσις, [ἐξ]αγοράζω)—Christ's death as a payment or a ransom that purchases the freedom of captives or slaves; "you were bought with a price" (1 Cor 6:20; 7:23);

- **martyrdom**—several different versions of a "dying formula" similar to such formulas in Hellenistic literature and hortatory rhetoric, stating that Christ died "for us" or "for me."

The premier biblical example of curse-transmission ritual, the scapegoat, has often been conflated with sacrifice by scholars. A recent study by McLean[9] helpfully distinguishes sacrifice from expulsion rituals, but mislabels the latter as "apotropaeic," thus confusing the terminology further, for that term (in Greek and in English) refers primarily to charms or rites that *avert* some evil, not to rites where an animal or person takes on the community's evil and carries it away. "Expulsion ritual" may be the best term for the latter type of

---

[8] This is my term, partly based on J. Dyneley Prince's term, "transmission rites" in "Scapegoat (Semitic)," in *Encyclopaedia of Religion and Ethics*, ed. James Hastings (Edinburgh: T&T Clark, 1920), 11:222. His Babylonian examples involve the transference of an evil influence or illness to a human or animal victim, which is then driven out of the community.

[9] B. Hudson McLean, *The Cursed Christ: Mediterranean Expulsion Rituals and Pauline Soteriology*. JSNT Sup 126 (Sheffield: Sheffield Academic, 1996).

ritual, but "curse transmission" is more useful in this dissertation because it draws attention to the particular *part* of the ritual that seized Paul's imagination: the act of *transfer* (Christ "becoming a curse").

McLean's thesis is that Paul did not represent Christ's death as a sacrifice but as a curse transmission ritual. My thesis is that Paul used both of these as conceptual models for Christ's death, and other models as well. Even with this quite major correction, McLean's thesis calls for serious rethinking of sacrificial understandings of Pauline theology. Since McLean, Stowers, and others call into question the presence of sacrificial metaphors in Paul, it is necessary to search Paul's writings with this in mind.

In addition to these models for interpreting the death of Jesus, there are also some that he uses to describe the *result* of the saving transaction. "Redemption" can also be listed here, in that the redeemed person has a new status: *free* (while paradoxically being also the slave of righteousness). The other models are:

- **reconciliation** (καταλλαγή) of alienated humanity to God, using the term commonly designating reconciliation between estranged spouses or diplomatic settlement between states;
- **justification** (δικαίωσις and related words): either a judicial "rightwising" that declares one to be right, that is, acquitted, thus normalizing one's civil standing, or a morally transformative "rightwising" that actually makes a person just;
- **adoption** (υἱοθεσία) into the status of children of God, which, for Paul, means becoming joint-heirs with Christ, and receiving the Spirit of God (Rom 8:13–17, 23).

I will endeavor to understand Paul's soteriology by exploring the interplay between these metaphors. It is necessary to unfold the theo-logic of the rituals Paul uses metaphorically, and then to make sense of Paul's usage of them. Since sacrifice is so fundamental to Paul's metaphoric vocabulary, it will be necessary to examine sacrifice in Jewish and non-Jewish cultures, to see if there are themes or concepts common to sacrificial cultures, that may therefore be implicit in Paul's teachings.

It is important to preserve the distinction between sacrifice and the scapegoat: rites that are as different from each other as are Yahweh and Azazel, the beings to whom they are offered. Yet Paul juxtaposes these two rites, and also the judicial model, in a densely mixed metaphor in Rom 8:3. The new ideas of Paul are expressed through his unique mixing of metaphors.

Spiritualization

In the chapter on sacrifice I will undertake a thorough analysis of the six major ways that scholars have used the term "spiritualization," but it is necessary to offer a brief summary of this list, since the subject has already come up, and it is a term that I use for understanding not only Paul's metaphors, but also the history of sacrifice.

Any far-reaching examination of sacrifice in the Jewish, Greek, or Indian cultures must take notice of an interesting pattern of change in these practices over time. One development that can be observed throughout the Greek-speaking world from the sixth century B.C.E. to the fourth century C.E. is a steady devaluation of sacrificial practice, sometimes accompanied by allegorizing interpretations of ritual that discover its "real" meaning, other times expressing a pointed rejection of the whole idea of sacrificial offerings. A severe criticism of sacrificial practice occurs frequently in Hebrew literary records from the eighth century B.C.E. to Paul's time, sometimes focusing on the need for the sacrificer to have the right attitude, and other times frankly mocking or denigrating sacrificial actions.

Various strategies are applied for the reinterpretation, reassessment, alteration, and sometimes the rejection of rituals. And "spiritualization" applies to concepts as well as to practices; in fact, the reassessment of previous interpretations of ritual is an important part of both their alteration and their preservation. The Eucharist, we are now told, signifies the "unity of God's People," and should help them to "live joyfully" and "do good works."[10] Moral meanings are attached to the interpretation of the ritual. Spiritualizing preserves while it transforms ancient religious practices. "Who sublimates, does not abolish"[11]—but he *does* change.

Both Jews and Gentiles found the mere practice of sacrificial ritual insufficient. They spiritualized the cult, that is, focused on righteousness or rationality, either in contrast to the cult, or in connection with it in a new rationalization of cult; either:

- making a distinction between ethical motivations and ritual procedures; emphasizing that ethical values or spiritual attitude have primary validity, and expressing some degree of disdain for the outward cultic practice; or

- attributing new ethical and spiritual meanings to the cult, importing new values into the cultic ideology.

---

[10] Giacomo Cardinal Lercaro, et al, *Instruction on Worship of the Eucharistic Mystery* (Boston: Daughters of St. Paul, 1967), 9, 13.

[11] Ina Willi-Plein, *Opfer und Kult im alttestamentlichen Israel: Textbefragungen und Zwischenergebnisse* (Stuttgart: Verlag Katholisches Bibelwerk, 1993), 156.

Ritual preserves social order and organization,[12] so its critique is also a social critique. On this subject, Paul is politically wise rather than unnecessarily radical. Paul emphasizes the typological fulfillment of cultic practices and religious hopes. He never attacks the sacrificial cult, but does speak of "a new covenant," a (new) place of atonement (1 Cor 11:25; Rom 3:25). The fact that the old cult seems mainly to matter because of what it *foretold*, does seem to reduce its literal value—while raising its *symbolic* value.

Material for Soteriological Metaphors

One of Paul's methods of argument was to present concepts that could be accepted by both Jews and Gentiles. The beneficial death of Jesus, interpreted with cultic metaphors, was a crucial bridging concept. The Greek tragedians had developed the idea of self-sacrifice for one's city or for a religious principle into a major literary/religious theme. The Jews spoke in their scriptures of the selfless suffering of a prophet or righteous one, bordering on self-sacrifice (in Psalm 22 and 69, Isaiah 53, Zechariah 11 and 13, Wisdom 2).

Under the pressure of anti-Semitic Seleucid cultural repression, and also of rising anti-Jewish feeling in Egypt, the theme of martyrdom became increasingly important in Jewish thought, and along with it came Judaism's first clear expressions of belief in an afterlife. Wisdom 1:15 through 3:10 assert that righteousness, and the righteous, are undying.

Drawing upon Greek concepts of noble death, Second Maccabees[13] and *Fourth Maccabees*[14] develop a theology of martyrdom and vindication in the afterlife. Especially in the latter book, the utterances of the martyrs as they were put to death are sometimes couched in sacrificial terms, even to the point where one character says that the martyrs were a "ransom" or "life-substitute" (ἀντίψυχον) for the sin of the nation, and Israel was saved by their "propitiatory (ἱλαστηρίου) death" (*4 Macc.* 17:20–22). The self-sacrificial speeches in this book seem intended to outdo the heroic lines of characters from the plays of Euripides, and the ἱλαστηρίου line brings Rom 3:25[15] to mind.

Sacrifice was a theme ripe for further rhetorical development for a cross-cultural audience, and Paul successfully exploited it. Cultic metaphors

---

[12] Rituals can establish, maintain, or restore order; Yom Kippur, for instance, annually purifying the temple, is restorative (Frank H. Gorman Jr., *The Ideology of Ritual: Space, Time and Status in the Priestly Theology*. JSOT Sup 91 [Sheffield: Sheffield Academic, 1990], 59, 61).

[13] 2 Macc 6:18–7:41; afterlife: 7:9, 14, 36.

[14] 4 *Macc.* 6:27–29; 18:3–4. Since this is not a biblical book, it is italicized, while Second Maccabees is part of the Catholic Bible, and so is abbreviated in Roman type.

[15] See chapters 3 and 5.

interpreting the noble deaths of brave persons were a potential point of contact between Greek and Jewish thought.

The Scope of This Study

I will be concentrating on Paul's use of sacrifice and scapegoat metaphors, but that does not mean that I think it possible to reduce his theology to these two themes. Paul's is a great synthetic theology in which many themes are brought together. Redemption, adoption, and justification are often closely related to the cultic models, and these soteriological metaphors are to be examined. But some important Pauline eschatology receives little or no attention here, such as the change of epochs entailed in the *arrival* of faith ("now that faith has come," Gal 3:25), and the epochal change involved in the idea of Christ as the second Adam—the new Man who makes a new creation within human nature possible ("everything has become new!" γέγονεν καινά, 2 Cor 5:17).

I begin with a cross-cultural analysis of sacrifice and scholarly theories of sacrifice. Sacrificial practices are examined for possible motivations or concepts that can be observed cross-culturally. The various purposes of Hebrew sacrifice are explored. In the second chapter, I survey the types of curse transmission rituals found in ancient Israel and surrounding Gentile regions, and also review Paul's use of the widely recognized curse transmission/sin-bearing image. I test the thesis of Bradley McLean that (1) the scapegoat was used metaphorically by Paul in his soteriology, but (2) that sacrifice was not. This study of sacrifice and of scapegoat may tell us why these metaphors were so compelling.

In the third chapter I treat what I consider to be the most important (and difficult) cultic metaphor in the letters of Paul, and assess the work of Dan Bailey on this passage. The fourth chapter summarizes the redemption metaphor and substitutionary themes in the central chapters of Romans. The fifth chapter examines martyrological themes in Greek and Jewish literature, and how Paul utilizes them, interpreting them *through* his metaphors. Throughout, I make observations on Paul's continuity and discontinuity with what went before him.

I spend considerable time on cultic backgrounds, but the real goal is to tie together Paul's soteriological metaphors into a coherent system.

1.
The Logic of Sacrifice

I undertake here a condensed survey and assessment of scholarly theories about sacrifice in cultures around the world. I will assemble a list of frequently encountered purposes for sacrifice. These questions are relevant since, if there are any universal or near-universal intuitions, concepts, or motives underlying sacrifice, Paul's sacrificial metaphors would evoke these concepts in Gentile and Jewish readers alike. Whatever ideas inform Paul's understanding of sacrifice, they affect the content of Paul's theology, and need to be identified.

As with N. T. Wright, there is a "question which I for one would like to press: according to what inner rationale was the killing of animals or birds thought to *effect* the atonement and forgiveness . . . ?" but unlike Wright, I am not satisfied that they function as a "pointer back to the great acts of redemption such as the exodus, and equally as a pointer forward to the great redemption still to come."[1] Animals were ritually slaughtered, and the deity invoked, long before the development of such an intellectual theology. Sacrifice bespeaks ancient beliefs about the life-force residing in the blood, and the priestly ability to manipulate that life-force. The metaphysical logic originally supporting the ritual was transformed as worldviews changed, but the old logic is still covertly present within the new rationalization. Both the ancient (pre-Pentateuch) concepts and the various rationalizations overlaid upon them are necessary material for our study of sacrifice, if we are to avoid superficial summaries.

Sacrifice dramatized an ancient concept of the supernatural that was no longer understood in Paul's time. The reason for sacrificing given by Josephus[2]

---

[1] N. T. Wright, *The New Testament and the People of God*, volume 1 of *Christian Origins and the Question of God* (Minneapolis: Fortress, 1992), 274.

[2] *Ag. Ap.* 2.193–98. Hans Wenschkewitz, *Die Spiritualisierung der Kultusbegriffe: Tempel, Priester und Opfer im Neuen Testament*. Angelos-Beiheft 4 (1932) (Verlag von Eduard Pfeiffer), 21–22.

and the rabbis[3]—we sacrifice because we are commanded to do so—bears witness to the fading out of the supernatural concepts that gave rise to the practice. Even as early as Sirach (second century B.C.E.), we are told "all that you offer is in fulfillment of the commandment" (35:7 NRSV; 35:5 in RSV).

To inquire into Paul's sacrificial idea requires some examination of ancient sacrificial ideas and of their transformation or replacement by other ideas, that is, to the discourse of spiritualization: the replacement of animal sacrifice by symbolic substitutes, the ascription of new values to the cult, the increasing recognition of inward religious disposition as more important than outward ritual, the metaphorical appropriation of cultic language, and (for some) the rejection of cult practices and their replacement with a philosophy of spiritual progress. Cross-cultural study enables one to see "biblical lines of thought converg[ing] with Greek 'spiritualization'"[4] in inter-testamental works such as *The Testaments of the Twelve Patriarchs* and *Wisdom of Solomon*, and again in Paul. Paul draws upon both Jewish and Gentile patterns of spiritualization, but makes much less use of recognizably Middle Platonic patterns of spiritualization than does the Epistle to the Hebrews.

1.1 Theories of Sacrifice

1.1.1 Tylor: Sacrifice as Gift

An important nineteenth century theorist was Edward Tylor, who drew attention to the element of self-interest in sacrifice: the concept of *do ut des*, "I give that you may give meant the god's favor was won."[5] Although known for his "gift-theory" of sacrifice, Tylor actually mentions "the gift-theory, the homage-theory, and the abnegation-theory" held by those who practice sacrifice (he is not talking about scholars); of the three, "the gift-theory ... properly takes the first place."[6]

The gift-theory also has the strength of building upon one of the most important social actions of ancient societies: the complex system of gift exchange, whereby potential conflict is avoided through mutual gift-giving.

---

[3] *Num. Rabbah* 19; cf. *Pesiq. Rab. Kah.* 4,7. W. D. Davies, *Paul and Rabbinic Judaism: Some Rabbinic Elements in Pauline Theology* (rev. ed.; New York: Harper, 1948), 235.

[4] William Horbury, "Land, Sanctuary and Worship," in *Early Christian Thought in Its Jewish Context*, eds. John Barclay and John Sweet (Cambridge: Cambridge University Press, 1991), 214.

[5] Rick Franklin Talbott, *Sacred Sacrifice: Ritual Paradigms in Vedic Religion and Early Christianity* (New York: Peter Lang, 1995), 40; also affirmed by Emile Durkheim, *The Elementary Forms of the Religious Life*, tr. Joseph Ward Swain (London: Allen & Unwin, 1915), 341, 347.

[6] Edward Burnett Tylor, *Religion in Primitive Culture*, vol. 2 of *Primitive Culture* (New York: Harper & Bros., 1958), 462.

Gift-exchange was involved in all kinds of social contracts, contributing to both the formation and the conceptualization of social relationships. In covenants between unequal parties, exchange usually took the form of the weaker party offering a gift (tribute) to the stronger, and the stronger offering military protection and political concessions to the weaker.

Gift-exchange has often informed the conceptualization of relationship with gods. Ancient Greeks generally understood sacrifice as a gift, and authors like Plato and Lucian were severely critical of the more literal-minded and selfish developments of it, where "dolts" thought to bribe the gods.[7]

Old Testament scholars have long noticed the gift element of sacrifice. In Num 15:25 the sacrifice is described as a קָרְבָּן, a gift, and there are many other passages where "*kipper* stands for a process of making atonement by the offering of a suitable gift."[8] There is the blunt command that Israelite males shall make the religious pilgrimage three times a year, and "they shall not appear before the Lord empty-handed" (Deut 16:16).

Despite other notions of sacrifice, the gift idea is hard to deny. Levine writes, "The notion of sacrifice as a *gift* . . . tells us most about the purposes of such worship."[9] The word that means "gift" in secular usage (מִנְחָה) indicates a grain offering in such passages as Gen 4:3–5; Judg 6:18.[10] Another word for gift (שַׁי; δῶρα) is used for offerings brought to the Lord (Ps 68:30; Isa 18:7). Josephus summarizes the cult thus: God "receives his accustomed sacrifices!"[11] Though not enthusiastic about the gift theory, Milgrom concedes that it "seems to be the only one that manifests validity in all sacrificial systems."[12]

One aspect of gift that is not often noted is that it involves feeding the god and, at a primitive level, *strengthening* the god with food. In studying Iranian religion, Pancino notes that "sacrifice [is] seen as a means of 'strengthening' the object of veneration," and he cites an important instance where Ahura Mazda, the supreme God, sacrifices to the demigod Tistrya to strengthen him for his battle against a demon.[13] Gods strengthen other gods with sacrifices in

---

[7] For Lucian's "dolts," see *On Sacrifices* 1–2, quoted in Bruce J. Malina, "Mediterranean Sacrifice: Dimensions of Domestic and Political Religion," *BTB* 26 (1996): 38. The Plato passage referred to here is *Laws* 10.885C.

[8] Leon Morris, *The Apostolic Preaching of the Cross* (3rd ed.; Grand Rapids: Eerdmans, 1965), 168.

[9] Baruch A. Levine, *Leviticus: The Traditional Hebrew Text with the New JPS Translation* (Philadelphia: Jewish Pub. Society, 1989), xxiv.

[10] Levine, *Ibid.*

[11] *J.W.* 6.99.

[12] Jacob Milgrom, *Leviticus 1–16* (AB 3; Garden City, N.Y.: Doubleday, 1991), 440.

[13] Antonio Pancino, "An Aspect of Sacrifice in the Avesta," *East and West* n.s. 36 (1986): 272.

the Vedas.¹⁴ A feeding idea also appears in ancient Chinese religion: "Nourished by the reverence of propitiation and sustenance of the sacrifices, the gods requited (*bao*) the living with blessings (*fu*)."¹⁵

Meat-eating was associated with taking on strength, whether the consumer was human or divine. This can be detected in the admonition that "the food for my offerings by fire, my pleasing odor, you shall take care to offer to me" (Num 28:2), followed by a list of the most delectable products of animal husbandry and agriculture. God is given a "food offering" (Lev 3:11; Num 28:24), a fire offering (אִשֶּׁה) in MT, a fruit-offering (κάρπωμα) in LXX. Leviticus 21:8 and 17 speak of "the food of your God," and Lev 21:6 and 21 speak of "the Lord's offerings by fire, the food of their God." The Hebrew and Greek need to be examined here. We find that the Lord's fire offerings (plural, אִשֵּׁה, and called sacrifices, θυσίαι, in LXX) are followed by God's *bread*: לֶחֶם, translated "food" in NRSV (τὰ δῶρα, *offerings/gifts*, in Greek). The bread is the Bread of the Presence, or showbread, perpetually present in the sanctuary. Do we have here a synonymous parallelism, with the bread (לֶחֶם) being identified with fire offerings (אִשֶּׁה), in order to identify both as the food of God?

כִּי אֶת־אִשֵּׁי יְהוָה לֶחֶם אֱלֹהֵיהֶם הֵם מַקְרִיבִם

γὰρ θυσίας κυρίου δῶρα τοῦ θεοῦ αὐτῶν αὐτοὶ προσφέρουσιν Lev 21:6

Or is there, instead, a *differentiation* going on, since the sacrifices are *the Lord's* (יְהוָה, κυρίου, in vv. 6, 8, 17, 21, but not in v. 21 in the Greek), while the bread is *God's* (אֱלֹהֵיהֶם or אֱלֹהֶיךָ, and θεοῦ in all four verses)? This option seems more likely. It may be that two different traditions are being distinguished by Leviticus,¹⁶ *sacrificing* to Yahweh, and *offering of bread* to Elohim. It is usually the name Yahweh that is associated with sacrificing, while moral injunctions applicable to Israelite and Gentile alike usually utilize the name Elohim.¹⁷ One rabbi makes it very clear: "In all the sacrificial contexts of

---

¹⁴ Cf. Rg veda 10:90:16; 1:64:50; Bruce Lincoln, *Death, War, and Sacrifice: Studies in Ideology and Practice* (Chicago: University of Chicago Press, 1991), 167. In the Vedic commentary, the Satapatha Brâhmaṇa 3.9.1.8, we read that "Pragâpati . . . . does . . . now become strong by food; food turns into him" (*The Satapatha-Brâhmaṇa According to the Text of the Mâdhyandina School, Part II*, tr. J. Eggling [Oxford: Clarendon, 1885], 219).

¹⁵ Thomas A. Wilson, "Sacrifice and the Imperial Cult of Confucius," *HR* 41 (2002): 251.

¹⁶ But not in Num 28:24, where לֶחֶם and אִשֶּׁה are identified. Therefore, the above is an observation about Leviticus alone.

¹⁷ Milgrom, *Leviticus 17–22* (AB 3A; Garden City, N.Y.: Doubleday, 2000), 1803–04.

the Torah *'elohîm*" and related words "never appear, only the special name YHWH."[18]

So the distinctions between Elohim's bread and Yahweh's fire offerings are important for Leviticus, but in both cases, the food is explicitly demanded to be offered to Elohim or Yahweh on a regular basis. Piety requires consistent maintenance of the cult of feeding the god. It is likely that all of this food *strengthened* the deity, at least in the priestly traditions upon which Leviticus draws, and whose anthropomorphic implications are partly suppressed by Leviticus. The notion of strengthening the God, however, can persist in altered form; worship itself may be unconsciously thought to strengthen God. Even in the NT, God is worthy "to receive glory and honor and power" (Rev 4:11). God apparently needs to receive power from human worshipers, in this conception.

Primitive cultic assumptions, though partly suppressed and spiritualized, persist and shape the rationalizing theologies of later eras of human development. Acknowledgment of this process meets with resistance due to the largely unconscious appeal of spiritualized primitive ideas. The thinker who first spiritualizes a cultic form or idea knows that he or she is transforming its meaning, adding new insight, but the people who inherit and transmit these traditions usually have no idea how many layers of theology are contained in the expressions they transmit.

I use the old term "animism" to describe a naturalistic concept of spiritual power, where trees and rivers are indwelt by (often dangerous) spirits or pixies. Spirits (like animals and people) can usually be placated, fed, won over. Homer says the gods are pliable (στρεπτοί), they are persuaded by pleasing meat-smell (*Il.* IX.497–500).[19] Similarly, "when the Lord smelled the pleasing odor" of Noah's sacrifice, he promised not to curse the ground (Gen 8:21). Such naturalistic notions were ancient, and had not been completely displaced by more moralized concepts of sacrifice, when Saul of Tarsus was growing up.

1.1.2 Smith—Sacrifice and Tribal Identity

A rival theory arose around the turn of the century, championed by William Robertson Smith, who saw totemism and the sacred meal as the basis of all ritual systems. His contribution was to highlight the *communal* aspect of sacrifice: "the kinship of gods with their worshippers. . . . [and] sacrificial animals were originally treated as kinsmen."[20] Further, "private sacrifice is a

---

[18] *Sipre* Num. 143; Milgrom, *Leviticus 17–22*, 1804.

[19] John Pairman Brown, "The Sacrificial Cult and Its Critique in Greek and Hebrew (I)," *JSS* 24 (1979): 162.

[20] William Robertson Smith, *Lectures on the Religion of the Semites: The Fundamental Institutions* (3d ed.; New York: Macmillan, 1927), 288–89.

younger thing than clan sacrifice."²¹ The most serious concern was not the welfare of the individual soul but protection of the community from pollution. Many of Smith's insights are now common fare in anthropological studies.

It has been widely recognized that his theory is too narrow to account for the many societies that show no sign of totemism.²² Further, Smith's resistance to the gift idea of sacrifice because of its supposed lack of logic, is exposed by Durkheim as overlooking the many examples where people think of sacrifices as gifts to the deity, while yet acknowledging that the deity had supplied these goods in the first place; this is an aspect of reciprocity between sacrificer and deity. Such "logic" is widespread in human religion, and the gift idea is ancient.²³

A dubious contribution to the legacy of Smith is made by Bruce Chilton. First, he says, we should know that "The grand design of explaining sacrifice is itself a product of modern mystification."²⁴ We should reject all scholarly "myths of sacrifice,"²⁵ all attempts to explain it from "outside" the event, since "no such explanation exists"²⁶—except, of course, the one he supports! Chilton backs Smith's analysis of sacrifice as "a feast with the gods . . . . the celebration of consumption and of being consumed."²⁷

However, ancient texts from India, Israel, and Iran give minimal attention to the meal, mainly stipulating what is to be eaten and by whom. Of more concern in the texts are matters of preparation and manipulation of spiritually significant substances, which our next scholars refer to as "introduction and consecration."

1.1.3 Hubert and Mauss

More sophisticated than the gift theory, and with more universal applicability than the totem-meal theory, is Hubert's and Mauss's "communication theory," named for the idea of the victim as a mediator of sacred power. Their complex definition is sensitive to the metaphysics of sacrifice. Analyzing primarily Vedic sacrifice and secondarily Hebrew

---

[21] Smith, *Lectures*, 421.

[22] William Beers, *Women and Sacrifice: Male Narcissism and the Psychology of Religion* (Detroit, Mich.: Wayne State University Press, 1992), 25; Talbott, *Sacred Sacrifice*, 41–43.

[23] Durkheim, *Elementary Forms*, 341–42.

[24] Bruce Chilton, "The Hungry Knife: Toward a Sense of Sacrifice," in *The Bible in Human Society: Essays in Honour of John Rogerson*, edited by M. Daniel Carroll R., David Clines, and Philip R. Davies. JSOT Sup 200 (Sheffield: Sheffield Academic, 1995), 137.

[25] Bruce Chilton, *The Temple of Jesus: His Sacrificial Program within a Cultural History of Sacrifice* (University Park: Pennsylvania State University Press, 1992), 39.

[26] Chilton, "The Hungry Knife," 136.

[27] Chilton, *Temple of Jesus*, 41.

sacrifice, they note the great care taken with the *consecration* (making-holy) of the sacrificial space and participants.

> Sacrifice always implies a consecration; in every sacrifice an object passes from the common into the religious domain. . . . The thing consecrated serves as an intermediary between the sacrifier[28] . . . and the divinity to whom the sacrifice is usually addressed.[29]

There are three stages in sacrifice: introduction, consecration, and exit. The introduction involves rigorous and precise preparations which result in a progressive impartation of sacredness to the animal victim. The consecration increases by stages the religiosity of both the sacrifier and the victim, up "to a maximum degree of religiosity, where it remains only for a moment."[30] When it is slaughtered, there is an actual transfer of spiritual power "from the victim to the sacrifier."[31] There is a quasi-physical transfer, whereby the "sacrifier" gets "religiosity" from the victim.[32]

After the slaughter and the transfer that it effects, according to Hubert and Mauss, there is an "exit" procedure for returning to normal life, closing down the connection with the divine and disposing of things that have been "infected" with the divine.[33]

Transfer can go in either direction. In expiatory sacrifice, "the sacrifier's religious impurity" is transferred to the victim.[34] Hubert and Mauss recognize that there is diversity in the conceptualization of sacrifice, but they insist that sacrifice always consists of "establishing a means of communication between the sacred and the profane worlds through the mediation of a victim."[35] In all ancient religions, the sacred world is profoundly dangerous. Only the sacrificial victim is able to venture into this domain.[36]

---

[28] This is the spelling used in Hubert and Mauss to denote the person for whose benefit the sacrifice was performed, who does not necessarily perform the slaying.

[29] Henri Hubert and Marcel Mauss, *Sacrifice: Its Nature and Function* (trans. W. D. Halls; 1898; repr., Chicago: University of Chicago Press, 1964), 9, 11.

[30] Hubert and Mauss, *Sacrifice*, 45.

[31] Hubert and Mauss, *Sacrifice*, 52.

[32] Hubert and Mauss, *Sacrifice*, 44.

[33] Hubert and Mauss, *Sacrifice*, 45, 99.

[34] Hubert and Mauss, *Sacrifice*, 53.

[35] Hubert and Mauss, *Sacrifice*, 97. Maurice Bloch strongly rejects the idea that the separation between sacred and profane is universal (*Prey Into Hunter: The Politics of Religious Experience* [Cambridge: Cambridge University Press, 1992], 28). But it is, at the very least, strongly present in Indian, Zoroastrian, Jewish, and Christian symbolic systems.

[36] Hubert and Mauss, *Sacrifice*, 98.

At the very end of their work, Hubert and Mauss express a thoroughly sociological theory of sacrifice: "The sacred things in relation to which sacrifice functions, are social things. And this is enough to explain sacrifice."[37]

Hubert and Mauss set the agenda for academic discussion of sacrifice, even to the present day, to some degree. Criticism of their theory is often the starting point for development of a new one. Beers rejects their idea of the victim as mediator between human and divine; rather, the victim is "the substitute for the one guilty of transgression . . . or impurity."[38] Beers admits that neither the gift-idea nor the substitute-idea are universal, but what they have in common *is* universal: "the idea of exchange . . . to substitute one moral condition for another."[39] I would rephrase his insight thus: *sacrifice is a self-interested technique for obtaining an improved metaphysical environment.* People in many religious cultures have thought of sacrificial exchange as a *transaction*, often in the nature of an appeasing gift ("a sweet-smelling oblation to the Lord" Lev 1:9 NAB). Valeri astutely observes that what motivates sacrifice is "a perceived lack"; transgression is *one* variety of lacking. Sacrifice is thought to remedy "imperfection or even disorder."[40]

Malina accepts that "inducement" is the operative principle behind sacrifice, but he rejects as anachronistic the notion of the animal as substitute victim: "it is only individualists who can consider the sacrifice as substitutionary. . . . Individualism looks to punishment of the individual culprit [but] in collectivist societies, any ingroup life will do for any life owed."[41] Malina is right to take ancient collectivism into account, but wrong to deny any notion of individuality, treating the Hellenistic Age as though it were the Paleolithic Age. The idea of individual culpability was certainly known to Paul, having been debated by the prophets (Jer 31:29–30; Deut 24:16; Ezekiel 18).

There are other notions of substitution than the strictly Christianized one against which Malina is reacting. Substitution recurs in sacrificial systems, differently conceived by different cultures. Perhaps even, "It is substitution . . . that defines sacrifice as sacrifice. . . . The sacrifice *is* a sacrifice, and not a suicide (or a 'murder'. . .) because of this displacement and replacement."[42] The sacrificial victim stands for the god as well as for the worshipper.[43]

---

[37] Hubert and Mauss, *Sacrifice*, 101.

[38] Beers, *Women and Sacrifice*, 27.

[39] Beers, *Women and Sacrifice*, 27.

[40] Valerio Valeri, *Kingship and Sacrifice: Ritual and Society in Ancient Hawaii* (Chicago: University of Chicago Press, 1985), 71.

[41] Malina, "Mediterranean Sacrifice," 40.

[42] Brian K. Smith and Wendy Doniger, "Sacrifice and Substitution: Ritual Mystification and Mythical Demystification," *Numen* 36 (1989): 217, 201.

[43] Smith and Doniger, "Sacrifice," 190.

What emerged prominently in Christian doctrine is the notion of penal substitution, and Christian scholars have sometimes projected it onto ancient texts. That is reason to learn *more* about the nature(s) of substitution, not to close down the subject. I struggle for a label to assign to Vedic/Hindu substitution; it could be called *symbolic*, but *all* substitution is symbolic, actually, so that will not do. Therefore I settle on the term *abstract* substitution. Abstract substitution is the "confusion of identities necessary to the sacrificial operation and to the series of substitutions integral to sacrifice"[44] in the Vedic culture, and the same concept continues in the Hindu ritual, which only mimes sacrifice. This is not a judicial substitution. The initial threat comes not from a judicial sentence, but from a violent deity. The Vedic gods are aggressive, like Vedic warriors themselves. The sacrificer's goal, then, is not acquittal, but appeasement, subterfuge and sometimes counter-aggression. A few stories in the Pentateuch show similar ideas, for instance "the Lord ... tried to kill" Moses, but was appeased by the blood of circumcision that Zipporah was able to produce (Exod 4:24–26). Such notions were rejected by later biblical authors.

Once again, to stress this point: I think the following is at least theoretically true about sacrifice in all cultures: "The ultimate paradigm underlying all sacrifices [is] the sacrifice of oneself."[45] However, the essence of the threat (in most ancient times) was not legal but simply vital, so the oldest substitution is *abstract*, not penal, substitution. Its effect is to appease the deity, which seems to be the intent of the Hebrew notion of *feeding* Yahweh.

1.1.4 Bloch's Theory

Maurice Bloch criticizes Hubert and Mauss for universalizing upon Vedic sacrifice, yet he also claims a universal or near-universal basis for his theory. In all the cultures he examines, he finds that sacrifice has the elements of identification and substitution, "spirit mediumship and meal" or "invocation and feast,"[46] and "the triumphant penetration of a transcendental being into the conquered body of a medium."[47]

Bloch claims that only the physical part of the person offering the sacrifice is identified with the animal. Identifying with the animal as it weakens and dies, is a form of self-renunciation; but with the death of the animal, the person becomes wholly identified with the transcendental,[48] and may experience spirit

---

[44] Smith and Doniger, "Sacrifice," 207.
[45] Smith and Doniger, "Sacrifice," 190–91.
[46] Bloch, *Prey,* 42–43.
[47] Bloch, *Prey,* 35.
[48] Bloch, *Prey,* 5, 30–31, 35–36.

possession or other types of spirit communication. After this, the sacrificer needs to revitalize his physical aspect by consuming the animal.[49] From that moment, revitalization becomes the dominant theme: eating the meat restores vitality, and this then "becomes a legitimation of outwardly directed aggression,"[50] including military conquest. Bloch calls this "rebounding violence."[51]

Bloch weakens his case when he denies that this reveals "an innate aggressiveness in humans"; instead, "violence is itself a result of the attempt to create the transcendental in religion and politics."[52] This attempt to blame religion for aggression is psychologically shallow and methodologically unsound. If there is no innate aggressive tendency, how does Bloch explain the emergence of this aggressive pattern in unrelated cultures around the world? How can he make generalizations about ritual forms, but not about their psychological underpinning? Bloch does uncover the use of religion to mandate aggression, but this does not prove that religion generates consumption in presumably noble and vegetarian Rousseauists to whom ideas of domination would never occur were it not for the dastardly influence of religion.

Bloch's theory works well for describing aggression in primitive cultures. One of his best examples of social violence following upon sacrificial violence is when God commands the sacrifice of Isaac (a self-renouncing sacrifice on Abraham's part), supplies a substitute, and then promises Abraham that his descendants will "possess the gates of their enemies" (Gen 22:17).[53] Similarly, in the Agamemnon and Iphigenia story, the commanded sacrificing of his daughter constitutes "partly self-inflicted violence" by Agamemnon. "But then the violence rebounds and, from having been the victim, Agamemnon becomes a violent actor towards others,"[54] taking and pillaging Troy.

Bloch finds an experience of spirit possession occurring in the sacrificing cultures he examines: the Dinka in Africa, the Buid in the Philippines, and the Japanese.[55] His data confirm that sacrifice *strengthens* the participants, although he overlooks the probability that the deity is also strengthened by the sacrifice. He shows how expansive aggression accompanied sacrifice in Vedic and Shinto cultures,[56] and in a few Greek and biblical texts. However, he fails to notice that there are numerous examples of spirit-mediumship that involve

---

[49] Bloch, *Prey*, 35–43.
[50] Bloch, *Prey*, 45.
[51] Bloch, *Prey*, 4–6, 18–23, 50, 64–69, 88–89, 93.
[52] Bloch, *Prey*, 7.
[53] Bloch, *Prey*, 27.
[54] Bloch, *Prey*, 26.
[55] Bloch, *Prey*, 35, 41–43, 63.
[56] Bloch, *Prey*, 49–50, 61–63.

no violence, and his complicated theory of self-weakening and attachment to "the transcendent" can hardly be argued for sacrifice around the world.

Bloch's theory is useful for analyzing warrior cultures, but does not work for societies advanced beyond the tribal stage, whose cults manifest an important *centralizing* symbol such as a national shrine vulnerable to contamination by sins committed in the nation, as in Babylon or Israel. He says nothing about purity or sacred space, not to mention any kind of moral or reflective theology. He takes no notice of the sea change in Indian religion, from the bloody cult of aggressive warriors to the purely metaphoric "sacrifice" of vegetarian priests. He notices no spiritualization in religion. His theory is overly political, completely ignoring how people reckon with the powers of nature and of divinity.

Sacrificial ideology itself changes over time, with less emphasis on violence and more on relationship to the deity. In Second Temple Judah, sacrifice comes to resemble complex economic exchanges and vassalage relationships; sacrifice is thought of as gift or payment—an *exchange* that builds a relationship. In Christianity, sacrifice becomes a metaphor, and the notion of self-giving is highlighted. Advancing civilizations seek more noble motivations than aggression; of course, that primitive aggressiveness is still present, but some of it is directed inward, in a battle for self-conquest.

Theory must try to take account of continuity and change in religious conceptualization. No inkling of this is found in Bloch. What *is* useful in Bloch is evidence of sacrifice functioning as spirit-mediumship for the appropriation of supernatural power, which is linked with organized aggression in primitive cultures.

1.1.5 Douglas on Impurity

The influential anthropologist Mary Douglas emphasizes that rituals and purity systems reflect concerns about social boundaries and distinctions, about safety and power. "Ritual recognizes the potency of disorder.... Danger lies in transitional states.... Danger is controlled by ritual."[57] Ritual restores order, conceptually and socially. "Physical crossing of the social barrier is treated as a dangerous pollution.... The danger which is risked by boundary transgression is power."[58]

Douglas notes that primitive beliefs "imply lack of differentiation ... animism ... failures to discriminate ... confusion of internal and external, of ... self and environment.... Such confusions may be necessary and universal stages in the passage of the individual from the chaotic, undifferentiated

---

[57] Mary Douglas, *Purity and Danger: An Analysis of Concepts of Pollution and Taboo* (New York: Frederick A. Praeger, 1966), 94, 96.

[58] Douglas, *Purity*, 139, 161.

experience of infancy to intellectual and moral maturity."[59] Maturity demands the making of distinctions, "correct definition, discrimination and order."[60] Purity rules articulate such discrimination and organization.[61] What Douglas shows us is that this social thinking has very primitive roots (and "primitive" is not a pejorative term for Douglas).

Douglas describes the social dimension that underlies religious ideology. High-group, high-grid societies (those that are highly structured in terms of control and classification) have a strong proclivity toward ritualism in religion,[62] since ritual preserves social order. Therefore, social change leads to anti-ritualism: "Every conversion generates some anti-ritual feeling."[63] Readers and hearers of Hosea, Micah, and Jeremiah would have heard just such a conjunction of anti-ritualism and social/moral critique.

A study of Christian history would bear out Douglas's statement that, in social settings with high levels of social control and classification, "magical efficacy [is] attributed to . . . sacraments,"[64] but that ideas of sin and atonement are weak when group boundaries are weak.[65] In high-group, high-grid situations, "theories of Natural Law flourish, doctrines of atonement flourish."[66] In low-group, low-grid modern societies, "the move away from ritual is accompanied by a strong movement towards greater ethical sensitivity."[67] Such movement away from ritual and toward ethics was also expressed in ancient times.

Hendel observes that prophets like Isaiah, Amos, and Jeremiah showed a heightened ethical concern and a lowered concern with social boundaries; they had low group/low grid notions of social identity, while the priestly hedging-about with rules shows "high group/high grid" thinking.[68]

---

[59] Douglas, *Purity*, 88.

[60] Douglas, *Purity*, 53.

[61] "A central element of the Priestly duties is to make distinctions"; (Gorman, *Ideology of Ritual*, 51). Sacrifice has to do, in part, with order: Colin E. Gunton, *The Actuality of Atonement: A Study of Metaphor, Rationality and the Christian Tradition* (Grand Rapids: Eerdmans, 1989), 118.

[62] Mary Douglas, *Natural Symbols: Explorations in Cosmology* (New York: Pantheon, 1982), 35, 54, 144.

[63] Douglas, *Natural Symbols*, 145.

[64] Douglas, *Natural Symbols*, 73.

[65] Douglas, *Natural Symbols*, 142.

[66] Mary Douglas, *In the Active Voice* (London: Routledge & Kegan Paul, 1982), 211.

[67] Douglas, *Natural Symbols*, 20.

[68] Ronald S. Hendel, "Prophets, Priests, and the Efficacy of Ritual," in *Pomegranates and Golden Bells*, eds. David P. Wright, et al (Winona Lake, Ind.: Eisenbrauns, 1995), 189–91; cf. 196 n.45.

Stowers has written an article that shows Greece as a stunning example of sacrificial custom reflecting lines of social control: "An extreme fragmentation into independent sacrificing groups characterized classical Greece."[69] Distribution of the animal parts was metaphoric for distribution of rights.[70] Women were excluded from "the actual killing, carving, and distribution. . . . Sacrifice actually caused what it signified[:] membership in an all male line."[71]

Stowers leaves many questions unanswered and he shows almost no interest in the different natures of the different gods worshipped. But by showing how the wielding of the knife was linked to political power, he demonstrates a connection between ritual violence and authority structures.

The linkage of sacrifice with rigid power structures is most interesting, and suggests that authoritarian thinking underlies the doctrines of sacrificial atonement. God is understood to be rigidly authoritarian and violent, and society is structured upon that assumption. "The sacrificial reading has no problem with God as the source of violence."[72]

1.1.6 Sacred Violence: Girard and Hamerton-Kelly

One of the most arresting theories is that of René Girard. Girardian theory starts with the idea of mimetic (that is, imitative) desire, asserting that people learn what they "should" desire from their elders and peers. By thus desiring the same things they put themselves into rivalry with others; rivalry leads to anxiety, and anxiety to violence. Societies learn to control this violence by channeling it onto a (human) scapegoat. At a later stage of social development, animal sacrifice is instituted, allowing an animal to stand as a "surrogate victim" for the scapegoat. Since human socialization itself originates from the "scapegoat mechanism," it can be said that: "human culture [is] an effacement of bloody tracks, and an expulsion of the expulsion itself."[73]

---

[69] Stanley K. Stowers, "Greeks Who Sacrifice and Those Who Do Not: Toward an Anthropology of Greek Religion," in *The Social World of the First Christians: Essays in Honor of Wayne A Meeks*, eds. L. Michael White and O. Larry Yarbrough (Minneapolis: Fortress, 1995), 308.

[70] Stowers, "Greeks Who Sacrifice," 306.

[71] Stowers, "Greeks Who Sacrifice," 327–28; similar point made by Marcel Detienne ("The Violence of Wellborn Ladies: Women in the Thesmophoria," in *The Cuisine of Sacrifice among the Greeks*, eds. Marcel Detienne and Jean-Pierre Vernant [Chicago: University of Chicago Press, 1989], 132, 136, 143), but he shows that women *do* have limited sacrificial rights (135–42, 145).

[72] James G. Williams, "Steadfast Love and Not Sacrifice," in *Curing Violence*, eds. Mark I. Wallace and Theophilus H. Smith. Forum Facsimiles 3 (Sonoma, Calif.: Polebridge Press, 1994), 98.

[73] René Girard, *Things Hidden Since the Foundation of the World* (London: Athlone, 1987), 50.

This failure to distinguish between sacrifice and scapegoat is one of several serious errors with this theory. In fact Girardian theory requires that all sacrifice be, at bottom, a form of scapegoating. But any cross-cultural survey of sacrifice will show that violence is strictly limited; the animals are not abused or beaten, but are killed quickly and without anger. They represent the careful and controlled presentation to a deity of symbols of the community's wealth and livelihood. They are not the focus of community wrath or resentment; there is no mock trial, no accusation of sins, no calling down of curses on their heads, at least *some* of which we would expect if Girardian theory were accurate on this point. Instead, these are actions that are done to the scapegoat and other curse transmission victims in rituals that can be described as *cathartic* in both the ancient sense (purifying) and the modern sense (emotionally discharging). Even a vestige of this remains in the Hebrew ritual, where the animal is cursed, abused,[74] and driven out to the wilderness demon, Azazel.

Girardians make dubious assertions about the origin of god-concepts. Hamerton-Kelly says, "the god is the transfigured victim" and, "the mob ... makes the victim a god. ... the mob's stupefaction turns to awe."[75] But the strongest support for this supposed deification of the victim is a fictional work, *The Bacchae* of Euripides. To make scapegoating the basis of religion is to eliminate all other factors that contribute to it: concerns about food supply, disease, infertility, impurity, justice, social solidarity, ghosts, the afterlife, and the desire to communicate with the god. Of the many religious intuitions that can be observed, Girard and Hamerton-Kelly see only one. How could people ever respond to the gospel, if its value system is really not human? Further, why did the Divine Man voluntarily call himself "Son of Man" if "man" is never anything but a victimizer?

If "all religion is essentially a cloak for human violence,"[76] what possible basis is there for reform? How could even Jesus ever break through such programming? The mere *exposé* of the victimization mechanism would not lead to its reform; a datum of knowledge can hardly overthrow a million years of systematic mendacity and violence.

But in fact, religions have always involved some degree of ethical reflection and restraint of violence; it is wrong to assume that religion has been

---

[74] Barnabas 7:7–9; Lester L. Grabbe, "The Scapegoat Tradition: A Study in Early Jewish Interpretation," *JSJ* 18 (1987): 158, 162–63.

[75] Robert G. Hamerton-Kelly, *Sacred Violence: Paul's Hermeneutic of the Cross* (Minneapolis: Augsburg Fortress, 1992), 16–17, 26.

[76] Robert G. Hamerton-Kelly, "Sacred Violence and Sinful Desire: Paul's Interpretation of Adam's Sin," in *The Conversation Continues: Studies in Paul and John in Honor of J. Louis Martyn*, eds. Robert T. Fortna and Beverly R. Gaventa (Nashville: Abingdon, 1990), 38.

the unceasing co-conspirator of the cruel side of human nature. It is also wrong to assume that scapegoating is the basis of all societies, or of any society. This is unduly cynical (although it is certainly understandable as a reaction against the systematic scapegoating that had just devastated Europe).

Scapegoating, when it involves mob mistreatment of a defenseless human victim, is a subset of bullying, and bullying behavior has always been recognized by the mature adults in any society as morally repulsive. This reaction against bullying shows the worldwide presence of values diametrically opposed to the scapegoating mechanism.

If we purge Girardian theory of this mistake, in fact its "foundational" mistake, the theory then becomes quite useful for noticing the connections between sacrifice, violence, and a fatalistic view of the universe. Sacrificialism is profoundly conservative and uncritical, accepting the "inevitable" structures of domination and consumption that seem to rule life, as non-Girardians have pointed out as well: "Sacrifice as a whole is but a replica of cosmic processes quite out of reach of direct human control."[77] Girardians point out that the Bible contains both this viewpoint and vigorous opposition to any notion of God as instigator of violence. The OT is full of debate on fundamental theological concepts, and it is in noticing this, that Girardian exegetes excel.

Support for a semi-Girardian theory may be found in ancient India, where there was a highly agonistic sacrificial culture, reflected in the Vedas, and where the ritual texts are quite forthcoming. The sacrificial contests in which warriors engaged were a "violent and destructive contest for the goods of life and access to heaven."[78] The violence of these sacrificial contests was not focused on the animal but on other warriors. Anticipation of violence from rival warriors is reflected in the traditional story of a warrior band that was "attacked and plundered on their place of sacrifice" by another warrior band dressed for sacrifice.[79] The ritual constitutes a violent attempt to break down the barrier between gods and men, giving an experience of "the terror and contradictoriness of the confrontation with the transcendent"; even when actual violence it reduced, intellectually "it remains a violent attempt at gaining access to the other world."[80] Religious achievement is linked with an aggressive and acquisitive drive. The sacrificing male anticipates actual violence from other sacrificers, and imagines meeting violent resistance from the gods. Here, religious reflection involves internalization of violence.

---

[77] Smith and Doniger, "Sacrifice," 204.

[78] J. C. Heesterman, *The Inner Conflict of Tradition: Essays in Indian Ritual, Kingship, and Society* (Chicago: University of Chicago Press, 1985), 100.

[79] Heesterman, *Inner Conflict*, 99, 86.

[80] Heesterman, *Inner Conflict*, 85, 98.

Combining these observations of social violence and violent imagination directed heavenward, it seems safe to say that *primitive sacrificial ideology reflects a violent social environment*. The animal is not so much a safety valve as a magnet for community violence. This was disturbing to many Hindu thinkers, so much so that the main Hindu epic from the period contemporary with early Christianity, the Mahabharata, is largely a series of critiques of sacrificial violence and of concepts of divine violence. There had evolved the recognized role of "reviler" of the sacrifice, "and in each case the fault in question is the violence of the rite."[81] In the Ashvamedhika Parvan portion of the Mahabharata, "the success of the sacrifice is assessed . . . in terms of the ability to avoid fighting."[82]

Hindu ritual comes to perform *symbolic* rather than actual acts of violence. The sacrificer becomes an ascetic who imitates the gods' own ascetic feats in a mental struggle for self-renunciation. Thus, both Vedic sacrifice and Hindu non-sacrifice *reflect* and *dramatize* existing beliefs about what is required, whether violence or self-conquest.

Even though "violent conflict and death were the essence of sacrifice,"[83] this evolves into *imagined* violence and grain offerings. The mental preparations accompanying Vedic sacrifice are those of a warrior preparing for battle. The sacrifice is more a danger-game than a safety valve. It provides a setting around which martial exercises (which become increasingly symbolic) are enacted. Violence is diminished by being converted to a ritual and ascetic exercise. Finally, "the mere *recitation* of the Veda . . . is regarded as . . . the actual performance of a Vedic sacrifice."[84]

Heesterman's insights provide a metaphysical angle from which Girardian theory could benefit. Heesterman brings out the role of *imagined* violence replacing real violence in the past. The conceptualization of violence probably has a greater role than Girard (or anyone else) recognizes. Even in our modern culture, where combatants in movies are able to endure dozens of knockout blows, we (men, that is) seem to have an intense need to *imagine* violence, to construct a story out of it.

Sacrifice ritualized a belief in the inevitability of violence, domination, and consumption, beliefs that underwent a complicated transformation over time. A theory is needed that can account for the discourse about—and against—sacrifice in Indian, Jewish, Greek, and Christian cultures, and I attempt a start

---

[81] Tamar C. Reich, "Sacrificial Violence and Textual Battles: Inner Textual Interpretation in the Sanskrit Mahabharata," *History of Religions* 41 (2001): 150–51; cf. Heesterman, *Inner Conflict*, 82.

[82] Reich, "Sacrificial Violence," 152.

[83] Heesterman, *Inner Conflict*, 91.

[84] Smith and Doniger, "Sacrifice," 208.

at this with my theory of spiritualization. Girardian *exegesis* has done a good job of noticing the discourse of violence and non-violence in the Bible, but Girardian *theory* makes it difficult to accept that there can be any *real* repudiation of violence by societies.

The overemphasis on something that really does exist—the scapegoating mechanism—does not render Girardian theory useless, but shows its weakness *as a systematic theory*. However, there is no denying that Girard has put his finger on a pattern of dissembling and violence that can be seen in all religions—precisely one of the things Paul noticed about "the present evil age" (Gal 1:4)[85]! Girardian theory helps to uncover the base motives that do show up in religion. As Ted Peters writes, "God does not demand sacrifice. We do. Yet in order to hide our own penchant for blood from ourselves, we attribute it to the divine. We create the illusion of a sacrifice-demanding God."[86]

Girardian theory is adequate only within a certain scope. Some of the best work on violence and the repudiation of violence in biblical texts is done by Girardians, and I will consult them later in this work.

1.1.7 Assessment and Theory

To articulate my own theory of sacrifice I begin with the simple observation that ethnography shows us that sacrifice has something to do with human *livelihood*, with the means of getting it and maintaining it. People sacrifice a portion of their livelihood in order to insure its perpetuation, to secure good crops, good hunting, and a good spirit environment. Given the assumption that the gods perpetuate the food supply and that they respond to sacrificial gifts, placating them is a thoroughly logical activity. Metaphysical belief systems shaped the understandings of the transaction. Frustratingly for us, such understandings are not well-preserved in the texts, probably because they were so obvious to the original authors.

There is a danger in focusing on the act of killing, which in fact is not the focus of attention in any of the ancient ritual texts (Israelite, Vedic, Zoroastrian[87]) that I have examined. There is much more attention to "introduction and consecration," and sometimes to praise and supplication. In other words, there is more attention to approaching and communicating with the god than there is to killing the animal or to making the animal "stand for" anything. The offerer considers the animal to be a valuable item.

---

[85] Cf. 1 Thess 2:2–4, 14–18; 3:4; 2 Cor 4:4–11.

[86] Ted Peters, "Atonement and the Final Scapegoat," *PRSt* 19 (1992): 181.

[87] In classical Greece, too, there is little attention to the moment of killing; violence is not "examined," and "men seek no omen in it" (Jean-Louis Durand, "Greek Animals: Toward a Topology of Edible Bodies," in *The Cuisine of Sacrifice among the Greeks*, eds. Marcel Detienne and Jean-Pierre Vernant [Chicago: University of Chicago Press, 1989], 91).

I offer a composite theory of sacrifice, accepting the fact of spirit-mediumship as noted by Hubert and Mauss and by Bloch; adapting the communal solidarity idea of Smith; and accepting the gift idea that Tylor and countless others have observed. Finally, some concept of substitution is often involved in sacrifice, although by no means is *penal* substitution as widely present as Christian scholars often assume.

Sacrificial ritual demonstrates and reinforces lines of social power in classical Greece (Stowers, Detienne), but to explain the social structure is not to explain the ritual practice. Religious symbols speak of far more than just social structure; society itself exists within a cosmos, and religion purports to explain the cosmos, including things that, as of yet, have no social reflection.

I greatly alter the violence-channeling ideas of Girard and Bloch, because the problem is significantly more complex than they concede. I end up with more cautious conclusions, taking note of the importance of *imagined* violence (against rivals, spirits, gods, even oneself) in connection with sacrifice. In Vedic and Greek cultures, sacrifice was an arena for reflection on violence and struggle, and on the inculcation of (male) character values. The Vedic stories point out the need for proper attentiveness, the Greek ones for proper submission. The agonistic notion, connected with a purely spiritualized sacrificial pantomime, outlived actual sacrifice in India, while agonistic asceticism persists in Greek and Roman Christianity nearly two millennia after the cessation of animal sacrifice. This allows some cautious cross-cultural observation of how violence and struggle are conceptually connected with sacrifice, confirming Bloch's and Girard's intuitions, but not their systematic theories.

I do find that sacrificial ideas are most prominent in societies with the most coercive structure. This is my synthesis of anthropological data about Greece and India, and the finding that: "magical ... sacraments"[88] and "doctrines of atonement"[89] are common in societies with high levels of social control. Similar instincts about social control are present even when sacrifice has become metaphorical, and spiritualization has generated social adaptations. It is no surprise to find structures of "high group" social control (priesthoods or sacred professionals) continuing to emerge from any sacrificial theology. These are the social results of a theological idea: God as a sacrifice-demander. A ritual-demanding God generates ritual professionals.

Speaking cross-culturally (and tentatively), I can say that sacrifice *usually* involves the offering of a gift to a god, is *usually* associated with some ideology of spirit-mediumship or communion, *often* involves substitutionary ideas, and *often* includes an ideology of violence or struggle that tends over

---

[88] Douglas, *Natural Symbols*, 73.
[89] Douglas, *In the Active*, 211.

time to turn into asceticism. I will add to this explanation of sacrifice after I discuss the Hebrew ritual.

I am particularly interested in the concept of Deity implied in the rituals and the texts. This is necessary background to approaching the question of whether Paul's sacrificial metaphors entail any notion of ritual as a means for spirit-mediumship, of ritual as something required by God, or of the sacrificial victim as a substitute or a payment.

1.2 Hebrew Sacrifice

We move to Hebrew sacrifice which, at first glance, has much less to do with spirit-mediumship or struggle than does Indo-European sacrifice, and more to do with guilt, debt, and impurity (and its correlate: forgiveness). I will begin my analysis with an observation of historical and theological stages of development in Hebrew religion, then proceed to a discussion of the most important rituals of the Second Temple period.

In the premonarchic period, Hebrew sacrifice was not much different from that of its neighbors. Sacrifice was originally for *appeasement*, mollifying the gods with gifts: What the priests offer is "the food for my offerings by fire, my pleasing odor" (Num 28:2). The "pleasing odor" (here רֵיחַ נִיחֹחִי; thirty-six times elsewhere without the possessive suffix, רֵיחַ נִיחֹחַ, and five times in other forms) signifies sacrifices that satisfy God. The phrase refers to God's sensory experience and to the mollifying effect the offering has on him, it is "the smell of pacification."[90] People understood sacrifice to be propitiatory, whether directed at God or at idols, as in Ezek 6:13 (*Ibid.*).

Wenham favors "soothing, pacifying" odor over "pleasing odor," because God is actually *appeased* by the aroma, as is shown by its first usage in the OT, when the Lord decides not to "curse the land again" after Noah sacrifices to him (Gen 8:21).[91] That such propitiatory notions are embarrassing to certain scholars is evidenced by the strategies of denial they employ: Milgrom says that the notion of caring for and feeding a shrine-resident god was ancient and widespread, but that, in the Bible:

> only rare linguistic fossils survive, such as that the sacrifices are called "God's food" ([Lev] 22:25) and "pleasing aroma to the Lord" (1:17). The altar is also called "the Lord's table" (Ezek 41:22; 44:16; Mal 1:7, 12).[92]

---

[90] Douglas McC. L. Judisch, "Propitiation in the Language and Typology of the OT," *CTQ* 48 (1984): 225.

[91] Gordon J. Wenham, "The Theology of Old Testament Sacrifice," in *Sacrifice in the Bible*, eds. R. Beckwith and M. Selman (Carlisle, U.K.: Paternoster, 1995), 80.

[92] Milgrom, *Leviticus 1–16*, 250.

Forty-two instances of God (or gods) being soothed by the smoke of burning flesh, constitutes a *standard* Pentateuchal usage, not a *rare* one. Despite Milgrom insisting that "provid[ing] food for the god . . . . [is] not found in Israel,"[93] his own evidence shows that it was fundamental. Theology is moving away from such anthropomorphic notions, but in the Pentateuch, it has not moved very far. Even prayer is conceived of in a naturalistic manner, as Milgrom notes: "their prayer will travel to God along a trajectory that passes through their land, city, Temple, and then, at the altar, turns heavenward (1 Kgs 8:44, 48)."[94] Milgrom admits that the notion of the gift is present in many of the Hebrew sacrifices,[95] but he downplays the fact that the gifts are, in fact, the best available food items, just what an anthropomorphic god would want.

Feeding, housing, and mollifying a god, and praying in his direction, are only some of the naturalistic notions that occur in pagan and Hebrew traditions alike. Sacrifice in ancient societies often involved defense against spirit-wrath and infectious impurity. The same concerns are reflected in Jewish texts, where God strikes dead a man who innocently put out his hand to steady the ark of the covenant (2 Sam 6:6–7), and in the conviction that accumulating impurity could drive God out of the temple.

These primitive mythemes decline in importance when they are subjected to the notion—and set within the literary context—of *law*, and even of the elaborate ritual technology for the manipulation of sacred substances. The obsession with cultic purification tends to converge with an emerging perception of lawfulness in the universe. Sin as ethical violation entails reliability in divine dealings. Law means consistency.

In the Hebrew priestly religion we see a thorough mixture of moral and ritual categories: "Many technical terms can mean both 'sin' and 'impurity' "; *ma'al* can signify anything from accidental misuse of sacrificial animal parts to adultery and lying.[96] Whether the infraction is ritual or moral, the solution lies in *cultic procedure*, creating a need for meticulous ritual correctness.

Ritual has to do with establishing, maintaining, and restoring order. Impurity means disorder, a break in the spiritual defenses, which opens up the community to spirit-wrath. Ritual restores purity, that is, order and safety. Hebrew ritual also demonstrates anxiety about impurity. "Israel was part of [an ANE] cultic continuum which abounded in purifications both of persons

---

[93] Milgrom, *Leviticus 1–16*, 440.
[94] Milgrom, *Leviticus 1–16*, 251.
[95] Milgrom, *Leviticus 1–16*, 441.
[96] Levine, *Leviticus*, 19, 30.

and buildings."[97] By wiping away impurity, sacrificial ritual averts disorder, which in a theistic milieu means the wrath of God. Ritual restores order and prevents vulnerability to spirit forces.

God shows interest in properly organized ritual by his fiery manifestation at some sacrificial events, igniting the burnt offering on his own initiative,[98] or annihilating those who offer wrongly, as when he slays the sons of Aaron for offering "illicit fire" (Num 3:4), and when he incinerates Korah and 250 supporters while they are lighting incense (Num 16:35–38 in NRSV). These incidents are followed by commands to "bring the tribe of Levi near" (3:6), and that "no layman ... should approach the altar" (17:5 NAB; cf. 3:10). The authority of the priests is backed up by stirring miracle stories and chilling horror stories.

1.2.1 Temple Purification

It is necessary to take a look at the main categories of animal sacrifice, of which the most important for Pauline studies is the חַטָּאת.

The main kinds of sacrifice were:

- The whole- or burnt offering (עֹלָה) was an ancient rite to attract the deity's attention, "to show one's consummate devotion.... Another level of meaning in the 'ola is that of .... the food of the deity,"[99] as shown by the persistent reference to "a pleasing odor to the Lord" (Num 15:7, 9, etc.). Originally the burnt offering atoned or expiated, but, with time, that function was taken over by "the חטאת and אשם."[100]
- As the burnt offering was food for God, the peace offering (שְׁלָמִים זֶבַח) was food for people, as mentioned in the Mekilta and other rabbinic sources.[101] The peace offering had nothing to do with atonement, but was a "celebrative sacrifice," frequently offered on feast days, and sometimes associated with the fulfillment of vows.[102]
- The two sacrifices that provide expiation in the post-exilic period were formerly referred to in English as the sin offering and guilt offering, but Milgrom calls them "purification offering" and "reparation offering," respectively, a suggestion accepted now by many, but not all, scholars.

The most important sacrifices in the Second Temple period are these last two.

---

[97] Jacob Milgrom, *Studies in Cultic Theology and Terminology* (SJLA 36; Leiden: Brill, 1983), 69.
[98] Lev 9:24; Judg 6:21; 1 Kgs 18:38; 1 Chr 21:26; 2 Chr 7:1; 2 Macc 2:10.
[99] Gary Anderson, "Sacrifice and Sacrificial Offerings (OT)," in *ABD* V:878.
[100] Jacob Milgrom, "Further on the Expiatory Sacrifices," *JBL* 115 (1996): 513.
[101] Anderson, "Sacrifice (OT)," 879.
[102] Anderson, "Sacrifice (OT)," 879.

Hebrew	LXX	Milgrom	NRSV, NAB	others	e.g.
ḥaṭṭā't (חַטָּאת)	(περι) ἁμαρτία	purification offering	sin offering	expiation offering	Lev chap. 4; 6:25ff[103]; 16:5–15; Exod 29:36; Ezek 43:21
āshām (אָשָׁם)	πλεμμέλεια	reparation offering	guilt offering		Lev 7:1–7; Isa 53:10

The difference between these types of sacrifice became confused even in certain Pentateuch passages (in Lev 7:7 they are said to "be alike," and in 5:6 the two terms are actually used interchangeably), but they continued to be recognized as separate sacrifices. Milgrom insists that "these two sacrifices should never be . . . confused. The אשם expiates for desecration; the חטאת for contamination."[104] Desecration results when temple property is misappropriated,[105] while contamination results from sin and other causes of impurity. The main difference for Levine is that the ḥaṭṭā't "was to remove the culpability borne by the offender," while "the 'āshām . . . was actually a penalty paid in the form of a sacrificial offering to God," often accompanied by monetary restitution plus fine (*Ibid.*).

Despite these real distinctions, exceptions can be found; in fact, they are not always animal sacrifices: the חטאת can sometimes be a grain offering, while the אשם was sometimes *just* the monetary restitution, without the sacrifice.[106]

Jacob Milgrom has called for a rethinking of the purposes of sacrifice by focusing on the cleansing of impurity from the inner sanctuary, on Yom Kippur, with חטאת blood. He describes the contamination of the temple:

> The dynamic, aerial quality of biblical impurity is best attested by its *graded power*. . . . The wanton, unrepented sin not only pollutes the outer altar and penetrates into the shrine but it pierces the veil to the holy ark and *kapporet*, the very throne of God. . . . Sin . . . is certain to mark the face of the sanctuary, and unless it is quickly expunged, God's presence will depart.[107]

Milgrom describes three different levels of purification to handle different levels of pollution: application of the blood of the חטאת sacrifice to the horns of the outer altar will purge the impurity caused by the voluntary sin *of an individual*; חטאת blood on the inner altar purges involuntary sin by the *community*; deliberate and wanton sin by either an individual or the community

---

[103] This is 6:17ff in the MT (followed by NAB, but not by most English translations).
[104] Milgrom, "Further," 513.
[105] Levine, *Leviticus*, 18.
[106] Anderson, "Sacrifice (OT)," 880.
[107] Milgrom, *Studies*, 78, 83.

requires the sprinkling of הַחַטָּאת blood on the *kapporet,* and can only be done once a year.[108]

The "priestly theodicy" meant protecting the community against God-abandonment, a viewpoint similar to that of Israel's pagan neighbors: "The sanctuary needs constant purification lest the resident god abandons [sic][109] it."[110] Ezekiel's program also focuses on the impurity concern. The rites in Ezek 43:20, 26 כִּפֶּר, "purge," and חִטֵּא, "decontaminate," and טִהַר, "'purify,' the altar so as to make it fit for the regular worship."[111]

Milgrom argues that Hebrew sacrifice is not a matter of substitutionary death, but concerns the purity of the temple, which was a kind of spiritual barometer registering the degrees and kinds of sin committed in Israel. But the ritual inside the temple also has to do with sins; it is not only "because of the uncleanness," but also "because of their transgressions (מִפִּשְׁעֵיהֶם[112]), all their sins" (חַטֹּאתָם, Lev 16:16). The text links uncleanness with its cause: sinning.

If "sin-sacrifice" is too narrow a term for the *hattat* ritual, so also is "purification sacrifice" if it is meant to drive out the possibility of sin-purgation or expiation. Milgrom imposes a new narrowness of meaning upon a ritual whose name is, after all, the same as the word for sin (חַטָּאת). By insisting on "purification" alone, Milgrom is minimizing the fact that it is *sin-caused* impurity that is being cleansed. In fact, the Hebrew חַטָּאת had a broader meaning than the English "sin"; חַטָּאת was not always a moral transgression; the defilement incurred by a Nazirite when someone dies suddenly in his presence is also called חַטָּאת (Num 6:11).[113]

Milgrom has correctly exposed a (former) scholarly neglect of purity concerns in Leviticus, but he has tried to impose a new hegemony of meaning upon actions that were really understood in a dual sense, as cleansing both the symbols (the sancta) and the things symbolized (the priests and people). Cleansing of individual, community, priests, and temple are homologous, or parallel. Just as the temple suffers pollution whenever sin is committed in

---

[108] Milgrom, *Studies,* 38–43, 77–79; idem, "The Priestly Laws of Sancta Contamination," in *"Sha'arei Talmon": Studies in the Bible, Qumran, and the Ancient Near East Presented to Shemaryahu Talmon* eds. Michael Fishbane, and Emanuel Tov (Winona Lake, Ind.: Eisenbrauns, 1992), 142.

[109] Because of the conditional "lest," the verb should be subjunctive: "abandon."

[110] Milgrom, *Studies,* 82.

[111] All in Piel form; Moshe Greenberg, "The Design and Themes of Ezekiel's Program of Restoration," *Interpretation* 38 (1984): 194.

[112] פֶּשַׁע is a strong term for "revolt" or "rebellion"; Angel G. Rodriguez, *Substitution in the Hebrew Cultus* (Berrien Springs, Mich.: Andrews University Press, 1979), 148.

[113] John Dennis, "The Function of the חַטָּאת Sacrifice in the Priestly Literature," *ETL* 78,1 (2002): 111.

Israel,[114] so does purification of the temple signify purification of people. The high priest makes "atonement for himself and for the people" (16:24). Cultic actions *affect* the things symbolized. If it were not too clumsy, I would argue for the label "expiation and purification sacrifice."

Milgrom interprets the חַטָּאת sacrifices of Leviticus 4 and 5 through the lens of the Yom Kippur temple cleansing. Some critics of Milgrom, however, overstate their case: "Milgrom's position is only valid for the Day of Atonement.... In Lev 4 nothing is said about the cleansing of the sanctuary."[115] But cleansing *is* in view there; the priest "shall ... sprinkle some of the blood seven times before the Lord in front of the curtain of the sanctuary" (Lev 4:6), and on the two altars and at the base of the holocaust altar. This supports Milgrom's assertion that different levels of cleansing are required for different degrees of sin-infection. The cleansing in Leviticus 4 does not reach into the inner sanctum, where the ark of the covenant was kept, but it does cleanse all of the lesser installations.

However, forgiveness of the individual is clearly in view in Leviticus 4. *Four times* we get a clear indication that the sacrifice results in forgiveness: "they shall be forgiven [נִסְלַח].... The priest shall make atonement on his behalf for his sin, and he shall be forgiven.... atonement on your behalf.... you shall be forgiven" (Lev 4:20, 26, 31, 35). Dennis and Kiuchi point out that in every one of these cases in Leviticus 4, and again in 5:10, 13, 18, the ritual is performed, and *then* the text says that the person is forgiven.[116] "Forgiveness of sin is the *direct* result of the ritual."[117] The text has a personal emphasis; it does not say that *sin* is forgiven, but "*he* shall be forgiven,"[118] and this includes the deliberate sins of Lev 5:1–3.[119]

It is quite clear that "The *hattat* indeed deals with חַטָּאת (sin) (Lev 4.1–5.13)"[120]—securing forgiveness on days other than Yom Kippur. But even as regards Yom Kippur, Milgrom unjustly suppresses the consequential or parallel expiation of the sinners when he says "the purification offering purges the sanctuary but not the wrongdoer."[121] For the Yom Kippur sacrifice also "make[s] atonement for the priests and for all the people" (Lev 16:33). The

---

[114] Milgrom, *Studies*, 78–79.

[115] Rodriguez, *Substitution*, 128–29.

[116] Dennis, "The Function," 117; N. Kiuchi, *The Purification Offering in the Priestly Literature: Its Meaning and Function.* JSOT Sup 56 (Sheffield: Sheffield Academic, 1987), 35 n.21.

[117] Dennis, "The Function," 118.

[118] Kiuchi, *Purification Offering*, 37.

[119] Dennis, "The Function," 118–19.

[120] Kiuchi, *Purification Offering*, 161; cf. 65.

[121] Milgrom, *Leviticus 1–16*, 441.

individual undoubtedly feels released when the stain made by his sin is purged. "The *hattat* ritual deals with both the act of sin and its consequence."[122]

The blood rites then have a two-fold function: to cleanse the sanctuary from the pollution of sin and to release the offerer from the penalty for his sinning.[123]

Anderson and Levine opine that some sacrifices purify, and others forgive.[124] On the contrary, Kiuchi says, "Sin . . . is a kind of uncleanness . . . . [T]here is no essential distinction between purification and expiation,"[125] an overstated position, in my view. I think the Hartley-Dennis view (that the חטאת had two purposes) is best here.

All the scholars mentioned in the previous paragraph challenge Milgrom's tendency to make totalizing claims about temple-purification. When Milgrom insists that the חטאת deals only with purification and not forgiveness, this contradicts his other statements that the *consequence* of sin is forgiven.[126] He distorts the meaning of *forgiveness* when he says, "the inadvertent offender needs forgiveness not because of his act per se . . . but because of the *consequence* of his act."[127] By bringing forgiveness into the equation *at all*, Milgrom should concede—and *has* conceded, in more recent communications[128]—that forgiveness of sins is part of the חטאת process. Milgrom considers "forgiveness" too weak and narrow a term; the person "seeks more than forgiveness"; he seeks to "be once again restored to grace."[129] This concedes my point that a sacrificing person experiences a spiritual change.

There is more than a semantic problem here; his resistance to the terms "forgiveness" and "sin" really stands for a resistance to Christian ideas of substitutionary atonement that depend upon Christ as the fulfillment of the "sin sacrifice." This has led him into a rhetorically one-sided explication of חטאת and כפר, and so his work, while crucial, stands in need of correction.

This leads to a discussion of the key verb in these texts.

---

[122] Kiuchi, *Purification Offering*, 52; cf. Dennis, "The Function," 112–15.

[123] John E. Hartley, *Leviticus*. WBC 4 (Dallas: Word Books, 1992), 65; similarly, David P. Wright, "Day of Atonement," in *ABD* II (New York: Doubleday, 1992), 74.

[124] Anderson, "Sacrifice (OT)," 879–80; Baruch A. Levine, *In the Presence of the Lord: A Study of Cult and Some Cultic Terms in Ancient Israel* (Leiden: Brill, 1974), 103–6.

[125] Kiuchi, *Purification Offering*, 65.

[126] Anderson, "Sacrifice (OT)," 880.

[127] Milgrom, *Studies*, 77.

[128] In conversation with me in June, 2000, Professor Milgrom agreed that forgiveness was part of the *hattat* process.

[129] Milgrom, *Leviticus 1–16*, 245.

1.2.2 The Meanings of כפר

The rituals described in Leviticus 16 (the goat purification sacrifice, the scapegoat, the bull purification sacrifice, and the two burnt offerings) are described without a pause, with the priest going from one set of animals to another, and back again. First the bull purification sacrifice is mentioned but not carried out (v. 6). Then the two identical goats are brought forward and their fates mentioned but not carried out (vv. 7–10). Next the bull is slaughtered and its blood sprinkled on the *kapporet* (vv. 11–14), followed by the goat slaughter and the sprinkling of its blood (15), then by a description of the reason for the purification sacrifices (16–17), and by further actions with the blood of the two sacrifices (18–19). Next comes the scapegoat ritual (21–22), then a change of clothing and some washings (23–24a), the burnt offerings (24b), a further action with the blood of the purification sacrifices (25), a cleansing of the person who had driven out the scapegoat (26), disposal of carcasses and further washings (27–28), and another description of the reason for the ritual (29–34).

Atonement (כפר) is mentioned in connection with the purification sacrifices (6, 16–17, 20, 27), the burnt offerings (24), the scapegoat (10), and the whole process (30, 32–34).

This key verb, כפר, covers more than just temple-cleansing; the priest and "all the assembly of Israel" (Lev 16:17) are also cleansed. Impurity-cleansing and sin-purging are part of the same procedure: "[Aaron] shall make atonement for the tent of meeting and for the altar, and he shall make atonement for the priests and for all the people of the assembly" (16:33). McLean wants to argue that כפר was strictly focused on the temple furniture; "When *kipper* is used with a person, it always requires the preposition *'al* (Lev 16:24 . . .) or *b^e'ad* (Lev 16:6) . . . signifying agency ('on behalf of')."[130] But this does not mean that individual cleansing was a purely Hellenistic idea. The prepositions do not sever the people from the experience of atonement,[131] or make forgiveness unrelated to temple-cleansing.

To say, "atonement of sins was accomplished through repentance alone,"[132] is to treat the spiritualizations of second to fourth century rabbis as though they were normative for the functioning cult. In fact, people poured into the temple with their sacrifices, seeking purgation even when the city was about to fall. The spiritual doctrine of repentance became dominant in the rabbinic period—because there was no longer any temple to encourage a literal interpretation!

---

[130] McLean, *Cursed Christ*, 38.
[131] Cf. Levine, *In the Presence*, 64 n.29.
[132] McLean, 38–39.

Milgrom helpfully drew attention to the neglected role of purification, but by posing his findings in a dichotomous manner—temple, *not* people—he opened the door to such one-sided interpretations as McLean's. McLean artificially excludes persons from the atonement process, failing to recognize that the temple stands for the priests and people. Cleansing the temple *mattered* because it symbolized the cleansing of the people.

In fact, forgiveness is prominent in the views of Jewish writers in the century leading up to 70 C.E. For Jews such as Philo and Josephus, its *main* purpose is to deal with sin, as Milgrom himself points out, although he tries to restrict their reference to the sacrifices in Leviticus 4 and Numbers 15.[133] Both the schools of Hillel and Shammai understood the daily lamb sacrifice to represent forgiveness of sin.[134]

The ancient way of thinking, which attaches supreme importance to symbols, for instance the cleanness of a temple, is profoundly alien to modern ways of thinking. In studying the sacrificial cult, Christian scholars had emphasized sin, substitution, and forgiveness, and in reaction to them Milgrom over-stated his case for purification. Forgiveness is a correlate of temple cleansing, whether on Yom Kippur or throughout the year, in connection with which forgiveness is explicitly mentioned (Leviticus 4 and 5).

Milgrom's main interest in one book, *Cult and Conscience*, is to show that the priestly religion emphasized repentance as well as cult. Personal repentance, remorse, and reparation were absolutely necessary for an effective אשם sacrifice;[135] "without sacrifice, however, it does not suffice to obliterate sin."[136] Stowers overlooks this stress on personal confession when he writes: "The person did not receive forgiveness for a sinful act itself but dealt only with the consequences of such acts on the temple."[137]

I cannot help but detect an ideological motive in the position of Stowers. He wants to depict Christians as dreadful misinterpreters of Judaism, "from Hebrews and Barnabas to Origen."[138] Stowers insists that forgiveness was derived only from repentance and was not thought to have any connection with

---

[133] Milgrom, *Studies*, 68 n.1–2.

[134] Alfred Edersheim, *The Life and Times of Jesus the Messiah* (Peabody, Mass.: Hendrickson, 1993), 237–38 (Book 3.3).

[135] Jacob Milgrom, *Cult and Conscience: The* Asham *and the Priestly Doctrine of Repentance* (Leiden: E. J. Brill, 1976), 108–19; cf. 10–11.

[136] Milgrom, *Cult and Conscience*, 123–24.

[137] Stanley K. Stowers, *A Rereading of Romans: Justice, Jews, and Gentiles* (New Haven, Conn.: Yale University Press, 1994), 208.

[138] Stowers, *Rereading*, 206.

sacrificial ritual ... except on the Day of Atonement![139] Such views probably take Milgrom's slant further than Milgrom intended.

NT scholars are particularly interested in the meaning of *kipper*, because this impinges on the meaning of NT sayings about the death of Jesus that utilize the ἱλάσκομαι word group. Scholars have debated whether ἱλάσκομαι has primarily the sense of *propitiation* (appeasing or conciliating God) or of *expiation* (removing or wiping away sin).

Lyonnet defends an expiatory meaning, noting that ἐξιλάσκεσθαι can translate "the Hebrew verb *ḥiṭṭeh* ... 'to remove sin,'"[140] or it can translate כִּפֶּר with the meaning "purify. The more usual Greek word for purify, καθαρίζω, can also translate כִּפֶּר.[141]

In defending "expiate" as the meaning of כִּפֶּר, Dunn writes:

> In Hebrew usage God is never the object of the key verb (*kipper*). Properly speaking, in the Israelite cult, God is never "propitiated" or "appeased." The objective of the atoning act is rather the removal of *sin*. ... acting on the sin rather than on God.[142]

This is correct, as long as it does not overlook the more literal meaning, "purge."[143] Of course, propitiation is another implication of כִּפֶּר; God's anger is a factor in many of the passages where כִּפֶּר is used.[144]

Hartley minimizes propitiation. "Not God's kindled wrath but his potential wrath is the direct focus of the expiating sacrifices,"[145] and there is no need to propitiate a God who is not yet angry. But propitiation certainly *is* present if God's anger will swiftly follow any letup in the regimen of ritual feeding. This is the arrangement: God agrees to withhold his wrath if humans remember to keep up their offerings. Here sacrifice resembles a tribute payment to a demanding sovereign, and this is an implication of sacrifice that remains attached to it, even in its metaphorical transformations in Paul and Hebrews.

---

[139] Stowers, *Rereading*, 208.

[140] Stanislas Lyonnet, "The Terminology of Redemption," in *Sin, Redemption and Sacrifice: A Biblical and Patristic Study*. Analecta Biblica 48 (Rome: Biblical Institute, 1970), 137.

[141] Lyonnet, "Terminology," 130–31.

[142] Dunn, *Theology*, 214; cf. Hartley, *Leviticus*, 64–65.

[143] Milgrom contrasts "purge" with "expiate" (*Leviticus 1–16*, 1079), but later (1083) acknowledges "the final stage in the evolution of the verb[:] the abstract, figurative notion 'atone' or 'expiate.'"

[144] e.g., Exod 32:10–14; Ps 78:38; Morris, *Apostolic Preaching*, 148, 160, 171; Klaus Koch, "The Translation of *kapporet* in the Septuagint," in *Pomegranates and Golden Bells*, eds. David P. Wright, et al (Winona Lake, Ind.: Eisenbrauns, 1995), 68–70.

[145] Hartley, *Leviticus*, 65.

There are numerous non-cultic usages of the verb כִּפֶּר where it means "conciliate" or "appease," including appeasing humans (Gen 32:20–21; Prov 16:14). One of these was the "righteousness" (Psalm 106:31) of Phinehas in killing a man and his pagan girlfriend. The Lord specifically says that this act "made atonement" and "turned back my wrath from the Israelites," earning for Phinehas "a covenant of perpetual priesthood" (Num 25:11, 13). The gold offered to the Lord after the victory over Midian, the intercession of Moses after the Golden Calf, the setting aside of the Levites in Num 8:19, all accomplish atonement.[146]

Milgrom lists numerous passages where כִּפֶּר indicates a ransom payment (Exod 30:16; Num 31:50), sometimes averting God's wrath (Num|1:53; 8:19; 18:23) or human wrath (2 Sam 21:3–6), and more.[147] Payment conciliates a creditor; ransoming appeases an angry sovereign. A theme of conciliation underlies all these passages. Substitution does not always have a moral or penal setting; it may be simply a matter of buying-off a demanding sovereign.

Looking mainly at the non-cultic usages, Schenker wants to emphasize a moral or interpersonal meaning, insisting that reconciliation between feuding parties is the fundamental meaning of כבר. He claims that "preventing the hard punishment or disastrous vendetta is the original meaning of atonement [*Sühne*] in the OT."[148] Looking at the Jacob and Esau story, he notes that, "for reconciliation to be possible" there must be "willingness to forgive" by both parties.[149]

Schenker argues that reconciliation is also at the basis of cultic atonement. "In the blood of the atonement liturgy," men encounter "the *reconciling mercy of God*. . . . men can only accept reconciliation when they gain an insight into their guilt."[150] This evidences "God's readiness to reconcile," not "substitutionary violence."[151] Yet his survey of כבר must include OT contexts of *kofar*-payments,[152] and the same idea in the NT: "Christ pays the necessary price."[153]

---

[146] Herbert Chanan Brichto, "On Slaughter and Sacrifice, Blood and Atonement," *HUCA* 47 (1976): 29.

[147] Milgrom, *Leviticus 1–16*, 1082–83.

[148] Adrian Schenker, *Versöhnung und Sühne: Wege gewaltfreier Konfliktlösung im Alten Testament mit einem Ausblick auf das Neue Testament* (Freiberg: Schweizerisches Katholisches Bibelwerk, 1981), 59.

[149] Schenker, *Versöhnung*, 39–40; cf. 53.

[150] Schenker, *Versöhnung*, 117.

[151] Schenker, *Versöhnung*, 119.

[152] Schenker, *Versöhnung*, 55–59.

[153] Schenker, *Versöhnung*, 125.

One could question whether the notion of *payment* at the heart of all *kippering* really keeps the idea at the high level of moral repair of relationships. Sometimes *kippering* is quite baldly self-interested. Schenker's emphasis seems to be a spiritualizing move, suppressing the give-to-get logic of *kipper*.

1.2.3 The Logic of Kipper

It turns out there was more than one kind of logic of sacrificial atonement in the Pentateuch. The Priestly author (P) occupies a central place in the Pentateuch, being preceded by two authors (J and E) and followed by one (H). Knohl sees the P source as standing in tension with earlier, popular anthropomorphic notions of God smelling the sacrifice,[154] of "God receiving pleasure from the sweet aroma and his anger subsiding as a result," as in Gen 8:20.[155] God actually "smells" (יָרַח) the offering (as in 1 Sam 26:19). P, however, avoids using "pleasing odor." The central feature becomes the sprinkling of blood instead of the sending up of smoke, and it is understood to purify rather than to appease. Purification becomes an impersonal operation.[156]

Neither J nor P make any reference to moral change; *atonement is not a moral experience*, but depends on properly offered goods desired by the Lord (J) or on properly executed manipulation of a spiritual substance, blood (P). J and P fit animism into theism in two very different ways.

In reaction to P's idea of an impersonal atoning mechanism, the Holiness Code ("H") re-personalizes the cultic transaction,[157] deliberately reintroducing anthropomorphism. It is the attitude of the personal God that matters the most for H. The role of blood is retained, but demoted in importance; sacrifice is "an אִשֶּׁה, a gift, 'a pleasing odour to the Lord.'"[158]

Schwartz picks up where Knohl leaves off, noting that the P doctrine of blood as cleansing is changed by H; in Leviticus 17, the key H chapter, "the action of the blood is a ransoming one," which is "a new and unique theory."[159]

---

[154] Gary Anderson, "The Interpretation of the Purification Offering (חַטָּאת) in the *Temple Scroll* (11QTemple) and Rabbinic Literature," *JBL* 111 (1992): 27 n.18, summarizing a Knohl article in Hebrew.

[155] Israel Knohl, "The Sin Offering Law in the 'Holiness School,'" in *Priesthood and Cult in Ancient Israel*, eds. G. Anderson and S. Olyan. JSOT Sup 125 (Sheffield: Sheffield Academic, 1991), 199.

[156] Knohl, "The Sin Offering," 199.

[157] The opinion that H is more recent than P is steadily gaining more scholarly adherents; see Knohl, "The Sin Offering," 200, and, in the same volume, Milgrom (188–90) and Schwartz (60).

[158] Knohl, "The Sin Offering," 203.

[159] Baruch J. Schwartz, "The Prohibitions Concerning the 'Eating' of Blood in Leviticus 17," in *Priesthood and Cult in Ancient Israel*, 59.

H "diverges radically" from the decontamination belief.¹⁶⁰ So we have three clearly distinct concepts:

- the anthropomorphic notion of God enjoying the "sweet aroma" of burning (J), sacrifice as food-bribe;
- the impersonal process of purification with blood (P), sacrificial blood as magic detergent;
- sacrifice as ritual payment (H).

I would alter Schwartz slightly by saying that H blends the other two ideas: blood has both a material and supernatural value. This brings us to the tantalizingly simple and centrally important verse, Lev 17:11: "For the life of the flesh is in the blood; and I have given it to you for making atonement for your lives on the altar; for, as life, it is the blood that makes atonement."

The concepts at the beginning of the verse seem fairly clear, but not the last major point. To take them in order:

- The life-force of a living creature is in its blood;
- God is telling Moses to tell Aaron to perform blood-sacrifice and sprinkle the blood on the altar;
- This ritual action will "mak[e] atonement [לְכַפֵּר] for your lives";
- Blood makes atonement *because* the life is in the blood.

The last part, translated word-for-word, would read "because the blood, it for the life will atone" (כִּי־הַדָּם הוּא בַּנֶּפֶשׁ יְכַפֵּר). Manipulation of blood is effective because "the life of the flesh is in the blood"—*obviously* (but not to us). The metaphysical logic that was obvious to the H author and his readers was soon forgotten in the Jewish tradition. The text became normative, but its animistic assumptions were no longer understood.

Why should the sprinkling of life-force accomplish atonement? There is clearly some equivalency between blood and life, but the exact nature of the equivalency is not spelled out. Deuteronomy 12:23 takes the equivalency literally: "the blood is the life" [*nephesh*]. H does say "the life of every creature is its blood" (and Lev 17:14), but Lev 17:11, I think, is more clear: life is a force *within* the blood, and ritual, carefully performed, can harness this dangerous force.¹⁶¹ Blood, carrying the life-force, can somehow reverse the anti-life of sin and pollution. When the blood is poured on a ritually-polluted temple installation, the life-force cleans away the anti-life force, pollution.

---

¹⁶⁰ Schwartz, "Prohibitions," 59.

¹⁶¹ Despite some differences, all three passages "revolve around" the equivalency between blood and life (Rolf Rentdorff, "Another Prolegomenon to Leviticus," in *Pomegranates and Golden Bells*, 24–25).

This is an animistic idea, the notion of a spirit-force inhabiting something. A theistic overlay has been added; God ordains the ritual technique for undoing spiritual pollution. The life-force can be manipulated (animism), but only because God has allowed it.

This focus on vitalism or animism is one of the two main ways that scholars have tried to make sense of this passage. Just as natural forces can, within limits, be manipulated, so spirit-forces can be manipulated with ritual; here, *ritual is a technology of spirit*. And this reflects a truth about cultic ritual: cult takes the power of *symbols* literally. In fact, one could define cult as the systematic taking of religious symbols literally—as literal conduits of power. Inasmuch as it involves the belief that acting upon the symbol will have an effect on the thing symbolized, cultic ceremony is inherently magical. For example, cleansing the temple will *actually* cleanse the nation. Later interpreters will say that it *symbolizes* the cleansing of land and people—and it does, but the early practitioners took the symbol literally. God would strike dead (or strike with leprosy) those who transgressed priestly space. Even Mary Douglas says she sees no point "in making any distinction between magical and sacramental."[162]

What of the possibility that the life-force is diverted from its usual function (keeping the animal alive) into the function of carrying away pollution/disorder with it on its journey to the other world—a spirit-transportation quality? This is not likely; the theology surrounding sacrifice is not eschatological and does not concern a distinction between spirit and body. The theology is, however, highly dualistic, even symbolizing the process of *making distinctions*, which is essential to priestly religion.

This dualism encourages an analogy to electricity. The positive life-charge in the blood *neutralizes* the negative death-charge in the pollution, wherever it has penetrated into the temple. Another analogy would be the Midas touch: the blood transforms and purifies the defiled symbols. If this is the logic of *kippering*, it is an animistic, not substitutionary, operation. And this does seem to be the logic of the author of Lev 17:11. Of course, this author is not an "animist," but a theist who uses an animistic notion. Ancient religious ideas are frequently re-shaped by theists.

The other option is to see the animal as a substitute. By Augustine's time, Christians understood sacrifice legalistically, with the animal as a penal substitute for the person. Either a supernatural or a legal interpretation can be given to the Lev 17:11 passage, the animal is "for atonement for your lives" (לְכַפֵּר עַל־נַפְשֹׁתֵיכֶם): either it cleans up the spiritual pollution you created, or it *stands in* for the accused human.

---

[162] Douglas, *Natural Symbols*, 8.

The legal concept is that of *penal substitution*—although this particular phrase is now unpopular. Two rabbis take this approach, seeing it as the payment of a judicial penalty—"the innocent effects atonement for the guilty"[163]; or "let the soul of an animal come and atone for the soul of man."[164] Some current scholars argue that Levitical texts present the animal straightforwardly as a penal substitute for the human:

> [T]hrough the laying on of hands [in sacrifice] sin and guilt is [sic] transferred to the animal which dies as the offerer's substitute.... [S]in but also its penalty was [sic] transferred to the sacrificial victim.[165]

Rodriguez takes animistic "transfer" and turns it into legal substitution, without noticing how he has changed the logic of the transaction. This notion of "expiation through substitution"[166] does nothing to account for the blood applications, for how the life force cleanses the temple sancta from anti-life forces. Penal substitution did become prominent in rabbinic and Christian understandings, but it seems to be subsidiary, *at most*, in Leviticus.

To the extent that there is substitution in Levitical sacrifice, it is *monetary*, not penal. Gorman, partly agreeing with Milgrom, notes that, "the use of כפר in this verse [Lev 17:11] is related to *kôpher* and the idea of 'ransom'.... *kôpher* [is] compensatory payment."[167] Brichto also says the underlying concept of *kipper* is compensatory. In non-sacrificial passages, the verb כפר means *to serve as a kopher* (כֹּפֶר), that is, as a payment[168] (e.g. Exod 21:30), even a bribe (Amos 5:12). The Lord demands all the first-born of Israel, but is happy to accept the tribe of Levites as a substitute (Num 8:17–19); this is political, not judicial; it is payment to a sovereign, not substitution for a convict.

All monetary transactions are substitutionary in a pragmatic, not moral, sense. Hebrew sacrifice does not involve the animal substituting for one who has been justly convicted of sin. Rather, it is a payment; after all, foodstuffs have *value*. Various texts speak both of kippering and of making restitution plus one-fifth (Lev 5:24 [6:5 NRSV]; Num 5:7), or of paying double

---

[163] *m. Yoma* 43b; Hans-Joachim Schoeps, *Paul: the Theology of the Apostle in the Light of Jewish Religious History* (London: Lutterworth, 1961), 132.

[164] Rashi on Lev 17:11, from the Sapirstein edition; similar translation in Schoeps, *Paul*, 130.

[165] Rodriguez, *Substitution*, 201, 232.

[166] Rodriguez, *Substitution*, 192.

[167] Gorman, *Ideology*, 184. Gorman politely demolishes Milgrom's other point, that this verse supposedly concerns only the *shelamim* (Milgrom, *Leviticus 1–16*, 441). Rather, the focus is to place *all* blood "outside of the prescribed human bounds" (Gorman, 187).

[168] Brichto, "On Slaughter," 28, 34.

(Exod 22:7–9). כפר, then, has this connotation of payment, which does not negate its denotation, its primary meaning, of purging or cleansing.

If animistic temple-cleansing and frank tribute-payment were the basis of Pentateuchal concepts of sacrifice, they must have also been present, at least to *some* degree, in the mind of a first century person whose own emphasis was more legalistic. By no means do I assume that Paul's concept of sacrifice was identical with the Levitical concept(s) written down centuries earlier, but I also cannot imagine that his concept was utterly devoid of the notion of atonement as sacred procedure dealing with sacred substance, nor of the idea of sacrifice as payment. These have animistic and propitiatory implications, however uncomfortable these are to modern theologians.

We must recall that Paul's doctrine of atonement was aimed at appealing to Gentiles as well as Jews. His notions of cultic atonement may have resonated with certain Gentile concepts, even the idea that sacrificial blood could be "cleansing and sanctifying."[169]

The saving transaction that Paul describes with sacrificial metaphors, then, implies at least three associated themes: a judgment of sin, a cultic procedure performed with sacred blood, and a payment to God that removes God's resentment. Theologians cannot give an adequate account of Paul if they leave out any one of these elements; an emphasis on the judgment and defeat of sin cannot afford to leave out the fact that it is done *through* a martyr's death that is reckoned (by God) as an acceptable sacrifice. A Pauline theology that emphasizes Jesus' heroic death, must also notice that this is said to avert God's wrath. The Messiah's death is a payment and a cultic action. These are ideas that are not found in the gospels, and are quite difficult to reconcile with the sayings of Jesus.

1.2.4 An Intercultural Theory of Sacrifice

Pulling together now our survey of Gentile and Jewish sacrificial practice, we saw three widespread conceptualizations by practitioners of sacrifice. They are the notions of the sacrificial victim as gift or offering (*payment*), as substitute (which, in the Hebrew setting, would have penal implications), and as means of spirit-mediumship.

Hebrew sacrifice often resembles a gift or payment, but mediumship is also present, despite Judaism's major differences from pagan religions. The initiative in Jewish belief is always the Lord's, and he established the sacrificial cult in the first place, but he does respond to cultic situations, therefore the cult does involve (a Jewish form of) spirit mediumship. In fact, the Lord is *dangerously* present in the cult, as is shown in the foundational stories where

---

[169] καθαῖρον καὶ ἁγνίζον, in Pseudo-Hippocrates; David E. Aune, *Revelation 1–5*. WBC 52 (Dallas: Word, 1997), 47.

"Fire came out from the Lord and consumed the burnt offering" (Lev 9:24), where the Lord ignited "with fire from heaven" the offerings that David had placed on an altar (1 Chr 21:26), where he answered Solomon in the same way (2 Chr 7:1), and again when he slew those who offered "illicit fire" (Num 3:4). These stories resemble pagan theophanies in that there is a special manifestation of the god at the peak moment of the ritual.

Josephus repeats the stories about God's literal presence above the tabernacle,[170] about the divine incineration of sacrifices, and the burning of those who deviated from proper liturgical practice.[171] One of the jewels on the high priest's shoulder "shined out when God was present at their sacrifices."[172] These statements give evidence of *cult* in its definitive sense: the taking of symbols literally, and belief that the god is present at, and responds to, the cultic environment.

The motivations of sacrifice were pragmatic, and the technology was practical, even if metaphysical. In fact, the technique of sacrifice (in any culture) could be described as a practical system for improving or maintaining a beneficial metaphysical environment. Sacrifice was a ritual for communal and individual self-maintenance, based upon religious assumptions. Sacrificing peoples are not dealing with impersonal spirit forces, but with divine persons. In fact, what distinguishes sacrifice from certain other rites, such as expulsion ritual, is the consciousness that it is conducted "before" and "for" personal gods. Sacrifice evidences theological reflection.

The development of *covenant* is in some ways parallel to the development of sacrifice. As social relations became more complicated, covenant became a central ingredient of inter-tribal peace. Covenants are transactional, something is given by both sides, even when one is a superior power. In Judaism, sacrifice becomes a projection of this transactional thinking onto the religious realm; God blesses and forgives if he gets what he demanded from his people, either material or volitional; being fed (as in Leviticus and Numbers), seeing a sufficient demonstration of worshipful submission (as in Psalms), or seeing unpolluted and unblemished offerings offered by honest and educated priests (Mal 1:7–8; 2:6–7). Enlightened critics such as Plato (see below) and Micah reject the idea, all too common among their peers, that one can induce the deity to be favorable.

The supplications that are connected with rituals always show a concern for the insurance of present and future well-being, and they take place when there is believed to be a special connection with the divine. Even Judaism,

---

[170] *Ant.* 3.202; 20.166; *J.W.* 5.459; God dwelt in a cloud that "dropped a sweet dew" (*Ant.* 3.203).

[171] *Ant.* 3.207 and 209–10.

[172] *Ant.* 3.215.

which originally had no supplications connected with sacrifice, came to incorporate them, reflecting the notion that, "the times ordained by God for sacrifices were propitious for prayer as well."[173]

To draw out the supplication theme, one could say that three elements recur in sacrifice in many different cultures: *appeasement* of the deity (which can include the notion of strengthening the deity), momentary connection or *communication* with the divine, and *supplication* for well-being. This approach-to-deity triad is not identical to my earlier kind-of-sacrifice triad (gift, substitute, spirit-medium). The gift or substitute *appeases* the deity and opens up the moment of communion, at which time urgent supplication is made.

Can it be said, then, that there is spirit-mediumship in Hebrew cult? This involves the animal as "a means of communication between the sacred and the profane worlds,"[174] or as the means for being penetrated by "a transcendental being."[175] Certainly the last element is absent, but the notion that sacrificial ritual opens up access to the divine realm certainly seems to be implied in God's ignition of the sacrifice, his taking punitive action against those who infringe on priestly territory or perform improper ritual,[176] his lighting up a jewel of the priest (Josephus). In the Hebrew system, any elements of "possession" were eliminated very early on, but the notion that ritual worked to gain the Lord's attention persisted to the end of the sacrificial cult; the Lord was believed to extend forgiveness and magnanimity if the system was properly maintained.

As the culture evolves, religion evolves, and sacrifice is subjected to continuing reinterpretation and alteration. Theories about evolution of religion are currently out of favor because they were linked with the concept of progress, and the West, demoralized by the horrors of war and totalitarianism, has lost confidence in that concept. But a truly cross-cultural description of sacrifice must be trans-temporal, must take notice of the change or evolution that sacrifice and religion undergo. From Greece to Asia Minor to Israel we can see that a heightening of intellectual culture brings a heightening of moral sensibility, and calls bloody sacrifice into question. This is especially visible in the Hebrew and Greek cultures, which both moved toward an emphasis on the inward religious attitude.

As cultures enter a stabilization phase, cultic tradents standardize the cult. Under their influence, ritual practices are reinterpreted, changed, or even

---

[173] Shaye J. D. Cohen, *From the Maccabees to the Mishnah*. LEC (Philadelphia: Westminster, 1987), 68.

[174] Hubert and Mauss, *Sacrifice*, 97.

[175] Bloch, *Prey*, 43, 35.

[176] Lev 10:2; Num 3:4; 12:10; 16:35–38; 26:10; 2 Sam 6:6–7; 2 Chr 26:16–21.

suppressed. The original metaphysical conceptions motivating the ritual were already being de-anthropomorphized by the P editors of Leviticus. The metaphysical conceptions motivating many rituals were forgotten by the time the procedures were inscribed in texts.

1.3 Spiritualization

Various kinds of spiritualization can be observed in any religious culture. The continuous reinterpretation of cult, along with spiritual reflection apart from cult, can result in a strong dynamic of religious reflection over against cult (particularly in Greek and Jewish religion) or with highly developed metaphorical interpretations of abandoned cult practices (Hinduism). Since, with Paul, we are dealing with metaphorical spiritualizations of the cult, it is necessary to look at the complex processes of spiritualization.

1.3.1 Levels of Spiritualization

The term "spiritualization" has been used several ways by scholars: the progressive transformation of ritual through substitution and symbolization, the allegorical or symbolic interpretation of ritual and of texts, the increasing abstraction and internalization of concepts ("circumcision of the heart," for instance), or the usage of ritual imagery to describe non-ritual experiences. Although these meanings can often overlap or combine, "spiritualization" has been used by scholars to mean six things:

1.3.1.1 The First Four Levels

1. TRANSFORMATION OF RITUAL THROUGH SUBSTITUTION, especially the replacement of human sacrifice with animal sacrifice, reflected in Yahweh's claim on the first-born ("whatever is the first to open the womb among the Israelites, of human beings and animals, is mine," Exod 13:2; cf. 22:29) and his subsequent allowing of their "redemption" by payment (Exod 13:13; 34:20; Num 18:15). Jon Levenson finds that the narratives and ideology of human sacrifice in the Bible reflect an actual practice of sacrificing first-born sons.[177] Such substitutions are frequent in Greek literature, sometimes being left unexplained, as when Pausanias tells what he heard at Potniae in Boeotia, where an oracle of Dionysus had demanded the sacrifice of a boy, "but not many years later they say that the god substituted a goat as victim instead of the boy."[178]

---

[177] Jon D. Levenson, *The Death and Resurrection of the Beloved Son: The Transformation of Child Sacrifice in Judaism and Christianity* (New Haven, Conn.: Yale University Press, 1993), 4–6, 20–23. An example of actual human sacrifice is shown in 1 Kgs 16:34.

[178] Pausanias 9.8.2; Dennis D. Hughes, *Human Sacrifice in Ancient Greece* (London: Routledge, 1991), 82.

Other times, the revulsion that reformers feel for human sacrifice is clearly expressed, as by the heroes of Euripides[179] and Plutarch,[180] and by Jeremiah (7:31; 19:5; 32:35) and the Psalmist (106:37–42).

Studying Babylonian, Canaanite, and biblical texts, Hooke notes that substitution ranges all the way from a kind of magical "exchange of personality" with a "dying and rising god" in the Babylonian *puḥi ameli* ritual[181] to the ethical meanings in Isaiah 53 and Ezekiel 4.[182] Hooke lists four ancient religious intuitions that enable substitution, and each one involves "the principle of exchange": first is "belief in the psychical nature of inanimate concepts" (what I call *animism*), second is "the assumption that the part may stand for the whole," third is the notion that a person's place can be taken by symbols or clay or wooden images, and fourth is the "conception of corporate personality."[183] His third level describes some of the things that are literally substituted for human or animal sacrifices in many cultures. The ideas underlying such substitution did not sit well with all biblical authors, however, as we shall see below.

2. INCREASINGLY SYMBOLIC AND MORALIZING INTERPRETATION OF RITUAL; attributing new spiritual and abstract meanings to the cult practice; for instance, adding morality to the notion of purification ("he will purify the descendants of Levi. . . . Then I will draw near to you for judgment . . . against those who swear falsely, against those who oppress the hired workers"—Mal 3:3, 5), in fact inserting new and ethical meanings into discussion of the cult, as when Gese says that "damaged being is reconstructed and healed"[184] in sacrifice, or when Milgrom says the Jewish "dietary system rests on foundations that are essentially ethical, and ethical in the highest sense."[185] Philo reinterprets the cult by means of a moralizing hermeneutic that derives from Greek philosophy. He transcendentalizes cultic imagery, describing the priestly garments as "an 'icon' of the All" or imagining the worship service as corresponding to a heavenly service.

---

[179] Iphigenia questions that a goddess should "take pleasure in sacrificial murder." Rather, it is men who "lay their own guilt on the gods. No god, I am sure, can be evil"—*Iph. taur.* 389–99; from *Ten Plays by Euripides,* tr. Moses Hadas and John McLean (New York: Bantam Books, 1960), 251.

[180] Especially by the character Themistocles; see Carl Pfluger, "Progress, Irony, and Human Sacrifice," *The Hudson Review* 48 (1995): 67–70, 73, 88, 90.

[181] S. H. Hooke, "The Theory and Practice of Substitution," *VT* 2 (1952): 8.

[182] Hooke, "Theory," 11–13, 16.

[183] Hooke, "Theory," 3.

[184] Hartmut Gese, *Essays on Biblical Theology* (Minneapolis: Augsburg, 1981), 110.

[185] Milgrom, *Studies*, 108. Mary Douglas makes the same move ("Justice as the Cornerstone: An Interpretation of Leviticus 18–20," *Interpretation* 53 [1999]: 348–49).

Hayward says that Philo is extending the transcendent ideas that are already implicit in the ritual;[186] Daly says this process is: "to emphasize the true meaning . . . or ethical significance of the cult."[187] Hayward and Daly are supporting the Spiritualization Two strategy of their sources when they find the cult to have said ethical significance; in fact their sources have imported those meanings into the cult. Spiritualization Two is a strategy of pouring new wine into old wineskins, new values into old forms.

3. INTERNALIZATION of religious values, asserting that what matters to God is the right attitude: "a clean heart . . . and right spirit within me. . . . The sacrifice acceptable to God is a broken spirit" (Ps 51:10, 17). A Chinese text says that "sacrifice . . . originates from within"; only the "trembling" of the heart is "able to realize the aim of sacrifice."[188] Indian texts[189] say that "the five (sacrificial) fires are contained in the sacrificer . . . he offers only in the self"; this is "mental sacrifice (*manasa yajna*)."[190]

Cultic terms are made to apply to the religious attitude, as in, "Let my prayer be counted as incense before you, and the lifting up of my hands as an evening sacrifice" (Ps 141:2). Sometimes the correct attitude *takes the place* of cult: "Penance is my fire; life my fireplace; right exertion is my sacrificial ladle" (from a Jain Sutra[191]).

Some denigration of cult is frequently present in Level Three expressions: "Does the Lord demand . . . sheep or oxen or any kind of sacrifices at all? That is nothing, but he demands pure hearts."[192] No handmade temple can suffice for God, "but a pious soul is his fitting abode."[193]

Implicit in many of these remarks is a rejection of anthropomorphism. The LXX tones down some (but by no means all) of the MT's anthropomorphic images, finding a way to distance God from the images by inserting a term (as when "word of" is inserted in front of "anger" in Isa 30:27) so that an

---

[186] C. T. R. Hayward, *The Jewish Temple: a Non-biblical Sourcebook* (London: Routledge, 1996), 116 (quoting Philo, *Spec. Leg.* 1.96). Cf. 87–88 (on *T. Lev.* 30:14; 31:14); 148 (Josep., *Ant.* 3.180); cf. George Buchanan Gray, *Sacrifice in the Old Testament: Its Theory and Practice* (Oxford: Clarendon, 1925), 148–78.

[187] Robert J. Daly, S.J., "Is Christianity Sacrificial or Antisacrificial?" *Religion* 27 (1997): 238.

[188] *Li Ki* 22.1; Wilson, "Sacrifice and Imperial," 276. The *Li Ki*, also called the Book of Rites, is one of the Confucian classics.

[189] *Bṛhad-Āraṇyaka Upaniṣad* 1.4.17; *Manusmṛti* 6.25, 38.

[190] Heesterman, *Inner Conflict*, 39.

[191] Brian K. Smith, *Reflections on Resemblance, Ritual, and Religion* (Delhi: Motilal Banarsidass, 1989), 212.

[192] *2 Enoch* 45:3, in *OTP* 1:46.

[193] Philo, *Cher.* 100. Hendrickson edition, page 90.

anthropomorphic expression is linked with an *emanation* of God rather than with Godself.[194]

It is often difficult to decide whether a statement belongs to Level Three or Five (rejection of ritual). *Sometimes* it is true that "interiorization of a symbol does not ruin or discredit it,"[195] but sometimes redefinition of a ritual term does indicate impatience (conscious or unconscious) with the ritual, as with the Jainist and Buddhist identification of "true sacrifice" or "the highest sacrifice" with "the way of life of the monk."[196]

Clooney implies that spiritualization is incipient in sacrifice, since a certain *attitude* is implied in the practice: "The 'sacrifice,' the basic sacrificial alienation of one's own property, is ultimately a mental resolution."[197] This may be true, but the ethical implications he wants to draw out, cannot be found in the earlier, unspiritualized, ritual texts.

The process of spiritualization among Jewish sages was strongly affected by the destruction of the temple. The study of the laws concerning sacrifice was understood to take the place of sacrifice.[198] One rabbinic quotation will suffice; the *'Abot de Rabbi Nathan* (9b) states that when one has expounded Scripture, it is "as though he had offered up fat and blood on the altar."[199]

4. METAPHORICAL APPLICATION OF CULTIC TERMS TO NON-CULTIC EXPERIENCES, as when a Maccabean martyr's death is a "purification" and a "ransom," an "expiatory death" that "purifies" (*4 Macc.* 6:29; 17:21–22; 1:11), or when Paul says he is "poured out as a libation over the sacrifice and the offering of your faith" (Phil 2:17).

Level Four spiritualizing sometimes hints at a devaluing of cult-practice. Consider Sirach's metaphors: "To keep the law is a great oblation. . . . In works of charity one offers fine flour, and when he gives alms he presents his sacrifice of praise" (35:1–2 NAB). This highlights not the literal sacrifice, but acts of charity and loyalty, implying a certain distance between the recommended actions and the cult actions used as a metaphor. But we would be wrong to

---

[194] Markus Bockmuehl, *Revelation and Mystery in Ancient Judaism and Pauline Christianity* (Grand Rapids: Eerdmans, 1997), 139.

[195] David Lindsay Olford, "Paul's Use of Cultic Language in Romans: An Exegetical Study of Major Texts in Romans Which Employ Cultic Language in a Non-literal Way" (Ph.D. thesis, Sheffield, 1985), 30.

[196] Heesterman, *Inner Conflict*, 42.

[197] Francis X. Clooney, "Sacrifice and Its Spiritualization in Christian and Hindu Traditions: A Study in Comparative Theology [Jaimin, Ramanuja, Srivaisnava]," *HTR* 78 (1985): 369.

[198] E. P. Sanders, *Paul and Palestinian Judaism* (Philadelphia: Fortress, 1977), 165.

[199] Bockmuehl, *Revelation and Mystery*, 112 n.53.

conclude that Sirach looks down on cult-practice; in fact, the author values the cult highly (e.g., 45:15-24).

Paul's Level Four spiritualizing can simply re-use cultic terms metaphorically (Rom 3:25; 1 Cor 6:19), or can set out to redefine terms, as when he says that "true" circumcision is defined by ethical behavior (Rom 2:26–29) or by spiritual worship (Phil 3:3). If the ritual *idea* can be carried out without the ritual, that tends to make the latter negligible.

For a cultic image to carry metaphoric power requires that the referent be *recognized*, not that there be unquestioning faith in the cult's literal efficacy. When Paul characterizes his activity as "priestly service of the gospel of God, so that the offering of the Gentiles may be acceptable" (Rom 15:16), he is saying that *something else* now accomplishes what sacrifice was alleged to accomplish. Those who are open to metaphoric expression in connection with religious reflection will not find such rhetoric blasphemous. Spiritualization is part of a sophisticated dialogue between author and audience.

1.3.1.2 Rejection of Sacrifice

5. REPUDIATION OF SACRIFICE. When interiorization of religious attitude is affirmed as the direction of progress mandated by God, a widespread rejection of the ritual can develop, as in Hindu ritual where Vedic sacrificial texts are chanted but the sacrifices no longer performed.[200]

Sacrifice is even disparaged: "The fools who delight in this sacrificial ritual .... go round in a circle like blind men."[201] Even when using "quite sharp satire" to discredit Vedic sacrifice, this is done *with* the rhetoric of sacrifice, which gives the anti-sacrificial position "legitimation."[202]

Greek thinkers are especially critical of sacrifice. In fact, the most "technically correct description of classical cult is already a critique," that of Empedocles.[203] Other pre-Socratics reject it, notably Heraclitus and Pythagoras. Heraclitus attacks the logic of sacrifice, comparing the idea of sacrificial blood that purifies with the notion of washing in mud to cleanse from mud.[204] Logic increasingly called sacrifice into question, repeating an insight that was at least as old as Euripides: "God, if indeed he truly is God, has need of nothing."[205]

---

[200] Smith, *Reflections on Resemblance,* 212, 216–17; cf. Heesterman, *Inner Conflict,* 42, 82.

[201] *Mundaka Unpanishad* 1.2.2; *Sources of Indian Tradition, vol. 1,* ed. Wm. Theodore de Bary (New York: Columbia University Press, 1958), 26.

[202] Smith and Doniger, "Sacrifice," 209, 215.

[203] Brown, "Sacrificial Cult," 159.

[204] Valentin Nikiprowetzky, "La Spiritualisation des sacrifices et le culte sacrificiel au Temple de Jérusalem chez Philon d'Alexandrie," *Semitica* 17 (1967): 99.

[205] Euripides, *Heracles fur.* 1345. The Greek is given in Everett Ferguson, "Spiritual Sacrifice in Early Christianity and Its Environment," *ANRW* 23.2:1152.

Plato does not quite condemn sacrifice, but he indicates that it is only profitable for the good man,[206] and that it is stupid to think that the gods "are easy to win over when bribed by offerings and prayers," by "offerings and flatteries."[207] Only haters of men teach "that the gods are negligent or open to bribes."[208] Plato condones only the most inexpensive sacrifices and the most humble materials in the construction of sanctuaries.[209]

Plato focuses on a particularly objectionable motive that some people were bringing to sacrifice, but his position seems circumspect compared to the objections of his later disciples: Clement of Alexandria sees Plato as rejecting material sanctuaries altogether; Porphyry thinks that not only sacrifice, but "even a word is too material."[210] The move "away from the material cultus may be said to stem from the ethicizing of religion."[211]

In the Hellenistic period, this movement is encouraged by the general tendency of the universalizing super-culture that *is* Hellenism: national concepts of identity were being replaced by more universalistic ways of construing identity, and national cults were under pressure from more universalizing cults which, to one degree or another, promulgated the values of Hellenism. But that is another thesis.

Sacrifice may begin to look outdated whenever people start focusing "on the divine origin of the soul and on the gods' rationality and good."[212] These latter ideas were not in place when ancient peoples developed sacrifice. Sacrifice assumes divine hunger, temper, and authority rather than rationality and goodness, and the Greeks increasingly made observations such as this. Level Five spiritualization is often accompanied by a philosophy about becoming more spiritually enlightened, which I treat as Level Six spiritualization.

Level Two reformism and Level Five rejectionism are the two opposing strategies available to religion for handling customs that have become embarrassing or even revolting to the civilized consciousness; the former is the strategy more commonly chosen. Reformist spiritualization "civilizes," transforms, and reinterprets outmoded practices and beliefs. Gradual change is

---

[206] Plato, *Alcibiades* II 149E.

[207] Plato, *Laws* 10.885C; 10.948C (Bury, LCL).

[208] Plato, *Laws* 10.909B (Bury, LCL).

[209] Plato, *Laws* 12.955E; cf. 10.910D; James W. Thompson, "Hebrews 9 and Hellenistic Concepts of Sacrifice," *JBL* 98 (1979): 574.

[210] Thompson, "Hebrews 9," 574–75.

[211] R. J. McKelvey, *The New Temple: The Church in the New Testament* (Oxford: Oxford University Press, 1969), 56.

[212] J. H. Liebeschuetz, "Religion," in *The Cambridge Ancient History, Vol. XI: The High Empire,* Second edition (Cambridge: Cambridge University Press, 2000), 1003.

instinctively preferred by all cultures to the continuity-breaking option of rejecting established practice. Even when cultural values demand that a practice be rejected, it is most often altered and re-interpreted rather than rejected outright. Religions, East and West, are far more likely to tone down and domesticate the radical demands of rejectionist prophets than to follow them. And so a strategy of gradual reform and spiritualization (Levels 1–3) becomes the main avenue for philosophic development in traditional religions.

There were some strongly rejectionist strains in Judaism. The following passages indicate, at the very least, a frank disrespect for the sacrificial cult:

Deliver me from bloodshed, O God. . . . For you have no delight in sacrifice. Ps 51:14, 16

Honoring God . . . . is not done with gifts or sacrifices, but with purity of heart and of devout disposition. *Aristeas* 234

The more radical formulations openly mock the cultic concept:

I will not accept a bull from your house, or goats from your folds. . . . If I were I hungry, I would not tell you, for the world and all that is in it is mine. Do I eat the flesh of bulls, or drink the blood of goats? Ps 50:9, 12–13

Will the Lord be pleased with thousands of rams, with ten thousands of rivers of oil? Shall I give my firstborn for my transgression, the fruit of my body for the sin of my soul? Mic 6:7

The positive advice in Mic 6:8, to do justice, to be kind, and to walk with God, is set in *contrast* to sacrifice, which is parodied with "a sequence of exaggerated images."[213]

It is fashionable to deny that any of the prophets actually attacked the cult, to claim that they only criticized cult unaccompanied by reverence and morality. Certainly that is the emphasis of *some* of biblical passages, for instance of Malachi 1 and 2 where priests are exhorted to observe both ritual correctness (1:8, 13–14) and moral integrity (2:6–7). Another *reformist* passage that brings moral principles into the ritual realm is Ps 4:5: "Offer right sacrifices (זִבְחֵי־צֶדֶק) and put your trust in the Lord."

I have a separate category when there is a glaring absence of support for the cult: "The sacrifice of the wicked is an abomination to the Lord, but the prayer of the upright is his delight" (Prov 15:8). Sacrifice is conspicuously

---

[213] Hendel, "Prophets, Priests," 194; where also: "Micah vehemently rejects a relationship between ritual and ethics."

absent from the positive side of the statement; the sacrifice of the upright *may* be acceptable, but it is not worth mentioning! I call such passages *strictly moral*, since they *only* assert the value of the moral or spiritual. They do not openly attack cult, but their conspicuous non-support implies, at least, some demotion of cult.

My next category is *critical* sayings, where cult is clearly give an inferior status: "to obey is better than sacrifice" (1 Sam 15:22); "To do righteousness and justice is more acceptable to the LORD than sacrifice" (Prov 21:3).

Finally, the *radical* sayings go further, openly ridiculing the sacrificial mentality—"Whoever slaughters an ox is like one who kills a human being . . . whoever presents a grain offering, like one who offers swine's blood" (Isa 66:3). "Bringing offerings is futile; incense is an abomination to me" (Isa 1:13).[214] Sometimes an alternative to sacrificing may be asserted—"for I desire steadfast love and not sacrifice" (Hos 6:6); "Sacrifice and offering you do not desire, but . . . . I delight to do your will" (Ps 40:6, 8).

The assaults of Amos and Jeremiah are the most important because they attack the doctrine that God established the sacrificial cult, undermining its whole legitimacy:

> I hate, I despise your festivals. . . . The offerings of well-being of your fatted animals I will not look upon[215] . . . . But let justice roll down like waters. . . . Did you bring to me sacrifices and offerings the forty years in the wilderness, O house of Israel? Amos 5:21–25

> In the day that I brought your ancestors out of the land of Egypt, I did not speak to them or command them concerning burnt offerings and sacrifices. But this is what I commanded them, saying, "Obey My voice, and I will be your God." Jer 7:22–23

Hermisson tries to make Jeremiah's contempt for sacrifice apply only to certain times and situations, and even to be evidence of the cult's "holy and venerable origin."[216] Venerable to whom? Not to Jeremiah. If mere reformism were the prophet's goal, he would not have *contrasted* true piety to cult practice. People who really believe in the supernatural effectiveness of cult or in its venerable lineage do not show such disrespect for it. The purpose of this

---

[214] The Isaiahs are not consistently "anti-sacrificial"; Isa 19:21 is reformist, linking the acceptability of sacrifice to the right disposition of the offerers.

[215] The nouns (עֹלוֹת, שֶׁלֶם, זֶבַח) and the verb אָרִיחַ (from רִיחַ), "smell" in v. 21 indicate *animal* sacrifices.

[216] Hans-Jürgen Hermisson, *Sprache und Ritus im Altisraelitischen Kult: zur "Spiritualisierung" der Kultebegriffe im Alten Testament* (Neukirchen-Vluyn: Neukirchener Verlag, 1965), 141–42.

whole speech, as Anderson points out, is "to undermine the grounding of the mythic nature of the temple."[217]

Hermisson insists that Hosea's remarks represent a polemic against the Baalized cult, and not an attack on *"des legitimen Jahwekultus."*[218] Hosea does, indeed, fight a Baalized cult (4:10–18; 10:1; cf. Jer 2:8), but that is not his only complaint with the cult, or he would have expressed an interest in seeing it purified. When he attacks the altars at Bethel and Gilgal, he never hints of any pure altar in Jerusalem, past, present, or in an "ideal future."[219] He does speak of an idealized past (2:14–15; 11:1), but not an ideal cult. In fact, he makes fun of that step in the *hattat* sacrifice where the priests eat the meat: "they feed on the sins of my people and relish their wickedness" (4:8 NIV). He rebukes the priests for not *teaching* (4:6), not for not *sacrificing*. God wants kindness, *not* sacrifice (6:6).

God rejects their cult because of *false* piety (not just "Baalized" piety): "Their heart is false . . . the Lord will break down their altars, and destroy their pillars" (10:2). Their "altars to expiate sin" have become "altars for sinning" (8:11), which they value more than God's written instructions (8:12)! Hosea's problem is this "sinning," not (as with Malachi) carelessness about cultic procedure. Ephraim's violence, apostasy, and worship are all of a piece. It is no accident that the famous passage at 6:6 is surrounded by a "judgment (6:5) directed against those . . . implicated in murder (6:8–10)."[220]

Hosea and Jeremiah do undertake a "polemic against sacrifice and temple worship."[221] Of course, their point is not "you should never sacrifice," but rather "you have abandoned God and your activities show it; your sacrificing is hypocrisy." God rejects the means—cult—by which people convince themselves that their sinning is not a problem:

Will you steal, murder, commit adultery . . . . then come and stand before me in this house . . . and say, "We are safe!" . . . Has this house, which is called by my name, become a den of robbers? Jer 7:9–11[222]

---

[217] "Sacrifice (OT)," 882.

[218] Hermisson, *Sprache und Ritus*, 135, where he also speaks of his "distinguishing between legitimate and illegitimate cult," but there is no evidence that Hosea had any yearning for a "legitimate" cult.

[219] Correctly: Hendel, "Prophets, Priests," 196.

[220] James G. Williams, *The Bible, Violence, and the Sacred: Liberation from the Myth of Sanctioned Violence* (San Francisco: Harper, 1991), 151.

[221] William McKane, "Prophet and Institution," *ZAW* 94 (1982): 259. On temple worship, see Jer 7:4 and Micah 6.

[222] Of course, this passage was quoted by a later prophet in *his* temple sermon (Matt 21:13).

The whole people have become unworthy. The point is moral. When Hosea uses cultic language to describe the people as polluted (נִטְמָא; 5:3; 6:10), the point is not their *cultic*, but their *moral* condition—"Their deeds do not permit them to return to their God" (5:4)—and their abandonment of the covenant—"There is no faithfulness or loyalty, and no knowledge of God in the land," only killing, stealing, lying, adultery (4:1–2). This undermines the argument that a prophet who uses cultic terms supports the cult.[223] Hosea and Jeremiah use cultic terms *against* their listeners in order to make cult a source of anxiety rather than comfort. Cult is really of no importance. The people perish "for lack of knowledge" (Hos 4:6), not for lack of ritual (8:11–14). Only moral repentance will do any good: "amending your ways," not "trusting in . . . the temple of the Lord . . . the temple of the Lord" (Jer 7:4–5).

Hosea sees cult as self-deception: "Though they offer choice sacrifices, though they eat flesh, the LORD does not accept them. Now he will remember their iniquity, and punish their sins" (Hos 8:13). Why such an interest in attacking the cult? Sociologically speaking, it was inevitable: "All movements of religious renewal have had in common the rejection of external forms"; "a new viewpoint produces a revulsion against dead ritual."[224]

There was clearly a division of opinion on this subject within Judaism; there was a heavy traffic in sacrifice up to the destructions of each of the two temples. But, at the very least, Amos, Hosea, Micah, and Jeremiah were quite contemptuous of the sacrificial cult, as were the authors of Isaiah 1 and 66, and of Psalms 40, 50, and 51.

Scholars who try to deny or minimize the intensity of the prophetic renunciation of ritual, who "reduce the prophets to ordinariness by making them conform to somewhat conventional ideas of piety, by domesticating them,"[225] are attempting a Spiritualization Two strategy, but it will not work. Amos cannot be turned into an altar boy, or Jeremiah into a temple prophet.

The attempt to dampen down the radicalism of the prophets has been a thriving industry in professional circles from the time of that priest who complained that the land could not bear the words of Amos (7:10), to academics who still claim that the prophets in no way opposed the cult. There is a social-political agenda at work here. Opposition to cult is (correctly) perceived as opposition to an authority structure and its ideology.

Of course, prophetic radicalism is always theistic; it is not proto-Marxism. Nor does the prophetic teaching fit into today's ideological categories of

---

[223] As argued by Hermisson, *Sprache und Ritus*, 142–43.
[224] Douglas, *Natural Symbols*, 52, 145.
[225] McKane, "Prophet and Institution," 253. "Scholarship ha[s] been . . . too facile and complacent" (265).

"liberal" or "conservative" (although there is an undeniable conservatism to Hosea and Jeremiah, and a radical flavor to Amos, Micah, and Isaiah 1).

It is quite likely that "Jesus adopted the prophetic attitude," shown by his approval of the scribe's remark that love is greater than burnt offerings (Mark 12:33), and his twice quoting Hosea's "I desire mercy and not sacrifice" (Matt 9:13; 12:7).[226] In these incidents, Jesus is rejecting Pharisaic ritual strictness (Sabbath rules) and purity boundaries (prejudice against tax collectors). Jesus has a strong prophetic emphasis on religious disposition over outward semblance. He affirms Micah's prioritizing of justice, mercy, and faith above sacrifice (Matt 23:23; Mic 6:6, 8). We also find him citing Jeremiah's bitter critique of the temple (Matt 21:13; Jer 7:11). It seems quite likely that "Jesus had no place for the cult in his theological schema."[227] His anti-temple sayings and actions may have fueled the conspiracy against him.

To offer a simple summary of views on sacrifice, I list five groups of remarks about sacrifice by ancient writers—supportive (Level 2 spiritualizing), reforming (Level 3 ethical emphasis, but with some Level 2 rationalizing), strictly moral (Level 3, with Level 5 implications), critical, and frankly rejectionist (the last two manifest on Levels 3 and 5, and hint at Level 6).

It has become commonplace for scholars to depict many rejectionist passages as mildly critical, and strictly moral ones as reformist. The NAB moves Amos 5 three rungs, trying to turn this plainly rejectionist passage into a reformist one by inserting a whole phrase at the end of 5:23: "if you would offer me holocausts, then," completely changing the force of what follows: "but let justice roll." This is blatant distortion, but not as bad as the violence done to Jer 7:22 by the NIV, which reverses the prophet's meaning by inserting the word "just" into his rejectionist pronouncement, having God say that, in the wilderness, he did not *just* give instructions on sacrifice. Those who distort the prophets' words in this way are like those who remove a boundary marker.

Approaching Paul's own usage requires a look at cult-critical trends in Jewish writings of the Hellenistic period. The Jewish Sibyl, writing around 300 B.C.E., looks ahead to a time when "They will reject all temples when they see them; altars too, defiled with blood."[228] A different attitude is taken by the *Psalms of Solomon*, 250 years later. The author reveres the temple, is shocked by careless acts of ritual polluting (*Pss. Sol.* 1:8; 8:12) but does not connect atonement with the cult,[229] only with humility (3:8) and confession (9:6).

---

[226] Frances M. Young, "Temple Cult and Law in Early Christianity: A Study in the Relationship between Jews and Christians in the Early Centuries," *NTS* 19 (1972–73): 336.

[227] J. McGuckin, "Sacrifice and Atonement: An Investigation into the Attitude of Jesus of Nazareth towards Cultic Sacrifice," *Remembering for the Future* (Pergamon, 1989), 1:649

[228] *Sib. Or.* 4:27–30, from *OTP* 1:384; temple-rejection is distinctive of this work.

[229] Wenschkewitz, *Spiritualisierung*, 15.

Similarly, in Judith 16:19–20, a positive attitude toward sacrifices is expressed, but v. 16 (NAB) says "the sweet odor of every sacrifice is a trifle." Some degree of distance from the cult had become the norm, even among supporters.

Even such a pro-cultic document as *Sirach* says: "Do not say, 'He will consider the great number of my gifts, and when I make an offering to the Most High God, he will accept it'" (7:9).

Philo dips into, but finally draws back from, Level Five rejection of sacrifice. He speaks of "true sacrifice" as "the piety of a soul which loves God,"[230] and says "the only sacrifice [is] plain truth,"[231] but he also ascribes value to the cult: the flawless animals are "a symbol of the flawless soul offered to God."[232] He seems to have dueling strategies. Allegory in the Hellenistic period was a passport of universal citizenship, redefining local custom as universal truth, rescuing it from the accusation of provinciality, and he uses it that way. But Philo is not prepared to allow allegory to eclipse Jewish cult. He allegorizes circumcision, but does not allegorize it away; it is still an essential rite for full male membership in Israel.

In Paul's time, there was considerable philosophizing about traditional cult practice by Jews and Gentiles alike. It could be described as symbolic, thus diminishing but not discarding its literal importance; strictly moral sayings implied a reduction in importance of the outward cult; or traditional cult could be rejected altogether in place of "rational" sacrifice—piety alone—as in Hermeticism. The Hermetic philosophy condemns sacrifice; even the burning of incense is "regarded as an abomination."[233] Instead, God is beseeched to "receive from all their rational sacrifice"[234] (prayer). Moule argues that "rational," in this connection, means "*spiritual* or *immaterial*," and is virtually synonymous with πνευματικός, meaning that it is "spiritual" *as opposed to* literal sacrifice.[235] Here the spiritualized idea has been liberated from the cultic form (or at least the *old* cultic form).

---

[230] *Vit. Mos.* 2.108. The Greek of this and other passages is given by Harold W. Attridge, "Philosophical Critique of Religion Under the Early Empire," *ANRW* 16.1:72.

[231] *Det.* 21 ("The Worse Attacks the Better"); cf. Thompson, "Hebrews 9," 577.

[232] A paraphrase of *Spec. Leg.* 1.166ff by Erwin R. Goodenough, *Goodenough on the History of Religion and on Judaism*, eds. Ernest S. Frerichs and Jacob Neusner. BJS 121 (Atlanta: Scholars Press, 1986), 57.

[233] Young, "Temple Cult and Law," 328, referring to *CH* 1.31; 12.23; 13.21ff.

[234] δέξαι ἀπο πάντων λογικὴν θυσίαν (*CH* 13.19; see also 13.18); Ferguson, "Spiritual Sacrifice," 1154.

[235] C. F. D. Moule, "Sanctuary and Sacrifice in the Church of the New Testament," *JTS* 1 (1950): 34. Christopher Evans ("Romans 12.1–2: The True Worship," in *Dimensions de la Vie Chrétienne [Rm 12–13]*, ed. Lorenzo De Lorenzi [Rome: Abbaye de S. Paul, 1979], 18–19) thinks λογικὴν really means "rational," but this is more convincing as regards the intellectualizing Philo than as regards Hermeticism or Paul. Moule's view is to be preferred.

Paul uses some of the same wording in Rom 12:1: "present your bodies as a living sacrifice (θυσίαν ζῶσαν), holy and acceptable to God, which is your spiritual worship (λογικὴν λατρείαν)." A similar concept of spiritual sacrifice had already been articulated by a Hellenistic Jewish writer in the *Testament of Levi* 3:6, where, in the heavenly temple, "archangels . . . . present to the Lord a pleasing odor, a rational (λογικὴν[236]) and bloodless oblation." The *best* worship, heavenly worship, was bloodless.[237] The spiritualizing influences to which Paul responded came "from both Greek and Jewish traditions."[238] Both factors are present in the *Testaments of the Twelve Patriarchs*, a work that is able to engage in spiritualization without abandoning eschatology, messianism, or asceticism—and therefore a work after Paul's own heart. In both the *Testaments* and in Paul, the Jewish hope takes on a universalizing scope and a hellenizing form of expression, but conservative moral values are staunchly defended.

Some branches of early Christianity were strongly anti-cultic: *Barn.* 16:2 rejects the temple ritual; the Ebionite literature goes further, rejecting the notion of Christ as a sacrifice (*Ps.-Clem. Rec.* 1:37, etc.).[239] An Ebionite document says that believers are not to think carnally, for to drink the blood of Christ would be "to drink the blood of corpses. . . . In so doing they treat me as an idol."[240] Such hostility to sacrifice may, ironically, be combined with metaphorical appropriation of sacrifice (Level Four spiritualization), as when Jesus says "I will become an altar for them"[241] in this same document.

The Qumran community is a special case; there, "the 'offering of the lips' takes the place of the material sacrifices," but still they desired the restoration of the Jerusalem cult.[242] Obedience to God's words makes one "acceptable by God, offering the sweet savor of atoning sacrifice. . . . They shall be an acceptable sacrifice, atoning for the land."[243] The community's

---

[236] *The Greek Versions of the Testaments of the Twelve Patriarchs*, ed. R. H. Charles (Oxford: Oxford University Press, 1908, 1966), 34.

[237] McKelvey, *New Temple*, 31–32.

[238] McKelvey, *New Temple*, 122.

[239] William Horbury, "New Wine in Old Wine-Skins: IX. The Temple," *ExpT* 86 (1974–75): 38; this rejectionism may "derive from a strand in pre-Christian Judaism" (*Ibid.*); cf. John J. Collins, "The Place of the Fourth Sibyl in the Development of the Jewish Sibyllina," *JJS* 25 (1974): 378–79.

[240] *Testament of Our Lord Jesus in Galilee* 8, from John J. Gunther, *St. Paul's Opponents and Their Background: A Study of Apocalyptic and Jewish Sectarian Teachings*. NovTSup 35 (Leiden: Brill, 1973), 151, 161. This apocalyptic testament is preserved in Ethiopian (Gunther, 23–24), and apparently has not been translated into English.

[241] *Testament of Our Lord* 7; Gunther, 151.

[242] McKelvey, *New Temple*, 50, 53; *Manual of Disc.* (1QS) 9.3–6; CD 4.1–3.

[243] 1QS 3.10–11 and 8.10; Wise, et al, 129 and 138.

dispute with the ruling priesthood prevented their participation in the sacrificial cult, so they accepted prayer as a theoretically temporary substitute, but this substitute was a matter of daily practice, while the possibility of participation at the temple was a distant hope.

Hinduism used sacrificial language "to *traditionalize innovations*."[244] Similarly, Paul's spiritualizing (interiorizing and metaphorizing) of sacrifice serves to legitimate his sacrificial doctrine, despite its factual severance from the Jewish sacrificial cult. Religious innovation is doomed to be rejected unless one finds a compelling rhetoric of spiritualized usage of established religious symbols. The spiritualizing of existing religious symbols is the medium for importing new teachings.

Paul unifies new and old through his typological teaching: what the OT cult was thought to do, is now accomplished in Christ. Cultic terms are used to describe the death of Christ and also the suffering and rejection undergone by apostles (1 Cor 4:13; Phil 2:17). Many OT stories are re-interpreted as prophetic of the church or of Christ (see "Typology," below).

1.3.1.3 Spiritualization as Transformation

6. AFFIRMATION OF SPIRITUAL TRANSFORMATION AS THE REAL GOAL OF PIETY. On this level, "spiritualization" means "to make spiritual," a meaning that only occurs when there is movement beyond blood rituals, when Level Three and Five spiritualization are functioning.

Examples include all Middle Platonic philosophies, Hermeticism, and any form of Christianity that speaks about becoming perfect. The patristic and Eastern Orthodox concept of *theosis* suggests this kind of spiritualization: "the *restoration* of mankind and the universe by the renewal of their harmony with God in which all creation becomes a faithful likeness of the Godhead,"[245] "the incarnation of the divine idea, or the deification of all that exists."[246]

Level Six spiritualization is a *philosophy of spiritual progress or transformation*. Here, interiorization is seen as a real transformation of human character toward godly character, and devolution of ritual is usually affirmed as evidence of said religious progress. Interiorization of religious attitudes has proceeded so far that the transformation of human character has become the principal goal of religious faith.

Ciholas is clearly speaking of this level functioning in Paul when he writes,

---

[244] Smith and Doniger, "Sacrifice," 216.

[245] Vladimir Solovyov (but spelled Solovyev), *God, Man and the Church: The Spiritual Foundations of Life,* tr. Donald Attwater (London: James Clarke, 1938), 168.

[246] Vladimir Solovyov, *Lectures on Divine Humanity,* tr. Peter Zouboff, revised by Boris Jakim (Hudson, New York: Lindisfarne, 1995), 137.

> The concept of the whole creation yearning for redemption is unique for Paul for whom man's salvation was contingent on a total spiritualization of reality.... In a totally spiritualized world the distinction between the phenomenal and the spiritual ceases.[247]

Each of the stages of spiritualization (substitution, moralizing, interiorization, metaphorical appropriation, rejectionism, and making-spiritual) in its different way embodies some kind of transformation of sacrifice. We can also observe an increasingly reflective and literary component as we proceed up the scale from Level One to Six. In fact, this scheme can be used to describe different literary strategies and different strategies for socializing religion, as well as different ways of transforming sacrifice.

1.3.2 The Meanings of Spiritualization

Scholars have used the term "spiritualization" in each of the six ways I have listed above, sometimes with a clear reference to one of these meanings, and quite often joining two or more of these levels. "Spiritualization" is like many religious terms ("faith," for instance) in that it has a range of meanings, and any particular usage will probably weave together several of the basic meanings.

Moule seems to have in mind Levels Three and Four, and a hint of Five, when he says "St. Paul has come to take a certain delight also in 'sublimating' the Levitical terms ... into purely spiritual senses, wholly on the level of personal relationships .... the spiritualization of sacrifice into its mental and volitional equivalents of prayer, praise, and obedience."[248]

Dalferth has Level Four in mind, and brings in Level Three at the end:

> Spiritualization ... is a process of symbolization by which ... things ... and actions [are] used as interpretative symbols ... [T]he meaning which things, events or actions have acquired in one context is used to ... articulate or to represent the meanings of things or events in some other context .... the concentration on the *notion* of sacrifice rather than on sacrifices themselves.[249]

Chilton seems to have Levels Four and Five in mind when he writes, "Myths, ancient or modern, may be understood as attempts to replace sacrifice."[250] Strenski intends a Level Three process with Level Five

---

[247] Paul Ciholas, "Knowledge and Faith: Pauline Platonisms and the Spiritualization of Reality," *PRSt* 3 (1976): 199–200.

[248] Moule, "Sanctuary and Sacrifice," 36, 38.

[249] I. U. Dalferth, "Christ Died For Us: Reflections on the Sacrificial Language of Salvation," in *Sacrifice and Redemption: Durham Essays in Theology*, ed. S. W. Sykes (Cambridge: Cambridge University Press, 1991), 307.

[250] Chilton, "The Hungry Knife," 137.

implications when he refers to spiritualizing as minimizing the place of sacrifice.[251] Boyarin's provocative book examines a spiritualizing hermeneutic that includes Levels Three through Six:

> [F]or Paul truth lies in the spiritual, allegorical interpretation of text, history, and world, while the physical is but a shadow of this truth.[252]

This subject often seems to arouse scholarly irritation. Roetzel criticizes Räisänen's use of the term,[253] yet he himself uses it to signify manifestations on both Levels Three ("Philo ... spiritualizes the sacrifice, emphasizing the importance of inner preparation necessary to legitimate the sacrifice")[254] and Four ("the church as the temple, an explicit spiritualization of the temple").[255] An examination of Räisänen shows that he uses the term in some of the same ways Roetzel does ("ναός in a spiritualized sense")[256] but he relates this Level Four rhetoric to the Level Five strategy of the Hellenists whose "spiritualized view of the Torah" led them to give up circumcision.[257]

Roetzel is tending in an opposite direction: "spiritualization of the cult recognizes the axiomatic nature of the sacrificial cult."[258] Roetzel connects Levels Four and Two in order to affirm the cult, while Räisänen links Levels Four and Five in order to bring out the theme of rejection of cult. Both types of spiritualizing do occur, and their advocates are often at odds with each other, as are these two scholars. Such disagreements do not render the term useless, but necessitate a clarification in usage, which I am attempting with this sixfold differentiation.

Käsemann notes that Paul spiritualizes (Levels Three and Four), but refuses to use the term to explain what Paul is doing in Rom 12:1: "Its sharpness is missed if one seeks to understand it in terms of a spiritualizing of cultic motifs and terms."[259] When we read on, we see that Käsemann wants to emphasize

---

[251] Ivan Strenski, "The Social and Intellectual Origins of Hubert and Mauss's Theory of Ritual Practice," in *India and Beyond: Aspects of Literature, Meaning, Ritual and Thought; Essays in Honour of Frits Staal*, ed. Dick van der Meij (London: Kegan Paul, 1997), 526.

[252] Daniel Boyarin, *A Radical Jew: Paul and the Politics of Identity* (Berkeley: University of California Press: 1994), 86.

[253] Roetzel, *Paul*, 192 n.86.

[254] Roetzel, *Paul*, 28.

[255] Roetzel, *Paul*, 193 n.99.

[256] Heikki Räisänen, *The Torah and Christ* (Helsinki: Kirjapaino Raamattutalo, 1986), 292.

[257] Räisänen, *Torah*, 300.

[258] Roetzel, *Paul*, 192 n.93.

[259] Ernst Käsemann, *Commentary on Romans*, tr. Geoffrey W. Bromiley (Grand Rapids: Eerdmans, 1980), 327.

that Paul does not deny embodied living. Thus, Käsemann is reacting against a common characterization of spiritualization as ethereal. He *does* accept that Paul uses cultic metaphors to emphasize interiorization, but he wants to avoid the docetism that he thinks "spiritualization" implies.

Robert Daly speaks of three phases of spiritualization. Corresponding to my Levels Two and Three is his "sacrifice .... performed with proper religious-ethical dispositions."[260] Daly's next two levels move from (my) Level Five to Six, and both incorporate Level Three: "it moves beyond the second phase where ceremonial action becomes almost superfluous, to a third phase ... incarnating proper dispositions in human actions."[261] I think that the sixfold division I delineate is clearer than Daly's three levels. If Daly had done more to clarify the *kinds* of spiritualization, he could answer Attridge's complaint that he should not use the same term to describe different phenomena.[262]

Indeed, there are significant differences between substitution, moralizing, interiorization, metaphor, rejectionism, and making-spiritual. There is also good reason to see a connection between them—besides the common historical occurrence of several of these levels in the sequence listed—and this is that each level causes or registers[263] a change in sacrificial practice or ideology. Levels Two and Four need not *intend* any change in the cult, but both do *rethink* cult by reinterpreting the cult's rationale, and Level Four describes a non-cultic reality accomplishing a cultic result. In different ways, each of the levels registers *transformation through representation*, although Level Four may or may not be accompanied by any intended change in the cult.

This does not imply that the six approaches are harmonious. In fact, it is common for advocates of one type of spiritualization to be very much at odds with those who articulate a different type. The hostility between Level Two spiritualizing defenders of the cult and Level Five critics, is proverbial. One cause of tension is that Christianity committed itself to Level Three spiritualizing from the beginning, but toned down its rejectionist attitude toward the Hebrew cult so that typology could be brought to the fore. One can hardly be happy with typological fulfillment if one has utterly discredited the system within which the *type* occurs. The attitude of Christianity is supersessionist, simultaneously seeing "death" and "glory" in the old system (2 Cor 3:6–9).

One could very well argue that "spiritualization" is too broad a term if it is able to describe such diverse strategies. In fact, it *is* too broad if the term is not

---

[260] Robert J. Daly, S.J., *The Origins of the Christian Doctrine of Sacrifice* (Philadelphia: Fortress, 1978), 79.

[261] Daly, *Origins*, 138.

[262] H. W. Attridge, review of Robert Daly, *Christian Sacrifice*, *JBL* 100 (1981): 147.

[263] Depending on where one assigns the causative factors. It is safest to refer to the six levels as *registers* of a transformative process already taking place.

qualified as has been attempted here. By daring to use this term to cover such a range of interpretive activities, I am indeed asserting that they are related in the long historical process whereby cult is transformed, and inward principles are made paramount. My sixfold delineation is meant to illuminate, not deny, the complexity of the process. I also aim to reduce unnecessary conflict among scholars, who could manifest a closer reading of each others' usages. We either need to reject the term altogether or clarify its different usages.

When I use the term "spiritualization" to signify literary symbolization, Levels Three and Four are chiefly indicated. But I do not want to allow the term to become a purely abstract or *literary* notion. Spiritualization expresses an inward movement toward increasingly personal interaction with God or divinity, and it exerts on ritual practices a pressure for change in response to this inward demand. Unless we have contempt for numerous religious thinkers who speak of responding to an inward or divine demand for "true" piety above and beyond cultic observance, we must accept that they are responding to a genuine spiritual mandate. Spiritualization emerges from reflection on religious ritual in the light of the highest religious values. Every spiritualizing strategy is motivated by conclusions about what those highest values are.

Cult relies on traditions that stretch back beyond memory, often embodying a forgotten or rejected metaphysical logic. Old rites receive new explanations. Heightened appreciation of relational values, along with declining belief that all affliction is caused by purity infractions, leads to a reassessment of cult practices and to a rejection of beliefs and practices that are deemed crude, brutal, or childish.

1.3.3 Spiritualization of Rites

Throughout history, and in all cultures that have been studied, rituals change through a process of substitution and reinterpretation. Human sacrifice was replaced by symbolic human sacrifice, usually the substitution of an animal for a human victim, and is inscribed in numerous narratives, such as the story of Abraham's being stayed from executing his son: when he noticed a ram caught in a thicket, he took it, and "offered it up as a burnt offering instead of his son" (Gen 22:13). There are similar stories in Greek mythology. A whole series of substitutions can take place, following a line of imaginative equivalencies.[264]

Numerous Vedic texts speak of a series of sacrificial substitutions comprising five creatures, from man to goat: "The gods offered man as sacrificial victim. Then the sacrificial quality passed out of the offered man. It entered the horse," and when it passed out of the horse it went down the line, to

---

[264] Described as a "play of sliding substitutions" by Jean-Pierre Vernant, *Mortals and Immortals: Collected Essays* (Princeton, N.J.: Princeton University Press, 1991), 216.

cow, to ram, to goat, and finally to the rice and barley, which embody "the sacrificial quality of all *paśus*."[265] It is taken for granted that "man is the first of the *paśus*"[266] (creatures to be offered), although the substitutions prevent him actually offering himself.

Greek myths provide abundant evidence of sacrificial substitution of animals, where humans had previously been sacrificed. There are many Greek myths that follow "the pattern (transgression, plague, oracle, institution of human sacrifice, abolition of human sacrifice)."[267] A few scholars (for instance, Hughes) see it as purely a literary fiction. But this asks us to see the historiography of Plutarch and Pausanias as utterly devoid of historicity, and to imagine the Greeks resorting to a fiction in order to make themselves feel ashamed about their past. Such hyper-skepticism, though fashionable, is obtuse as regards the historical consciousness of the people who gave us the word "history." The claim that human sacrifice stories were simply used to show the barbarism of foreigners [268] runs aground on the numerous stories about human sacrifice in Athens, Sparta, Thebes, Lesbos, Abdera, Rhodes, and other Greek cities.

Local lore preserved a memory of the transition from human sacrifice to animal sacrifice, as when Pausanias (3.16.10–17) tells how "Lycurgus replaces ancient human sacrifice by sprinkling the altar during the flagellation of the young men."[269] A Boeotian myth tells how a goddess thwarts a falsified oracle demanding a human sacrifice; she sends a golden ram to rescue the intended victims; later the ram is sacrificed.[270]

In fact, the ideology of replacement did not always sit well with the more radical thinkers. Some biblical authors strongly dissent from the idea of God ever commanding sacrifice of the first-born, or arranging the killing of the Egyptian first-born. These authors (Jeremiah, Ezekiel, Deuteronomy, and the Holiness Code) refuse to repeat the story of the slaying of Egyptian first-born and the apotropaic blood-swabbing. Deuteronomy 16 even allows the Passover sacrifice to come from the flock or the herd,

> in evident contravention of the corresponding law in Exodus .... These sources ... aimed not simply at the *substitution* of animals for the first-born sons, but at the *elimination* of the very idea that God has a special claim upon

---

[265] Aitareya Brâhmana 2.8–9; Smith and Doniger, "Sacrifice," 201, 203.
[266] Satapatha Brâhmana 6.2.1.1; Smith and Doniger, "Sacrifice," 200.
[267] Hughes, *Human Sacrifice*, 82.
[268] Hughes, *Human Sacrifice*, 89; cf. similar view of J. Rives, "Human Sacrifice Among Pagans and Christians," *JRS* 85 (1995): 68.
[269] Vernant, *Mortals and Immortals*, 214.
[270] Apollodorus, *Bibliotheca* 1.9.1; Hughes, *Human Sacrifice*, 83.

the first-born son that had to be honored in the cult. The sources that are most outraged at child sacrifice do not allow for the substitution of a sheep for the doomed son.[271]

Deuteronomy and Jeremiah reject "substitutionary etiology" because it implies some legitimacy for human sacrifice in the first place. The P source preserves sacrificial ideology by transforming it, says Levenson, as when it incorporates into Exodus 12–13 a Phoenician institution allowing for "substitution of an animal for the child marked for sacred slaughter."[272] There are serious differences in the strategies of different biblical authors.

1.3.4 A Spiritualized Theory of Sacrifice

One scholarly strategy is entirely based on a spiritualizing argument, although the term does not occur. This is Harmut Gese's highly Christianized interpretation of atonement in the Pentateuch, a clear example of Level Two spiritualizing. Gese relentlessly defends the Levitical cult. He admits that "atonement [is] a substitutionary offering of life,"[273] but not that it is penal or animistic. The operative power that causes the transaction to be successful is the presence of God's holiness in the sanctuary:

> The animal is not killed in order to bring about a destruction of the sinful object . . . but rather a holy ritual of blood is performed. . . . [A]tonement . . . is . . . accomplished . . . by the . . . contact with holiness.[274]

Thus, the animal is not a "sinful object," but it is "substitutionary." Gese may, then, recognize the presence of animism in the ritual, but he overlays it with Christian idealism:

> The sin offering . . . . was to deal with the depraved *being* of humans, into which they came without any conscious act. . . . By means of the sacrifice for atonement, the damaged being is reconstructed and healed. . . . Atonement . . . is coming to God by passing through the sentence of death . . . . substitutionary total self-surrender.[275]

But one can hardly speak of *total* self-surrender when it is the animal that must die, while humans must *dine*. Gese has developed some interesting Christian existentialism here, but Leviticus has nothing about "depraved

---

[271] Levenson, *Death and Resurrection*, 45.
[272] Levenson, *Death and Resurrection*, 177.
[273] Gese, *Biblical Theology*, 110, 98.
[274] Gese, *Biblical Theology*, 106.
[275] Gese, *Biblical Theology*, 110, 114.

The Logic of Sacrifice

being," "total self-surrender," or even moral recovery. What *are* mentioned in a key atonement chapter like Leviticus 17 are blood-guilt incurred by non-sacrificial slaying of stock animals (vv. 3–5), the guilt of sacrificing to goat-demons (שְׂעִירִם, v. 7), injunctions against eating blood or leaving the blood of hunted animals lying uncovered on the ground (vv. 10, 12–13), the explanation that blood atones because it contains life (v. 11), and the datum that one remains unclean until evening if one eats carrion (v. 15). The two injunctions against eating blood surround the key verse (v. 11). It seems quite imaginative to discover here a reconstruction of damaged being. Gese is reading two millennia of Christian theology into this antique list of impurity data. At most one could say that the text speaks of a reconstruction of ritual purity.

But Gese is correct that the offering is "brought into contact with the holy"—a numinous power located at the altar. This affects a person because of the "identification of the *nephesh* of the one making the offering with the sacrificial animal."[276] However, Gese does not tell us how the holy effects atonement. He brings us to the altar and leaves us there, as it were. Or rather, at that point he pours in ideas about "reconstructed being" that have nothing to do with Leviticus:

> Atonement is the sacrifice of life for the sake of making life whole. It brings the abyss of human life into union with the highest divine *doxa*.[277]

Gese's hyper-spiritualized understanding of sacrifice leads him to distance himself from the scapegoat ritual "which does not represent cultic atonement ... but a removal of sin. It is a rite of elimination belonging to popular culture"[278]—and it receives no further attention from him. He cannot find a way to spiritualize this rite of "popular culture." Gese will not dignify it with the label "cultic atonement" since its metaphysic for the riddance of sin is too crudely physical.

This is one of several places where Gese makes a sharp separation between expiation or forgiveness, on the one hand, and atonement, on the other. Atonement, for him, deals not with specific instances of sin, but with human depravity, with "damaged being." People are "worthy of death. But God opens a way to himself through symbolic atonement, which takes place in the cult that God has revealed to us."[279] Gese seems to be saying that the Torah embodied everything we need to know about God.

---

[276] Gese, *Biblical Theology*, 107.
[277] Gese, *Biblical Theology*, 115.
[278] Gese, *Biblical Theology*, 112.
[279] Gese, *Biblical Theology*, 109.

Thus dedicated to *symbolic* atonement, Gese is uninterested in ancient or modern debates that set ethics against cult. Apparently, symbolism is sufficiently ethical, cult is above critique, and Torah is teacher enough. With Levitical technique providing restoration of damaged persons, one must ask what need there is for prophet or Messiah?

Gese's defense of the Jewish cult—a Spiritualization Two strategy—is not as orthodox he seems to think. Among ancient Christians, only the so-called Judaizers attribute literal value to the Jewish cult; Paul certainly does not. With Paul, cultic ideas operate *in a new form*—through the *comprehension* of the believer who knows that "Christ is the end of the Law," and who knows that "these things . . . were written down to instruct us" (Rom 10:4; 1 Cor 10:11). This is supersessionist, implying some form of rejectionism even while exalting the *symbolic* significance of the old cult. Paul's method of interpretation and expression is typological.

1.3.5 Typology

Level Four spiritualization of cult finds its fullest expression in the reinterpretation of narratives through typology and allegory. Typology posits an earlier event as a *prefiguration* or "stamp" (τύπος) of a later event, while allegory involves a spatial or ontological correlation, seeing a "higher" level of reality reflected in the "lower." In my analysis, typology correlates temporal levels, while allegory relates spatial or ontological levels. For instance, Paul sees Abraham's faith as prefiguring the faith of believers. Philo, on the other hand, finds hidden meanings in the narrative: the decision to leave Ur is said to stand for the rational mind turning away from the sensual life: "he means by Abraham's country the body, and by his kindred the outward senses."[280]

Both typology and allegory look for a secondary meaning behind the literal meaning of a narrative. Allegory finds the "hidden" or "real" meaning of the narrative in some cosmological scheme or moral teaching, thereby (to some degree) discounting the literal narrative. Typology, asserting the repetition and transformation of event-patterns, lends itself to narrative theology, seeing the action of God in a pattern of events; this is a transformation of the literal meaning, but not a negation of it. Allegory, looking for the higher realities encoded in the narrative, lends itself to ontological theology.

Typology and allegory involve two different metaphysical viewpoints. The typologist sees evidence of the activity of the divine in time, in *events*; the allegorist believes the divine exists at a higher ontological level of reality; the divine is in the higher *level*.

Typology, then, has a stronger sense of history, while allegory has a stronger sense of ontological differentiation. Of course, typology is not

---

[280] *Migr.* 2.7, 10.

historiography in the modern sense; it makes a link between *narratives*, not between facts.[281]

Typology links up to Level Four spiritualization in my scheme. It can lean in either a Level Two or Level Five direction, but it often avoids taking sides in that bitter struggle. Allegory lends itself to a Level One-Three-Five complex: a strategy of *replacement* of the lower with the higher. Typology sees *fulfillment* where allegory sees replacement.

Paul pulls off a remarkable blending of these two competing strategies; he teaches a doctrine of replacement, but it is *replacement through fulfillment*. Paul says that the old foretold the new: cult and Torah[282] were prefigurations of the Messiah and the Messianic community, but the glory of the old is outshone by the glory of the new (2 Cor 3:7–11). He does not claim that all of the new glory was already there in the old (which would be a Level Two strategy). Paul's ideology struck a consistent middle road between the extremes of Level Two conservatism and Level Five radicalism, although after his lifetime the conservative side (represented by the Pastorals) won out.

In fact, neither "conservative" nor "radical" are adequate labels for what Paul did with cult. His consistent fulfillment typology results in a new kind of cultic ideology. Impurity and holiness still exist, cultically represented death and revival still happen—but they happen in Christ. Paul's cult enacts participation in the Messiah's death and resurrection. The Christ-event becomes a cultic event!

Paul utilizes both Jewish and Hellenistic thinking: he sees a deeper meaning hidden beneath the OT narrative (a Hellenistic viewpoint), and this meaning was prophetic (a Jewish intuition). I mean "prophetic" in both senses: the *type* foretells the future, and God speaks through it: "For whatever was written in former days was written for our instruction" (Rom 15:4). Discernment of the real meaning of Scripture depends on recognition of the Messiah, both in the OT text and in the proclamation about the life of the Messiah, Jesus. The real meaning of the OT is hidden from those who do not read *spiritually*. "Only in Christ" (2 Cor 3:14) can the spiritual meaning of the Scriptures be discovered.

Paul mostly inclines toward typology, but he also uses allegory, as he admits when he says, of the details of the Hagar/Sarah story, that "these things are allegories (ἀλληγορούμενα)" (Gal 4:24; my tr.). He uses the language of allegory, not typology, when he says Hagar *is* (ἐστίν) Mount Sinai, the free

---

[281] Richard B. Hays, *Echoes of Scripture in the Letters of Paul* (New Haven, Conn.: Yale University Press, 1989), 161.

[282] Which was a *"narrative of promise"* (Richard B. Hays, "Three Dramatic Roles: The Law in Romans 3–4," in *Paul and the Mosaic Law,* ed. J. D. G. Dunn [WUNT 89; Tübingen: J. C. B. Mohr, 1996], 160). Cf. Hays, *Echoes,* 99, 157.

woman *is* (ἐστίν) the Jerusalem above (4:25, 26), and the fleshly child "persecuted the child who was born according to the Spirit, so it is now also" (v. 29). It is no coincidence that in this, his most radical letter, he departs from typology and uses allegory. The language of fulfillment is rare in Galatians, since fulfillment implies some legitimacy to the original, something that he is reluctant to concede while he is arguing so vehemently against those who would compel circumcision of Gentiles.

Typology can have the effect of relativizing the significance of the original, in favor of the much more important antitype. Meyer points out that the typological interpretation of Jewish Scripture may raise the value of Israelite history to a Gentile mind, but relativizes it to a Jewish mind: "the effect of interpreting it typologically might be to deprive it of any meaning apart from its reference to Christ."[283] Indeed, when once the antitypes are recognized, "The shadowy prototypes... fall away."[284]

When Olford remarks that "the Temple is [not] rendered meaningless, even if typological,"[285] he is failing to notice that it certainly does render the temple of only *temporary* and *derivative* significance. Olford underrates the implied criticism of cult in Paul's teaching: "[Rom] 9:4 would seem to rule out total disrespect for the cultus."[286] In that verse Paul includes ἡ λατρεία among the Jewish advantages, but the chief gifts (the ones that Paul links to salvation) are the sonship, the promises, and the Messiah—all of which come from the Abrahamic, not the Mosaic, covenant. "The worship" has only typological significance, foretelling the λογικὴν λατρείαν to come; but such worship is still described with cultic terms: it is "a living sacrifice, holy and acceptable to God" (Rom 12:1).

1.4 Paul's Sacrificial Typology

Some of the most important examples of sacrificial typology (Rom 3:25; 8:3), and all my examples of scapegoat typology, must await the analysis in the coming chapters. But three interesting passages can be examined now.

Paul boldly says: "our paschal lamb, Christ, has been sacrificed" (1 Cor 5:7). This summons up the image of Christ's blood averting the wrath of God just as the apotropaic blood on the doorposts caused the Angel of Death to "pass over" the Jews. The remark is made in passing, when he is making a non-soteriological point, but it probably shows that typological equations of Christ with Jewish rituals would not be shocking to his readers.

---

[283] Ben F. Meyer, "The Pre-Pauline Formula in Rom. 3:25–26a," *NTS* 29 (1983): 205.

[284] Leonhard Goppelt, *Typos: The Typological Interpretation of the Old Testament in the New* (Grand Rapids: Eerdmans, 1982), 114.

[285] Olford, "Paul's Use," 58.

[286] Olford, "Paul's Use," 321.

The Logic of Sacrifice

Paul probably alludes to the covenant-sacrifice on two occasions, and the author of Ephesians does so, explicitly, once (1 Cor 11:25; Gal 3:14; Eph 2:13–15). Animal sacrifice was commonly used to seal covenants and treaties between tribes or individuals who otherwise would be enemies.[287] I think there is an echo of such a political result in Gal 3:14; the blessing of Abraham is there extended to the Gentiles, just as peace is achieved between tribes in a covenant sacrifice. It would be difficult to prove this connection, but the next example is much more certain.

The covenant sacrifice was used as the paradigm for the covenant with God. The Lord makes such a covenant with Abram in Gen 15:9–21, and Moses carries out this kind of ritual to bind the people to Yahweh in Exod 24:6–8. In his wording of the Lord's Supper, Paul inserts Jeremiah's "new covenant" into an Exodus-style covenant-sacrifice. Rather than using Exodus, Paul uses Zechariah's restatement of Exod 24:8 (in the Septuagint, of course) as his base text. In Zech 9:11, God promises to "bring forth your prisoners" because he remembers "the blood of your covenant."[288] To this Paul adds the great promise in Jeremiah, "I will make a new covenant. . . . I will write it on their hearts."[289] These phrases are combined in 1 Cor 11:25, but with "in the blood of your covenant" changed to "the new covenant in my blood" (predicate nominative).[290] Christ fulfills the uplifting prophecies of Zechariah 9 and Jeremiah 31, as well as being the antitype of the covenant sacrifice in Exodus.

As Jews do with Passover, Christians are to *remember* and *commemorate* the covenant-founding. Previous covenants provide an imaginative background for the Christian liturgy, and solemnity is communicated through cultic metaphors.

Paul's use of cultic language heightens a sense of continuity between his innovations and the tradition from which he emerged. New teachings may be accepted if they are presented through a spiritualization of existing religious symbols. Paul promotes a transformed, spiritualized, sacrificial ideology.

Paul's is a *metaphorical* system, but one could still attempt to argue that Paul's thinking is "fundamentally cultic."[291] Of course, cultic theologians such as the Sadducees would hardly comprehend, much less accept, Paul's transmogrified cultic thinking. But the cultic mode still applies; the

---

[287] Jer 34:18–20; Gen 15:9–21.

[288] This is the NAB translation. The NRSV of Zech 9:11 changes one pronoun and adds another to make the passage conform to 1 Cor 11:25.

[289] Jer 31:31, 33 (returning now to NRSV, my default translation).

[290] Zech 9:11a LXX: ἐν αἵματι διαθήκης . . . σου. 1 Cor 11:25b: ἡ καινὴ διαθήκη ἐστὶν ἐν τῷ ἐμῷ αἵματι. Jer 31:31 (LXX 38:31): διαθήκην καινήν.

[291] Renwick, *Paul, the Temple,* 74; see "Is Paul's Thinking 'Fundamentally Cultic'?" in chapter 5.

fundamentals of salvation are experienced in the new cultic actions: one dies to sins and is reborn in Christ when one rises from the baptismal water; one partakes of Christ's body and blood in the Eucharist (Rom 6:6; 1 Cor 10:16). This is the form that spirit-mediumship takes in Paul's cult: participation in Christ (in his suffering and vindication, and in his righteous character) and reception of the Spirit (which is simultaneously Christ's Spirit and God's).

The relevance of the Mosaic cult fades when compared with the Messianic cult, but Paul's cultic metaphors indicate that God is still approachable through cultic means; through the *new* Passover lamb. The new cult brings about an intense social experience, usually described by Paul in terms of *unity* across class, gender, and ethnic lines. Bousset was certainly right to look for the basis of Pauline doctrine in shared religious experience: "the spiritual-religious grows out of the cultic."[292]

The next cultic model to be discussed is the scapegoat. There are certain aspects of sacrifice that cannot be clarified until we investigate curse transmission rituals, along with Paul's metaphorical usage of them.

---

[292] Wilhelm Bousset, *Kyrios Christos* (trans. John E. Steely; 1913; repr., Nashville: Abingdon, 1970), 205; cf. 210.

2.
Curse Transmission Rituals and Paul's Imagery

This chapter examines curse transmission rituals and argues that Paul makes use of this image in several soteriological metaphors and two non-soteriological illustrations. Analysis of curse transmission and how it differs from sacrifice gives me the opportunity to explicate the metaphysical assumptions underlying the two rituals. This chapter brings my comments on sacrifice to completion, while beginning my in-depth examination of Paul's use of cultic metaphors.

The best term for the scapegoat type of rite is probably "expulsion ritual," but I also use my own term, "curse transmission ritual," because it focuses on the *transfer* of curse or sin, which is what Paul seems to be focusing on in three soteriological passages. He also uses the scapegoat image in two passages that are not soteriological.

In examining curse transmission rituals in Hebrew and Gentile cultures and Paul's use of this image, I am also assessing the theory of Bradley McLean, that scapegoat is the *only* soteriological image used by Paul. Actually, it is relatively easy to overturn McLean's one-sided thesis. My endeavor is to discover whether Paul uses scapegoat imagery *at all*.

If Paul used curse transmission as a metaphor for the salvific effect of Jesus' death, then at least some of the content of Paul's interpretation is supplied by the theology behind that ancient rite. Metaphor is not just a medium for a message; it also supplies part of the message. A particular metaphor is chosen because the author finds something in the image to be a vivid characterizer of some aspect of his subject. For example, an evangelist is a *fisher of people*, for he seeks to "hook" some people and pull them out of the "sea" of humanity. The image of snagging a fish can be used to say something truthful about what an evangelist does. When a metaphor is effective, it establishes a heuristic link between the image and the referent that becomes established in the interpretive tradition; subsequent readers will always think about evangelism as a type of "fishing." The content of the metaphor has an enduring influence upon readers' understanding of the referent. If Paul used scapegoat imagery, then at least some of the metaphysics of ancient scapegoat theology must have influenced subsequent Christian theology.

Apotropaism and Its Assimilation to Sacrifice

McLean considers expulsion rituals to be a kind of apotropaic rite, but the term apotropaic has long designated an amulet or figure that diverts evil *from the community*.[1] The curse transmission ritual, on the other hand, involves the expulsion of an evil force that is *already present in the community*, its redirection onto a victim that is made to carry it out of the community. Although one can see some similarity between apotropaic *diversion* and expulsive *ejection*, the latter is to be distinguished from apotropaic devices such as gargoyles that can be kept in place permanently, without ritual attention. Gargoyles are stationary guardians; the scapegoat is not a guardian but a porter, and—once the community's pollution has been transferred to it—it is anything but stationary. Apotropaic devices function automatically. Expulsion rituals are not automatic, but must be carried out in times of emergency (Greece), before battles (Hittites), or on the highest of holy days (Israel). Apotropaism is prophylactic toward danger; expulsion ritual is radical surgery after the danger has penetrated the social body.

The notions of *keeping out* and *throwing out* evil are close enough, however, that at least one Greek author confused the two concepts. McLean revives the idiosyncratic use of Photius (ninth century C.E.) who, in describing a Greek expulsion ritual, says, "This purification was of the nature of an apotropaeic ceremony to avert pestilential diseases."[2] The Greek word (ἀποτρόπαιος) is an adjective meaning averting evil; the verb ἀποτρέπω means to hinder; to avert evil; or to desist (LSJ). They signify devices that ward off evil influences. In Ezek 16:21 LXX, idolators think their sacrifices will ἀποτροπιάζω. The prime biblical apotropaism is the daubing of lamb's blood on the door lintels at Passover to ward off the Angel of Death[3]—it causes the LORD to *pass over* (Exod 12:23).

---

[1] Such as an "apotropaic eye" painted on a wine-vessel "to ward off evil" (*The New Encyclopaedia Britannica, vol. 1, Micropaedia* [1991], 489).

[2] Helladios 5 in Phot. *Bibl.* 534a (McLean, 89).

[3] Norman H. Snaith, *Mercy and Sacrifice: A Study of the Book of Hosea* (London: SCM, 1953), 112. Apotropaic background is rejected by Rogerson, who maintains a blanket opposition to any notion of ancient survivals in contemporary religions, coupled with a contempt for "evolutionistic" approaches (J. W. Rogerson, *Anthropology and the Old Testament* [Oxford: Blackwell, 1978], 38, 12).

This apotropaic rite is assimilated to sacrifice in Deut 16:2 where the instructions for utilizing the lamb's body and blood resemble sacrificial protocol, and the lamb is even called the "Passover sacrifice." It has been conceived of sacrificially ever since, including by Paul—"Our paschal lamb, Christ, has been sacrificed" (1 Cor 5:7).

When ritual is subjected to systematization, divergent rituals are (at least partly) assimilated to the dominating ritual. Primitive rites reflecting variant ideas about the workings of the spirit world are absorbed by an emerging system and subjected to the explanations associated with the dominant practice. Scholars unconsciously replicate this process when they subsume scapegoat into sacrifice. McLean correctly rejects this, but he himself assimilates apotropaism to the expulsion ritual, while using a peculiar spelling ("apotropaeic"). Out of 27 dictionaries and articles consulted, I found only one that considered the scapegoat to be apotropaic.[4] Rather, it is correct to signify "apotropaic powers" as "avert[ing] a supernatural threat."[5]

Despite this terminological problem, McLean contributes to Pauline studies by making a useful distinction between sacrifice and expulsion ritual.

2.1 The Ritual Practice

2.1.1 Curse Transmission in the OT

Israel's most important expulsion ritual occurs on Yom Kippur, linked with the most important sin-sacrifice of the year. Besides the goat to be sacrificed, there is another goat. "Aaron shall lay [or *press*: סָמַךְ] both his hands on the head of the live goat, and confess over it all the iniquities of the people of Israel, and all their transgressions, all their sins, putting [נָתַן] them onto the head of the goat, and sending it away (שִׁלַּח, ἐξαποστελεῖ) into the wilderness .... The goat shall bear [נָשָׂא] on itself all their iniquities [כָּל־עֲוֹנֹתָם] to a barren region" (Lev 16:21–22) where the wilderness demon Azazel[6] lives. The verbs show the literalness of the laying-on and sending-away. Further, "the fact that it is devoted to the demon would seem to show that behind the moralized form of the ritual there lies an earlier, non-moral, stage."[7]

---

[4] *Dictionary of Religion and Ethics*, eds. Shailer Mathews and Gerald Birney Smith (New York: Macmillan, 1921), 24.

[5] Speaking of "the paschal blood": William H. C. Propp, *Exodus 1–18: A New Translation with Introduction and Commentary*. AB 2 (New York: Doubleday, 1999), 436.

[6] Verse 26: "The satyr-demon Azazel," Milgrom, *Studies*, 81; cf. Levine, *Leviticus*, 251–52.

[7] Hooke, "Theory," 9.

The divergence of sacrifice and sin-transmission is dramatized by the different fates of "the goat ... for the Lord" and the one "for Azazel" (Lev 16:8–9, 26). Of the first goat, Aaron is to "offer it as a sin offering; but the goat on which the lot fell for Azazel shall be presented alive before the Lord to make atonement over it, that it may be sent away into the wilderness to Azazel" (Lev 16:9–10).

Even the most famous spiritualizer of Jewish theology, Philo, understood the antique essence of the rite; the goat "was sent out into a pathless and inaccessible desolate place carrying on himself the curses of those who had committed offenses."[8] The Septuagint slightly heightens the goat's sin-carrying function by adding "on itself": "it shall bear on itself all their iniquities."[9]

The notion that a curse was transferable is seen in the vision in Zechariah 5, where a curse travels over the land, ready to lodge in the house of the liar or thief.[10] And there are cross-cultural instances beyond number of transmissible luck, *churingas*, curses, and maladies, from the "blessings" gained by touching a relic or being touched by a holy person, to the "cooties" that little boys get if they touch a girl.

Jewish expulsion rituals differ from those of the Assyrians and Hittites in that the latter two seek to appease the god, but this is absent from Leviticus[11] (and also from Greek religion). Jewish and Greek expulsion victims bear away evil without deity involvement. In Mesopotamian and Anatolian usage, since the affliction was thought to have been sent by a god, it was necessary to plead with the god not to re-apply the punishment or disease.

I know of only two other Hebrew rituals that "express the phenomenology of riddance" as does the scapegoat ceremony.[12] First is the rite for keeping a leper in a state of remission of his disease, involving two birds (Lev 14:1–7). One bird is slain and the second is dipped in its blood and released. There is a double transference: the pollution presumably is first conveyed to the sacrificed bird, then to the other bird by contact with the first one's blood.

Here the concepts underlying sacrifice and expulsion ritual are blended, yet the two different kinds of ritual are still distinguishable. Shortly thereafter, the two-bird rite occurs again, this time for decontaminating a house infected with leprosy (Lev 14:48–54). Despite the Torah's rejection of divination, "there is

---

[8] Philo, *Spec. Leg.* 1.188.

[9] Καὶ λήψεται ὁ χίμαρος ἐφ' ἑαυτῷ τὰς ἀδικίας αὐτῶν (Lev 16:22); cf. Hayward, *Jewish Temple*, 138.

[10] McLean, *Cursed Christ*, 83.

[11] David P. Wright, *The Disposal of Impurity: Elimination Rites in the Bible and in Hittite and Mesopotamian Literature*. SBLDS 101 (Atlanta: Scholars Press, 1987), 49.

[12] Levine, *Leviticus*, 251.

no explicit objection to certain forms of therapeutic magic,"[13] and these rites exemplify that.

On the whole the Hebrews relegated expulsion ritual to a secondary position, behind sacrificial practice. In the leprosy-cleansing rites, curse transmission has been conjoined with sacrifice, while the scapegoat is surrounded by the numerous sacrifices of Yom Kippur. Sacrifice became more important in Jewish thought than did curse transmission because it was more *personal*: the response of the personal God to the offering was the matter of central concern.

The key verb כִּפֶּר occurs many times in connection with the sacrifices and once with the scapegoat (16:10), but we have already seen that כִּפֶּר is not an exclusively sacrificial term. Milgrom thinks that its earliest meaning was expulsive/purgative: *kipper* began "as an action which eliminates dangerous impurity by absorbing it through direct contact (rubbing) or indirect (transference)."[14] Milgrom compares the Mesopotamian rite whereby "dirt" is transferred into dough and the dough thrown away, with the scapegoat as "*kipper*-carrier."[15]

Thus it is possible that כִּפֶּר, in the pre-literary period, meant "wiping off," and was associated with expulsion rituals, but that the sacrificial system gradually took over the term. Some of the ideas in Hebrew sacrifice seem to owe something to the (presumably older) rite of expulsion. But at the level of the HB text there are crucial differences between these rites: sins are *put* (נָתַן) on the scapegoat's head, and nothing comparable is said about sacrifice; one goat is violently driven *out* to Azazel, the other is carefully brought *in* to Yahweh. The scapegoat is an impure thing, but the sacrifice is pure. Therefore, scholars should cease to assimilate the scapegoat ritual to sacrifice, unless they can demonstrate the degree and limits of any such assimilation. The theological and ritual differences in the texts need to be taken seriously.

2.1.2 Gentile Expulsion Rituals

Since a large percentage of Paul's readers were Gentiles, an examination of Gentile expulsion rituals is necessary preparation for approaching the question of Paul's usage of expulsion metaphors.

The Greeks, Hittites, and Mesopotamians show a particularly high number of expulsion rituals, some involving no victim, some with an animal victim,

---

[13] Levine, *Leviticus*, 250.

[14] Jacob Milgrom, "Kipper," in *Encyclopaedia Judaica*, vol. 10 (New York: Macmillan, 1971), 1041.

[15] Milgrom, "Kipper," 1040.

and some with human victims. The Ashella ritual of the Hittites[16] was used when there was a disease in the army; a number of rams adorned with colored twine and rings and a woman bedecked with jewels were driven out into the enemy land while the priests prayed, "Whatever evil has been ... these rams, behold, and the woman have carried it away from the camp; the country which accepts them shall take this evil plague."[17]

Wright delineates five key ingredients. There is the element of "concretization," with the placement of the rings and the colored wools "signif[ying] the transfer of evil to the animals."[18] "Disposal" is obviously present, but there is also "prevention," ensuring that the victims do not return; "substitution" is seen in the prayer to the devouring god to be "satisfied with the rams instead of their human flesh."[19] Finally, in "appeasement," the god who is devouring the soldiers by plague is twice asked to be pleased with the adornments of the rams and the woman.[20]

The Hittites had many elimination rites. The ritual of Pulisa, also meant to drive a plague out of the army, involved a bull, a ewe, a prisoner clothed in the king's attire, and a woman; the persecuting god is asked to be appeased with "this decorated man."[21] Several more Hittite rituals "use live animals as bearers of the evil." The Huwarlu ritual involves waving a live dog over the king and queen and then having the dog "carry away evil." The Ambazzi rite involves tying a string on the hand and foot of "those suffering evil," and then tying the string to "a mouse with the request: 'Let this mouse take it [the evil] to the high mountains ... (and) the distant ways.'"

David Wright emphasizes that these animals are not *punished*, but carry something away, and this is what he means when he says these rites "lack the motif of substitution."[22] This is most clearly seen in certain rites of wiping, as when a ram carcass is used to wipe impurity (the verb is *kuppuru*) off of cult items in the cella of Nabu in Marduk's temple, the carcass being thrown in the river; again, "a patient who has been seized by a 'curse'" is wiped with bread, which is then taken out of the city and "placed near a bush" (*Ibid.*)

---

[16] Wright, *Disposal*, 50–55.

[17] Walter Burkert, *Structure and History in Greek Mythology and Ritual* (Berkeley: University of California Press, 1979), 61; cf. Wright's translation, *Disposal*, 51; and McLean's, *Cursed Christ*, 88.

[18] Wright, *Disposal*, 52. On concretization itself, see 41–42, 48.

[19] Wright, *Disposal*, 53.

[20] Wright, *Disposal*, 50–51, lines 14 and 23.

[21] Wright, *Disposal*, 46. Cf. the similar ritual of Uhhamuwa (55–57).

[22] All these examples are from Wright, "Day of Atonement," 74.

Speaking of Hittite elimination rituals, Janowski refers to the "spatial elimination of the evil transferred at that time onto the substitute creature,"[23] and sees the same principle in the Hebrew scapegoat.[24] Schenker stresses that the scapegoat's "task is confined to transport"; it has nothing to do with repentance; "It is purely a carrier . . . . It was not killed for its burden of guilt, but was expelled with its unwanted freight. . . . The scapegoat is, accordingly, no sacrifice . . . . it portrays the spatial departure of guilt."[25]

Expulsion rituals are attested in ancient Egypt, France, Assyria, Rome,[26] but those involving a human victim (the φαρμακός) were particularly common in Greece. At Abdera, the victim was fed well, led "all around the walls of the city, and then chased across the frontier with stones"; during the Thargelia festival at Athens, two men designated as *pharmakoi* were garlanded with figs[27] and driven out after "ritual mistreatment"; in Leukas, a man was hurled off a cliff and then rescued from the sea, but banished from the island.[28]

Hengel mentions Greek accounts of *pharmakoi* being led "round the city. . . . coupled with a curse," and then either stoned[29] "or—as a humane mitigation—be driven out."[30] Hengel places the *pharmakos* ritual within that category of ritual human sacrifice. But these are not sacrifices since they are not part of a controlled presentation to a deity at a central temple. They are not always well-controlled, show little interest in a deity, and reflect a primitive level of social complexity, before the group had developed a central shrine. The emergence of a single temple of premier importance indicates the development of a higher level of social consciousness than in societies where the main concern is simply the boundary of "inside" or "outside" the community, which is all that matters spatially in elimination rituals. Sacrifice shows a much higher degree of conceptualization of sin, atonement, and especially of the will of the deity. A deity seems to be essential in sacrificial rituals in all cultures, but many expulsion ritual texts do not even mention a deity.

---

[23] Bernd Janowski, *Sühne als Heilsgeschehen: Studien zur Sühnetheologie der Priesterschrift und zur Wurzel KPR im Alten Orient und im Alten Testament* (WMANT 55; Düsseldorf: Neukirchener Verlag, 1982), 213.

[24] Janowski, *Sühne als Heilsgeschehen*, 210.

[25] Schenker, *Versöhnung und Sühne*, 115–16.

[26] Bradley McLean, "On the Revision of Scapegoat Terminology," *Numen* 37 (1990): 170.

[27] Burkert, *Structure and History*, 65.

[28] Adela Yarbro Collins, "Finding Meaning in the Death of Jesus," *JR* 78 (1998): 184.

[29] Martin Hengel, *The Atonement: The Origins of the Doctrine in the New Testament* (London: SCM, 1981), 25.

[30] Hengel, *The Atonement*, 27.

Elimination rituals were not sacrifices, and, in Greek sources, the verb θυειν is not used to refer to these rituals by any text earlier than the twelfth century C.E.[31] They all show the "strange mechanism of reversal";[32] they are, in fact, "reversal rituals,"[33] depicting in vivid fashion the transfer of a bad condition from a group onto the victim(s), and of the healthy condition of the victim(s) onto the group.

2.1.3 Purification and Separation

The Greeks believed these rituals accomplished καθάρσις, "purification," and this is naturalistic. It has nothing to do with the Hebrew or Babylonian idea of a central shrine taking on pollution as a result of infractions committed in the whole country. The Greek concept of impurity is simpler and represents any spiritually perilous force, not necessarily resulting from an infraction. Καθάρσις has to do simply with expelling a spiritual danger.

Writing on Greek and Hittite expulsion rituals, Burkert lists three stages common to expulsion rituals: "(1) selection ... (2) rites of communication ... then (3) rites of contact and separation to establish the polar opposition, those active and safe on the one side, the passive victim on the other."[34] McLean speaks of "selection, degradation and alienation."[35] Although it is important to distinguish expulsion from sacrifice, we notice a distant similarity to Hubert's and Mauss's three stages of sacrifice: introduction, consecration, and exit.[36] The content is very different, of course; the careful consecration of sacrifice is the opposite of the wild actions of degradation in an expulsion rite.

McLean notes eight different Greek terms by which these human victims were named: φαρμακός, κάθαρμα, συβάκχος, περίψημα, καθάρσιον, καθαρμός, καθαρισμός, and δημόσιος.[37] Photius, relying on Helladios, said:

> It was the custom at Athens to lead in procession two pharmakoi with a view to purification (καθαρμός); one for the men, one for the women.... He says

---

[31] McLean, *Cursed Christ*, 75 n.38.
[32] Burkert, *Structure and History*, 62.
[33] McLean, *Cursed Christ*, 74.
[34] Burkert, *Structure and History*, 67.
[35] McLean, "On the Revision," 170.
[36] Hubert and Mauss, *Sacrifice*, 45–52.
[37] McLean, "On the Revision," 170, 173. Except for φαρμακός and κάθαρμα, which are more widely attested, the main literary sources are Photius, the Byzantine grammarian John Tzetzes, and a scholiast on Aristophanes (McLean, *Cursed Christ*, 89–93, 209–14). Cf. Hughes, *Human Sacrifice*, 245 n.47.

they were called *Subachoi*. This purification was of the nature of an apotropaeic[38] ceremony to avert pestilential diseases.[39]

Simply put, the rite was "to purify the city."[40]

In short, expulsion rituals were extremely common in Hittite and Greek societies, and even if their actual practice had greatly declined by the time of Paul, the image of the expulsion ritual was recognizable and could provide rich fodder for metaphorical usage. The diversity of expulsion rituals (even in Jewish society, where there were the two rites with the doves, as well as the one with the goat) enabled a metaphorical reference to this *kind* of ritual without specifying one particular rite. Even many modern readers feel a recognition-response when they read descriptions of a mob focusing upon a victim, of the *moment of exchange* or transmission, and of the final expulsion; it is a theme that recurs in popular fiction (for instance in Shirley Jackson's "The Lottery," and in the movie *Suddenly Last Summer*). We feel a chill of recognition in such actions, whether or not we have ever heard of the theories of René Girard. There is something about the process of "selection, degradation and alienation" that we recognize.

2.2 Analyzing Expulsion Ritual

2.2.1 Distinguishing Expulsion Ritual From Sacrifice

If clarity about Paul's metaphorical usage is to be attained, there must be some clarity about the concepts utilized, and therefore it is necessary to distinguish expulsion rituals from sacrifice. Sacrifices are pure offerings made reverently to the deity; expulsion victims are made to be impure and are not directed to the deity but to a wilderness demon. Sacrifices are *sent to God*. Scapegoats are *sent beyond the pale*. Sacrifices are perfect offerings, sending up a "pleasing odor," which means a positive reaction is desired from God. Scapegoats are loathsome things that have nothing to do with God, being merely a sin-bearing mechanism; God is not asked to do anything, is not even called upon to witness the process.

A Christianizing interpretation sometimes assimilates scapegoat to sacrifice under the all-dominant notion of "substitution." One can then say "the Azazel goat itself is the *hattat*," and "the ritual is the special form of the burning of the

---

[38] To my knowledge, this is the only ancient source that uses this word (ἀποτροπιασμός) in connection with expulsion rituals.

[39] Helladios 5 in Phot. *Bibl.* 534a. McLean, *Cursed Christ*, 89.

[40] πόλιν καθαίρειν; Hipponax fragment 4 (from *Poetae Lyrici Graeci* [1882]); McLean, *Cursed Christ*, 210.

hattat."⁴¹ This confuses both the terminology and the function of two rituals that deal (at least directly) with two different problems—impurity and sin—and in two entirely different ways. Hebrew sacrifice must be performed in the temple, and it is used to cleanse the temple, which is the center and symbol of the community. The scapegoat concept has nothing to do with the temple, but with expulsion of sin beyond the borders of the community. Gaster helpfully points out that it is not a substitutionary rite; the animal does not have *blame* shifted to it. The rite did not pay an individual's debt, or cleanse the temple for a particular transgressor; it just removed "the collective taint"; the rite "was representative, not substitutional."⁴² This may be an overly fine distinction as regards these English terms, but it expresses a valid distinction as regards the nature of the rite. It should not be conflated with sacrifice under the rubric of "substitution," and the notion of a judicial penalty, which is not correct.

Sacrificing tended to become routine, but expulsion rituals in Greece and the Ancient Near East were often "emergency rites."⁴³ In Jewish usage, the main expulsion ritual was performed once a year, bringing a primitive rite under the control of priestly law, taming and controlling a religious practice that could—and *did*, in Greek practice—give rise to frenzied behavior expressive of anxiety about evil influences.

Many scholars classify the ritual expulsion of humans in Greece as a kind of human sacrifice, but this does not aid understanding. If one seeks a category into which to fit curse transmission, it would be a *ritual for the transfer and banishment of a curse or disease*, and such transfer can be thought of as "purification," although quite different from the highly symbolic action of temple purification. Sometimes this involves animal or human victims, and sometimes it does not, as with the rituals of wiping and discarding.

The Greeks would purge the community by projecting the imagined "off-scourings" onto the human scapegoats who would transport them, and who were themselves referred to as "off-scourings" (*katharmata*).⁴⁴ There is a reversal of status, with the healthy victim becoming cursed or diseased, and the cursed or diseased community becoming cleansed. Any kind of threat that could be imagined to have penetrated the social boundary can be banished by

---

⁴¹ Kiuchi, *Purification Offering*, 164.

⁴² T. H. Gaster, "Sacrifices and Offerings, OT," in *The Interpreter's Dictionary of the Bible, Vol. 4*, ed. George Buttrick (New York: Abingdon, 1962), 153. Gorman also preserves a distinction (*Ideology*, 96–97).

⁴³ Ida Zatelli, "The Origin of the Biblical Scapegoat Ritual: The Evidence of Two Eblaite Texts," *VT* 48 (1998)261.

⁴⁴ Robert Parker, *Miasma: Pollution and Purification in Early Greek Religion* (Oxford: Clarendon, 1983), 24, 258.

an expulsion ritual. The reasoning is quite literal-minded, ejecting the danger, defending the boundaries by hardening the boundary between community and victim. Banishment is an emergency restoration of boundaries, a naturalistic restoration of spiritual order; there is no need to involve a divinity.

Greek expulsion ritual "was not intended to please or appease any spirit or god. It was ... a καθαρμός, a purification."[45] Expulsion of sins is "more akin to animistic demonology than to religion.... there is hardly any need for a high god in the matter."[46]

The distinction between expulsion ritual and sacrifice, as McLean points out, "is implicit in the difference between 'offering up' and 'forcing out.' 'A sacrifice is an oblation, something offered up, an image of value, of man's best self; a scapegoat is ejected out, an image of no value, of man's worst self.'"[47] The Greek human scapegoat, the φαρμακός, "is utterly impure."[48] It does not "rate as a sacrifice,"[49] because it is defiled, unclean.[50] If we fail to notice the distinction between expulsion ritual from sacrifice, we will fail to understand the dynamics underlying Pauline soteriological metaphor.

The scapegoat ritual involves something not seen in Hebrew sacrifice, and almost never seen in any sacrificial culture: cruelty to the animal. The Mishnah tractate *Yoma* says "the 'Babylonians' (common people) would pull the hair of the Azazel goat as it was led away."[51] The *Epistle of Barnabas* mentions its being spat upon and stabbed, while Tertullian says it was "cursed and spit upon and pulled about and pierced, was by the people driven out of the city into perdition."[52]

---

[45] Jane Ellen Harrison, *Prolegomena to the Study of Greek Religion* (Cambridge University Press, 1903), 103. Regarding the Greek φαρμακός ceremony, "it is not a human sacrifice to Apollo or to any other divinity ... it is a ceremony of physical expulsion" (108). Usually "there is no pretence that any god is worshipped" (106).

[46] Lewis Richard Farnell, *The Cults of the Greek States* (New Rochelle, NY: Caratzas Brothers, 1977), 280; cf. Levine, *Leviticus*, 250: the rites show the "magical objectives of demonology."

[47] Bradley H. McLean, "The Interpretation of the Levitical Sin Offering and the Scapegoat," *SR* 20 (1991): 353. He quotes W. Blissett, "The Scapegoat in Art," paper presented at University College Symposium on Post-Modernism, Toronto, 20 January, 1987.

[48] Harrison, *Prolegomena*, 101.

[49] Milgrom, *Leviticus 1–16*, 441.

[50] M. C. Sansom, "Laying on of Hands in the Old Testament," *Expository Times* 94 (1983): 324.

[51] *m. Yoma* 6:4; Grabbe, "Scapegoat," 158.

[52] *Barnabas* 7:7–9; Tertullian, *Adv. Marcion* 3.7.7 which = *Adv. Jud.* 14.9; Grabbe, "Scapegoat," 162; cf. Daniel Stökl Ben Ezra, *The Impact of Yom Kippur on Early Christianity: The Day of Atonement from Second Temple Judaism to the Fifth Century*. WUNT 163 (Tübingen: Mohr Siebeck, 2003), 31.

Perhaps a good way to relate the rituals to each other is provided by the four-fold functional division conceived by Beattie. Borrowing the distinction of Hubert and Mauss between rites of sacralization (taking on a sacred quality) and those of desacralization (getting rid of a sacred quality), he calls these "conjunctive" and "disjunctive," respectively. He then adds the distinction between those rites that involve the concept of "personalized spiritual beings," and those that focus on an "impersonal, diffused quality or force."[53] Combining these distinctions yields four purposes for rites: to obtain closer contact with God or gods, to achieve "separation from such spirits," to obtain spiritual power, and to achieve separation from spiritual forces. The last category is appropriate for a description of expulsion rites. It differs from Hebrew sacrifice in that it is concerned with an impersonal power rather than with the attitude of God, and it is disjunctive rather than conjunctive. Thus, scapegoat is the opposite of sacrifice along both axes.

Janowski observes that the scapegoat ritual is not a sacrifice and does not involve vicarious atonement, but involves the "magical principle of identification ... the interchangeableness of original and copy," and it evolved from thirteenth—fourteenth century B.C.E. Anatolian and Syrian practices.[54]

A variety of Christianizing strategies has contributed to the tendency to co-mingle the meanings of sacrifice and of scapegoat. It may be that Paul, also, has engaged in such co-mingling, but we cannot intelligently comment on that process unless we first distinguish between the cult practices possibly being conflated. If we say there was no difference between the two practices in the first place, we fail to notice whatever conflation may have taken place.

On the other hand, McLean has failed to notice that the dominant cult practice (sacrifice) did partially absorb, or rather *surround*, the scapegoat ritual. In Leviticus, an assimilation of *placement* has transpired: the scapegoat rite is inserted into the Temple service and surrounded by sacrifices. One must assume neither a lazy blending of scapegoat and sacrifice nor an absolute separation with no relationship, since both were performed on Yom Kippur. One must discern the *extent* and *nature* of any assimilation.

2.2.2 Allegations of Sin-bearing in Sacrifice

The debate about whether there is sin-*bearing* in sacrifice, is actually two debates: one about the hand-laying (to be discussed shortly), and one about the alleged sin-bearing described in Lev 10:17. The dueling interpretations of this verse are reflected in some leading translations. In RSV, Moses wants to know

---

[53] J. H. M. Beattie, "On Understanding Sacrifice," in *Sacrifice*, ed. M. Bourdillon (London: Academic Press, 1980), 38.

[54] Janowski, *Sühne als Heilsgeschehen*, 213; cf. the whole argument from 210–19.

whether two priests realize that the sin sacrifice "has been given to you that you may bear the iniquity of the congregation, to make atonement for them before the LORD?" Here נָשָׂא עָוֹן is translated quite literally as "bear iniquity," but the NRSV treats this as a term for the whole priestly function: "God has given it to you that you may remove the guilt of the congregation."

Rodriguez takes נָשָׂא literally: "the priest bears the sin of the people" when he eats the sin-offering in Lev 10:17, although he admits that this phrase can "also mean 'to become guilty' (Lev 5:1, 2)."[55] Probably the most articulate opponent of the traditional figurative readings of נָשָׂא עָוֹן, "forgive" or "endure," is Baruch Schwartz, who insists that נָשָׂא עָוֹן always means "'to bear', that is, hold up, haul about, carry sin."[56] The sinner himself first bears the sin, which refers to the guilt that *weighs* upon him; the same phrase is then used for someone else bearing *away* the sin.[57] So, "'sin-bearing' is a metaphor for guilt and not punishment . . . . the 'objective' fact of legal guilt."[58]

Kiuchi takes this sin-bearing even more literally: "it can be assumed that Aaron bears the guilt of the Israelites when he makes atonement for sancta" and, further, he bears it when he lays it upon the scapegoat: "Aaron is regarded as guilty on a substitutionary level. . . . he bears the guilt of both priests and the people."[59] This locks Kiuchi into a very literal interpretation and prevents him from being able to explain such actions as the blood-applications.

Schwartz's vehement insistence on a literal reading is undermined by his eventual allowance of a figurative reading of his verb: "It is not that Aaron 'takes upon himself' the liability, or worse, the punishment, for the cultic sins of the community; rather, he is charged with their removal, their elimination."[60] And this idea, *responsibility for removal*, is how many people have understood the phrase. Milgrom has expressed this viewpoint: "assuming the responsibility (*nāśā' 'āwōn*) of guarding the sanctuary."[61] The same phrase occurs in

---

[55] Rodriguez, *Substitution*, 131–32.

[56] Baruch J. Schwartz, "The Bearing of Sin in the Priestly Literature," in *Pomegranates and Golden Bells*, 8–9; essentially supporting this interpretation is Rolf Rentdorff, *Studien zur Geschichte des Opfers im Alten Israel*. WMANT 24 (Düsseldorf: Neukirchener Verlag, 1967), 215–16.

[57] Schwartz, "The Bearing," 10.

[58] Schwartz, "The Bearing," 12, 15.

[59] Kiuchi, *Purification Offering*, 153.

[60] Schwartz, "The Bearing," 16.

[61] Milgrom, *Leviticus 1–16*, 623; cf. "bearing the responsibility of the community by performing purgation rites" (*Studies,* 71). Kiuchi (*Purification Offering*, 51) is overly literal when he says that עָוֹן does not mean responsibility; Milgrom does not claim that it does, rather he claims that נָשָׂא עָוֹן signifies bearing responsibility for carrying out the expiation procedures.

non-cultic situations, where it means "remove iniquity" in the sense of "forgiving,"[62] as when the brothers hope Joseph will forgive them (Gen 50:17), and when Pharaoh asks Moses to forgive him (Exod 10:17). But Milgrom also says things that sound like Schwartz's position, allowing that "the officiating priest absorbs the impurities of the Israelites by means of the *ḥaṭṭa't*,"[63] and even that "the *ḥaṭṭa't* is the embodiment of impurity."[64] Milgrom's position on this point, then, is unclear.

Examination of these passages, cultic and non-cultic, reveals that נָשָׂא עָוֹן is a fixed phrase meaning either "bear responsibility" or "take away blame, forgive," depending on context, and that Schwartz's attempt to force the term to have only literal meaning, falls to the ground, especially when he *does* allow it to mean "charged" with responsibility. This partly abstract meaning makes the most sense: the priest "bears" the responsibility of carrying out atoning rites. The *putting* and the *bearing* in the scapegoat ritual is more literal.

2.2.3 The Different Laying-on of Hands Gestures

In order to better understand Paul's cultic metaphors, we need to understand the cultic actions being utilized metaphorically. It is necessary to see if there is difference between scapegoat and sacrifice as regards the meaning of the laying-on of a hand or hands.

In the sin-sacrifice, the person who has brought the animal lays his "hand" on its head, while in the scapegoat ceremony, the priest lays *both* hands on the animal's head (Lev 16:21). McLean notes that the two goats are virtually identical up to that moment, but that their status and fate diverge from this moment; he argues that the two-hand gesture *transfers* sin, just as Moses laying his hands (plural) on Joshua in Deut 34:9 transferred authority.[65]

Comparing Hittite and Hebrew texts, David Wright affirms this meaning of the laying on of a single hand: "Handlaying serves to ritually identify the offering material as coming from the handlayer."[66] It is particularly apparent in Hittite rituals where a person lays his hand on the offering and someone else carries out the procedure, though it "is to be ritually attributed to the one who

---

[62] Milgrom, *Leviticus 1–16*, 623.
[63] Milgrom, *Leviticus 1–16*, 624.
[64] Milgrom, *Leviticus 1–16*, 638.
[65] McLean, *Cursed Christ*, 79.
[66] Wright, *Disposal*, 54. This point is confirmed by Roland de Vaux, *Ancient Israel: Its Life and Institutions; Volume 2: Religious Institutions* (New York: McGraw-Hill, 1961), 416, 449.

performs the gesture."⁶⁷ The god recognizes that it is from the person who made the gesture, not from the "cultic postman who delivered it" (*Ibid.*).

I argue that, while scapegoat ceremony involves a transfer of sin-stuff, sacrifice does not; the one-hand gesture simply identifies the giver. The metaphysical assumptions of sacrifice are *different* from those of the scapegoat ritual. "The scape goat was considered to be unclean after the imposition of hands on it, the flesh of the *ḥaṭṭa't*, most holy."⁶⁸ Most importantly, sacrifice involves a *theistic* metaphysic; scapegoat is based on a naturalistic or animistic metaphysic where sin is a substance that can be physically transferred and literally banished. Theism assumes the controlling activity of a divine person, and sacrificial texts are constantly making reference to the deity and the deity's instructions.

The two ceremonies are differently conceived, the animals differently treated, the sacred landscapes differ, and the theology is different:

> The dispatch of the Azazel-goat carrying the indebtedness of Israel into the wilderness is not to be understood as a sacrifice but rather as an *eliminatory rite*, whose basis consists in the *magical transfer (contagious magic) and subsequent elimination of the material of sin [materia peccans] through an earmarked substitute.*⁶⁹

The nature of the two animals is conceived quite differently: one is a spotless offering or gift to God, the other a cursed thing that is not even called to God's attention, much less offered to him, but is driven out to the realm of the wilderness demon, bearing the community's sins. Sacrifice offers a community's valuable commodities to a deity; expulsion ritual does not offer *anything*, it dumps "off-scourings" or sins onto a being that acts as a burden-carrier.

Sacrificial instructions culminate with application of blood to the correct sanctum. The Temple sancta are irrelevant to the scapegoat. The laying on of hands in the purification sacrifice certainly signifies some kind of connection between offerer and offering, but probably not the *transfer of sin*. Only in the case of the scapegoat does the biblical text say that sin-transfer has taken place. Laying on of hands in sacrificial rituals seems to signify *who* is making the necessary payment (*kopher*).

---

⁶⁷ David P. Wright, "The Gesture of Hand Placement in the Hebrew Bible and in Hittite Literature," *Journal of the American Oriental Society* 106 (1986): 443; similarly, Schenker, *Versöhnung und Sühne*, 115.

⁶⁸ Robert J. Daly, S.J. *Christian Sacrifice: The Judaeo-Christian Background before Origen* (Washington, D.C.: Catholic University of America Press, 1978), 104.

⁶⁹ Janowski, *Sühne als Heilsgeschehen*, 210.

Gese denies that the transfer in the scapegoat ceremony is quasi-physical. The sins are "given" to the scapegoat not by the hand-laying, but by the accompanying confession; there is "an identification in the sense of a delegated succession, a serving in the place of, and not a transferal of mere 'sinful material' [*bloßem Sündenstoff*]."[70] Dunn agrees, and he points to the laying-on of hands in non-cultic connections as proof: in the transfer of Moses' authority to Joshua (Num 27:18, 23), in the legal appointment of Levites (Num 8:10), and in the sacral-judicial gesture made over a blasphemer before he is stoned (Lev 24:14).[71]

If cultic hand-laying always means a (non-physical) attribution of guilt, this would make the peace-offering and the whole offering to have the same meaning as the *hattat*, but in fact they have different functions. If, on the other hand, "the meaning of the hand-laying is not transference but an attestation"[72] of source, there is no difficulty in the fact that these sacrifices have different significance.

Unlike Gese and Dunn, Janowski frankly acknowledges that the scapegoat ritual involves "the magical motive of elimination of impurity," and that a "magical transfer"[73] takes place. The ancient rite does use literal, physical terms; the priest is "putting them" (נָתַן אֹתָם, Lev 16:21) on the head of the goat, and "sending away" the goat (שָׁלַח, ἀποστεῖλαι once, and ἐξαποστελεῖ twice; vv. 10, 21–22), who "shall bear on itself all their iniquities" (נָשָׂא, λαμβάνω, v. 22). *Putting*, *sending*, and *bearing* are literal physical actions.

The enormous care taken to ensure that the sins were *literally* carried away belies the notion that the transfer of sin was merely symbolic; the Mishnah says ten booths were set up, from which men signaled the passing-by of the goat, the man at the last booth pushing it over a cliff, then signaling back that it had been killed.[74] The Mishnah further says that the red thread that had been tied to the sanctuary door will turn white at the moment the goat is pushed off the cliff, symbolizing that the sins, which were as scarlet, had been made white as snow.[75] This evidences a quasi-physical concept of sin in the scapegoat rite.

---

[70] Gese, *Biblical Theology*, 105–6.

[71] James D. G. Dunn, "Paul's Understanding of the Death of Jesus," in *Sacrifice and Redemption: Durham Essays in Theology*, ed. S. W. Sykes (Cambridge: Cambridge University Press, 1991), 44. The same scriptures are cited by David Daube (*The New Testament and Rabbinic Judaism* [London: University of London Press, 1973], 225–27) and Gese (105).

[72] Sansom, "Laying on of Hands," 325.

[73] Janowski, *Sühne als Heilsgeschehen*, "motive": 213; "transfer": 210 and 219.

[74] McLean, *Cursed Christ*, 81; cf. *m. Yoma* 6:4ff.

[75] *m. Yoma* 6.8, citing Isa 1:18; McLean, *Cursed Christ*, 82.

Dunn acknowledges that only in connection with the scapegoat does the text actually depict the laying on of hands as "laying the sins of the people on the head of the goat" (Lev 16:21), but he insists that "the two layings on of hands [were not] seen as quite distinct," even though (he admits) this means going against "the most recent full-scale treatment [of scapegoat, by] B. Janowski"; for Dunn, "the second goat demonstrated what the sin-offering normally did with their sins anyway."[76]

Dunn's evidence is one Qumran text and two Mishnah texts, "where the language of expiation/atonement is used for both goats,"[77] and this "calls in question the sharp distinction between the functions of the two goats, maintained, e.g., by Kraus, *Tod Jesu* 45–59."[78] But the mere occurrence of כפר in connection with the two goats does not make the rites identical, any more than the numerous non-sacrificial things to which כפר is applied make these things identical to a *kippering* sacrifice. The presence of a כפר-word does not make two rituals equivalent to each other. We need to attend to the context, since even the verb has various meanings: "Kipper is not limited to purgation but serves a wider function," such as an apotropaic effect.[79] The distinction between scapegoat and sacrifice is widely recognized in German scholarship.[80]

Further, the preponderance of Mishnaic and later rabbinic evidence is against a complete blending of scapegoat with sacrifice. The very verse preceding the one that Dunn quotes clearly distinguishes the impurity cleansed by sprinkled blood, and the transgressions atoned for by the scapegoat.[81] *Yoma* and *Sifra* do so as well, and at some length.[82]

---

[76] Dunn, "Paul's Understanding," 45.

[77] Dunn, *Theology*, 221; citing 11QT 26–27, *m. Shebuoth* 1:7, and *m. Yoma* 3:8.

[78] Dunn, *Theology*, 221 n.77, referring to Wolfgang Kraus, *Der Tod Jesu als Heiligtumsweihe: Eine Untersuchung zum Umfeld der Sühnevorstellung in Römer 3,25–26a* (WMANT 66; Düsseldorf: Neukirchener Verlag, 1991) [see chapter 7 as well].

[79] Milgrom, *Studies*, 155.

[80] Janowski, *Sühne*, 209–21 (and see his citations of Koch and others); Gese, *Biblical Theology*, 112; Willi-Plein, *Opfer*, 105–6; Schenker, *Versöhnung und Sühne*, 115–19; Notker Füglister, "Sühne durch Blut—zur Bedeutung von Leviticus 17,11," in *Studien zum Pentateuch: Walter Kornfeld zum 60*, ed. Georg Braulik (Vienna: Herder, 1977), 146–47.

[81] "'For impurity that befalls the temple and its sancta through wantonness, atonement is made by the goat whose blood is sprinkled .... For all other transgressions ... the scapegoat makes atonement' (Mishna, *Shebuoth*, I, 6)" (Milgrom, *Studies*, 81); cf. McLean, *Cursed Christ*, 82.

[82] *Sifra* 181.2.9 distinguishes between the goat that "shall bear all their iniquities" and the one dealing with "uncleanness to the sanctuary"; *m. Yoma* 4:2; 6:1–8 and Philo also make the distinction; McLean, 79–83.

David Wright concedes that the presence of כפר in both rites connects them,[83] but, crucially, "the blood and scapegoat remove two different evils—impurity and sin, respectively."[84] "Impurity is merely the effect flowing from the ... transgression."[85] The scapegoat does something the חטאת, when it cleanses the stain of inadvertent sins, does not: it carries away the "deliberate, wanton sins (עונות)."[86] The notion that the scapegoat does nothing different than the חטאת, "makes the scapegoat ritual superfluous."[87]

Finally, the Qumran community cannot control our understanding of a Temple cult in which it did not participate. The sectarians were not interested in how the rites worked, but in decrying the Jerusalem cult as absolutely corrupt.

Dunn allows that, "just how the sacrifice effected atonement remains an unsolved riddle,"[88] yet he is confident that the scapegoat ceremony travels the same unknown path. His explanation of sacrifice incorporates the logic of scapegoat. This has been a common aspect of Christian understanding of sacrifice and atonement since early deutero-Pauline times. After all, Christian preaching was focused on Christ, not on precisely distinguishing OT cultic activities.

Paul's use of multiple models to describe the saving effect of Christ's death contributed to a blending of these models in the Christian mind, and to the attitude that the differences could hardly be very important if they could be used to describe the *same* event. Even today, most Christians think of sacrificial imagery when they use the *economic* term "redemption." So it is not surprising that ideas associated with scapegoat (and with redemption, and with acquittal) helped shape the Christian understanding of OT sacrifice. Thus Christians came to understand the sacrificial animal as a penalty bearer and sin-carrier. And so, even in scholarship, the familiar doctrine of penal substitution (though without this now-unpopular label) is common:

> The hand laid on the animal ... symbolizes the offering of his own life....
> The essence of atonement is thus mitigation of punishment.[89]

---

[83] Wright, *Disposal*, 20.
[84] Wright, *Disposal*, 79.
[85] Wright, *Disposal*, 18.
[86] Schwartz, "The Bearing," 20.
[87] Schwartz, "The Bearing," 19; *contra*, Kiuchi, 145–54, and Rodriguez, 117–18.
[88] Dunn, *Theology*, 218.
[89] B. Lang, "כפר kipper," *TDOT* 7:295.

It shows an animal suffering vicariously in a man's place.... [a]s a substitute for the worshipper.... Its immolation on the altar quietens God's anger at human sin."[90]

This assumes something that is never stated in Hebrew texts: that the animal is being somehow *punished*. On the contrary, no abuse is poured on the sacrificial animal as there is on the scapegoat; it is treated with great care and is sacrificed *to God*, while the sin-carrying scapegoat is abused[91] and driven out *to Azazel*, something that never happened with sacrificial animals. Beating and stabbing and spitting would alter the animal from its previously "spotless" condition, rendering it impure. But a sacrificial animal remains spotless, it brings no impurity into Yahweh's house. The wilderness, on the other hand, is an appropriate repository of impurity.

By treating sacrifice as a ritual of penal substitution and treating scapegoat as a sub-species of sacrifice, it becomes easy to attribute scapegoat themes to sacrifice, to speak of "the sin offering as somehow embodying the sin of the one who offered it ('made sin'—2 Cor 5:21)."[92] "[T]he animal becomes sin in the literal sense."[93]

Here sacrifice is made to take on the animistic metaphysic of the scapegoat rite. The corollary of this non-distinction between sacrifice and scapegoat would be a non-distinction between Yahweh and Azazel, between the holy sanctuary at the center of the community and the accursed wilderness, and between careful handling and raucous mistreatment.

Dunn describes the first part of the atonement process, the part regarding the connection between offerer and victim, as quite animistic or quasi-physical. Sin is transferred to the animal, becomes commingled with its life-force—its blood—and so is spilled out with the blood. "The equivalence between offerer and sacrifice lay exclusively in the *blood* of the victim,"[94] Dunn writes. Since sin drains out with the blood, the bloodless meat is not polluted with sin and so is edible.[95] Thus, the first stage of the sacrifice reflects the animistic metaphysic of the scapegoat rite, the notion that sin can be physically transferred to another body. But Dunn does not stay with animistic logic, he switches to the logic of penal substitution. The animal's death becomes an effective *punishment*: "the

---

[90] Wenham, "Theology of Old," 80, 82.
[91] Grabbe, "Scapegoat," 158, 162–63, on *Barnabas* 7, Tertullian, *Yoma*, etc.
[92] Dunn, *Theology*, 219. Two pages earlier he had admitted that 2 Cor 5:21 probably intended the scapegoat image.
[93] Klaus Koch, "חטא *chatá*," *TDOT* 4:317.
[94] Dunn, *Theology*, 221.
[95] Dunn, "Paul's Understanding," 46.

manner in which the sin-offering dealt with sin was by its death,"[96] "by the destruction of the sin-laden sacrifice."[97]

Dunn uses animism to account for the projection of sin into the animal's blood, which would require that something be *still alive in the blood* after it is spilled. However, Dunn abandons animism at this point; suddenly we have a substitutionary "destruction," and the blood-pouring is not because of any force still alive in the blood or any special usage to be made of the blood, but only to show that the animal has died: "The sprinkling, smearing, and pouring away of the sacrificial blood in the sight of God indicated that the life was wholly destroyed, and with it the sin of the sinner."[98]

Dunn is changing his metaphysical logic; he leaves behind the animistic notion that "equivalence . . . lay exclusively in the *blood*,"[99] and starts treating the animal's death as the key moment. But if mere death deals with the sin, why the stringent regulations that the blood must be poured out (*šapak* or *yaṣaq*), squeezed out (*maṣâ*), applied (*natan*), sprinkled (*hizza*), or dashed (*zaraq*),[100] and on precise locations: the altar of holocausts, the incense altar, the curtain, the mercy seat? We cannot afford to ignore the text's focus on applying blood in a certain way to certain temple sancta. We cannot treat this, the climax of the sacrificial act, as irrelevant, which is tantamount to treating the temple itself as irrelevant.

The end of the animal's life is not the end of the scholar's problem. If animism transferred sin to the animal's blood, it is still operative after the blood is spilled, and the careful gathering and disposition of the liquid seems to evidence this. Spilling the animal's blood is merely the beginning of the procedure.

Milgrom says the blood is applied to different sancta in order to deal with different "degrees" of contamination.[101] Milgrom accounts for the different levels of contamination and the different remedies taken. Blood application performs a key role, cleansing the sanctuary from pollution. Here is where we need to change our habitual way of looking at the ritual. We must stop thinking of the blood as carrying a sin-charge; rather, the temple has impurity, and the blood takes it away. *It is not the blood that has been corrupted by sin, but the temple.* Blood washes away temple impurity.

---

[96] Dunn, "Paul's Understanding," 46.
[97] Dunn, *Theology*, 221; the death of Jesus has the same meaning: 343 n.35.
[98] Dunn, *Theology*, 221.
[99] Dunn, *Theology*, 181.
[100] Wright, *Disposal*, 147–48; Daly, *Christian Sacrifice*, 88–89.
[101] Milgrom, "Priestly Laws," 142, 146.

In sacrifice, the life-force is momentarily liberated, and it is used to wash the stain of sin from the holy furnishings. Thus, the analogy of life-blood as "detergent" suggested itself, but we also saw how Milgrom overemphasized one aspect of the ritual (cleansing the temple) and suppressed the other (forgiveness for people). Further, "detergent" is somewhat vapid; rather, the life-force in the blood eliminates the death-force in the pollution. The animal is pure and its blood is good (nothing like the impure scapegoat).

Seeing the animal as a sin-carrier obscures the fact that its blood is not corrupt, but is a cleansing agent. This is still animistic, but it is a different logic than the usual Christianizing logic about guilt and substitution. Rather, it involves an idea of the magical power of blood, and also a logic of payment; the offerer must give up something valuable, something that has *cost* him. Sacrificial animals must be costly to the owner: "I will not offer burnt offerings to the Lord my God that cost me nothing" (2 Sam 24:24).[102]

2.2.4 Blended Concepts of Atonement

Christian scholarly interpretation of the OT is sometimes redolent of Christian atonement doctrines, as here: "The animal had to be holy, without defect, precisely so that both priest and offerer could be confident that the death it died was *not its own.*"[103] Instead of labeling this as penal substitution, Dunn asserts that "any thought of *punishment* is secondary," and offers an analogy of vaccination: Jesus was given a "shot" of the consequences of sin, but was able to rise up again, "germ-resistant."[104] Since the ancient world did not know vaccination, what is the *ancient* thought pattern being described here? Is it not a scapegoat that takes a "shot" of sin, freeing the community from sin?

Vaccination is a modernizing description of the scapegoat mechanism. Dunn's interpretation of Levitical sacrifice (and he assumes Paul has the same understanding) is a combination of scapegoat-logic (sin transferred to a victim) and penal substitutionary logic (a substitute for one's own deserved fate).

A downplaying of penal language is seen in many current interpretations of Pauline atonement teaching, only one of which will be examined here. Stephen Travis wishes to deny penal implications when he says that Jesus "'was judged in our place' . . . he experienced divine judgment on sin. . . . But this is not the same as to say that he bore our punishment."[105] If there is no punishment, what

---

[102] Milgrom, *Leviticus 1–16*, 441.
[103] Dunn, *Theology*, 221.
[104] Dunn, "Paul's Understanding," 50.
[105] Stephen H. Travis, "Christ as Bearer of Divine Judgment in Paul's Thought about the Atonement," in *Jesus of Nazareth: Lord and Christ*, eds. Joel B. Green and Max Turner (Grand Rapids: Eerdmans, 1994), 344–45.

is meant by saying "he was judged in our place"? Travis's answer is that "God's judgment" refers to an automatic judgment on sin, built into reality, and Christ experienced *that*, not direct divine punishment. "He endured the God-ordained consequences of human sinfulness[, b]ut . . . not . . . punishment."[106]

This is a spiritualizing strategy, rejecting the terminology of "punishment" while retaining the logic of legal penalty and of substitution ("judged in our place"). Travis is on more solid ground when he utters the truism that, for Paul, sin is alienation,[107] and Christ "absorbed" this alienation, rather than *paying* for sins. This goes partway toward establishing his point, but cannot explain passages that *do* speak of payment for sins, such as, "you are bought and paid for" (1 Cor 6:20; 7:23), "you are storing up wrath for yourself on the day of wrath," when "he will *repay*" with "wrath and fury" (Rom 2:5–8).

Travis tries to envision judgment without punishment, and sin-elimination without sin-transfer. Dunn was not thus evasive; he allows that there was a dynamic of sin-transfer, and there was punishment. We need *some* explanation of the dynamic of sin-transfer, if it is present. One must ask: What *happens* to the sin? If the animal receives a legal punishment, then it is a penal stand-in. If there is no retribution, but the departing life-force takes our pollution into the other world, then it would be a magical haullier of sin, but Travis will not even mention that possibility. He uses penal substitutionary logic without admitting it. Saying that Christ "absorbs" human alienation, while denying punishment and evading scapegoat, leaves the mechanism of "absorption" unexplained.

If magic and retribution both are to be rejected, then the theory of sin-transference must also fall. If one wishes to argue against animism while retaining sin-transfer, then penal substitution is implied (otherwise, why would killing the animal accomplish atonement?). If one rejects retribution while retaining the theory of sin-transference, then the animism entailed in sin-transfer must be recognized.

Do we get a better alternative by staying closer to the metaphysics of the Levitical texts? They indicate that sin (a form of un-life) is cleansed by the life-force that is found in the animal's blood. The logic is magical more than penal, although the sacrifice does involve an economic burden. But this makes it difficult to see why sacrifice would suggest itself to Paul as a possible metaphor. Would Paul be saying that killing a martyr releases a cleansing life-force, and killing the Messiah releases the most life-force? This cannot be found in Paul; rather, he has set his cultic formulas within judicial and participationist frameworks; but that does not mean that Leviticus had only

---

[106] Travis, "Christ as Bearer," 345.
[107] Travis, "Christ as Bearer," 345.

judicial and participatory, but no animistic, meanings. Paul has reduced the animism, but it is still present in the logic of his metaphors.

In fact, Paul does seem to utilize both the notion of vicarious punishment ("was handed over to death for our trespasses," Rom 4:25) and a scapegoat-like bearing away of pollution ("for our sake [was] made to be sin," 2 Cor 5:21), along with his other soteriological metaphors. Carroll and Green detect *eight* soteriological models for the death of Christ in Gal 3:11–14—and they do not distinguish scapegoat![108] Therefore it is no surprise that Christian theology and scholarship have tended to interpret the sacrificial victim as a sin-bearer. But to understand the OT on its own terms, we must remove these deeply ingrained assumptions.

Since Paul does, in fact, conflate different OT images,[109] Dunn's conflation of sacrifice and scapegoat in fact signals his sensitivity to Paul's own synthetic method. But if we are to explicate the OT background, we need to notice the distinctions that the OT makes. Dunn is highly perceptive of Paul's own motifs, but the viewpoint of Pauline theology may have unduly shaped his interpretation of OT sacrifice.

A reassessment of the cultic concepts upon which Paul drew may give us a deeper understanding of how the metaphors are constructed. If we are to make the term "conflation" meaningful, we must distinguish between the elements being conflated. Paul found it rhetorically profitable to conflate models of sacrifice, noble death, scapegoat, and redemption-price; that does not mean that he saw no difference between cultic, martial,[110] and economic realms. He *does* want to assert that Jesus' death was a cleansing gift to God (a sacrifice), a sin-bearing departure (a scapegoat function), a heroic dying *for* others, a payment of a price to obtain freedom for others. He does want people to understand Christ's death as performing all those functions, but that does not mean that he saw no difference between sacrifice and scapegoat, any more than it means that he saw no difference between a redemption payment and a heroic death.

---

[108] "Christ as the *representative* of Israel . . . *justification* . . . *redemption* . . . *adoption* . . . *substitution* . . . *sacrifice* (implicitly, Gal 3:13); the *promise of the Spirit* (Gal 3:14); and the *triumph over the powers*" (John T. Carroll and Joel B. Green with Robert E. Van Voorst, Joel Marcus, and Donald Senior, *The Death of Jesus in Early Christianity* [Peabody, Mass.: Hendrickson, 1995], 126). Scapegoat probably fits under "substitution" here.

[109] See especially the section on Rom 8:3, below.

[110] The "noble death" motif arises from military and political loyalty; see chap. 5.

2.3 Paul's Usage

2.3.1 The Insistence on One Model

McLean, like many scholars, wants to find only one interpretive model for Paul's soteriology, and he attempts to expel the sacrificial one. But Paul used multiple models. An example of McLean's logic is this: "Paul's emphasis on Christ's suffering is irreconcilable with the fast, painless death of a sacrificial animal."[111] But this is altogether rigid and misinformed. Paul also emphasizes Jesus as Messiah, something never associated with animals; but that is beside the point. Whether or not Paul focuses on Christ's suffering, he does draw attention to the death, and that one point of contact is sufficient to allow sacrifice to function as a metaphor, regardless of other details. Metaphors need only draw on one point of similarity. Jewish tradition had already equated noble death with sacrifice (2 Macc 6–7, Isaiah 53).

McLean's approach is sometimes dogmatic; having decided that Paul does not use sacrificial imagery, he dismisses the Maccabean martyr thesis in a footnote when he finds that it is a sacrificial concept.[112]

It is not necessary to be so one-sided in assessing the themes of Pauline theology. Paul—of all people—is more than capable of utilizing more than one soteriological model, and McLean recognizes this, but he does not allow Paul to draw upon the sacrificial model. He fails to see that in Rom 8:3 Paul synthesizes the sacrificial model ("sacrifice for sin," περὶ ἁμαρτίας) with a judicial setting (God condemning) with the scapegoat metaphor (the focalization of wrath on a particular piece of flesh). This does not negate the distinction of scapegoat and sacrifice—or of the judicial metaphor. Examples of conflation can only be identified *as such* when one recalls the standard and recognized *distinction* of the things being conflated. Conflation departs from standard usage.

Sometimes conflation is due to ignorance about one of the rites; Plutarch uses the word for sacrifice when describing expulsion rituals in which he had participated.[113] The Byzantine grammarian John Tzetzes does the same when he says "they led out as to sacrifice the ugliest of all the citizens to be an expiation and pharmakos (εἰς καθαρμόν καὶ φαρμακόν) of the diseased city. And having set the sacrifice at such a spot . . . ."[114] After φαρμακός rituals became rarer or were ceased altogether in certain localities, it was easy for people to begin to conflate them with the more well-known practice of

---

[111] McLean, *Cursed Christ*, 48.
[112] McLean, *Cursed Christ*, 51–52 n.92.
[113] McLean, *Cursed Christ*, 103–04.
[114] Tzetzes, *Chiliades* 729–31; McLean, *Cursed Christ*, 93–94.

sacrifice. But the biblical text shows the clear differences between sacrifice and scapegoat, and a Pharisee like Paul would have known these differences. The Mishnah also preserves the differences.

2.3.2 Gentile Expulsion Terms in 1 Corinthians 4:13

In 1 Cor 4:13 Paul uses explicitly Gentile cultic terms when he says he and his fellow apostles "have become like the rubbish of the world, the dregs of all things" (ὡς περικαθάρματα τοῦ κόσμου ἐγενήθημεν πάντων περίψημα). This translation hides the cultic background of περικαθάρματα and περίψημα; both can mean "off-scourings" or "refuse,"[115] and both terms can signify a price or ransom, as in Prov 21:18[116] and Tobit 5:19.[117] More importantly, these terms can refer to φαρμακός victims on whom were laid "a μίασμα or (religious) impurity"[118] to rid a city from disaster. Even the related terms κάθαρμα and κάθαρσις can refer either to the debris from various forms of purifications or to the human scapegoats who were the purificatory debris of the community.[119]

Eventually the main candidates for περίψημα came to be criminals and rejects, so it came to be a general term of abuse or polite "self-abasement,"[120] but the ritual background is still in view, because these "scum of society (περίψημα in the first sense) were used as expiatory offerings (περίψημα in the second sense)."[121] "The notion of expiatory substitution must have clung to the word" [περικαθάρμα].[122]

The implications of this verse are "that the apostles accepted like Christ the rôle of victims for the sins of the world,"[123] but a number of scholars recoil from accepting this aspect of Paul's idea of participation in Christ.[124] Moulton and Milligan want to see in περικαθάρμα and περίψημα in 1 Cor 4:13 merely

---

[115] BAGD, 647. According to James H. Moulton and George Milligan, *The Vocabulary of the Greek New Testament Illustrated from the Papyri and Other Non-Literary Sources* (London: Hodder & Stoughton, 1929), 510, περικαθάρμα was the "rinsing" and περίψημα the "'scraping' of a dirty vessel."

[116] Joseph Henry Thayer (tr. and enlarged by), *A Greek-English Lexicon of the New Testament* (from Grimm) (4th ed.; Edinburgh: T&T Clark, 1901), 503.

[117] BAGD, 653.

[118] Gustav Stählin, "περίψημα," *TDNT* 6:84, 85.

[119] Parker, *Miasma*, 24, 219, 258–59, 299.

[120] Stählin, *TDNT* 6:89.

[121] Stählin, *TDNT* 6:86–87.

[122] Anthony Tyrrell Hanson, *The Paradox of the Cross in the Thought of St. Paul*. JSNT Sup 17 (Sheffield: JSOT Press, 1987), 33.

[123] Hanson, *Paradox of the Cross*, 35.

[124] Such as Stählin.

terms of self-deprecation, "much like, 'your humble and devoted servant.'"[125] This is far more polished than is likely for these gritty words. The occurrence of these two terms in the same sentence, and the presence of cultic imagery in succeeding chapters of the letter, increase the likelihood of a cultic resonance to these terms.

First Corinthians 4:13 is the first of many cultic or redemption images in a lengthy paraenesis: expelling someone (a scapegoat image, 5:5), casting out old leaven (5:5–8), body as temple (6:15–19), being bought with a price (6:20; 7:23), husbands and wives "being made holy" (ἡγίασται; 7:14; a cultic term in Num 3:13, etc.). Stählin says the likelihood of a cultic sense is strengthened by "the association with πάντων," recalling that the περίψημα "must perish for a whole city or people," and by the choice of the verb γίνεσθαι, just as in texts describing the Greek rite (Photius, Suidas).[126]

Paul's labeling himself and his fellows as περικαθάρματα and περίψημα reminds of Christ's role as an expulsion victim, to be replicated by his apostles. "The cross of Christ" (1 Cor 1:17) embodied selfless service for others; Christ died for weak brethren (1 Cor 8:11); he died for our sins (15:3); in fact, Christ "died for all" (2 Cor 5:14). The idea of Christ as ransom-payer or punishment-bearer may not be present in every one of these instances of ὑπέρ and διά, but it is impossible to banish it from all of them. That the punishment-bearer should be the rescuer is part of the astounding ironic reversal that Paul wishes to emphasize. Even "God's weakness" can "shame the strong" (1 Cor 1:25, 27).

It is hard to believe that Paul the Pharisee would not know the difference between sacrifice and scapegoat, or that he would be unaware that he is applying the language of scapegoat when he speaks of apostles as περικαθάρματα or when he speaks of Christ being cursed (Gal 3:13). I think Paul knows what he is doing when he applies various cultic metaphors to Christ and to the apostles.

2.3.3 The Scapegoat Image in 2 Corinthians 5:21

In 2 Cor 5:14–15, Christ dies "for (ὑπέρ) all," and in v. 21, Christ is *made sin* (ἁμαρτίαν ἐποίησεν) *for* (ὑπέρ) *us*. McLean argues that this image comes from curse transmission, not sacrifice.[127] This cannot be sustained as a principle for all uses of ὑπέρ, but McLean is right about this verse, and Dunn also sees a scapegoat allusion here.[128] As another Durham scholar noted, the scapegoat

---

[125] Moulton and Milligan, *Vocabulary of the Greek*, 510.
[126] Stählin, *TDNT* 6:90–91; he quotes Photius and Suidas on 85.
[127] McLean, *Cursed Christ*, 110–12.
[128] Dunn, *Theology*, 217.

"becomes in a certain sense the impersonation of the sin and of the curse."[129] Such a shameful *becoming* does not happen to the sacrificial animal, which remains pure, but only to the expulsion victim.

In curse transmission there is an *exchange*; the victim's initial well-being becomes the community's well-being after the victim takes on the community's ill. They could be called "reversal rituals." In the *pharmakos* ritual, the human scapegoats are selected, consecrated, "clothed in sacred garments" and subjected to "ceremonial whippings," before the sudden pouring of curses upon them, at which point they take on the sin and misery of the population.[130] So is the transforming event described in this verse—Christ takes on our sin, and we "become the righteousness of God."

What is the basis of the exchange process? Hooker thinks it hinges on incarnational theology. Christ is not "an outside Saviour"; his entering into human nature has transformed that nature.[131] "He who is Son of God was born of a woman in order that those who are born of woman might become sons of God."[132] The second Adam takes on the form of the first Adam so that men can take on his likeness, can become sons of God.[133] Thus does Hooker help us fit these images into the big picture of Paul's theology, but she does not mention that the model for the exchange is the curse transmission ritual. She does not discuss the darker side of exchange: magical transfer and vicarious victimization.

Yet Paul imposes joyful and liberating meanings upon this primitive image. In his whole corpus, this chapter is probably Paul's most moving metaphor. "The love of Christ urges us on, because . . . one died for all," so that we might learn to live for him who died for us (5:14–15). This surely tugs at the reader's conscience. Then comes the explosive passage: "there is a new creation . . . everything has become new! All this is from God, who reconciled us to himself through Christ" (vv. 17–18). God has found a way to call back estranged humanity: "God was reconciling the world to himself" (v. 19). This is crucial for understanding Paul's thinking; it tells us clearly that God is not changed in any way; it is humanity that gets reconciled—re-oriented—to God. God's kindness is emphasized, and Paul makes an emotional/spiritual appeal: "we entreat you on behalf of Christ, be reconciled to God" (v. 20). As a culmination, there is a soteriological formula: "For our sake he made him to be

---

[129] J. B. Lightfoot, *St. Paul's Epistle to the Galatians* (Rev. 3rd ed.; London: Macmillan, 1869), 138.

[130] McLean, *Cursed Christ*, 74.

[131] Morna D. Hooker, "Interchange in Christ," *JTS* n.s. 22 (1971): 358.

[132] Hooker, "Interchange," 352.

[133] Hooker, "Interchange," 355.

sin who knew no sin, so that in him we might become the righteousness of God" (v. 21).

One cannot adequately interpret this passage without noticing the cultic *exchange* that it describes. The final verse unfolds the cultic implications of v. 19: the transgressions not reckoned in v. 19 had to be imposed on a ritual victim in v. 21, as though it could not have happened any other way. "All this is from God" (v. 18) shows that Paul does not envision any kind of inducement of God—God is not bribed by Christ's death—but v. 21 seems to imply that only through a reversal ritual and with a ritual victim, could God make us righteous. Reconciliation was intended by God, but its actualization derives from the making-sin event. Our being made righteous is a great reversal, and requires a reversal ritual; it is "in Christ"—in the ritual victim—that God was reconciling the world to himself, not reckoning their transgressions (a judicial category). A judicial end was accomplished by ritual means, making this passage fully consistent with the sin-elimination described in Rom 3:24–25 and the redemption by curse-bearing in Gal 3:13.

God's generosity is unbounded, but it seems that God is bound to use cultic forms—even making an innocent man to become sin—to accomplish God's ends. The scapegoat mechanism is a given; it is already in place when God uses it. This places the cultic form on the divine level. Paul seems to share ancient instincts about cult as the interface between the human and the divine, and of God acting always through a cultic pattern. Reconciliation and righteousness apparently *require* the scapegoat mechanism, the victimization of Christ, who dies for all. Thus, God reconciling the world with Godself is simultaneously a personal and a cultic action. God's personal attitude is emphasized in vv. 18–20, but the cultic nature of God's action is shown in the *making-sin* and the magical status-reversal for "us."

2 Corinthians 5:21 shows us how inadequate for explaining Pauline soteriology is a purely judicial model of being "rightwised" in the sense of being acquitted.[134] Mere acquittal would not empower people to *become the righteousness of God* (γενώμεθα δικαιοσύνη θεοῦ), and would not explain the need for cultic metaphors describing radical reversal.

N. T. Wright's explanation for this passage is also inadequate, in that it ignores the cultic exchange. He insists Paul speaks as an ambassador, and an ambassador "*becomes* the living embodiment of his sovereign"; so "becoming the righteousness of God" means "substantially the same thing" as being "a

---

[134] Bultmann (*Theology*, 1:272–87) gives a good account only of the judicial aspect.

minister of the new covenant" in 2 Cor 3:6.[135] But the focus of the made-sin death is *salvation* ("one died for *all*" in v. 14), not apostleship. Wright does not explain the two *exchanges* of status going on in the verse, from "no sin" to "sin," from needing reconciliation to "becoming righteousness." The exchange is so jolting, so unexpected, that it needs an explanation that has *exchange* at its core. Wright allows, but downplays, cultic elements. He accounts for radical transformation with the notion that "new covenant" implies "new creation," but this does not explain one being *made-sin* while another is *made righteousness*. Only scapegoat seems adequate as a model for such a strange, actually magical, reversal.

Paul makes reconciliation his central theme in only one other passage, Rom 5:8–11. Paul's reconciliation words, καταλλάσσω and καταλλαγή, have their ancestor in ἀλλάσσω, which "originally meant . . . 'exchange,' of hostility, anger or war for friendship, love, or peace,"[136] and was often used of political diplomatic aims. It seems correct to say that here "the NT language is more dependent on the Hellenistic world . . . and less on ancient Judaism."[137] Paul uses "reconciliation from the political-social realm, expiation from the cultic realm, justification from the forensic realm, and redemption from the area of human rights."[138] My caveat is that the cultic ones are at the peak of Paul's metaphorical heap, as can be seen in a passage where a common expulsion theme, the curse, is highlighted.

2.3.4 Galatians 3:13

The first thing to notice about Gal 3:13 is how utterly shocking it must have sounded: "Christ redeemed [ἐξαγοράζω, "ransomed" in NAB] us from the curse of the law by becoming a curse for us." It still sounds shocking, and leaves readers asking questions.

The phrase "for us" (ὑπὲρ ἡμῶν) could have either of its usual meanings, "for our benefit" or "in our place," and still be consonant with Paul's atonement teachings elsewhere. His dying "in our place" could embody a substitutionary idea, or it might mean he died while living *in the human place*: an idea of "inclusive place-taking."[139] If he died "for our benefit," releasing us from the

---

[135] N. T. Wright, "On Becoming the Righteousness of God: 2 Corinthians 5:21," in *Pauline Theology, volume II: 1 & 2 Corinthians*, ed. David M. Hay (Minneapolis: Fortress, 1993), 206.

[136] H. Merkel, "Καταλλάσσω, κτλ.," in *Exegetical Dictionary of the New Testament*, vol. 2, eds. Horst Balz and Gerhard Schneider (Grand Rapids: Eerdmans, 1991), 261.

[137] Merkel, "Καταλλάσσω," 262.

[138] Merkel, "Καταλλάσσω," 262; cf. Dunn, *Theology*, 231, 328–33.

[139] Otfried Hofius, *Paulusstudien*. WUNT 51 (Tübingen: J. C. B. Mohr [Paul Siebeck], 1989), 41. See my section 4.6, "Correcting the Atonement."

law's curse, this looks like release from a judicial penalty, but there is no provision in Hebrew law for substitutionary bearing of a legal "curse" due to another. Where does such a sudden reversal of condition for "us" ever take place? It is logical to ask what type of religious action involves the transfer of a curse, and release for the community?

2.3.4.1 McLean on Curse-Transfer

McLean's focus is that "God transferred this curse from humanity to a substitutionary victim, Christ."[140] The exchange was therefore *substitutionary*. But since the scapegoat was not a penal substitute but an animistic sin-bearer, I prefer not to call it "substitutionary." Gaster also stresses that it was not a substitute for known transgressors; "What it removed ... was miasma, not responsibility."[141] There may have been some potential responsibility, but since the perpetrator is not known, what is left is a miasma in the community. The word "substitutionary" tends to suggest individual penalty, and that is not, in fact, associated with the OT scapegoat. The scapegoat is not condemned or convicted, and the confession over the animal is "a collective, blanket confession of sins and then saddling the collective taint upon some one deputed being. . . . The scapegoat was representative, not substitutional."[142]

McLean correctly eliminates sacrifice from Gal 3:13. Sacrifices do not involve the transfer of curses.[143] That an expulsion ritual can transfer a curse is seen in many examples from the Gentile world. There was a disease, "the manifestation of a *curse* (ἄγος)"[144] infecting Athens, that was removed by an expulsion ritual. Similarly, *Oedipus Rex* has a king praying that the curse may be transferred to him, who is "'bearing the curse' in order to save the city."[145]

The element of *exchange* is clear; the economic term ἐξαγοράζω in Gal 3:13 refers to purchasing the freedom of those who were slaves of sin, death, and the law. "The unprefixed form ἀγοράζειν (derived from ἀγορά) means literally 'to buy' in a commercial sense,"[146] and is used soteriologically in 1 Cor 6:20 ("you were bought with a price"). So we have a cultic metaphor conflated with an economic one; Christ's scapegoat action *buys* people's freedom.

---

[140] McLean, *Cursed Christ*, 124.

[141] Gaster, "Sacrifices," 153.

[142] Gaster, "Sacrifices," 153.

[143] McLean, *Cursed Christ*, 51.

[144] McLean, *Cursed Christ*, 72; from Diogenes Laertius; ἄγος can also be translated "pollution," as McLean does in footnote 24.

[145] *Oed. tyr.* 1290–93; McLean, *Cursed Christ*, 72.

[146] McLean, *Cursed Christ*, 127.

One of McLean's central points is sound (that Paul used scapegoat metaphors), while the other is insupportable (that Paul did not use sacrificial metaphors). McLean's assertion that the expulsion paradigm and "the resurrection paradigm" are "independent,"[147] is overextended, especially when he attempts to assign certain letters of Paul to one paradigm (and one period of Paul's life), and other letters to the other. Such an artificial barrier overlooks the linkage of death and resurrection in such passages as Rom 4:25; 8:34; 1 Cor 15:4; 2 Cor 5:15, and in his common label for Jesus ("him who has been raised from the dead," Rom 7:4). Thus, McLean's thesis is idiosyncratic and often extreme, but his insight into the scapegoat theme in the ancient world and in Paul, is basically sound.

I would add that Paul's emphasis in Gal 3:13 is not on the judicial status of Christ's death but on its ritual status (accursed) and on its result: Christ bears away the curse and opens up salvation for the Gentiles. Elsewhere Paul uses sacrificial, judicial, and redemptive metaphors. No matter that these images cannot be perfectly harmonized; for Paul they capture a truth in that they picture Christ's death as a ritual act with universal saving consequences. Paul has an intuition that Christ's death fulfills a cultic pattern, perhaps all the basic cultic patterns, since he can equate him to the spotless sacrifice, the accursed scapegoat, or the Passover lamb.

Barnabas 7:7, 9 and *m. Yoma* 6:4 both describe the scapegoat as accursed; this is not what Leviticus says, but obviously it has support in the tradition.

The saving death of Christ is depicted in Gal 3:13 as a (metaphoric) curse-bearing and resultant exchange of conditions: the scapegoat takes on the curse of "us," so that "the blessing of Abraham" (which Jesus embodies) "might come to the Gentiles" (3:13–14). Of course, extension of salvation to the Gentiles is the central theme in Galatians. The Messiah brings about the promised blessing for all nations. What was promised to Abraham was not a numerous Israel but a singular σπέρμα, the Christ (3:16). For salvation, Paul gives a Messiah-answer, not an Israel-answer: "Those who believe (οἱ ἐκ πίστεως)," those who "belong to Christ ... are Abraham's offspring" (3:7, 29). And again, salvation is described with redemption and adoption metaphors (4:5).

2.3.4.2 Explanatory Limitations of the Deuteronomic Curse

In its two occurrences in Gal 3:10, "curse" summons up the image of the Deuteronomic curse against covenant breakers. It is the third occurrence, the one in 3:13, that cannot be explained by Deuteronomic categories. A brief examination of the Deuteronomic curse is in order.

---

[147] McLean, *Cursed Christ*, 125.

Morland places Paul's curse-language firmly within the Deuteronomistic rhetoric of curse-and-blessing: "Expressions like the 'curse of the law' are found only in [Deuteronomistic] traditions. Also the metonymic use of curse is a typical Deuteronomistic device."[148] The latter device is especially seen in Jeremiah: "I will make this city a curse" (26:6); "I will make them ... to be a curse" (29:18 [NAB]).[149] Now, with Christ, "the period of covenantal curses ... has come to an end."[150]

Morland draws our attention to the connection of curse formulas with the juridical realm. "It is probable that the ארור formula originated in *jurisdiction*. ... Most curses with a form identical or similar to Gal 3:10 ... have some connection with juridical procedure."[151]

Morland accepts a sacrificial or scapegoat background to Gal 3:13 (not distinguishing between the two!), seeing "a transference of identity" taking place with the laying of hands on the two goats.[152] Thus, Gal 3:13 implies expiation. He tells us, "expiation also in Hellenistic culture is regarded as the most appropriate means of eliminating the power of curses,"[153] but does not mention any specific ritual. The *pharmakos* ritual had become rare by Paul's time, but its rhetorical effectiveness depended on its being *recognized* when mentioned, not on its being continually practiced.

Paul conflates the Deuteronomic curse and the Levitical curse-expulsion. His first two mentions of curse in Galatians 3 would undoubtedly summon up the image of the Deuteronomic curse, but the third instance, where the community benefits from someone *becoming* a curse (3:13b), requires something outside the Deuteronomic scope, something beyond Morland's explanations. This summons up the Levitical and Greek expulsion rites—the frightening and ancient image of a being carrying away a community curse.

Attempts to account for the rhetorical background to Gal 3:13 using only the Deuteronomic curse, yield three inadequate explanations:

1) Christ has become the paradigmatic covenant-breaker, and is cursed by being put out of the community, even killed. But why is this salvific? Since when was covenant-breaking salvific? No logical answer has been given within a Deuteronomic setting.

---

[148] Kjell Arne Morland, *The Rhetoric of Curse in Galatians: Paul Confronts Another Gospel*. Emory Studies in Early Christianity 5 (Atlanta: Scholars Press, 1995), 71.
[149] Morland, *Rhetoric of Curse*, 256.
[150] Morland, *Rhetoric of Curse*, 225.
[151] Morland, *Rhetoric of Curse*, 63.
[152] Morland, *Rhetoric of Curse*, 222.
[153] Morland, *Rhetoric of Curse*, 223.

2) Christ receives the curse that every Jew receives because of a supposed impossibility of following the law perfectly. But this punishment would not be something that any Gentile would be expected to bear. This explanation has nothing to do with Gentiles. Unless:

3) The Deuteronomic curse is transmogrified into another kind of curse, one directed *against Gentiles*: "The curse which was removed by Christ's death therefore was the curse which had previously prevented that blessing from reaching the Gentiles."[154] With this interpretation, "under the curse" means "in the place of the Gentile!"[155]

However, the "blessings and curses" that "today I have set before you" (Deut 30:19), are set before a *particular* people from whom the Lord "obtains" an "agreement" (26:18). The Gentiles are not partners to this covenant, and are not expected to fulfill it. Nor does Paul, fond as he is of shocking reversals, ever say "God made him a Gentile in order to save the Gentiles." Anyone attempting to explain Gal 3:13 while utilizing only the Deuteronomic curse as background, will be forced to introduce innovations, since there is no hint of the Deuteronomic curse having a salvific effect, nor does it have anything to do with Gentiles.

Salvation in the Deuteronomic setting comes if the whole community repents (Deut 30:1–3). A Deuteronomic curse is not removed by someone "becoming a curse" for the community; this metaphor requires either a Levitical or a Greek (*pharmakos*) background. That is the image in Gal 3:13b, even though Paul starts out with the Deuteronomic curse in 3:10.

In Galatians 3, the image of expulsion ritual is piggy-backed onto the Deuteronomic curse. Paul is constantly trying to force his readers to do a double-take, but many have resisted it, even to the present day.

Observations about the *effects* of the curse-transfer often disguise an inadequate explanation of the underlying logic, leaving one still asking *how* Christ's death takes away the curse. It is metaphysically inadequate to skirt over the supernatural[156] transfer envisioned by Paul. For instance, Similarly Theissen says, "The redeemer takes the iniquity and doom of human beings upon himself so that they may achieve salvation."[157] This is vivid ... but

---

[154] James D. G. Dunn, *Jesus, Paul, and the Law: Studies in Mark and Galatians* (Louisville, Ky.: Westminster, 1990), 229.

[155] Dunn, *Jesus, Paul, and the Law*, 230.

[156] One is tempted to use "metaphoric" here so as to avoid being provocative, but that word seems to suggest a literary exercise, whereas Paul envisions a literal removal of whatever spiritual peril "curse" may suggest to his (mostly Gentile) readers.

[157] Gerd Theissen, *Social Reality and the Early Christians: Theology, Ethics, and the World of the New Testament* (Minneapolis: Fortress, 1992), 169.

incomplete. What religious practice involves "taking on" the people's doom?—the scapegoat exchange: the spotless goat takes on society's sin/curse, and sinful society gets the goat's spotlessness.

The supernatural transference of sin and its bearing-away, is a naturalistic or animistic transfer. Such an amoral notion does not sit well with many scholars, and they try to make it fit within a moral (Deuteronomic) framework. But it belongs in the cultic theology.

Greek literary tradition is heavy with curses and expulsions, including the very un-Jewish notion of an individual *becoming* a curse. Euripides has Medea say: "I have just now become a curse to your house."[158] The Oedipus of Sophocles dreads "a curse remaining on my house just as I am cursed."[159] This continues in Greek Christian literature, and in popular pieces such as the *Protevangelium of James* ("I have become a curse [κατάρα][160] in the opinion of the Israelites").[161]

In order that his remarks may resonate equally with Gentile and Jewish readers, Paul does not make his metaphor culturally specific—there is no mention of "the other goat," as the Bible calls the scapegoat—but a bit later he uses a verb from Leviticus 16, perhaps in order to evoke the correct image for Jewish readers. D. Schwartz points to the presence of the verb ἐξαποστέλλω in Gal 4:4, 6—the same verb used in Lev 16:10, 21, etc. for "sending out" the scapegoat and in the related rituals in Leviticus 14.[162] Paul uses the verb twice in Galatians (the only times he *ever* uses this verb) to refer to the "sending" of God's Son to be born of woman, and the "sending" of the Spirit into our hearts. Of course, the latter is not a scapegoat image, but the former may have that implication: the rejection suffered by Christ and by his imitators, the "sent-ones" (*apostles*), is a central Pauline image.

Paul may be envisioning several levels of salvific "sending": God's sending (ἐξαποστέλλω) of his Son to earth, where he must become a scapegoat; Christ's sending of his "sent ones" out to preach, with the result that they will become society's offscourings, sent away by unbelievers; and God's sending of the Spirit, which helps believers to become sons of God. Paul

---

[158] My translation of Eur., *Med.* 608: σοῖς ἀραία γ' οὖσα τυγχάνω δόμοις; compare the similar image in Aeschylus, *Ag.* 236, and in Sophocles, *Oed. tyr.* 246–54; cf. Parker, *Miasma*, 197–98.

[159] *Oed. tyr.* 1291: μενῶν δόμοις ἀραιὸς ὡς ἠράσατο. Notice the intriguing similarity of meaning and spelling of the Greek root ἀρα and the Hebrew root ארור.

[160] In TLG, this is located at 1637.001, 6.4.

[161] McLean, *Cursed Christ*, 124 n.57.

[162] In Lev 14:7 and 53; Daniel R. Schwartz, "Two Pauline Allusions to the Redemptive Mechanism of the Crucifixion," *JBL* 102 (1983): 261.

considers this pattern of rejection to be the inevitable result of proclaiming the gospel. Saving activity in human society takes on a scapegoat pattern, and Gal 4:4 may be alluding to this, as 1:4 alludes to the "evil age."

2.3.4.3 The Incorporative Messiah's Death

N. T. Wright tries to fit the Galatian curse firmly within a Messianic mold, with the Messiah being the one who fulfills Israel's destiny or destinies. "Because the Messiah represents Israel, he is able to take on himself Israel's curse and exhaust it," the curse being exile.[163] Even if Wright is right about the Messiah representing Israel, this does not explain why a curse gets "exhausted" by the Messiah "taking it on." Where, in Jewish history, does a figure take on a curse and exhaust it?[164] Only the scapegoat and possibly the scapegoat-like figure of Isaiah 53.

Wright does not rule out the cultic background, but makes it subsidiary to his notion that "Χριστός is incorporative": the Messiah "sums up his people in himself,"[165] and Israel stands for humanity in the same way. But as Brondos points out, this notion of "Israel as 'God's true humanity'" is "an abstract phrase never found"[166] in the Jewish literature. It seems dubious to claim that "Χριστός refers ... not merely to the Messiah as an individual but to the people of the Messiah.'"[167]

Despite Wright's masterful work, his explanations for how salvation is brought about are insufficient because he does not see that *cultic* themes are as fundamental as *Messianic* ones. He treats Paul's scapegoat and sacrificial models as incidental,[168] when actually they show the logic of how salvation was bought.

Wright's attempt to explain the logic of atonement in purely Messianic terms depends on each link in his chain of representation/incorporation holding fast: the Messiah representing Israel, and Israel "herself representative of the whole of Adamic humanity"; the Law censuring Israel for its sins, and therefore censuring all mankind; the Messiah being "able to draw on to himself Israel's

---

[163] N. T. Wright, *The Climax of the Covenant: Christ and the Law in Pauline Theology* (Edinburgh: T&T Clark, 1991), 150–51.

[164] David Brondos has exactly the same response: Wright does not explain how Jesus' becoming a curse "leads to 'our' being redeemed from the curse" ("The Cross and the Curse: Galatians 3:13 and Paul's Doctrine of Redemption," *JSNT* 81 [2001]: 23).

[165] Wright, *Climax*, 48.

[166] Brondos, "Cross," 11.

[167] Wright, *Climax*, 49.

[168] Wright, *Climax*, 153.

paradoxical destiny," and so to condemn "sin as a whole."[169] Even if this did not have some tenuous links, the logic would still be that of *sin-bearing*, which is not (fundamentally) Messianic, but cultic.

2.3.4.4 Elliott: Curses in Galatia; Paul's Dual Audience

Susan Elliott has shown that curses had a profound judicial, ethical, and theological import in Anatolian societies of Paul's time and in the earlier Phrygian civilization. (I do not find her mentioning the additional fact that curse transmission rituals were common in the earlier Hittite culture.) Elliott says the curse of Gal 3:13 "remains a strange concept within a Jewish framework"; it is "more intelligible when seen against the gentile religious background in Anatolia."[170]

Galatians believed in the profound *effectiveness* of curses, which carried metaphysical and juridical force, as demonstrated by the actions of both plaintiffs and defendants preserved in court documents. Lawsuits could be couched as curses,[171] and the defendant could appeal for settlement by making a confessional inscription. "Redemption" from the curse took place when the guilty party inscribed a confession stele, admitting his guilt and/or describing the punishment he underwent as a consequence of the curse lodged against him; "'Defendants' left a record of 'confession inscriptions' by which they apparently hoped to end the punishing action of the deities which had been let loose upon them."[172] So curses are thought to have supernatural and legal power.

Similarly, curses are given either rhetorical or judicial function in certain HB texts: curses are wiped into water that is then drunk in a judicial ordeal in Num 5:20–27, the curse of a servant can convict a slanderer (Prov 30:10), self-cursing was a standard procedure in oath-giving (Judg 9:20).[173]

While curses occur in many settings in the HB, they were probably interpreted differently by different segments of society,[174] but curses had a central importance in Anatolian societies. Curses inscribed on scepters were

---

[169] Wright, *Climax*, 207–8.

[170] Susan Margaret Elliott, "The Rhetorical Strategy of Paul's Letter to the Galatians in Its Anatolian Cultic Context: Circumcision and the Castration of the *Galli* of the Mother of the Gods." Ph.D. dissertation, Loyola University Chicago (1997), 143.

[171] Elliott, "Rhetorical Strategy," 160, 639.

[172] Elliott, "Rhetorical Strategy," 160; cf. 169, 191, 644; Franz Cumont, *The Oriental Religions in Roman Paganism* (New York: Dover, 1956), 40.

[173] Jeff Anderson, "The Social Function of Curses in the Hebrew Bible," *ZAW* 110 (1998): 232–34.

[174] Anderson, "Social Function," 236.

powerful protections for temple grounds and statues.[175] It may be this positive function of a curse that Paul intends, Elliott argues. The clearly positive intention of "becoming a curse *for* us" would likely evoke, for a Galatian audience, "something closer to 'standing as a curse on our side'. . . . a 'counter-curse' powerful enough to cancel the curse of the Law."[176]

Paul knows both Galatian and Jewish beliefs, and is used to speaking to mixed audiences. He had already used a term evocative of Gentile supernatural beliefs earlier in the chapter: "who has bewitched you" (βασκαίνω, 3:1),[177] alluding to the realm of witchcraft and the evil eye in order to embarrass the Galatians, who are trying to turn away from the paganism of their culture. This is nothing compared to his biting comparison of circumcision and castration, alluding to the horrifying rite of self-castration practiced by the γάλλοι priests[178] in the dominant belief system in the region, the Mother of God religion.[179] Thus, there is wit as well as impatience behind the brutal remark in Gal 5:21.

We cannot talk constructively about Paul unless we recognize his multivalency, his appropriation of ideas and styles from different realms, his ability to utilize halakhic reasoning one moment, and the hortatory method of a Hellenistic philosopher the next. If we notice his usage of OT scripture and messianic thinking, we need also to notice his appropriation of popular Hellenistic methods and styles of teaching.[180] His polemic sometimes echoes concepts found in Cynic epistles, for instance,

All are slaves either by law or through wickedness.[181]

Evil alone makes one a slave; virtue alone frees . . . . You yourselves are slaves on account of your desire.[182]

---

[175] Elliott, "Rhetorical Strategy," 168, 186–90.

[176] Elliott, "Rhetorical Strategy," 645.

[177] Jerome H. Neyrey, *Paul, in Other Words: A Cultural Reading of His Letters* (Louisville, Ky.: Westminster John Knox, 1990), 183ff.

[178] Susan Margaret Elliott, "Choose Your Mother, Choose Your Master: Galatians 4:21–5:21 in the Shadow of the Anatolian Mother of the Gods," *JBL* 118 (1999): 678–79.

[179] Elliott, "Rhetorical Strategy," 267–71; she was believed to administer justice, 286.

[180] Abraham J. Malherbe, *Paul and the Popular Philosophers* (Minneapolis: Fortress, 1989), 68, 72–77. Paul's style is Cynic in passages like 1 Thess 2:1–8 (*Paul and the Popular*, 5, 44, 47–48, 68, 72).

[181] Crates, *Epistle 29*, lines 10–11 (Hock). *The Cynic Epistles: A Study Edition*, ed. A. Malherbe, SBLSBS 12 (Missoula, Mont.: Scholars Press, 1979), 79.

[182] Heraclitus, *Epistle 9*, lines 32–35 (Worley). *Cynic Epistles*, 213.

Tomson says Paul's idea of being "all things to all.... involves a characteristic use of the Cynico-Stoic concept of freedom."[183] Engberg-Pedersen finds Paul's concept of conversion followed by identity-change and the joining of a new community, to resemble the Stoic concept of conversion to the life of philosophy.[184] Numerous scholars emphasize Jewish backgrounds, but these Gentile backgrounds are also important. Paul's familiarity with different belief systems is broad, and his rhetoric is many-sided so that he may reach different groups within his audience.

2.3.4.5 Summary

My exegetical finding is clear enough: this is a passage that begins with a reminder of the Deuteronomic curse against those who do not fulfill the law, but draws in an entirely different kind of curse, one that is ended by someone *becoming* the curse and so bearing it away (something that cannot be called Deuteronomic). It likely refers either to an expulsion victim who purges a community by bearing away its curse or sin, or to the protective legal curses common in Galatian society. Paul makes timely allusions that ring powerfully for a particular audience.

The curse in Deuteronomy is not directed against Gentiles and is not ended by a curse-bearer but by national repentance. Removal of a strictly Deuteronomic curse would not mean salvation for Gentiles (the subject of Gal 3:14). Curse-bearing summons up imagery that is recognizable in Leviticus, but also in Gentile religion.

Salvation of the Gentiles is indeed a major theme in Galatians, so it should not be surprising that Paul uses images that his Gentile readers would recognize. The curse-transmission ritual was particularly well-known in central Anatolia from ancient times, but was also recognizable to Jews as the curse-bearing scapegoat. It is likely that Paul meant to allude both to the protective curse in Galatian religion and law, and to the biblical scapegoat. Of course, Paul is not spelling out a detailed theology based on Galatian law, any more than his redemption metaphor means a point-by-point correlation with the law for manumission of slaves. Rather, he uses striking metaphors as they occur to him. Paul would not have become the most influential of all Christian preachers if he were unable to spin out a vivid metaphor, one that would resonate with a

---

[183] Peter J. Tomson, *Paul and the Jewish Law: Halakha in the Letters of the Apostle to the Gentiles* (Minneapolis, Fortress Press, 1990), 275. Tomson finds in Rom 14:20 and 1 Corinthians, "an unmistakable affinity to the Cynic view that food as such is religiously indifferent" (248; cf. 268).

[184] Troels Engberg-Pedersen, *Paul and the Stoics* (Louisville, Ky.: Westminster John Knox, 2000), 102–3, 109, 125.

given audience. Insufficient attention has been paid to the religious beliefs of the Galatian culture.

My investigations have shown me that good exegesis of Gal 3:13 requires an openness to cultural anthropology. Even to make my exegetical point requires me to speak of curses in Greek, Hittite, and Galatian tradition.

Educated Galatians may have seen Paul as a philosopher. Comparison of Paul's writings with ancient epistolary literature shows a remarkable similarity in style and, sometimes, in content to the Cynic Epistles. Paul puts himself in the role of authoritative philosopher, qualified to instruct and nurture his students[185] in the assemblies he had founded.

I have touched upon some suggestive Gentile patterns in Paul's expression. Paul's reconciliation words in 2 Cor 5:21 come from the realm of Hellenistic diplomacy. In Galatians 3 he alludes to Gentile religion. More Hellenistic themes will emerge in the discussion of Romans, an epistle that cannot be profitably interpreted unless Paul's dual audience (Gentile and Jewish) is kept in mind.

2.3.5 The Body of Sin

Paul's most complicated scapegoat image occurs in Rom 8:3. It will be helpful to approach it by first noticing some likely scapegoat themes in the two preceding chapters.

The scapegoat is a particularly *physical* kind of rite, in that sin or disease is loaded onto the body of a living creature, which is then abused and driven out. This image is particularly suggestive for someone who feels "that nothing good dwells within me, that is, in my flesh.... The flesh is hostile to God" (Rom 7:18; 8:7). Flesh and Spirit "are opposed to each other" (Gal 5:17). Paul's revulsion with the sinfulness of his flesh goes hand in hand with his notion of sin being expelled through Christ's body. Salvation means the expulsion of sin, which brings the body back to life. Even though "the body is dead because of sin, the Spirit is life [... and] will give life to your mortal bodies" (Rom 8:10–11).

Paul's soteriology includes the believer's deliverance from the sin in his own body. Christ died "so that the body of sin might be destroyed" (6:6). This is a deliverance from one's *own* body of sin, so that "we might no longer be enslaved to sin" (6:6b). Christ the scapegoat bears away the sin in my body. Sin needs to be *driven out* on the congregational level as well, and Paul uses a cultic metaphor to recommend the expulsion of a sinner from the Corinthian congregation (1 Cor 5:1–13).

---

[185] Abraham J. Malherbe, *Paul and the Thessalonians: The Philosophic Tradition of Pastoral Care* (Philadelphia: Fortress, 1987), 23–24, 68–72, 81–87.

When Paul asks, "Who will rescue me from this body of death?" (Rom 7:24)—the answer is, *someone else's body*!—Christ's—"you have died to the law through the body of Christ" (7:4).[186] This sentence and the one at 6:6 are incomprehensible without recognizing the link between Christ's death and the believer's rescue from sensuality, and it operates by the scapegoat mechanism. One actually experiences this mechanism when one believes in Christ the scapegoat, and then finds sin driven out of one's body. "What has died to the Law is the fleshiness."[187]

The only way to escape the enslaving influence of the body of sin is to be "united with him in a death like his" (Rom 6:5). This means the death of sensualism: "our old self was crucified with him so that the body of sin might be destroyed" (6:6). Again and again this message reappears: "if by the Spirit you put to death the deeds of the body, you will live" (8:13); "do not gratify the desires of the flesh. . . . those who belong to Christ Jesus have crucified the flesh with its passions" (Gal 5:16, 24). Christ enables the believer to die to his own "body of sin."

When we are really "dead to that which held us captive" (Rom 7:6), when we are actually "conformed to his death" (Phil 3:10 NAB), we have experienced the great participatory mystery. But it is only possible because God first condemned sin in *Christ's* flesh (Rom 7:4; 8:3).

In cultic symbolism, death stands for transition, and only metaphors of death can convey the intense metamorphosis that Paul envisions. Baptism is a symbolic death, standing for a life-changing event: the transition from fleshly loyalties to spiritual ones. The body does not enjoy any moral neutrality, for "whatever does not proceed from faith is sin" (Rom 14:23). Fornicators, adulterers, and sodomites will not inherit the kingdom of God, and "the body is meant not for fornication but for the Lord" (1 Cor 6:9–13). Sexual sinning (πορνεύω) means sinning against the Holy Spirit that dwells within (1 Cor 6:18–19), and this is followed by the formula, "you were bought with a price; therefore glorify God in your body." Salvation must lead to the holiness of the *body*.

Here is where Paul's soteriology and his ethics intersect. Sacrificial, juridical, and scapegoat metaphors articulate soteriology, while the image of sin-expulsion describes the breaking of sinful sensual inclinations. The expulsion image can describe both Jesus' act and the believer's consequent deliverance from sensualism.

---

[186] I am indebted to fellow Durham student, Bret Burrowes, for our conversations about Rom 6:6; 7:4.

[187] Boyarin, *Radical Jew,* 166.

Christians are to "no longer present your members to sin as instruments of wickedness" (Rom 6:13a). This is possible once they are no longer "under the law" (6:14). The law was an aid to sin not because it encouraged meritorious earning of salvation, but because it "causes sin as an inevitable consequence of its commandment to procreate."[188] The law's command to procreate proved to be its undoing: "Sin has used the commandment to procreate in order to arouse sinful desire."[189] Watson agrees that "the sin of sexual desire was first made possible by the law."[190] Paul equates being under the law with being swept into sin's control: "our sinful passions, aroused by the law, were at work in our members to bear fruit for death" (7:5). The "Jews bear fruit for death, that is, they have children who will feed the death machine, while Christians bear spiritual fruit." [191]

Boyarin convincingly argues that "The body of sin of which Paul speaks is the sexual body," reflecting the "extremely pessimistic notions of sexuality"[192] that had come into Judaism by this period, as seen in the *Testaments of the Twelve Patriarchs* and Philo. Roetzel's research confirms this; the prevailing view was that "repression of passions and desires distinguished the philosopher from the common lot," and "sexual chastity was a prerequisite for the divine encounter."[193] This thinking was associated with the Stoics, but had made major inroads into Judaism. Once again we see Paul drawing upon either Gentile ideas or Jewish adaptations of Gentile thinking.

Paul's radicalism can also be seen in the way he incorporates some standard rhetoric—about circumcision! In numerous Jewish sources, circumcision stood for the repudiation of the life of selfish sensuality: "circumcision portrays the excision of pleasure and all passions."[194] Borgen makes eminent sense when he suggests that Paul transfers this function of circumcision to the experience of being crucified with Christ (*Ibid.*). Rejecting circumcision for Gentiles, Paul retains what circumcision symbolized, offering a way for Jew and Gentile alike to repudiate sinful passions.

---

[188] Boyarin, *Radical Jew*, 176.

[189] Boyarin, *Radical Jew*, 164.

[190] Frances Watson, *Paul, Judaism and the Gentiles: A Sociological Approach* (Cambridge: Cambridge University Press, 1986), 156.

[191] Boyarin, *Radical Jew*, 177.

[192] Boyarin, *Radical Jew*, 169, 160.

[193] Calvin Roetzel, *Paul: The Man and the Myth* (Columbia: University of South Carolina Press, 1998), 138, 139.

[194] Philo, *Migr.* 16.92, quoted in Peder Borgen, *Philo, John and Paul: New Perspectives on Judaism and Early Christianity*. BJS 131 (Atlanta: Scholars Press, 1987), 258.

Besides expulsion of evil, there needs to be acquittal as well, since we stand condemned before a personal God. And so in Rom 8:3, Paul places the scapegoat image within a juridical framework. While the *body* of Christ carries away sin in Rom 6:6 and 7:4, the full story is that God carries out a judicial verdict against the sinfulness of the flesh: "There is no condemnation" *now* because God "condemned sin in the flesh" *then* (8:1, 3). Those who stood under a guilty verdict are now acquitted, because the sentence was carried out on Christ's body. Later Christian theologians, despite their tendency to exaggerate the punitive aspects of Paul's teachings, correctly understood that Paul saw Christ as a punishment-bearer (a conflation of the judicial and scapegoat metaphors).

2.3.6 Romans 8:3

> For God has done what the law, weakened by the flesh, could not do: by sending his own Son in the likeness of sinful flesh, and to deal with sin (καὶ περὶ ἁμαρτίας) (as an offering for sin—NASB), he condemned (κατέκρινεν) sin in the flesh. Rom 8:3

Here Paul has done what grammar teachers, weakened by the rule against mixing metaphors, are unable to do! There is a juridical word (κατακρίνω), the LXX term for the sin-sacrifice (περὶ ἁμαρτίας), and the notion of one flesh-creature carrying the burden of all flesh (scapegoat). We seem to have a conflation of metaphors from the juridical, sacrificial, and scapegoat realms.

The condemning of sin in his flesh is not the image of a spotless sacrifice. This flesh is execrable, as with the scapegoat. Yet we have what certainly looks like the technical term for purification sacrifice. Wright shows that anarthrous περὶ ἁμαρτίας has virtually the same meaning as τὸ περὶ τῆς ἁμαρτίας, or purification offering: "[W]hereas περὶ τῆς ἁμαρτίας usually means 'for sin', and τὸ περὶ τῆς ἁμαρτίας means '*the* sin-offering', περὶ ἁμαρτίας should almost always be translated either 'sin-offering' or 'as a sin-offering.'"[195] The NRSV's "to deal with sin" is too general and overlooks the LXX background.

The argument in Romans 6 to the first half of Romans 8, however, highlights the judicial and curse transmission metaphors more strongly than the sacrificial: there is a repeated mention of law's enslaving tendency (6:14; 7:6), and of "bodies" infected with sin (6:6, 12; 7:4, 24; 8:10, 13). Christ's *body* dies so that we may be rescued from the law; he takes away sin by taking on *sinful flesh* (7:4; 8:3)—these look like scapegoat notions. Christ takes on not just a

---

[195] Wright, *Climax*, 222.

"likeness" of flesh but the actual *form* of flesh.[196] Next, however, where we would expect an image of banishment, we get a judicial one—sin is "condemned" in 8:3.

The law, unintentionally "arous[ing...] sinful passions" (Rom 7:5), was unable to effectively condemn sin, but God condemned it through a cultic action carried out by his Son (8:3). Something outside the judicial realm was able to accomplish the κατάκριμα that the law intended.

Christ bears the punishment that all flesh, by virtue of allowing itself to be a gateway for sin, has incurred. In this sense, Christ is a penal substitute (by combining the scapegoat and judicial images). He becomes the thing that deserves the punishment: flesh. The penal theme is highlighted by the mention of condemnation in vv. 1 and 3, and of law *four* times in vv. 2–4. The dichotomy of flesh and Spirit dominates vv. 5–10, and so is likely present also in the condemnable flesh of v. 3.

The essential Pauline ideas of *exchange* (portrayed with cultic metaphors) and *participation* are linked in Rom 8:3–11. Christ bears the condemnation of sinful flesh, but God raises him up, just as God will raise up believers "through his Spirit that dwells in you" (v. 11). Christ, the ritual victim, is vindicated by God. Christians participate in both parts of the drama: the ritual death and the rescue from death's domain (Rom 6:4–5; 8:10–11). What is highlighted in Romans 8 is that believers are enabled to live by the Spirit rather than by the flesh; in fact, *this* is the meaning, for Paul, of sonship with God. Being led by the Spirit, and *not* by the flesh, constitutes one a child of God (8:12–14).

Paul clearly differentiates "the Spirit itself" (αὐτὸ τὸ πνεῦμα) from "our [individual] spirits" (πνεύματι ἡμῶν) in v. 16, though both testify that we are the children of God. Sonship is conditional upon being led by the Spirit, that is, the Spirit of God (v. 14). One would dearly like to know what "our" spirits are, and why they testify to sonship, but Paul leaves that concept dangling.

Romans 8:3 also shows Paul's differential reaction to flesh, sin, and law. The law was unable to bring about its "just thing" or "requirement" (δικαίωμα) because it had been sickened or weakened (ἠσθένει) by the flesh. Flesh is the instrument whereby sin disables the law. "Flesh . . . has caused the problem with the law."[197] Sin, then, is the real evil, and flesh is its secret weapon. The flesh was like a Trojan horse by means of which sin conquered the city. But Christ, by coming to indwell the flesh, pulls the same trick. When he takes on flesh, he enters disguisedly into sin-conquered territory, and God chose *that* moment to judge sin in the flesh. Thus, Christ does endure vicarious punishment. In fact, Wright's idea of the representative Messiah might be

---

[196] Cf. McLean, *Cursed Christ*, 140–41.
[197] Wright, *Climax*, 201.

present here, except that Christ is even more than a sacrificial Messiah, he is the antitype of sacrifice itself, and of sin-bearing itself. Only ritual has the power to effect such a reversal. Christ is the true place of atonement (Rom 3:25), the effective περὶ ἁμαρτίας, the real τέλος of the Law (Rom 10:4). Christ was there all along; he was the rock that watered the Israelites in the desert (1 Cor 10:4); he was the singular "offspring" promised to Abraham (Gal 3:16).

Christ's bearing of sin's "condemnation" means that he has broken sin's grip, which, for the individual Christian, means a metaphorical death of the flesh (Rom 6:6; 8:10, 13). The flesh is the battleground where sin has its greatest opportunity. There is a severe anti-cosmism in this. Paul, "the model ascetic,"[198] sees Christ as the supreme ascetic who, by his self-sacrificial example, enables the τέκνα θεοῦ to live by the Spirit (to repudiate the flesh).

Paul is not merely arguing in the realm of ethics here. He is making Christ's action into the ultimate cult action. Christ is the true sacrifice, the final scapegoat, the full price of redemption. In his usual manner, Paul moves from cultic imagery to ethical exhortation to participationist demand, each level reinforcing the other, but the cultic is not secondary to the others; it carries an intuitive and symbolic power that mere ethical exhortation does not.

Romans 8:3, like Gal 3:13 and 2 Cor 5:21, has a stated problem, a cultic solution, and a happy result communicated through a purpose clause. There is great variance among the three purpose clauses, but they all have to do with how Christ's death fulfills the highest hopes of righteousness, expressed in three different ways: bringing light to the Gentiles (Galatians), becoming the righteousness of God (2 Corinthians), conquering the flesh "so that the just requirement (δικαίωμα) of the law might be fulfilled in us" (Rom 8:4). Reversal is best communicated, for Paul, through the image of a reversal ritual.

Paul also uses an expulsion image (not exactly a metaphor) even in a non-soteriological passage. He attacks an instance of "a man living with his father's wife" (1 Cor 5:1), an ethical violation, serious enough to fall under Torah prohibition, and leading Paul to combine two Torah images. The man is to be handed "over to Satan for the destruction of the flesh" (5:5); with this is joined a Passover metaphor: "cleanse out the old leaven . . . . For Christ, our paschal lamb, has been sacrificed" (v. 7 RSV). Handing over to a demonic figure is reminiscent of scapegoat.

2.3.7 Participation and Atonement

Participation in Christ's sufferings, death, and resurrection is the main theme of Christian experience for Paul. The death of Jesus is not just

---

[198] Roetzel, *Paul*, 135–51.

"objectively" atoning; the believer must *participate* in it: "Christ's death for us involves us in dying with him,"[199] and only such participation enables our resurrection (Rom 6:5).

Sanders goes so far as to argue that "the *purpose* of Christ's death [for Paul is] that Christians may participate in it, *not* that their sins may be atoned for."[200] But atonement and participation should not be pitted against each other this way. It is probably true that Paul added participatory mysticism to the atonement idea that was already present in Christianity. But the two are integrally linked in Paul's soteriology, and Sanders too easily separates them: "Once we make the distinction between juristic and participationist categories, however, there is no doubt that the latter tell us more about the way Paul 'really' thought."[201] But if we look at the longest epistle, Romans, we find that juristic categories dominate chapters 1 through 10 and continue in 11 through 14, while participationism of *any* kind (in Christ, in Adam, in Israel, or in the body of Christ) is found in 4:14–18; 5:15–21 (although subordinated to a juristic image); 6:3–6, 11; 7:4; 8:2, 10–11, 16, 26–29; 11:18, 23; 12:4–9; 13:14; in other words, mainly in chapters 5, 6, 8, and 12. Juristic passages, having to do with righteousness or justification, would be too numerous to list, occurring in every chapter. Atonement formulas occur at key points throughout the four *Hauptbriefe*, notable more for their summarizing finality than for their number.

Sanders combines the participationist passages with those that mention "dying to the law" and argues that it is not so much atonement, as it is "*sharing in Christ's death*" that brings salvation.[202] I accept Sanders's *promotion* of participation, but not his *demotion* of cultic imagery to a secondary position. They both are "primary," but the cultic action is logically prior; there could be no participation in Christ's atoning death if atonement had not first been accomplished in that death. This is certainly entailed in the notion that we are "justified by his blood ... reconciled to God through the death of his Son" (Rom 5:9–10), and *then* are able to "be united with him in a death like his" and raised "with him in a resurrection like his" (6:5). To set "participation" against "atonement" is a false opposition.

Sanders concedes that "reconciliation is consistently in the past," that it "refers to sin as *human transgression* rather than to sin as power,"[203] and so is an exception to his argument. But the same could be said of the atonement,

---

[199] Morna D. Hooker, *Not Ashamed of the Gospel: New Testament Interpretations of the Death of Christ* (Grand Rapids: Eerdmans, 1994), 30.

[200] Sanders, *Paul and Palestinian*, 511.

[201] Sanders, *Paul and Palestinian*, 507.

[202] Sanders, *Paul and Palestinian*, 467.

[203] Sanders, *Paul and Palestinian*, 469–70.

redemption, and justification; all these transactions were achieved by Christ prior to believers' reception of them.

"Participation" answers *how* Christians are involved in the salvation event, but not *what* that event is. *What* Christians participate in is a judicial-ritual death (so depicted metaphorically). The salvation event comes first. "Atonement" conveys Paul's thinking on what Jesus accomplished, while "participation" encapsulates his thinking on Christian experience. The *theological* core involves the notion that God responded to Jesus' death as to a sacrifice, and the way of salvation was opened up.

Sacrificial soteriology is spiritualized ritual rectification, a solution that appeals to the consciousness that is consumed with "the horror of transgressions."[204] Further, it suggests a ritualization of experience, a common response to extreme stress. Atonement metaphors can be received on various theological, moral, and psychological levels.

Participation is a constant theme with Paul. The believer must offer up his whole self as a living sacrifice (Rom 12:1; 6:13), which represents Level Three and Four spiritualization. It is not so thoroughly spiritualized, however, as to lose the resonances either of ritual or of judgment. There are still spiritual accounts and balances, and God "will repay according to each one's deeds" (Rom 2:6). The future reality of Judgment Day exerts pressure on the present, giving a forensic cast to daily living: "the work of each builder ... will be revealed with fire" (1 Cor 3:13). The ancient reality of cult also affects the present, suggesting how impurity is to be cleansed and forgiveness to be obtained, even to a spiritualizing mind. Paul's sharp rhetoric of conflict with the flesh resembles the intense internalized conflict of Hindu sacrificial asceticism.

The sacrificial experience is all the more intense for being abstracted, internalized. The experience of facing down persecution, affirming a triumphant faith in the face of death, added new depths to the sacrifice idea. Christianity heightened the value of suffering servanthood as never before, giving rise to selfless heroism, but also to crippling self-condemnation and moralistic bullying.

For the olden ideas were not rejected. That which was taken literally in the Old Testament was rationalized and explained philosophically in the New Testament, and entered into the psychology of Christians. Christianity retains the sacrificial element in greater degree than Judaism or almost any other religion because it has idealized, psychologized, and internalized the sacrificial

---

[204] Paul W. Pruyser, "Anxiety, Guilt, and Shame in the Atonement," *Theology Today* 21 (1964): 19, 24.

idea in a complex and compelling fashion. This demonstrates the mixed blessing that is spiritualization.

2.4 Post-Pauline Usages

Christ as expulsion victim continues in the late NT period, first in the *Epistle of Barnabas*, a letter that was included after Revelation in the Codex Sinaiticus. The author says Christ offered himself as a sacrifice (προσφέρειν θυσίαν), thus fulfilling "the type ... of Isaac, who was sacrificed on the altar" (7:3), but his favorite typology is the scapegoat. As human evil was sent out to dwell with the demonic evil of Azazel in the scapegoat ritual, so also was human sin dumped onto Jesus. Here he quotes from an unknown document (possibly a Targum) whose implied author is God:

> "The other [goat]," He says, "shall be accursed"—note how Jesus is prefigured by it!—"and spit upon it, all of you, stab it, and put scarlet wool about its head; and so let it be driven into the desert." .... Observe, then, the type of Jesus, who was destined to suffer. *Barn.* 7:7–10

Barnabas states overtly what is implied in some Pauline sayings, and he uses a word in v. 7 (ἐπικατάρατος) found in Gal 3:13, although Paul uses that word when quoting Deuteronomy on the curse of the hanged person (3:13c), and uses κατάρα when referring to the curse of the law and Christ becoming a curse for us (3:13a and b).

Justin Martyr[205] makes the same connection when he spells out to his Jewish interlocutor how his forefathers "sent Him off as a scapegoat" (*Dial. Trypho* 40.4).[206] In *Dial. Trypho* 111.2 Christ was cursed (κατηράθη) by the law.[207] So, these equations are explicitly made:

Galatians: Christ=curse
Barnabas: goat=accursed—and—goat=Christ
Justin: Christ=scapegoat—and—Christ=accursed

---

[205] A work that came out after I had completed my dissertation covers much of the same ground and is quite thorough. On the usages in Barnabas and Justin: Stökl, *Impact of Yom Kippur*, 147–56.

[206] Bradley Hudson McLean, "A Christian Sculpture in Old Corinth," *Orientalia Christiana Periodica* 56 (1990): 203.

[207] Nancy Pardee, "The Curse that Saves (*Didache* 16.5)," in *The Didache in Context: Essays on Its Text, History, and Transmission*, ed. Clayton N. Jefford. NovTSup 77 (Leiden: Brill, 1995), 175 n.57.

These authors all use words formed from the same Greek root (καταρ). And an early Latin Father also saw the scapegoat as a type of Christ (Tertullian, *Adv. Marc.* 7:7).

Finally we have the intriguing "Curse" of *Did.* 16:5. This final chapter of the *Didache* has many similarities to, and interesting departures from, Matthew 24. *Didache* 16:5 says that, at the fiery trial, those who persevere will be saved "by the Curse himself [or itself]" (ὑπ' αὐτοῦ τοῦ καταθέματος). It seems the reader was expected to know who (or what) the curse was.

We notice that the author does not use a καταρ-word, but κατάθεμα. After a grueling perusal of the history of κατάθεμα, its sometimes-synonym, ἀνάθεμα, and their Hebrew ancestor, חרם, Pardee notes that they are often associated with the idea of a fiery trial. She allows two possible meanings for *Did.* 16:5: "Jesus as an 'accursed person,'" or "κατάθεμα is a reference to the fiery testing."[208] She favors the latter, agreeing with Draper, who says that the curse is the fiery trial.[209] In that case, the intensive pronoun αὐτοῦ would mean "itself."

Milavec is on the same wavelength, and argues that there is no evidence the *Didache* is even aware of the Pauline tradition.[210] Still, he admits that *Did.* 16:5 does "point toward some soteriological perspective that is based upon Jesus' death."[211] Indeed, the very next verse (16:6) recalls Isa 18:3 and Matt 24:30[212] when it refers to a sign in heaven, to "the trumpet's voice," and to "the rising of the dead." We do not know if κατάθεμα meant only a fiery trial or if the *Didache*'s readers were familiar with a metaphor of Christ as cursed, but Pardee is right to keep the latter possibility open.

2.5 Conclusion

In at least two passages (2 Cor 5:21 and Gal 3:13) and probably in three more (Rom 6:6; 7:4; 8:3), Paul pictures the salvific death of Christ with the scapegoat image: Christ as sin-bearer or curse-carrier; the "body of Christ" as victim that brings deliverance to others. In 1 Corinthians, he uses the scapegoat metaphor to describe the role of an apostle (4:13). That he uses this metaphor to describe different things indicates the liveliness of his allusive imagination and

---

[208] Pardee, "Curse that Saves," 175, 173.

[209] Jonathan Alfred Draper, "The Jesus Tradition in the *Didache*," in *The Didache in Modern Research*, ed. Jonathan A. Draper. AGAJU 37 (Leiden: Brill, 1996), 88.

[210] Aaron Milavec, "The Saving Efficacy of the Burning Process in Didache 16.5," in *The Didache in Context*, ed. Clayton N. Jefford (Leiden: Brill, 1995), 142–43.

[211] Milavec, "Saving," 144.

[212] Thomas F. Glasson, "Ensign of the Son of Man (Matt 24:30)," *JTS* n.s. 15 (1964): 300.

the fact that the same metaphor can have different meanings. That he can six times describe either the saving death of Christ or the mission of an apostle (which replicates Christ's ministry) with this image, shows that it lent itself to the soteriological transaction that took place on the cross. The scapegoat image is also useful for depicting the expulsion of sinful sensualism (Rom 6:6; 8:3–4; 1 Cor 5:5), the last instance blending a Passover and a scapegoat image (handing over to Satan).

Paul exploits the multivalency of cursing in a letter written to a culture where curses had protective power; for Galatian readers, Christ as curse in Gal 3:13 possibly summons up the image of a legally- and supernaturally-protective curse.

The image of Christ as antitype of the scapegoat persists in early Christianity. The *Epistle of Barnabas* and Tertullian identify Christ with the accursed scapegoat, Justin Martyr says Christ was the Accursed One, and the *Didache* refers to being "saved by the Curse." Paul's scapegoat metaphors have been influential. Even to this day, when some people say Christ gave himself "as a sacrifice," they often really mean "as a scapegoat": a being upon whom the sins of others may be unloaded, and who then carries them away. The concept of sacrifice has, for Christians, been heavily infected with expulsion theology, aided by Paul's conflation of scapegoat and sacrifice in Rom 8:3. Examination of Romans 3 will show that Paul blends a sacrificial, a judicial, and a redemptive image, and this explains why these notions are so co-mingled in later Christian thought.

3.
The Sacrificial Metaphor in Romans 3:25

In this chapter, I present my findings on the sacrificial metaphor that climaxes the first three chapters of Romans. I seek to clarify its liturgical connections and conceptual implications, and relate it to the economic and judicial metaphors in the same passage. To offer a satisfactory reading of this dense and important passage, it is necessary to do significant background research on several of the terms, ἱλαστήριον in particular.

My efforts amount to a refutation of McLean's and Stowers's assertions that there is no sacrificial imagery in Rom 3:25 or anywhere else in Paul's teachings. McLean is correct about the presence of a scapegoat metaphor in other Pauline passages, while Stowers makes many useful observations about Paul's rhetorical strategy. But both scholars mistakenly try to compel Paul's metaphors to fit one pattern, to deny Paul's imagery its full range of inventive flair, with all its shocking (even bloody) vividness and its blunt condemnation of common behaviors, Gentile and Jewish. Paul appears to have deliberately conflated metaphors from different realms of human experience—judicial with sacrificial, economic with salvation-historical, martyrological with scapegoat—and the significance of such conflation will be discussed. It is interesting to note that sacrificial metaphor always occurs near to, or conflated with, other types of metaphor.

I will seek to establish whether any of the ancient metaphysical notions of sacrifice—gift/payment, substitute, or spirit-mediumship—are carried forward into Paul's thinking, either overtly or implicitly.

In Rom 3:21–26 we find several key terms that Paul elsewhere uses to explain the salvation transaction, and one particular term that occurs nowhere else in Paul. The hinge of this passage is Rom 3:25, where Paul says God put Jesus forward as ἱλαστήριον, the term used in the Pentateuch for the lid of the ark of the covenant, and in Ezekiel and Amos for installations in some other temples.

> They are now justified by his grace as a gift, through the redemption (ἀπολύτρωσις) that is in Christ Jesus, whom God put forward as a sacrifice of atonement [*marginal reading:* place of atonement] (ἱλαστήριον) by his blood, effective through faith. He did this to show his righteousness, because in his divine forbearance he had passed over the sins previously committed.
> Rom 3:24–25

In this and the next chapter I will analyze ἱλαστήριον and ἀπολύτρωσις, a cultic and an economic term, and will situate justification (various δικαι- words) in relationship to the other two concepts, but will give in-depth lexical attention only to the first two. This examination will show that Paul conceived of a sequence of salvation: the justification of believers follows after the ἀπολύτρωσις, that itself results from the transaction taking place at the metaphorical ἱλαστήριον. But first it is necessary to investigate the background of ἱλαστήριον.

3.1 Meanings of ἱλαστήριον in the Literature

The study of ἱλαστήριον in Romans necessitates an examination of the occurrences of this word in the LXX and in pagan Greek literature. Dan Bailey has written a masterful dissertation on ἱλαστήριον in Romans and in the pagan literature.[1] He shows that traditional translations of 3:25b, such as NRSV's "sacrifice of atonement by his blood, effective through faith," are lexically insupportable, going against the usages of ἱλαστήριον in the literature.

Previous studies of this passage have focused either on the verbal cognates of ἱλαστήριον, namely ἱλάσκομαι and ἐξιλάσκομαι, or on ἱλαστήριον in the LXX, along with four instances of ἱλαστήριον in pagan Greek sources. Bailey found another four pagan sources not considered in previous studies, and argues that the pagan ἱλαστήριον and the LXX ἱλαστήριον have different origination and different meaning.

Bailey correctly points out that "the mercy seat is the object referred to in every one of the 21 occurrences of the term ἱλαστήριον throughout the LXX Pentateuch."[2] But the occurrences of ἱλαστήριον in Ezekiel and Amos, which do *not* refer to the mercy seat, go unmentioned at this point and are minimized by Bailey later on in his thesis.

---

[1] Daniel P. Bailey, "Jesus as the Mercy Seat: The Semantics and Theology of Paul's Use of *Hilasterion* in Romans 3:25" (Ph.D. Cambridge University, 1999). Whenever I cite the dissertation, I will note chapter, section, and manuscript page in this as-yet-unpublished work. When I cite the summary published in *Tyndale Bulletin* (which has the same title as the dissertation), there will be no such divisions, and I will note "*TynB*."

[2] Bailey, "Jesus," chap. 1 §1, page 1.

3.1.1 The Mercy Seat

Before discussing Bailey's thesis, I must say a few words about the mercy seat. In Exodus, Leviticus, and Numbers, the ἱλαστήριον (Hebrew: כַּפֹּרֶת) is the top-piece of the ark of the covenant[3] located in the Holy of Holies of the Mosaic Tabernacle. It was made of gold and carved into a pair of cherubim with overspreading wings (Exod 25:18–22). The כַּפֹּרֶת/ἱλαστήριον is also alleged for the First Temple ("the cherubim that spread their wings and covered the ark of the covenant" 1 Chron 28:18), though the cherubim are described differently in First Kings, as giant olive-wood statues "overlaid with gold" (1 Kgs 6:23–28). The ἱλαστήριον was only *symbolically* present in the Second Temple since it had been taken away by the Chaldeans. This hardly diminishes its importance, since it had always been a mental image rather than a seen object for the vast majority of Jews. Its centrality in the Pentateuch was sufficient to make it a vivid reality in the imagination.

The first mention of the ἱλαστήριον in the LXX is Exod 25:17, where Moses is told he will make a ἱλαστήριον ἐπίθεμα χρυσίου καθαροῦ, which could be literally translated as "a propitiation-place, a top-piece,[4] of pure gold."

In older English translations, it was usually called either "the mercy seat" or "the propitiatory." "Mercy seat" derives from Tyndale's "seate of mercy," itself derived from Luther's *Gnadenstuhl*.[5] The label "the propitiatory" has the advantage of reflecting the fact that ἱλαστήριον is cognate with ἱλάσκομαι which means "propitiate" or "expiate," but "propitiatory" is no longer widely recognized in English.

Blood was sprinkled on the mercy seat in the most important atonement/purification act of the year, on Yom Kippur. It is also the place from which God would speak with Moses; God speaks to him "from between the two cherubim" (Exod 25:22), "from above the mercy seat" (Num 7:89). To Moses alone does God "appear in the cloud upon the mercy seat" (Lev 16:2). Thus, one verse from each of these three books mentions the כַּפֹּרֶת as a place of revelation. These verses do not explain why God speaks from above the mercy seat; it is simply the *fact* that is highlighted. Exodus goes on to talk about the dimensions of the ark of the covenant, Leviticus about sacrificial offerings, and Numbers about lampstands. The three texts are simply claiming divine authority for the temple cult; they do not tell us anything important about revelation.

No one questions that Paul's use of ἱλαστήριον in Romans 3 is metaphorical, but there is no consensus as to whether the concrete referent is

---

[3] "You shall put the mercy seat on the top of the ark" (Exod 25:21).

[4] "Top-piece" is more accurate for ἐπίθεμα than is "cover," according to Bailey, "Jesus," Appendix B, Note A, page 236.

[5] Bailey, "Jesus," 1 §3.4, 8.

the ἱλαστήριον over the ark. Some scholars wish to see it as a reference to a general "place" or "means of atonement," analogously to θυσιαστήριον, the place where θυσία, sacrifice, is offered. There need not be a rigid either-or choice between a literal and a generalized reading; Manson, for instance, argues for a mercy seat reference, but also says that Paul's point is that Christ is the new place of atonement.[6] Some scholars who choose "place of atonement" do so in order to *deny* a specific reference to the ark's top-piece.

Despite Bailey's objections,[7] we must allow that Manson's option is certainly possible both grammatically and theologically: that the specific referent is the mercy seat, but that the real significance of the metaphor is seen in its etymological meaning ("place of atonement").

Now I will examine Bailey's dissertation in detail, later returning to questions about specific and generalized understandings of ἱλαστήριον.

3.1.2 Two Different Meanings

Fundamental to Bailey's findings is the assertion that "linguistic evidence for ἱλαστήριον up through the second century C.E. falls into two neat categories . . . . a biblical use that designates the golden plate above the ark as a 'place of atonement'. . . . Secondly there is the Hellenistic use of ἱλαστήριον . . . . [for] votive gifts dedicated to the gods."[8]

If Bailey is correct, previous linguistic investigations have erred when they have conflated the biblical and Hellenistic usages. Bailey argues that "every Hellenistic ἱλαστήριον is a type of ἀνάθημα or votive offering."[9] The Hellenistic term does not designate a sacrificial animal, nor the place where sacrifice takes place, but is rather "a propitiatory gift or offering," as in LSJ's definition (II 2). However, Bailey rejects LSJ's citing of Rom 3:25 as an example of this usage (*Ibid.*).

Bailey claims that Philo and Josephus were aware of the two different meanings, although his argument for Philo is completely unconvincing. He says Philo uses "only normal Greek words" in his initial listing of Tabernacle objects in *Life of Moses* 2.94, and then uses "special Septuagintal terms" such as ἱλαστήριον only later. "Later" turns out to be in the following paragraphs, in 2.95, 97.[10] I fail to see how this shows familiarity with the Hellenistic "votive offering" meaning. Rather, in those two instances, and in four more, Philo clearly refers to the mercy seat between the cherubim.[11]

---

[6] T. W. Manson, " 'ΙΛΑCΤΗΡΙΟΝ," *JTS* 46 o.s. (1945): 4.

[7] Bailey, "Jesus," 6 §2.5, 154.

[8] Bailey, "Jesus," 1 §3.2, 5–6.

[9] Bailey, "Jesus," 1 §3.3.1, 7.

[10] Bailey, "Jesus," Appendix B, Note A, 245.

[11] *Cher.* 25; *Fug.* 100–101; *Her.* 166.

Bailey's case with Josephus is more convincing. He says, "Josephus appears aware of the potential for confusion regarding the word ἱλαστήριον."[12] Conscious of his Gentile readers, he uses only the Hellenistic meaning, and refers to the golden top-piece of the ark as an ἐπίθεμα (*Ant.* 3.135, 137). He "appears purposefully to have avoided [the] special biblical sense" of ἱλαστήριον.[13]

There have been several arguments made for the part of speech of ἱλαστήριον. Büchsel confidently asserts that it is a "neuter noun from the adjective ἱλαστήριος."[14] Moulton and Milligan are equally confident that it is being used adjectivally—"of use for propitiation."[15] Bailey argues that the LXX noun did not "evolve through the stage of being an adjective in -τήριος," but arose earlier than, and independently from, the Hellenistic adjective ἱλαστήριος and its derivative neuter noun ἱλαστήριον;[16] the Hellenistic substantive ἱλαστήριον always designates a propitiatory gift or votive offering.[17]

Given that "there are no known uses of ἱλαστήριον denoting a victim,"[18] it is quite astounding that so many scholars and the two leading English translations (NIV and NRSV) state or imply that the term in Rom 3:25 refers specifically to a sacrificial victim, says Bailey.[19]

Bailey traces much of the mischief in the study of ἱλαστήριον to "Deissmann's faulty linguistic theory."[20] BAGD and its German parent, abbreviated BAA, reflect Deissmann's theory that a neuter substantive, meaning "that which expiates," underlies both Hellenistic and biblical usages. Bailey astutely comments that this would be equivalent to saying that θυσιαστήριον means "that which sacrifices."[21] The correct Greek term for the concept BAA is looking for, would be τὸ ἱλασκόμενον. Rather, ἱλαστήριον is a LXX neologism signifying the place where the action of ἱλάσκομαι is done,[22] just as θυσιαστήριον[23] (altar) is the place where one can θύω or

---

[12] Bailey, "Jesus," Appendix B, Note A, 245.
[13] Bailey, "Jesus," 4 §2, 79.
[14] Friedrich Büchsel, "ἱλαστήριον," *TDNT* 3:319. Cf. W. Sanday and A. C. Headlam, *The Epistle to the Romans*. ICC (Edinburgh: T&T Clark, 1900), 87.
[15] Moulton and Milligan, *Vocabulary*, 303.
[16] Bailey, "Jesus," Appendix B, Note A, 238, 240–46.
[17] Bailey, "Jesus," 1 §3.3.1–2, 7–8; chap. 3 throughout.
[18] Bailey, "Jesus," 2 §2.2, 20. Cf. §3.2, 24; §4.2, 29.
[19] Bailey, "Jesus," Appendix B, Note C, 248; chap. 2 §1–2, 16–17.
[20] Bailey, "Jesus," 1 §3.3.2, 7.
[21] Bailey, "Jesus," 1 §3.3.2, 8.
[22] Bailey, "Jesus," Appendix B, Note A, 235.
[23] Occurring 257 times in the LXX, including in Ezek 43:22, 26, 27.

θυσιάζω (offer sacrifice) and a φυγαδευτήριον is a place to which one can φεύγω (flee; thus, a city of refuge).[24] Most words ending in -τήριον designate *places*.[25]

Bauer follows Deissmann down this road, listing several German abstractions that have no support in the Greek literature, such as *das Versöhnende*, "that which propitiates." "Rather, only Bauer's concrete gloss *Sühnegabe* does justice to the Hellenistic meaning."[26] The conventional lexica follow Deissmann, citing Rom 3:25 but giving definitions appropriate to Hellenistic ἱλαστήρια.[27]

Bailey is on solid lexical grounds when he insists that the biblical ἱλαστήριον is not an animal victim but a temple installation, but he tends to overlook the reason that scholars have seen Paul's metaphor as extending to the animal whose blood is sprinkled there: because the animal, like a man, is a living being, and the animal was killed, as Jesus was. This is not to say that the NRSV is correct. Bailey's lexical work is a needed corrective, and those translations of Rom 3:25 that make an *explicit* equation of Christ with an animal victim need to be corrected, but the *implied* equation can hardly be avoided since the ἱλαστήριον is the place where the sacrificial animal's blood is sprinkled. However, a good translation refrains from extending the metaphor, making explicit what is possibly implicit. A more accurate translation would not prevent the English reader from taking the same imaginative step that the Greek reader probably did. Allowing the reader to make a connection, but not forcing the connection, is part of what a good translation does.

Bailey rightly argues that the mention of blood in Rom 3:25 does not make ἱλαστήριον into a word for the victim.[28] Still, the mention of blood and the usage of the technical term that is at the center of the sacrificial system, certainly suggest sacrifice; ἱλαστήριον is a synecdoche[29] for the atonement or purification process, and it is likely that "every pious Jew in Palestine and in the Diaspora knew what . . . . the *hilasterion* (that is, place of atonement) was."[30] Further, Paul's usage in Rom 3:25 is consonant with his other cultic equations: Christ as paschal lamb, curse-bearer, περὶ ἁμαρτίας, all suggesting that Christ's death was a cultic act, accomplishing what cult was thought to accomplish.

---

[24] Bailey, "Jesus," Appendix B, Note A, 237.
[25] Bailey, "Jesus," 3 §4.3.5.3, 64.
[26] Bailey, "Jesus," 3 §1.3, 36.
[27] Bailey, "Jesus," 3 §4.3.5.1, 58–59.
[28] Bailey, "Jesus," 2 §2.2, 21.
[29] Using a part as symbolic of the whole. See "3.3.6 The Place of Synecdoche."
[30] Peter Stuhlmacher, *Reconciliation, Law and Righteousness: Essays in Biblical Theology* (Philadelphia: Fortress, 1986), 61.

Bailey's work on the lexicography of ἱλαστήριον is unparalleled, but when it comes to the metaphoric implications of Rom 3:25, he tries to downplay the larger realm summoned up by Paul's metaphor, the sacrificial rituals of Yom Kippur. Bailey's work is strong lexically, but weak when he downplays the sacrificial resonances of the metaphor.

The mercy seat was the spatial pinnacle of the cult, and Yom Kippur its temporal peak. Sacrificial theology is indeed present in the αἵματι of Rom 3:25; the dative case indicates that it is the instrument by which the verbal action implied by ἱλαστήριον is accomplished. Bailey establishes that ἐν τῷ αὐτοῦ αἵματι goes with the noun ἱλαστήριον, and elsewhere but sidesteps the fact that this alludes to the verbal function, *expiating*, in ἱλαστήριον's cognate verb. The cognate verbs ἱλάσκομαι and ἐξιλάσκομαι can atone, expiate, propitiate, or purify, usually in connection with sacrificing, as will be explored below. The *reason* that a ἱλαστήριον is called that, is this cultic action performed there. Bailey's separation of ἱλαστήριον from the sacrificial *victim* does not remove it from the sacrificial *arena*.

While rightly exposing a certainly sloppiness in scholarly research into ἱλαστήριον, Bailey downplays the sacrificial implications of Paul's metaphorical usage of it. The more that Bailey strengthens his case for a reference to the mercy seat, the more he begs the question of the sacrificial ritual performed at that spot. However, there is no denying that Bailey performs a useful service by asking interpreters to explain what they mean by "sacrifice," instead of assuming that it is obvious, and going on to conflate sacrificial *victim* with sacrificial *act* and even with *place* of sacrifice.

3.1.3 Pagan Usage

Bailey informs us that the usage εἱλαστη[ρίο]υς θυσίας in Fayûm papyri no. 337 is the only "certain *ancient* instance of the adjective ἱλαστήριος,"[31] and can be translated "propitiatory sacrifices."[32] A number of scholars wish to assume a similar meaning in Rom 3:25. Lohse argues that ἱλαστήριον is an adjective in Rom 3:25 and that the word for sacrificial victim, τὸ θῦμα, was part of the pre-Pauline formula but was dropped by Paul.[33] Bailey replies that the expression ἱλαστήριον θῦμα *never* occurs in Greek literature and the word θῦμα never occurs in the NT, while the common term θυσία occurs 25 times as often as θῦμα in the LXX. But θυσία is disqualified as a likely elided term for another reason: if ἱλαστήριον is a third declension adjective, as the advocates

---

[31] Bailey, "Jesus," 2 §4.2, 30.

[32] Bailey, "Jesus," 2 §3.1, 22.

[33] Eduard Lohse, *Märtyrer und Gottesknecht* (Göttingen: Vandenhoeck & Ruprecht, 1963), 152.

of this position assume, its ending would be unable to signal the absence of the *feminine* noun like θυσία.

Aside from the previous example, the pagan ἱλαστήριον is a noun designating a propitiatory offering, like the Trojan horse (three times), four stone statues or monuments on Cos and in Jerusalem, a Rhodian inscription, a tripod dedicated to Apollo, and a drinking bowl dedicated to Athena.[34] Bailey rightly points out that a ἱλαστήριον is a concrete object, not an abstract noun such as "propitiation" is.[35]

Josephus applies the Hellenistic usage when he describes Herod's superstitious building of a monument to avert God's wrath after he had looted David's tomb.[36] *Cos* inscription 347 is a column with an inscription that is an incomplete sentence, "The people of Hales, to the August and Warlike Zeus ... ἱλαστήριον."[37] As is common in inscriptions and sometimes in literature, this Greek period leaves out both the verb and the direct object. Presumably a reader of the inscription would know that "the people [offer this object] to Zeus *as* a ἱλαστήριον."[38] The direct object was elided, but its complement (ἱλαστήριον) was not. In *Cos* 81, ἱλαστήριον is also an object complement, not the direct object. I will examine "object complements" in 3.1.5.

Bailey gives four more Hellenistic examples of ἱλαστήριον that highlight its propitiatory significance: examples from the *Odyssey* and from a scholion on the *Odyssey* where the Trojan horse is called an ἄγαλμα and a θελκτήριον, something delightful and charming for the gods.[39] Dio Chrysostom speaks of the Trojan Horse as "a Propitiation from the Achaeans,"[40] and another text gives ἱλαστήριον as the equivalent of μείλια, "propitiation," derived from μειλίσσω, "to soothe."[41] These are all propitiatory gifts.

Bailey cites "a widespread tendency among biblical scholars to fail to distinguish between material gifts and sacrificial victims, the former glossed by ἀνάθημα, the latter by θῦμα, ἱερόν, or ἱερεῖον."[42] We see this tendency in Lohse's insertion of a word for "victim" into a Hellenistic text. We see it again

---

[34] Bailey, "Jesus," 3 §1.1, 31–33. This includes the Rhodian variant, ἱλατήριον (lacking the sigma), seen in an inscription and in the drinking-bowl text.

[35] Bailey, "Jesus," 3 §4.3.3, 55.

[36] *Ant.* 16.182; Bailey, "Jesus," 3 §5, 66–67.

[37] Bailey, "Jesus," 3 §2.2, 41.

[38] Bailey, "Jesus," 3 §2.2, 42.

[39] *Odyssey* 8.509; Bailey, "Jesus," 3 §4–4.2, 47–50.

[40] *Or.* 11.121–124; *Dio Chrysostom*, LCL, tr. J. Cohoon (London: Heinemann, 1932), 1:539; Bailey, "Jesus," 3 §4.3.1, 53.

[41] A pre-Byzantine scholion on Apollonius of Rhodes; Bailey, "Jesus," 3 §3, 44.

[42] Bailey, "Jesus," 4 §3.3, 89.

in Meyer's lexicon, which calls ἱλαστήριον both a votive offering and a ἱερόν or θῦμα, an animal victim.[43]

Christian scholars have tended to read deutero-Pauline concepts of sacrificial atonement back into the texts of Paul. The notion of Christ's death as a sacrifice received extensive post-Pauline development, and this *Wirkungsgeschichte* came to dominate the interpretation of Paul. Any metaphor that even approached sacrifice tended to be drawn into its orbit. I hold that both scholars and believers have tended to import their understandings of Christological sacrificial atonement into their interpretations both of Paul and of OT cult. Sacrificial theology *is* present in Paul, but the fuller, later expressions of it often get projected onto Paul.

3.1.4 A Jewish Hellenistic Usage

The most important instance of Jewish use of ἱλαστήριον outside the Pentateuch is *4 Macc.*[44] 17:22. In *Fourth Maccabees*, as one Maccabean martyr after another refuses to renounce his faith, the evil Syrian king Antiochus Epiphanes has them tortured to death. The martyrs give Stoic-like speeches as they die; *4 Macc.* 17:22 says that their blood and their deaths act like a propitiatory gift, so that "divine Providence preserved Israel that previously had been afflicted" (RSV). There is an interesting textual variant between codex A and codex S of *4 Macc.* 17:22, which read διὰ ... τοῦ ἱλαστηρίου θανάτου αὐτῶν and διὰ ... τοῦ ἱλαστηρίου τοῦ θανάτου αὐτῶν, respectively. In the case of S, "the dependent genitive τοῦ θανάτου must be left as it is,"[45] and the passage is best translated "through the propitiatory gift of their death," while A can be translated adjectivally, "through their propitiatory death."

Again, Bailey is astute in observing that most scholars have failed to distinguish between the two codices, and between their chosen text and Rom 3:25. Most translations and lexica pay attention to the adjective in codex A without mentioning the neuter noun in codex S.[46] Bailey recommends understanding the genitive in codex S as epexegetic, "their death *as* a propitiatory offering."[47] This is different from the notion in Rom 3:25: "In 4 Maccabees it is the *death* of the martyrs that is the ἱλαστήριον, while in Romans it is *Jesus himself.*"[48]

---

[43] Bailey, "Jesus," 3 §4.3.5.2, 60–61.
[44] Although Bailey does not italicize the title of this book, I do, following SBL standards.
[45] Bailey, "Jesus," 5 §2, 94.
[46] Bailey, "Jesus," 5 §3–4.1, 97–98.
[47] Bailey, "Jesus," 5 §4.2, 99.
[48] Bailey, "Jesus," 5 §4.3.2, 106.

The author of *4 Maccabees* seems to have deliberately avoided sacrificial terms such as θυσία even though they were "used in his *Vorlage* in 2 Maccabees."[49] Much of the vocabulary in *Fourth Maccabees* is "generally Greek rather than specifically Jewish."[50]

These arguments are lexically sound, but misleading, since *Fourth Maccabees* does use cultic and temple-related terms in a spiritualized way (Levels 3 and 4). The author is inclined to explain the martyrs' deaths by applying cultic terminology to them, bearing a remarkable resemblance to Paul's usage. Given the web of meaning constructed out of cultic terms, it actually matters very little whether the origin of this author's ἱλαστήριον is independent of the LXX word of the same spelling. All of this will be discussed in the chapter on martyrdom. For now, I am allowing Bailey to establish his basically sound lexical arguments. I will then proceed to explain why his analysis does not do justice to Paul's highly creative mixture of metaphor.

3.1.5 Anarthrous Occurrence of ἱλαστήριον

In Rom 3:25, ἱλαστήριον is the complement of a direct object (a "predicate accusative"), and as such, does not take the definite article. This point effectively demolishes the errant assertion by some scholars that ἱλαστήριον would need to have the definite article if it referred to the "mercy seat." Bailey cites BDF §157 on the complement of a direct object, where all the examples are anarthrous.[51]

To clarify: a predicate accusative is a predicate (complement) of a direct object. An example in English would be: I appointed him *leader*. "Him" is the direct object, and "leader" is its complement. More examples include: You made Israel *a special people*. He considered my remark *agreement* with his position. I made him *a winner*. Each of the direct objects here have predicate accusatives (in italics), and the latter can occur with or without the article in English. But in Greek, the rule is that predicate accusatives are anarthrous. They do not function the same way as predicate nominatives, and scholars like G. Friedrich and D. Seeley have failed to make the distinction.[52]

In testing this thesis, I consulted the premier Classical Greek grammar's (that is, Smyth's) discussion of the "second accusative as a predicate to the direct object." Seventeen examples in 16 sentences were given, all of them anarthrous, with this remark: "The absence of the article generally distinguishes

---

[49] Bailey, "Jesus," 5 §7.3.2, 129.

[50] Bailey, "Jesus," 5 §7.3.2, 131.

[51] Bailey says an accusative complement "virtually never takes the article" ("Jesus," 6 §3.4, 160; cf. 163), perhaps writing while still searching for an exception. He never finds an exception, nor have I.

[52] Bailey, "Jesus," 6 §3.1–2, 155–57.

the predicate noun from the object."⁵³ I surmise that the word "generally" occurs only because the direct object can sometimes be anarthrous, not because the predicate accusative can have the definite article.

This grammatical fact makes nonsense of one of the main objections to the mercy seat interpretation, as articulated by Campbell, for instance, who repeats Deissmann's objection that ἱλαστήριον takes the article in almost every LXX occurrence, but does not have the article in Rom 3:25.⁵⁴ Even before Bailey's masterful thesis, Hultgren had pointed out that, "as in the case of the NT generally, Paul does not use the definite article before a noun in predicate position."⁵⁵

The object-complement construction is different from another type of double accusative, the "person-thing double accusative," exemplified by John 14:26, ἐκεῖνος ὑμᾶς διδάξει πάντα ("he will teach you all things"). "You" and "things" are both direct objects.⁵⁶ In the object-complement construction, however, the complement is *not* a direct object, but is identified with the direct object. My example is Heb 1:7, ʽΟ ποιῶν τοὺς ἀγγέλους αὐτοῦ πνεύματα καὶ τοὺς λειτουργοὺς αὐτοῦ πυρὸς φλόγα ("He makes his angels spirits,⁵⁷ and his servants flames of fire," TNIV). The angels (direct object) are *made* spirits (object complement), and the ministers (direct object) are *made* a flame (object complement).

3.1.6 ἱλαστήριον *in Ezekiel and Amos*

The term ἱλαστήριον occurs five times in Ezekiel 43, for two different ledges of the altar that the prophet sees in a vision, and once in Amos 9:1, for a cultic installation in the temple at Bethel. When he comes to the question of these ἱλαστήρια, Bailey abandons his usual lexicographic precision. He seems compelled to exalt the Pentateuchal ἱλαστήριον while reducing the prophetic ἱλαστήρια to a vanishing point. He uses a hyperbolic metaphor, saying that the Pentateuchal ἱλαστήριον is to all other ἱλαστήρια as the sun is to all other

---

⁵³ Herbert Weir Smyth, *Greek Grammar*, §1614. Revised, G. Messing (Cambridge, Mass.: Harvard University Press, 1920), 362.

⁵⁴ Douglas A. Campbell, *The Rhetoric of Righteousness in Romans 3.21–26*. JSNT Sup 65 (Sheffield: JSOT Press, 1992), 109.

⁵⁵ Arland J. Hultgren, *Paul's Gospel and Mission: The Outlook from His Letter to the Romans* (Philadelphia: Fortress, 1985), 60. In Philo, too (καλεῖ δὲ αὐτὸ ἱλαστήριον [*Fug.* 100] [Bailey, "Jesus," 6 §4, 161]), although Philo usually drops the article even when ἱλαστήριον is not an object complement (Daniel Bailey, "Jesus as the Mercy Seat: the Semantics and Theology of Paul's Use of *Hilasterion* in Romans 3:25," *Tyndale Bulletin* 51 [2000]: 158).

⁵⁶ Bailey, "Jesus," 6 §5.2, 165.

⁵⁷ Much to be preferred to "winds" (most translations), which does more justice to the Hebrew background than to the Greek text.

suns; when one hears "sun" one thinks of *our* sun, although the "word *sun* can refer to stars other than the one closest to us."[58] Likewise, allegedly, one will always think of the Pentateuchal ἱλαστήριον when one reads ἱλαστήριον in Ezekiel or Amos.

This analogy is misleading, both because it ignores the Christian preference for the prophets and because these ἱλαστήρια are clearly not the same one referred to in the Pentateuch. The prophets were not distant stars but were (along with the Psalms) the brightest source of prophecy and truth for early Christians, who quoted them far more often than they quoted the Pentateuch.

This is the weakest of Bailey's arguments, and causes us to favor what Bailey calls the "modified proposal,"[59] that ἱλαστήριον in Rom 3:25 means "place of atonement," which is, after all, the base meaning of the term, as Bailey admits.[60] Elsewhere, he allows two translations for ἱλαστήριον in the LXX: "place of atonement or place of mercy."[61]

In Ezekiel's vision, when the altar is erected, the blood of a bull is to be put on the ἱλαστήριον[62] and the base and the horns of the altar, "and they [the priests] will purify it" (καὶ ἐξιλάσονται αὐτό 43:20)—"it" being the altar as a whole, as v. 22 makes clear. The verb ἐξιλάσκομαι occurs three times, and the corresponding noun, ἐξιλασμός, once, in the verses 20–23. Clearly, purification is the prime activity taking place upon this ἱλαστήριον.

What enables Ezekiel to call the ledges of his envisioned altar ἱλαστήρια? They are not said to be located within the Holy of Holies; they are not copies of the mercy seat, they are not said to be golden, nor carved with cherubim. They are simply "ledges"—the underlying Hebrew is עֲזָרָה than כַּפֹּרֶת. Only the etymological, base meaning of ἱλαστήριον tells us what these ledges are: they are *place of atonement/expiation*. It is this base meaning that enables the same word to be applied to the quite different ἱλαστήρια in the Pentateuch and in Ezekiel: they are all places where the verbal action of ἱλάσκομαι is performed.

Presumably, the ἱλαστήριον in Bethel[63] was also a place where a purifying or atoning ritual was thought (by the Greek translator) to be carried out, even though ἱλαστήριον in Amos 9:1 seems to be a mistranslation, seeing כַּפֹּרֶת where the MT has כַּפְתּוֹר, a pillar's capital. Apparently a *place of atonement*

---

[58] Bailey, "Jesus," 6 §2.5, 152.

[59] Bailey, "Jesus," 6 §2.2, 149.

[60] Bailey, "Jesus," 7 §2.7, 200; 1 §3.2, 5–6; Appendix B, Note A, 237.

[61] Bailey, "Jesus," Appendix B, Note A, 239.

[62] Ezekiel LXX starts with two ἱλαστήρια, but before long the ἱλαστηρίου τοῦ μικροῦ (43:14) is dropped, and only τὸ ἱλαστήριον τὸ μέγα is intended.

[63] That Amos 9:1 refers to the Bethel temple is supported by de Vaux, *Ancient Israel, Volume 2*, 335 and by the NAB footnote.

came into the Greek translator's mind instead of the merely architectural feature of capitals. This confirms that a Greek reader *expected* to find a ἱλαστήριον in a temple. A reader of the LXX would hear God leveling his threat against Bethel's place of atonement.

As the ἱλαστήρια in Ezekiel and Amos demonstrate, the Jerusalem mercy seat is not the sole referent of ἱλαστήριον, which throws us back upon etymology ("place of atonement") as the base meaning of ἱλαστήριον in the LXX. Bailey tries to consign Ezekiel to the further regions of space, driven by his certainty that the Pentateuchal ἱλαστήριον is the only legitimate referent. Ezekiel, however, may support Bailey on another front. It seems that Ezekiel's ἱλαστήρια are of central significance in his imagined temple, thus supporting *that* theme of Bailey's (see subsection 3.3.4). Finally, the notion of a distinctly *biblical* meaning for ἱλαστήριον (place of atonement) is upheld, not threatened, by these other ἱλαστήρια, but the notion that there is only one biblical ἱλαστήριον is undermined.

The mercy seat is, indeed, the sole referent of כַּפֹּרֶת in the HB, but not of ἱλαστήριον in the LXX, as is clearly shown by the usages in Ezekiel and Amos. Ezekiel's ἱλαστήριον cannot simply be subsumed into the mercy seat. Some readers may indeed have thought of Ezekiel's description of a restored temple when they encountered the word in Rom 3:25.

Of course words, especially from scripture, have resonances, and Paul may have had many of these resonances in mind when he chose the word. The same holds true of other terms Paul uses, for instance of ἀπολύτρωσις in Rom 3:24, which means ransom payment, but which could be taken as an allusion to the biblical Exodus, since the related words like λυτρόομαι are used in Deut 7:8 and elsewhere to refer to the Exodus (see next chapter.)

3.2 Linguistic Relatives of ἱλαστήριον

Throughout the twentieth century, scholars debated whether ἱλαστήριον's verbal relatives, ἱλάσκομαι and ἐξιλάσκομαι, signified the *propitiation*, that is *appeasement*, of Deity, or the *expiation*, that is *cleansing*, of sinners. Bailey is correct when he says that these debates have been beside the point as regards the primary reference of ἱλαστήριον in Rom 3:25, but I contend that they *are* relevant to the questions of what was understood to be accomplished at the ἱλαστήριον and of what Paul is implying happened there.

Some scholars have made a radical distinction between propitiation and expiation, and tried to show that only one is present in ἱλαστήριον. In fact, they are not mutually exclusive, but do represent different points of view. *Expiation* is cleansing from ritual impurity, the stain of sin. This *stain* is an effective symbol of the sin itself—to eliminate the stain is to eliminate the sin. One might say that the lens is turned onto mortals. With *propitiation*, the lens is turned onto the deity: it means appeasing, soothing, or conciliating the angry deity. These terms describe two aspects of the same cultic transaction.

Büchsel offers three main meanings of the verbs ἱλάσκομαι and ἐξιλάσκομαι: to propitiate, to purge, to expiate, each followed by the accusative, while the last meaning can be followed by περί or ἀπό phrases. The first usage is common throughout Greek. The second and third usages are common in the LXX and NT, but not outside the Bible.[64] Büchsel notes that the term changed in the LXX, with more emphasis on expiation and on "the fact that God is gracious."[65]

LSJ and BAGD agree that ἱλάσκομαι means "appease" if the object is a god, "conciliate" if the object is a man, and "to be merciful" if the verb is passive, as in Exod 32:14; Luke 18:13.

The noun ἱλασμός signifies "means of appeasing" (LSJ; better than BAGD's "expiation"), and secondarily, "sin-offering" (both lexica). Both have "propitiate" for the related verb ἐξιλάσκομαι, which Morris indicates "means 'to appease, mollify.'"[66]

3.2.1 Dodd's Argument for Expiation

C. H. Dodd insists that propitiate is "the usual pagan use of ἱλάσκομαι," but it had evolved towards "meaning 'to cancel sin', 'to expiate'," as evidenced in Plato, *Laws* 862c, and that in the LXX it usually means "to forgive."[67] Dodd focuses on cases where כָּפַר (or a derivative) is translated with something *other* than a ἱλασ-word, and cases where ἱλασ-words translate something *other* than כָּפַר and its derivatives. He finds כָּפַר-words translated as καθαρίζω (purify), ἁγιάζω (dedicate cultically), ἀθῳόω ("pronounce free of guilt"), and once as ἀπαλείφω (wipe off); thus, as "meaning 'to sanctify', 'purify' persons or objects of ritual, or 'to cancel', 'purge away', 'forgive' sins."[68]

Similarly, he finds instances where ἱλασ-words translate חָטָא (to "un-sin"), סָלַח (forgive), נָחַם and רָחַם (have compassion), and חָלָה (appease, propitiate).[69] With the last example, which really does mean propitiate, "the translators have avoided the rendering ἐξιλάσκεσθαι" except for three occasions on which they revert to the usual "pagan" meaning of ἐξιλάσκεσθαι, with a "distinct tone of contempt: it is useless to think of 'placating' Jehovah!"[70] Zechariah 7:2 and Mal 1:9 might indeed carry this

---

[64] Büchsel, *TDNT* 3:316.
[65] Büchsel, *TDNT* 3:317, where he is actually talking about the noun, "ἱλασμός."
[66] Morris, *Apostolic Preaching*, 171.
[67] C. H. Dodd, *The Bible and the Greeks* (London: Hodder & Stoughton, 1935), 88–89.
[68] Dodd, *Bible and the Greeks*, 82–84.
[69] Dodd, *Bible and the Greeks*, 84–86.
[70] Dodd, *Bible and the Greeks*, 87.

meaning, but Zech 8:22 is the stirring promise of the day when "many peoples ... shall ... entreat the favor of the Lord"—a positive image, not a contemptuous one.

"Placate" is the normal meaning of כִּפֶּר[71] when involving human parties, and sometimes when involving a divine party. Dodd too quickly dismisses this usual meaning of כִּפֶּר, and downplays the propitiatory meanings of other ἱλασ-words. Propitiation is at the base of both:

> *kpr* ... make[s] someone bless someone else instead of nursing enmity ... in other words, propitiation. It is no wonder, then, that in the Septuagint *kpr* and its cognates are ordinarily translated with derivatives of *hileoos*, of which the basic meaning is "friendly" or "favorable."[72]

The concept of making-friendly is an inescapable part of the semantic range of ἱλασ-words, but one would not know this from reading Dodd. It is as though one were to insist that "putting the screws to someone" has nothing to do with torture, but only with strongly urging. It is the torture background that informs the newer, more general, meaning. Expiation emerges from propitiation in the same way: it is because the deity is thought to be appeased, that sin is thought to be cleansed. There would be no cleansing if the deity were still displeased. Cleansing takes place *before the Lord*: "from all your sins you shall be clean before the Lord" (Lev 16:30). The sequence is: "Have mercy on me .... cleanse me from my sin" (Ps 51:1–2).

It may be that Dodd wants to protect Christian theology from accusations of anthropomorphism, although this motive is more apparent in those who utilize Dodd than in his own careful writing. The logic seems to be that impersonal "expiation" does not imply primitive anthropomorphism, but propitiating, *persuading*, does.

Gundry-Volf wants to deny the presence of propitiatory notions in Christian atonement. She admits that the wrath of God is central for Paul, but argues: "that still does not mean that Christ's death propitiated God"; in consecutive sentences she says that the cross was not defined in terms of the wrath of God, and that Christ's death anticipates the "eschatological ... outpouring of divine wrath."[73] But the whole thrust of Romans 1–3 has been to establish that people lie under "the wrath of God .... deserv[ing] to die" (1:18, 32), "storing up wrath for yourself on the day of wrath" (2:5). Paul does not

---

[71] Lyonnet, "Terminology," 141.

[72] Judisch, "Propitiation in the language," 224.

[73] J. M. Gundry-Volf, "Expiation, Propitiation, Mercy Seat," in *Dictionary of Paul and His Letters*, ed. Gerald F. Hawthorne, Ralph P. Martin, Daniel G. Reid (Downers Grove, Ill.: InterVarsity, 1993), 282.

envision a mechanical expiation that has nothing to do with the personal attitude of God. Rather, "More than expiation is required, for to speak of expiation is to deal in sub-personal categories."[74] *In any monotheistic system, expiation implies propitiation*. The *stain* of sin suggests divine resentment, and its removal signifies a reconciled relationship with God.

3.2.2 Critics of Dodd's Position

Morris shows that some passages where Dodd sees only expiation actually involve averting the wrath of God, and so, propitiation.[75] Many of Dodd's eleven LXX instances of ἐξιλάσκομαι clearly involve *turning away the divine wrath*: God considered the Israelites "corrupt" (Exod 32:7, RSV) and wanted to "bring disaster" on them. Being "implored" by Moses (32:11), "the Lord changed his mind" (32:14). God is beseeched at some length to "turn away" his wrath (Dan 9:16–19).

Morris allows that ἱλάσκομαι is used differently in LXX than in pagan texts, but still concludes, "the averting of anger seems to represent a stubborn substratum of meaning from which all the usages can be naturally explained."[76] "Propitiate" was the long-recognized meaning of the term.[77]

Propitiation is documentable as part of the semantic range of ἱλασ-words.[78] The common usage ἵλεως γενοῦ is literally "be conciliated"; in context, it can mean (following NRSV:) "change your mind," Exod 32:12; "absolve," Deut 21:8; "forgive," Amos 7:2; "be merciful," *4 Macc.* 6:28. Similar expressions like ἵλεως ἔση occur in 1 Kgs 8:30; 2 Chr 6:21, 25 and many other verses. OT scholar Klaus Koch sees these texts as echoing Hellenic and Hellenistic texts; the translator may be choosing "to introduce a known motif of community prayer. . . . The wish 'be *hileos*' was already a common invocation to deities in the hellenistic world,"[79] occurring both in propitiatory and in purificatory rituals.[80]

These observations show that "there is the thought of divine wrath in the context" of a number of "expiatory" passages,[81] but this does not displace the assertion that expiate is the *primary* meaning of ἱλάσκομαι in the LXX. When

---

[74] Morris, *Apostolic Preaching*, 201.

[75] Morris, *Apostolic Preaching*, 157.

[76] Morris, *Apostolic Preaching*, 173; cf. 125–26.

[77] Morris, *Apostolic Preaching*, 148; cf. 160–61.

[78] C. E. B. Cranfield, *A Critical and Exegetical Commentary on the Epistle to the Romans, vol. 1*. ICC (Edinburgh: T&T Clark Ltd., 1975), 216.

[79] Koch, "Translation of *kapporet*," 68–69.

[80] Koch, "Translation of *kapporet*," 69–70.

[81] Leon Morris, *The Atonement: Its Meaning and Significance* (Downers Grove, Ill.: InterVarsity, 1983), 161.

we combine the valid observations of Dodd and Morris, we come to a position that neither of them was able to articulate: that *propitiation is implicit in expiation itself.* The state of uncleanness is displeasing to God, and it behooves the believer to obtain cleansing. Sacrifice is *inherently* anthropomorphic, whether one emphasizes propitiation, or seeks to rescue it from anthropomorphism by speaking of expiation or liberation. The notion that God can be driven away by impurity is anthropomorphic.

Morris's case needed to be made, because many spiritualizing theologians were poised to use Dodd's work, ignoring some evidence and arguing that biblical religion contains no trace of anthropomorphic appeasement of God. However, Morris's "propitiation" does not bargain away the presence of expiation, any more than Dodd's "expiation" wipes away all anthropomorphism.

One cannot pre-judge whether Paul is stressing the propitiatory, expiatory, or purificatory implications of the ἱλασ-semantic family. His distinctive emphasis (sin as a power) could grow out of any one of these precedents.

The argument between Dodd and Morris, in some ways, replays the different views of Pentateuchal authors P and H. P took a spiritualizing (Levels Two/Three) approach, making atonement an impersonal process with no anthropomorphic notion of God repenting of his wrath. This can be compared to Dodd's method. The H author revived the personal dynamic of the popular theology of appeasement. This re-personalizing/re-primitivizing resembles Morris's approach.

If Dodd is P (a spiritualizer) and Morris is H (a re-primitivizer), then James Dunn is D, drawing various OT threads together and imposing harmony on them, focusing attention onto a central image: expiatory sacrifice. Dunn's argument is the most complete; he successfully integrates MT and LXX evidence, and allows that Morris forces "some retreat at least from Dodd's" position, but he nevertheless thinks that "expiation" is a better translation, since "God is never the object of the key verb (*kipper*).... The atoning act thus removes the sin ... by acting on the sin rather than on God."[82] Actually it is *uncleanness* that is acted upon, but forgiveness is corollary to cleansing. Propitiation is implicit: after expiation the sinner "no longer experiences the wrath of God."[83] Further, God *is* the object of ἱλάσκομαι in the LXX[84] in a minority of the cases. With these caveats, "expiate" can be accepted as the primary meaning of ἱλάσκομαι, while "purge" is the best primary meaning for כָּפַר, with "expiate" next.

---

[82] Dunn, *Theology*, 214.
[83] Dunn, "Paul's Understanding," 49.
[84] Zech 7:2; 8:22; Mal 1:9; Ps 106:30; and in 2 Kgs 24:4 "The Lord was not willing to be propitiated" (οὐκ ἠθέλησεν κύριος ἱλασθῆναι).

I will return to Dodd and to spiritualizing strategies at the end of the next chapter, when I assess the larger implications of Paul's metaphors.

3.3 The Meaning of ἱλαστήριον in Context in Romans 3

Romans 3:21–29 is the answer to the question raised by 1:1–3:20, where Paul, with the intensity of a prophet, condemns human sinfulness and warns of imminent punishment. The generous God has provided a way out, "overlooking" or "holding back" (πάρεσιν) from punishing past sins, putting forward Christ as ἱλαστήριον in order to make salvation possible (3:25). This is Paul's good news after such sobering bad news about the fractured relationship between people and God.

Faith comes into focus from 3:22 through chapter 4, establishing that the true "seed of Abraham" among both Jews and Gentiles are those who believe, which seems to mean three things: believing God's promises (4:21), believing "in" (ἐπί) God (4:24), and believing *what* God did through the death and resurrection of Jesus (4:25). It is *through* Jesus Christ that "we have obtained access to this grace" (5:2). "Life for all" came from that "one man's obedience" (5:18–19). Everything points back to what this one man did on the cross, an event that Paul describes with cultic and economic metaphors.

McLean attempts to banish sacrificial meaning from Romans 3 by appeal to a common non-biblical meaning, "gift," citing the inscription at Cos of a statue offered as a ἱλαστήριον to Augustus. But the word cannot be confined to a secular nuance when it occurs in a document that is all about "the righteousness of God" and "the redemption that is in Christ Jesus" (Rom 3:22, 24). Further, the reference to blood in Rom 3:25 more likely pictures a sacrificial or a martyr's death (ἐν τῷ αὐτοῦ αἵματι) than a statue dedication.

Romans 3:25 does contain "the christological foundation of the Pauline gospel about justification," and it is expressed "in carefully thought-out, technical priestly terminology."[85] The cultic connection is first signaled by the verb προτίθημι, "put forward," which may be "a cultic term in the LXX for making a public presentation,"[86] including "setting out publicly the so-called shewbread (cf. Exod 29:23; 40:23)."[87] For some scholars[88] it calls to mind Moses' public presentation of the law, and his sprinkling of covenant blood on the congregation. Even though προτίθημι does not occur there in Exod 24:7–8, the action is a public display of a covenant-making sacrifice, which seems to be

---

[85] Stuhlmacher, *Reconciliation, Law*, 96, 61.
[86] Hultgren, *Paul's Gospel*, 56.
[87] Stuhlmacher, *Reconciliation, Law*, 102; cf. Bailey, "Jesus," 2 §2.2, 21 n.16.
[88] Frank Thielman, *Paul and the Law: A Contextual Approach* (Downers Grove, Ill.: InterVarsity, 1994), 181; relying on James D. G. Dunn, *Romans 1–8*. WBC 38A (Dallas: Word, 1988), 170.

Paul's point, and again in Gal 3:1 where Christ was "publicly exhibited" (προεγράφη) as crucified.

God is the subject of this verb, and "the Son is entirely passive," as Hultgren points out: "The stress is totally on the divine activity, not the 'work of Christ'" as in the martyr tradition,[89] where the stress is on the work of the martyrs, which can evoke a certain response from God (see chapter 5).

3.3.1 Translation Choices

A brief examination of the radically different translations ἱλαστήριον should be eye-opening, even though many of these are rendered obsolete by Bailey's work.

A. EXPIATION
expiation—NAB, RSV, Dodd[90] expiatory sacrifice—Sykes[91]
means of expiation—REB, Büchsel,[92] S. Williams,[93] Käsemann[94]

B. PROPITIATION
a propitiator—Jerome, Ambrose[95] means of propitiation—Morris, Ridderbos[96]
propitiatory sacrifice—Cranfield[97]
a/the propitiation—NASB, KJV, Sanday and Headlam[98]

C. MERCY SEAT
a covering of propitiation—Barth[99] the ark-cover—Anderson & Culbertson[100]

---

[89] Hultgren, *Paul's Gospel*, 57.
[90] Dodd, *Bible and the Greeks*, 94.
[91] Sykes, S. W. "Sacrifice in the New Testament and Christian Theology," in *Sacrifice*, ed. M. Bourdillon (London: Academic Press, 1980), 74.
[92] Büchsel, *TDNT* 3:319, 322.
[93] Sam K. Williams, *Jesus' Death as Saving Event: The Background and Origin of a Concept.* Harvard Dissertations in Religion 2. (Missoula, Mont.: Scholars Press, 1975), 40.
[94] Käsemann, *Romans*, 97.
[95] Cranfield, *Romans*, 1:216.
[96] Herman N. Ridderbos, *Paul: An Outline of His Theology* (London: SPCK, 1977), 187.
[97] Cranfield, *Romans*, 1:201, 216.
[98] Sanday and Headlam, *Epistle to Romans*, 92.
[99] Karl Barth, *The Epistle to the Romans* (Oxford: Oxford University Press, 1933), 104.
[100] Anderson and Culbertson, "The Inadequacy," 318.

mercy seat or place of atonement—Gundry-Volf,[101] Hengel,[102] Hultgren,[103] Lyonnet,[104] Meyer[105]

D. MULTIPLE CHOICE

Dunn: medium of atonement[106] —or—place of atonement[107]
Fitzmyer: means of expiation[108] —or—mercy seat of the new dispensation[109]
Stowers: act of conciliation[110] —or—a solution to the problem[111]
Black: *to Jewish readers*: mercy seat, *while to Gentiles*: propitiatory offering[112]
Stuhlmacher: *Sühnmal* (place of atonement)[113] . . . with the emphasis on "expiatory sacrifice" rather than on the literal *kapporet*-lid[114]

E. OTHER

sacrifice of atonement—NRSV, NIV, TNIV   atoning sacrifice—B. Longenecker[115]
reconciler—Erasmus[116]   gift—McLean[117]

3.3.2 The Implied Ritual Action

Which cultic connection is intended? We must allow that Gentile readers unfamiliar with the Bible might have thought first of a Hellenistic propitiatory gift when they heard of ἱλαστήριον, and that they were then filled in on the biblical background by their fellows who knew the Jewish scriptures. Black's surmise makes sense—"While for non-Jewish hellenistic readers the first

---

[101] Gundry-Volf, "Expiation," 283.
[102] Hengel, *Atonement*, 45.
[103] Hultgren, *Paul's Gospel*, 59–61.
[104] Lyonnet, "Terminology," 166.
[105] Meyer, "Pre-Pauline Formula," 204. Meyer also uses "the propitiatory."
[106] Dunn, *Romans 1–8*, 171.
[107] Dunn, *Theology*, 214.
[108] Joseph A. Fitzmyer, *Romans: A New Translation with Introduction and Commentary*. AB 33 (Garden City, N.Y.: Doubleday, 1993), 120, 349–50.
[109] Fitzmyer, *Romans*, 121.
[110] Stowers, *Rereading*, 223, 225.
[111] Stowers, *Rereading*, 195.
[112] Matthew Black, *Romans*. New Century Bible (London: Marshall, Morgan & Scott, 1973), 69.
[113] Peter Stuhlmacher, *Versöhnung, Gesetz und Gerechtigkeit: Aufsätze zur biblischen Theologie* (Göttingen: Vandenhoeck & Ruprecht, 1981), 101; idem, *Paul's Letter*, 57–58; *Reconciliation, Law*, 80, 102.
[114] Stuhlmacher, *Reconciliation, Law*, 96.
[115] Bruce W. Longenecker, "ΠΙΣΤΙΣ in Romans 3:25: Neglected Evidence for the 'Faithfulness of Christ'?" *NTS* 39 (1993): 479.
[116] Black, *Romans*, 69.
[117] McLean, *Cursed Christ*, 45–46.

meaning which would probably occur would be that of 'propitiatory offering', for Jews it would tend to be taken as 'the Mercy Seat'"[118]—and I would add that the God-fearers would probably have recognized both allusions. Paul was undoubtedly familiar with these dynamics in other congregations.

Bailey does not actually reject Black's suggestion, but downplays it, insisting that Paul himself, being Jewish, "will not have thought primarily of the Hellenistic meaning."[119] However, having preached the gospel to Gentiles for over 20 years, and now writing his lengthiest and most careful letter, Paul should have known what reference would come up in the minds of Gentile readers. Bailey himself concedes that "we must assume that this image entered the minds of at least a few of Paul's readers in Rome,"[120] and admits that "Ἱλαστήριον is not a rare word" and that at least one Jewish author, Josephus, "freely used ἱλαστήριον in its Hellenistic sense."[121]

Bailey does not actually examine Black's suggestion, but asks only "where does that leave readers today?"[122]—which contributes nothing to the question of whether Paul's usage could have evoked different interpretations in the Roman congregation. He finally decides that Black "underestimates Paul's Gentile readers," that they would have known to turn from the Hellenistic to the biblical meaning, "especially when Paul has instructed them to look in 'the law and the prophets' (Rom 3:21)."[123] This is unfair. Black's remark does not underestimate Gentiles; it simply assumes that some of them did not know the Bible. Their more biblically literate fellows *would* know where to look and would, presumably, direct their attention there. There is no necessary contradiction between Black's assertion of *initial* differences of perception, and Bailey's assertion of *eventual* recognition of a biblical metaphor. Admittedly, the questions of Pauline double entendre and the dynamics of audience reception do complicate exegesis, but we need to allow complexity where it exists. I would affirm Bailey's insistence that Paul's intended referent is the ark-lid, but precisely which function is Paul highlighting?

Since Yom Kippur is the *only* occasion on which the ἱλαστήριον is associated with sacrifice, and the overt focus of that ritual is *purifying*, we must consider the possibility that Paul's metaphor envisions Christ's death as purifying the temple—but *which* temple? Since Paul can refer to the community of believers as a new temple (2 Cor 6:16; 1 Cor 3:16), this raises

---

[118] Black, *Romans*, 69.

[119] Bailey, "Jesus," 4 §1, 77.

[120] Bailey, "Jesus," 4 §1, 78.

[121] Bailey, "Jesus," 4 §2, 79.

[122] Bailey, "Jesus," 4 §3.3, 90.

[123] Bailey, "Jesus," 4 §3.3, 91. On page 90 he does expose some carelessness with the Hellenistic meaning of the term ἱλαστήριον by Black.

the possibility that the implied temple is the community. But Romans 3 gives no hint of that, nor need there be any metaphoric temple; in Rom 12:1 believers are a "living sacrifice," but there is no metaphorical temple; the setting is believers' *lives*. By the next verse, the focus is "the renewing of your minds." A metaphorical ἱλαστήριον need not imply a metaphorical temple; Paul is talking about the whole human race ("all," "the whole world," "all"; 3:12, 19, 23). Jesus as ἱλαστήριον means Jesus is the new place of atonement for the whole human race.

The ancestral connotations of ἱλασ-words (propitiation, expiation, purification) are certainly present in Romans 3, where the cultic act offsets the wrath that is mentioned throughout the first three chapters. But when Paul gets to his soteriology, he offsets the potential harshness by emphasizing God's gracefulness (3:24–25), and grace is inherent in the concept of salvation by faith (4:4, 7; 5:1, 20). Propitiation, expiation, and purification are all implied in the Levitical rite. The concern was that if the stain of sin and impurity were not wiped away, God would be angry and would leave the temple; so purification was accomplished on Yom Kippur, when, and only when, the mercy seat was approached. It is there that good relations with the Deity were re-established, through cultic procedure.

How literally did Paul intend the metaphor to be taken? Newton says that Christ's death "parallels and replaces" the cultic action carried out at the *kapporet*, that is, it "cleanses the impurity" that sin has brought upon sanctuary (that is, upon the community) and *kapporet* (that is, on Christ), thus "guarantee[ing] that God will be forever present within the community."[124] Assuming that Paul has constructed a full-blown analogy, Newton identifies what corresponds to every element: to animal, blood, ἱλαστήριον, priest, and temple. Both Christ and believers are "not only performing a priestly function but also, paradoxically, presenting themselves as sacrificial offerings."[125] Christ, then, is animal, blood, priest, and ἱλαστήριον, while believers are animal, priest, and temple. Such dizzying role changing calls this interpretation into question. This is the same scholar who says that "ancient Judaism failed to perceive any difference between the ethical and the ritual."[126]

Metaphors need sufficient simplicity to be grasped quickly, and this usually means that there is one point of contact between reference and referent. In this case the point of contact is clear: *God has provided a place where sprinkled blood purifies*. If the further implication of community as purified

---

[124] Michael Newton, *The Concept of Purity at Qumran and in the Letters of Paul* (SNTSMS 53; Cambridge University Press, 1985), 76.

[125] Newton, *Concept of Purity*, 77.

[126] Newton, *Concept of Purity*, 3. This is refuted by Jacob Milgrom, "Rationale for Cultic Law: The Case of Impurity," *Semeia* 45 (1989): 107.

temple is intended, it is left unuttered. Only by importing imagery from the Corinthian literature is Newton able to read this as an analogy of the church community. We have no *Romans* evidence to support this conclusion. Before Rom 3:25, Paul had been talking about the sinfulness of *humanity*, Jewish and Gentile, not about the believing community. All have sinned but all can now be redeemed. If there is any "cleansed temple" in this metaphor, it is "the whole world," for God is not "the God of Jews only" (3:19, 29).

The implied ritual action that takes place at the ἱλαστήριον is the purgation of sin, which rectifies relations with God. So Paul is describing a new place of atonement, a new day of atonement. He brings up the ἱλαστήριον only after indicating that the righteousness of God has now been manifested *apart* from the law, although *attested to* by the law and prophets (3:21). The law has a fundamentally prophetic or typological purpose. Instead of a literal ἱλαστήριον, we now have a ἱλαστήριον of faith (ἱλαστήριον διὰ τῆς πίστεως, 3:25). Romans 3:25 is now "applying to Christ the properties of the *kapporet*."[127] "Christ crucified has become for the world what the mercy seat was for Israel."[128]

Campbell takes issue with this: "this is *not* a typological comparison, but a broader, metaphorical allusion."[129] Campbell allows that the usage is "metonymic" but "the point of the metaphor derives from the sacrificial associations *that surround the kprt, and not the kprt itself*."[130] But no one is treating the type in isolation; the type is evocative precisely because of its functional relations. The logic of fulfillment is that something new performs the old function. The emblems of Jewish worship (whether ἱλαστήριον or paschal lamb) are understood as prefigurations of Christ's expiatory and redemptive death.

3.3.3 A ἱλαστήριον *of Faith?*

The lexical challenges of Rom 3:21–26, a single Greek period that is dense with participial clauses, are daunting. What should the translator do with the two prepositional phrases that immediately follow ἱλαστήριον in Rom 3:25: διὰ [τῆς] πίστεως ἐν τῷ αὐτοῦ αἵματι? Which prepositional phrase, "through faith" or "in his blood," goes with the key word, ἱλαστήριον? These phrases seem always to be searching for, but never finding, a home, at least in the world of scholarship.

---

[127] Nico S. L. Fryer, "The Meaning and Translation of *Hilasterion* in Romans 3:25," *EvQ* 59 (1987): 106.

[128] A. M. Hunter, *The Epistle to the Romans: Introduction and Commentary* (London: SCM, 1955), 47.

[129] Campbell, *Rhetoric of Righteousness*, 113.

[130] Campbell, *Rhetoric of Righteousness*, 112.

The NAB offering, "an expiation, through faith, by his blood," leaves one wondering which is causing the expiation, the blood or the faith? And what is the other one doing? NIV adheres strictly with the word order, coming up with "atonement, through faith in his blood," but having faith in blood would have sounded as strange then as it sounds now. "The blood" either stands for the death,[131] or is a synecdoche for a *sacrificial* death,[132] so it could mean "faith in the death," but that is without parallel elsewhere in Paul.

Bailey has a sensible argument for this part of Rom 3:25. He finds that ἱλαστήριον διὰ πίστεως "refer[s] to the ἱλαστήριον of the age of faith or the ἱλαστήριον accessed by faith"[133] and that ἐν τῷ αὐτοῦ αἵματι "reads better with the verb."[134] He utilizes Rom 1:4, which is "*stylistically* parallel" to Rom 3:25a, to argue this. Just as ἐν δυνάμει ought to be taken with the noun in Rom 1:4, yielding "Son of God *in power*," and the other two prepositional phrases be related to the participle, so Bailey recommends that διὰ [τῆς] πίστεως be taken with its neighboring noun ἱλαστήριον, and the other prepositional phrase with the verb, yielding "God has set out Jesus openly in his blood (=death) as the mercy seat (accessible) through faith."[135]

The usage of διὰ πίστεως to modify a noun is somewhat rare in Paul, but not unparalleled. Usually it modifies a verb, as later in that same chapter (3:30–31). But in Phil 3:9 he uses "through faith" to modify "righteousness," and one can also compare 2 Tim 3:15 where a δια-phrase modifies σωτηρίαν.[136]

I follow Bailey in taking "through faith" with ἱλαστήριον, but I would suggest that it is, more simply, "a mercy seat of faith." For the half-verse 3:25a I offer: "whom God put forward in a bloody death as a mercy seat of faith." This has the advantage of inserting no words into the Greek, and of resonating with other spiritualized concepts of Paul's: the Jerusalem above, the inward or hidden (κρυπτῷ) Jew, circumcision of the heart, a living sacrifice (Gal 4:26; Rom 2:29; 12:1). Most of the examples of "spiritual" or "inward" realities are contrasted with fleshly or outward realities—ἐν πνεύματι οὐ γράμματι (Rom 2:29; cf. 2 Cor 3:6); ἐν καρδίᾳ [versus] ἐν προσώπῳ (2 Cor 5:12); οὐκ . . . ἐν λόγῳ μόνον ἀλλὰ . . . ἐν πνεύματι (1 Thess 1:5). Paul may use contrasting verbs ("do not be conformed . . . but be transformed"; Rom 12:2), or dueling instrumental datives ("a letter . . . written not with ink but with the Spirit"; 2 Cor 3:3). Examples could be multiplied. In Rom 3:25 the image of a ἱλαστήριον of faith builds upon the literal ἱλαστήριον, yet suggests a

---

[131] Fitzmyer, *Romans*, 401; it does not "connote anything sacrificial."
[132] Dunn, *Theology*, 217.
[133] Bailey, "Jesus," 7 §1, 177.
[134] Bailey, "Jesus," 7 §2.8, 203.
[135] Bailey, "Jesus," 7 §2.8, 204–07.
[136] Bailey, "Jesus," 7 §2.8, 207, including n.64.

transcendence of the latter. If the literal cult were sufficient, what would be the need for a ἱλαστήριον διὰ πίστεως?

In his other choice, "mercy seat *for the age* of faith," Bailey draws attention to "what unites rather than divides Jews and Gentiles"[137]—*faith*, which opens up the possibility for a new kind of society. I think the more straightforward "mercy seat of faith" is preferable, as it facilitates recognition of this as another instance of Paul's juxtaposing a *new* and *spiritual* antitype with an *old* and *fleshly* type.

The logic behind the term may be that believers have access to a "mercy seat" (that is, to cleansing from sin) by the exercise of faith, or it may be that believers derive their faith from Jesus' own *faithfulness*, which accomplished forgiveness before believers could practice faith. My translation allows for either interpretation. It is even possible that the faithfulness of God, Jesus, and believers are all included in the metaphor, faith being a current that flows between and connects these persons, so the ambiguity of "mercy seat of faith" may be an advantage.

It is not necessary for this thesis that this question be settled; still, it is interesting to inquire briefly into the sense of the genitives πίστεως Ἰησοῦ Χριστοῦ in 3:22 and τὸν ἐκ πίστεως Ἰησοῦ in 3:26, which might illuminate the implied subject of διὰ πίστεως in 3:25. Many scholars now argue for a "subjective genitive" reading: that these refer to the faith practiced by Jesus. The idea is that "Jesus' human faith is one that can be shared by others."[138] Advocates of this position compare Rom 3:26 with the similar phrase in 4:16, τῷ ἐκ πίστεως Ἀβραάμ, which means something like "to the one who shares the faith of Abraham," and claim that 3:26, then, should mean "the one who shares the faith of Jesus.[139] This position is interesting theologically: "The obedience of Jesus is God's way of saving other humans. . . . The faith of Jesus is soteriologically significant. . . . It provides the basis for the faith response of others."[140] One strength of Johnson's interpretation is that it makes both believers and Jesus active parties in this "faith."

But the "subjective genitive" argument is weak at many points. Johnson's translation "as a propitiation through his faithfulness unto death,"[141] is remarkably awkward. One notices that Keck leaves part of it untranslated, with

---

[137] Bailey, "Jesus as," Ph.D., 7.2.8, 208.

[138] Luke Timothy Johnson, *Reading Romans: A Literary and Theological Commentary* (New York: Crossroad, 1997), 60.

[139] Leander E. Keck, "'Jesus' in Romans," *JBL* 108 (1989): 456; Johnson, *Reading Romans*, 60.

[140] Luke Timothy Johnson, "Romans 3:21–26 and the Faith of Jesus," *CBQ* 44 (1982): 89; cf. Keck, "'Jesus' in Romans," 457.

[141] Johnson, *Reading Romans*, 59.

equally clumsy results: "whom God put forward as ἱλαστήριον, through [his] faithfulness [made concrete] in his blood."[142]

Romans 3:22 is at the end of a passage (vv. 20–22) highlighting the faith-law dichotomy, and ἐκ πίστεως' Ἰησοῦ in 3:26 is at the beginning of a passage that contrasts faith with works of the law. "Faith" and "works" refer to human options. Verses 20–22 and 26–30 contrast faith with law, while vv. 23–25 tell readers *what* to believe. If the faithfulness of Jesus is present at all, it is secondary to, and directed toward, believers' own faith-practice. After all, salvation depends on "believ[ing] in your heart" (Rom 10:9), on "hearing with faith" (Gal 3:5 RSV).

A believer's faith is the focus of Romans 4. Abraham's trust is emphasized (vv. 5, 9). We are to "follow the example of [Abraham's] faith" (Rom 4:12). Righteousness comes from practicing faith, from believing the promises of God. Abraham believed the initial promise, and we now get to believe in the *content* of the promise to Abraham: the Messiah. The stress is on *believing the promise*.

Dunn correctly points out that the subjective reading tends to make all instances of πίστις refer to Jesus' own faith, leaving us without a noun phrase to refer to the faith of believers, which is certainly the main theme of Galatians,[143] and crucial throughout Paul's writings.

It seems to me that the subjective genitive reading is an attempt to preserve an anti-works focus in Pauline interpretation, when, in fact, Paul does call for one "work": practicing faith. The "faithfulness of Jesus" argument may be theologically interesting but cannot bear the exegetical weight it is being asked to carry.

Currently the important point to stress is that Rom 3:25 is a metaphorical reference to the biblical mercy seat. The objection raised by some scholars that Paul could not be referring to the mercy seat because this had been carried away by the Chaldeans centuries earlier, is superficial. Even before that event, most Jews had never seen the mercy seat. The ἱλαστήριον had *always* been an object of imagination for every Jew except the high priest, and even he saw it but once a year. The ἱλαστήριον was a *literary* image, all the more evocative in metaphor for the fact of its never being seen. An object need not be physically visible in order to be intensely real to the imagination. It is the *significance* of an object in the *imagination* that gives it metaphorical power.

---

[142] Keck, "'Jesus' in Romans," 457.

[143] James D. G. Dunn, "Once More: ΠΙΣΤΙΣ ΧΡΙΣΤΟΥ," in *SBL 1991 Seminar Papers*, ed. Eugene H. Lovering, Jr. (Atlanta: Scholars Press, 1991), 736.

The Sacrificial Metaphor in Romans 3:25 149

The question of whether or not Paul incorporates a pre-existing salvation formula[144] in Rom 3:24–26 (and other places) calls for lengthy discussion, and will not be addressed. Even if he does so, he re-shapes it and makes it into his own argument. The texts as we have them represent *Paul's* theology, and can profitably be examined as such. He builds upon soteriological formulas.

It is now possible to look at interesting recent speculation on this passage, that affirms that a temple image is present, but attempts to downplay the sacrificial associations. Is the ἱλαστήριον a metaphor for a new temple, and if so, does this mean that something other than sacrifice is being emphasized?

3.3.4 Bailey on Christ as Center of a New Sanctuary

Bailey presents the interesting notion of an "exodus–new sanctuary tradition"[145] in Rom 3:25, which is a synthesis of some viewpoints of Horbury and Kraus. Kraus asserts that Paul has in mind the purification ceremony for inauguration or consecration of a new temple.[146] He cites two texts from *Jubilees* where a sanctuary is part of an eschatological scenario, and argues that this informs Paul's metaphor, and would have been recognized by his Jewish readers. In *Jub.* 1:27–29, God promises to build his sanctuary "in their midst forever," and in *Jub.* 4:24–26 Mount Zion will be sanctified, and "the earth will be sanctified from all sin" (*OTP* 2:63). Kraus also relies on the eschatological temple in 11Q19 (*Temple Scroll*) 29.8–10.[147] A passage that might strengthen Kraus's case but which he cites only in passing (162 n.82), is *Tg. Isa.* 53:5 where the Hebrew passage "was wounded for our transgressions" is interpreted "he shall build the sanctuary which was profaned for our sins."[148]

A good deal stronger for Kraus's case is Ezekiel 43, since here (and only here) is there a focus on the *consecration* of an eschatological sanctuary. In v. 18 blood is splashed on one of the two ledges (ἱλαστήρια) on the day of the

---

[144] Some who favor a pre-Pauline tradition here include Bultmann, *Theology*, 1:46; Williams, *Jesus' Death*, 6; Stuhlmacher, *Paul's Letter*, 59; and *Reconciliation, Law*, 104, 175. Some who oppose it include I. Howard Marshall, "The Development of the Concept of Redemption in the New Testament," in *Reconciliation and Hope: Essays on Atonement and Eschatology*, ed. R. Banks (Grand Rapids: Eerdmans, 1974), 164; and Hultgren, *Paul's Gospel*, 62–64 (who says that Paul inserted his own earlier material into Romans 3, including material for a Day of Atonement sermon).

[145] Bailey, "Jesus," 7, §2.6, 195.

[146] Kraus, *Tod Jesu*, 159–66.

[147] Kraus, *Tod Jesu*, 164–67. In 29.9, God says, "I Myself will create My temple"; Wise, et al, 469.

[148] Cf. Margaret Barker, *The Revelation of Jesus Christ Which God Gave to Him to Show to His Servants What Must Soon Take Place (Revelation 1:1)* (Edinburgh: T&T Clark, 2000), 135.

consecration of the altar,[149] then applied to the horns of the altar, and to the "four corners of the ledge, and upon the rim [βάσιν] all around; thus you shall ... make atonement for it" (ἐξιλάσονται αὐτό 43:20). The sacrificing goes on for seven days, making atonement, after which God says "I will accept you" (43:26–27).

This prolonged attention to consecration does not occur in *Jubilees* or 11Q19. Thus, the burden of Kraus's case must be born by Ezekiel 43, in my view, and he does cite it,[150] but seems to want to build more upon *Jubilees* than upon Ezekiel.

Bailey refuses to rely on Ezekiel 43 at all because of the problems it poses for his strictly focused "mercy seat" reading of ἱλαστήριον, and instead argues for Pentateuchal themes in Rom 3:21–25. He seems to be reaching for obscure allusions and avoiding the more evident relevance of Ezekiel 43. He argues that the "righteousness of God disclosed" (Rom 3:21) summons up Ps 98:2 ("he has revealed his vindication") and Isa 56:1 ("my salvation will come, and my deliverance be revealed").[151] But these passages do not even use the same verb as Rom 3:21, and hardly seem relevant. Bailey sees "he brought them to his holy hill" (Ps 77:54 LXX) as an example of the "exodus–new sanctuary" hope,[152] but this is a reminiscence of the historical sanctuary. Bailey is wary of the threat that Ezekiel 43 poses to his mercy seat interpretation, and therefore tries to depend upon Horbury's exegesis of Exodus 15 to prove the exodus–new sanctuary theme.

Relying on Horbury, Bailey claims that "the Song of Moses anticipates Paul's concept of the church. . . . [T]he song's introduction in Exod 14:31–15:1, where belief in God and Moses is followed by congregational praise, may be reflected in Rom 10:10,"[153] where one believes in one's heart and confesses with one's lips. At first glance, this connection looks weak, but Horbury does make a decent case for the wide influence of the Song of Moses (Exodus 15, Deuteronomy 32) in early Judaism, with the people *believing* God and *confessing* their belief as hymnodic praise, and for its reflection in Rom 10:10,[154] although his attempt to find it underlying nearly every instance of the common terms "beloved," "saints," and "inheritance" in the NT is completely

---

[149] Kraus, *Tod Jesu*, 61.

[150] Kraus, *Tod Jesu*, 184.

[151] Bailey, "Jesus," 7, §2.2, 183.

[152] As in Exod 15:17 ("Jesus," 7, §2.6, 197–98); Bailey relies on W. Horbury, here.

[153] Bailey, "Jesus," 7, §2.6, 195.

[154] William Horbury, "Septuagintal and New Testament Conceptions of the Church," in *A Vision for the Church: Studies in Early Christian Ecclesiology in Honour of J. P. M. Sweet*, eds. Markus Bockmuehl and Michael B. Thompson (Edinburgh: T&T Clark, 1997), 4–6.

unconvincing.[155] Faith in God *and* Moses is heightened by the LXX,[156] and Horbury claims it anticipates Paul's belief in one God and one Lord (1 Cor 8:6).[157] The resonances that Horbury hears may indeed be present, but it is hard to believe that they ring throughout the NT as loudly as he hears them. Paul can certainly use exodus themes (1 Corinthians 10), but it is more significant to note the number of times he does *not* refer to a Sinai-like revelation, does *not* make belief in Christ comparable to Israelite belief in Moses, and pays almost no attention to Jesus *as an instructor* or truth-teacher.

Bailey uses Horbury's argument for an echo of Exod 15:1 in Rom 10:10 as a "precedent for my suggestion of an echo of Exod 15:13 in Rom 3:24,"[158] claiming that Exod 15:13 and Rom 3:24 are the only places in their respective testaments "where God's saving righteousness and his activity of redeeming people (λυτρόω) are coupled in a single line"; thus, "the metaphor of salvation is not particularly judicial but involves the broad notion of deliverance."[159]

Several weak threads are themselves weakly linked. Bailey tries to use Horbury's "congregational praise" thread between Exod 15:1 and Rom 10:10 to weave a "righteousness/redemption" thread from Exod 15:13 to Rom 3:24. He then extends the latter thread to Romans 5, having just argued for its *uniqueness* in Rom 3:24 and Exodus 15! In fact, the association of righteousness and redemption is not rare; it occurs in Exod 6:6; Ps 119:154–165; Hos 12:7; and the absence of righteousness causes redemption to be withheld in Hos 7:13; 13:14. Bailey's linkage ends up resting on the presence of a δικ-word, a λυτ-word, and a sanctuary in Exod 15:13–17 and Rom 3:24–25.

Further, Bailey tries to use Horbury's assertion of a political land-based ideology and "a Christ-centered temple-theology"[160] in Rom 9:25–26; 11:26; Gal 4:27. All of these justify the calling of the Gentiles, doing more to undermine than to build a nationalistic ideology. Horbury wants to utilize Davies for his argument, while rejecting the insight of Davies that, in his *metaphoric* use of these themes, Paul "has cast off the Messianic significance of the earthly Jerusalem . . . in favour of the heavenly . . . . The Church here and now is part of the heavenly Jerusalem."[161] Instead, Horbury sees a persistence of Israelite political loyalties in the early church: "In 1 Cor 15 Paul

---

[155] Horbury, "Septuagintal," 12–13.
[156] Horbury, "Septuagintal," 8.
[157] Horbury, "Septuagintal," 5–6.
[158] Bailey, "Jesus," 7, §2.6, 195.
[159] Bailey, "Jesus," 7, §2.6, 194–95.
[160] Horbury, "Land, sanctuary," 219.
[161] W. D. Davies, *The Gospel and the Land: Early Christianity and Jewish Territorial Doctrine* (Berkeley: University of California Press, 1974), 197.

envisages a Zion-centered messianic reign."[162] Davies is more accurate in recognizing that Paul has "broken with the land."[163]

If Paul's teaching can be connected with Jewish nationalistic hope at all, it is his reversal of this hope that is important. Sinai is Hagar; there is no distinction between Jew and Greek (Gal 4:25; Rom 10:12). These things stand nationalism on its head. Horbury has a genius for discerning connections, but not for perceiving how fundamental is Paul's break with the views of those he calls "children of the flesh," "unenlightened," "ignorant" (Rom 9:8; 10:2–3).

Horbury's thesis cannot stand, and Bailey has not helped himself by leaning on it. Bailey himself does not assert a nationalist hermeneutic in Paul, but tries to use Horbury to strengthen his argument for a recognized eschatological "new sanctuary." In the end, the Horbury threads add nothing to the Kraus thesis.

There is no need for such complex intertextuality. The notion of Jesus as place of atonement is simpler, not requiring a complicated series of associations that take one far away from the ἱλαστήριον, to Jesus as a new Moses rescuing a new people, leading them to praise him and God and to build a new sanctuary where oracular revelation will take place—this is too much to ask from five key words in Rom 3:24–25 (δικαιούμενοι ... ἀπολυτρώσεως ... ἱλαστήριον ... πίστεως ... ἔνδειξιν). Only those already biblically literate—and able to detect the *right* biblical allusions—would have any chance of grasping it; the Hellenistic interpreters would miss it altogether, since the Hellenistic ἱλαστήριον is only sometimes placed in a temple, and certainly does not suggest a *new* temple. This string of allusions requires such precision of interpretation that it is hard to imagine Paul expecting his readers (whom he had not met) to grasp it.

Bailey asserts a "Pentateuchal narrative of salvation" in Rom 3:21–26, with a fall in v. 23, "redemption as from Egypt in v. 24," and a new sanctuary in v. 25: a "Pentateuchal narrative of salvation."[164] But if this is true, and the metaphor "is not particularly judicial," why does justification and law language dominate 3:24–31? No temple, metaphorical or otherwise, is mentioned when he hammers home his point about the universal sovereignty of God, and the single method of salvation, in vv. 29–30.

The case for a "new sanctuary" motif will remain weak as long as it cannot show: 1) more background: at least a few more intertestamental instances of an eschatologically significant temple-consecration; and 2) some NT examples of metaphors of Jesus as sanctuary or as center-of-the-sanctuary, perhaps an image of believers as worshippers in his courts, of sin polluting Christ the way it

---

[162] Horbury, "Land, sanctuary," 220.
[163] Davies, *Gospel*, 220.
[164] Bailey, "Jesus," 6 §2.4, 151–52.

pollutes the Temple—but there are no such examples, even when Paul uses ναός as an image for the community.

Rather, the ἱλαστήριον metaphor suggested itself to Paul at the end of his longest discussion of sin, by which time the need for purification or expiation had become a premier concern. It is immediately followed by the revelation (ἔνδειξις) of God's forgiving righteousness. Paul is tying together his major concerns: the saving death of Christ, faith, salvation of Gentiles. Justification by faith not by law is the point of vv. 26–28. The fact that God is God of the Gentiles dominates vv. 29–31. If Paul looks for a new temple, it is a spiritual one: a community of Spirit-bonded Jews and Gentiles.

Paul's main points are made clear in the subsequent chapters. He demonstrates the primary importance of faith in Romans 4, illustrates a new Adam and a new humanity (a new Israel would be too paltry) in Romans 5, explains how to be part of Christ in Romans 6, and spells out the enslaving power of the flesh and how to be free from it in chapters 7–8. If a Fall-and-Exodus narrative is present in Romans, it is just part of the mix of metaphors, and not a major part. The only utterly transparent Exodus reference is when he makes an analogy between the hard-heartedness of Pharaoh and that of the Jews, and how God makes use of both (9:17). There is also a reference to "the covenants" in 9:4, and he reworks the covenant concept throughout, but it is not modeled on the first covenant, whose glory has faded, whose letter kills, and whose circumcision may not be from the heart. It is a *new* covenant.

Paul constantly moves back and forth between his main themes, attempting to unify cultic typology, God's revelation, the juridical-eschatological solution (justification), the faith-bond with God that either takes the place of law or "fulfills the law," and the universality of God's sovereignty. No one of Paul's metaphors is able to capture the whole of his thinking. He has to chain them together to make his points, but he is not chained to any one of them.

The Bailey-Kraus-Horbury thesis makes too much of the temple's political significance. Paul's discontinuity with this symbolic universe is as important as his (typological) continuity with it. He utters a cultic metaphor in Rom 3:25, but he does not tie his gospel to a particular strand of political hope.

3.3.5 *Revelation at the Shrine*

Besides the new temple theme, Bailey's other argument is that *"revelation* [is] the primary purpose of the mercy seat."[165] He relies on three Pentateuch passages that have God speaking "from above the mercy seat."[166] This suggestion is made several times in the dissertation, but never argued thoroughly. This hardly convinces the reader that three Pentateuch verses

---

[165] Bailey, "Jesus," 7 §2.7, 202.
[166] Exod 25:22; cf. Lev 16:2; Num 7:89.

constitute "revelation" the primary meaning of a word that always occurs in a cultic connection or a cultic metaphor.[167] Further, Bailey poses his point in such a way as to suggest that his term relates to revelation *instead of* to sacrifice,[168] but when a priestly text mentions (in passing) revelation at a sacrificial location, this should be seen as an aspect of sacrificial ideology, not as a separate realm apart from sacrifice. Revelation is present but not prominent in Bailey's three passages; it is not the *content* of revelation that is mentioned, but its mere *fact*, to put a seal of divine approval on the surrounding cultic material. Moses heard from God here precisely *because* it was the place of expiation.

We have seen that sacrifice in Israel and around the world often involves spirit-communion at a key moment in the ritual. It is hardly surprising that priestly documents should make the place of cultic atonement also the place where Moses "would hear the voice speaking to him" (Num 7:89). It is the verbal equivalent of the fiery message from heaven igniting the sacrifices in 1 Chr 21:26 and 2 Chr 7:1.

Revelation is highlighted in Rom 3:21, 25b, and 26a, where God's righteousness is revealed in his canceling of sin, and revelation is a frequent biblical theme. The ἱλαστήριον is not introduced in order to inaugurate a revelation theme, which had already been mentioned; if God can reveal his righteousness apart from the law (3:21), he can reveal it apart from a piece of furniture. Further, if ἱλαστήριον is meant to suggest "place of revelation," this has failed to register with readers from patristic times to the present. Elsewhere, when Paul uses temple imagery, it does not stand for revelation as such, but for God's indwelling presence (1 Cor 3:16–17; 6:19; 2 Cor 6:16).

That Christ's shedding of his blood is now the "place" where sin is canceled is a notion that only makes sense if the sacrificial role of the ἱλαστήριον is recognized. In the Pentateuch, it is the sacrificial cult, not God's speaking or revealing himself, that brings forgiveness of sin. *Secondarily*, revelation may be present in the same way as in Pentateuch passages with theophanies at sacrificial altars, reflecting the olden idea that sacrifice opens up communion with the divine. In the Pentateuch as in the Vedas, revelation at a sacrificial location is strongly affirmative of cultic ideology. "Revelation" does not remove a text from the realm of cultic ideology.

---

[167] The term ἱλαστήριον occurs 22 times in the Pentateuch, six times in the prophets, and once in a metaphor in *4 Maccabees*.

[168] He asserts that, except for in Leviticus 16, "The mercy seat does not need blood.... The primary function of the mercy seat is still to be a symbol of revelation" ("Jesus," 7 §2.9, 210; cf. page 202).

In Paul, however, the cultic ideology itself has been transformed into an abstract and internalized sacrificial arena. One does not battle the gods here, as in Vedic sacrifice, but surrenders wholly to God, putting one's every thought and motivation in subservience to God, and recognizing this as a form of death to self. Paul's descriptions of the Christian cult always involve a symbolization of this experience of death of self through identification with the death of Christ.

But it is not just subservience to God and repudiation of selfishness that is being symbolized; there is also the element of new creation, freedom, encounter with a surprising revelation of divine love, none of which is manufactured by Paul, but which is experienced by him and, presumably, his fellows. Therefore, Paul's theology is highly original and creative. Merely describing it as "cultic theology," without distinguishing it from other cultic theologies, is inadequate.

3.3.6 The Place of Synecdoche

In considering Paul's soteriological metaphors, it is important to remember that they are linguistic devices designed to enhance comprehension, and not all-encompassing analogies wherein every detail of the metaphor is meant to refer to some reality. Overly literal interpretation of metaphors leads either to reductionistic theories or to conclusions about a supposed incoherence in Pauline metaphor.

It is essential to understand the linguistic devices called *synecdoche*, whereby a part is used to refer to the whole,[169] and *metonymy*, where a term is substituted for the person or office with which it is frequently associated (as "crown" for monarch[170]). The term "metonymy," however, is used in slightly different ways by different scholars, so I will utilize the more precise term, "synecdoche."

When someone says he dreads to stand before the bar, he is not afraid of a wooden railing, but of being called before a judge. The bar is a synecdoche for the court system or a court case. Similarly, Paul's reference to ἱλαστήριον is synecdochal. Paul is not saying that Christ is "a piece of Temple furniture"[171]; obviously it is a synecdoche for the temple and its rituals. This raises the subject of scholarly uneasiness about synecdoche. Campbell accepts that "ἱλαστήριον [is] metaphorical," but not that it is "an explicit reference to the

---

[169] Edwin J. Barton and Glenda A. Hudson, *A Contemporary Guide to Literary Terms with Strategies for Writing Essays about Literature* (Boston: Houghton Mifflin, 1997), 193.

[170] Barton and Hudson, *Contemporary Guide*, 104.

[171] Correctly noted by Brendan Byrne, who nevertheless is uneasy with the metaphor in *Romans*. Sacra Pagina 6 (Collegeville, Minn.: Liturgical, 1996), 127.

kprt,"[172] thus weakening his own earlier assertion of a *kapporet* and Yom Kippur reference.[173] Apparently "an explicit reference" cannot be a metaphor, for Campbell.

Leon Morris is also too literal in his interpretation of this metaphor. He says that "the Christian place of sprinkling is rather the cross than the Christ,"[174] and so, if anything could be called ἱλαστήριον, it would have to be the cross. Such rigidly logical methods of interpretation would prevent us from understanding most of the metaphors that occur in world literature. If we demand that metaphors be strictly logical, we rob them of their suggestive power. Who has not experienced a thrill of appreciation when "the light goes on" and one recognizes *which* feature has caused a metaphor to suggest itself to the author?[175]

There need only be *one aspect* of similarity for the metaphor to be effective; in fact, if there are too many correspondences, the allusive power is reduced, because the particular feature that is meant to be highlighted can be overlooked, and some other feature seized upon. The fact that blood is spilt or sprinkled on the ἱλαστήριον is sufficient point of contact to enable ἱλαστήριον to be a metaphor for Christ spilling his blood. The payoff of this metaphor is that it gives Christ's death a cultic significance.

Bailey points out the sloppiness of translating "place of atonement" as "sacrificial animal," but this does not remove the metaphor from the sacrificial realm. That would be like denying that "the collar" is a clerical metaphor since it does not designate the *cleric* but only his *office*. However, it certainly evokes the realm of persons and functions associated with that office. Likewise, ἱλαστήριον, being a place where sacrificial blood is sprinkled, evokes the sacrificial cult, and the events and beings associated with it.

The initial response of a Jewish reader to the image of a redemptive act taking place with blood on a ἱλαστήριον would be to think of the annual Yom Kippur festival rather than the rare event of founding a new temple. But we cannot afford to be dogmatic about this; "redemption" in 3:24 may enhance Kraus's case for the theme of new exodus, and a new sanctuary by implication. Still, we find nothing else to signal that a new temple is being founded. The emphasis through the first three chapters of Romans has been on the problem of

---

[172] Campbell, *Rhetoric of Righteousness*, 133.

[173] Campbell, *Rhetoric of Righteousness*, 131.

[174] Morris, *Apostolic Preaching*, 196. Deissmann makes the same point (Adolf Deissmann, *Bible Studies: Contributions Chiefly from Papyri and Inscriptions* [Edinburgh: T&T Clark, 1901], 129).

[175] The best metaphor should not be obscure but it should require "a bit of mental inquiry" on the reader's part; Aristotle, *Rhetoric* 1401b; cited in Umberto Eco, *Semiotics and the Philosophy of Language* (Bloomington: Indiana University Press, 1984), 102.

sin. In 3:25 Christ becomes the ἱλαστήριον where God cancels sins and manifests his kindly righteousness. It is the Yom Kippur cultic activity, not a new temple building, that expiates sin, and the ἱλαστήριον was the central installation in the sacred landscape on the most holy day in the calendar. Nor is this the only time that Paul uses a Yom Kippur image to characterize the death of Christ (cf. Rom 8:3; 2 Cor 5:21). It is the rightwising activity of God that is emphasized in these verses, transferred from Yom Kippur to Good Friday. The consecration of a new temple (*Heiligtumsweihe*) is possible, but seems much more obscure than the Yom Kippur option.

The gist of the cultic event comes through even if the metaphor is misinterpreted. If some readers thought of a Hellenistic propitiatory gift upon first hearing this passage, they would still correctly perceive that the death served as a *ritually effective* means of reconciliation with God. When the passage was later discussed in the congregation, Jewish and God-fearing readers would provide the biblical understanding of ἱλαστήριον, and those who had not known of this biblical background would have their understanding adjusted.

3.4 Justification in the Sequence of Salvation

In the next chapter I will examine ἀπολύτρωσις, redemption. That leaves δικαιόω as the next major term to look at. There is no space to undertake a deep examination here, but a brief look at the place of justification in connection with the other key ideas is now in order. The single complex sentence that goes from 3:21 to 26 describes the solution to the problem of sin. God has manifested his righteousness apart from the law, but in accordance with what the law and prophets foretold (v. 21). Even though all have sinned and lack[176] the glory of God, this righteousness is available to all through faith (vv. 22–23). Next come the key concepts, which I lay out here so as to give each important term its own line. Each of the two sections has an introductory clause, an adverbial element, an instrumental dative, and a concluding clause. I use NAB because it is the most literal translation here, and stays close to the Greek word order. Speaking of believers, Paul says:

They are justified (δικαιούμενοι)
    freely (δωρεὰν)
        by his grace (τῇ αὐτοῦ χάριτι)
        through the redemption (διὰ τῆς ἀπολυτρώσεως) in
            Christ Jesus,

---

[176] I prefer this neglected alternative to the usual translation, "fallen short of." That we have fallen short of God ought to be obvious, but that we are *lacking*, or needy, is interesting.

> whom God set forth as an expiation (ἱλαστήριον),
> through faith (διὰ τῆς πίστεως),
> by his blood (ἐν τῷ αὐτοῦ αἵματι),
> to prove his righteousness because of the forgiveness of sins
> previously committed. Rom 3:24–25 NAB

The motivation of God in this passage is not the problem; he acts from generosity ("by his grace as a gift" NRSV). What we need to explore is the sequence of events in the salvation process.

The three major events described in vv. 24–25 seem to occur in reverse order to that in which Paul names them. People are justified (present participle) *through* the redemption that is in Christ Jesus, whom God put forward (aorist tense) as a ἱλαστήριον. Thus, redemption took place at an already-existing ἱλαστήριον, while justification comes *through*—that is, *after*, or at least emerging *out of*—redemption. Everything emanates from the place of sacrifice.

The sacrificial death accomplished redemption, that is, rescue. Then follows justification, which is a legal ratification of the rescue. With Paul, salvation must be legally sanctioned by God. First, believers are snatched from the jaws of death, and only then are they let off by the divine court. One could argue that justification happens *by means of* redemption, that διά is purely instrumental. Still, justification and redemption come from different realms (legal and economic), suggesting that there must be some relationship or sequence from one to the other.

What is the legal basis for the acquittal? Is it the fact that the redemption was paid for by such a prestigious advocate, even an officer of the court? Will the Father acquit anyone whom He sees that the Son has rescued? This seems to be the implication, because there is no suggestion that the Son's advocacy is challenged, no hint of a legal hearing. This is where the terminology of Father, Son, and heirs, rather than Judge, attorney, and accused, might be appropriate. Why, then, does Paul use legal and sacrificial terms more often than family ones? Probably because of the deeply-ingrained Pharisaic notion of an afterlife lawcourt. Judgment Day is a compelling metaphor for Paul, where both God's justice and mercy can be highlighted.[177]

The terms "Father" and "Son" come to Paul from the Jesus tradition, but the "heirs" of the covenant promise are not natural heirs, they had to be adopted into such relationship. There is a contrast here with the Jesus tradition, where a Godlike love of enemies turns the practitioners of love into "children of the

---

[177] Of course, "the notion of a 'gracious' justice which creates salvation does not *transcend* the judicial sphere. It merely premises a different experience of justice" (Theissen, *Social Reality*, 167).

Most High" (Luke 6:35; Matt 5:45). Further, for Jesus, "we do not have to be 'acquitted' before the Judge in order to be reconciled to the Father,"[178] but that is precisely what is needed in Pauline soteriology: there needs to be a transaction (a trial, a purchase, a ritual, an adoption) that changes things. But while the logic of salvation seems to be different for Jesus than it is for Paul, the concept of the resultant state (faithful, righteous, generous to others) is the same.

Is the dominant idea in justification acquittal,[179] or is it the notion of being actually *made good*, as Goodspeed argues? It is not lexicography but theology, Goodspeed insists, whereby "the plain Greek word 'You have been made upright' is subtly transformed into meaning 'You have been declared upright, though you are not.'"[180] Barrett tries to affirm both "to make righteous" and "be acquitted," but he seems really to allow the forensic interpretation to be dominant.[181]

What is dominant in these soteriological summaries, Paul's *transactional* thinking or his *participationist* thinking? Is he thinking of a courtroom transaction of acquittal at a heavenly judgment, or of actually taking on Jesus' righteousness? (Or both?) Some passages suggest one, some the other, even within the same chapter: when he says "no one is justified before God by the law" (Gal 3:11), a (non-)acquittal is in view, but to "make alive" (v. 21), becoming "children of God" (v. 26), and being "clothed" with Christ (v. 27) suggest an inner transformation. Romans 8:1, 26–27, 33–34 envision a court scene with accusers and intercessors, but vv. 11 and 14 speak of being livened by the Spirit and being children of God. Evidently, the two themes are not mutually exclusive. One can be filled with the Spirit and transformed now, even "become the righteousness of God" (2 Cor 5:21), knowing that one will be acquitted on Judgment Day. Hope itself transforms us ("in hope we were saved," Rom 8:24), and the Spirit "intercedes" (a judicial term) for us (8:26). The inalienable love of God (8:39) accomplishes both.

Just as present hope and future acquittal intersect, so also do God's generosity and the need for a *transaction* that achieved salvation: "He who did not withhold his own Son, but gave him up for all of us, will he not with him also give us everything else?" (8:32). Acquittal is the most sensible meaning in a number of passages that entail deliverance from divine judgment: since we are justified, we have peace with God, and are saved from retaliation (Rom 5:1, 9); I am only acquitted if God acquits me (1 Cor 4:4).

---

[178] John Knox, *Chapters in a Life of Paul* (Nashville: Abingdon, 1950), 150.

[179] Among many is Bultmann, *Theology* 1:271–77.

[180] Edgar J. Goodspeed, "Some Greek Notes," *JBL* 73 (1954): 87.

[181] C. K. Barrett, *A Commentary on the Epistle to the Romans* (London: Adam & Charles Black, 1962), 75–76.

Thus, difficult as it is to reconcile the competing interpretations of justification, I think that both elements are present in Paul. When he thinks in terms of Judgment Day, "acquittal" is his meaning (Rom 8:33–34). But we can also "walk in newness of life" (Rom 6:4); even "we might become the righteousness of God" (2 Cor 5:21). The aorist subjunctive verbs in the apodoses of these conditional sentences point to real fulfillment. The apodosis can also feature a future passive verb to say that "the many will be made righteous" (κατασταθήσονται, Rom 5:19). Both concepts are visible in the remark that Christ's obedience confers both justification *and* life (Rom 5:18). Of course, any moral transformation happens *after* the legal/sacrificial action.

Still, Paul does speak of "a new creation" in Christ, enabling one to do "every good work" (2 Cor 5:17; 9:8). Believers *can* fulfill "the just requirement of the law" (Rom 8:4).[182] The notion of being merely *deemed* righteous while remaining loathsome is a distortion of Paul's teaching. It magnifies one aspect of Paul's doctrine out of proportion while overlooking his teaching about God's transformative *involvement* with the believer. The doctrine of total depravity takes some of Paul's rhetoric and makes it all-controlling. Rather, Paul draws together different and even *competing* concepts of God into one vivid and sustained argument.

I have now examined enough of the crucial Pauline passages to make some statements about Paul's use of cultic metaphors, and the direction of his spiritualizing strategy.

3.5 The Place of Cultic Formulas

Cultic formulas are not constantly reiterated in Paul's writings, nor are they ever given lengthy explication when they do occur. Rather, they occur at key moments, initiating narratives or summarizing them. Occasionally they seem out of place, but they are no more out of place than the pillars that hold up a building. For instance, the last line of Romans 4 is sometimes thought to be out of place, since it does not follow from the discussion of faith that precedes it. But Rom 4:25 ("was handed over to death for our trespasses") *does* follow from 3:21–26, and *that* passage itself is the answer to all of what precedes it.

The bulk of Romans 4 speaks only of the *necessity* and *lineage* of faith, saying nothing about the desired content of Christian faith. But in the last two verses of the chapter, Paul provides the content of faith, the reasons for Christ's death and resurrection. Those perplexed by v. 25 have often overlooked the transitional role played by v. 24. In the latter, Paul explains that the words about crediting righteousness to the believing Abraham were not intended for him alone, but "for our" sake also, if we "believe in him who raised Jesus our

---

[182] E. P. Sanders makes much of this fulfillment (*Paul, the Law, and the Jewish People* [Minneapolis: Fortress, 1983], 113).

Lord from the dead." So it is not surprising that the next verse should say more about what is to be believed. In v. 25, "for" (διά) is used in two different ways: He "was put to death for our trespasses" indicates causation, and probably implies penal substitution.[183] The second "for" shows purpose or fulfillment: he was raised *in order* to bring about our justification, thus answering the problem of sin raised by the first three chapters of Romans.

Other cultic formulas in Romans plug in various foundational elements of the atonement doctrine. They are the doctrinal bedrock upon which the rest of Paul's argument rests, and are often uttered in passing, in brief clauses: "since we are justified by faith" (Rom 5:1). This does not mean the cultic formulas are unrelated to the content of Paul's longer arguments, rather they are the tent-pegs that hold his more extended arguments together. His discussion of spirit, flesh, and suffering in Romans 8 is pinned at one end to the fact that God sent his Son in the flesh and there "condemned sin in the flesh" (v. 3), and at the other end to the statement that God gave up his Son "for all of us" (v. 32). These statements show the gravity of the flesh-Spirit battle: it necessitated the killing of God's own Son, but by that act, flesh and sin were defeated.

The doctrinal tent pegs of Paul's gospel concern the promise to Abraham and the Christ who fulfilled it, who was handed over for human transgressions, taking on the judgment that flesh and sin deserved, and then was raised up by God, leading the way for others. These are the things that believers need to "confess" and "believe," if they would "be saved" (Rom 10:9). The content of what is confessed and believed is conveyed through soteriological formulas.

"Faith" signifies both trust in God, *and* the belief that the sacrificial death of the Messiah brings justification and rescue: "We are justified by faith . . . through our Lord Jesus Christ, through whom we have obtained access to this grace in which we stand" (Rom 5:1–2). *Access* is cultic;[184] the word is προσαγωγή, a noun cognate to the verb for offering sacrifice in Lev 7:8 and Sir 34:20. To make that access possible, "Christ died for the ungodly" (Rom 5:6). This death is *cultically and judicially effective*. The spilt blood leads to judicial rectification, and aversion of God's wrath: "Now that we have been have been justified by his blood, will we be saved through him from the wrath of God" (5:9)

Paul also uses cultic images to describe a number of things other than the saving action. At least five terms signal the thoroughly cultic nature of Rom 15:16. Paul describes himself as a "minister (λειτουργόν[185]) of Christ Jesus to

---

[183] Theoretically, it could simply mean that human sin *caused* his death, but, given that he died *for the ungodly* (5:6–8), penal substitution is likely intended.

[184] This is challenged, but not utterly rejected, by Dunn, *Romans 1–8*, 247–48.

[185] Philo used this for heavenly (*Virt.* 74) and for earthly priestly servants (*Leg.* 3.135).

the Gentiles in the priestly service (ἱερουργοῦντα[186]) of the gospel, so that the offering (ἡ προσφορὰ) of the Gentiles "may be acceptable (εὐπρόσδεκτος), sanctified (ἡγιασμένη) by the Holy Spirit." Paul has an affection for the verb ἁγιάζω and its related nouns to refer to the need to be fit for membership in the community.[187] Ethical requirements are sometimes expressed as purity requirements; temple, Passover, and cleansing imagery is used to recommend moral purity (1 Cor 6:15–20; 5:7; 2 Cor 7:1). Ethical and ritual preparedness for the eucharist is paramount.[188] In Phil 2:15, believers are to be "without blemish" (ἄμωμος[189]).

In Rom 15:31, Paul makes himself an offering; in v. 16 the Gentiles are offered, elsewhere in Paul's literature Christ is offered. A metaphor need not have the same reference in each case; "first fruits" can refer to converts, to Christ, or to the Holy Spirit (1 Cor 16:15; 15:20; Rom 8:23). Neyrey finds that Paul uses common purity words over seventy times.[190]

Paul himself is "being poured out as a libation over the sacrifice (θυσίᾳ) and the offering of your faith" (Phil 2:17), and their gifts to him are also "a fragrant offering, a sacrifice acceptable and pleasing to God" (Phil 4:18).[191] Christians are Christ's "aroma" in 2 Cor 2:15. Paul can turn to cultic models to express an apostle's self-giving behavior and endurance of suffering, the holy character of Christians, foretastes of further experiences with the Spirit, and numerous other things. Whether or not this means that Paul's thinking is "fundamentally cultic,"[192] is a matter requiring analysis. It cannot simply be assumed, due to his use of cultic metaphors.

It is now time to examine the question of what kinds of "substitution" are stated or implied in Paul's metaphors.

---

[186] "perform the work of a priest . . . consistently in Philo and Josephus" (Dunn, *Theology*, 546).

[187] Rom 15:16; 1 Cor 6:11; 7:14; 1 Thess 5:23; Acts 20:28; cf. Lev 13:2; Num 3:12; 8:17; Ezek 37:28; Newton, *Concept of Purity*, 73.

[188] Frances M. Young, *The Use of Sacrificial Ideas in Greek Christian Writers from the New Testament to John Chrysostom* (Cambridge, Mass.: Philadelphia Patristic Foundation, 1979), 241.

[189] Exod 29:1, 42, and other Pentateuch cultic passages; Newton, *Concept of Purity*, 84–85.

[190] Neyrey, *Paul, in Other*, 54–55. Unlike Neyrey, I am counting examples only from the seven "undisputed" letters. This includes 50 instances from the *hagnos/hagiazo* group, ten *kathar*-words, and another ten words meaning spotless or blameless.

[191] On the technical sacrificial terms: Daly, *Origins*, 63.

[192] Renwick, *Paul, the Temple*, 74.

4.
Redemption and Substitution

This chapter involves a more comprehensive look at Paul's soteriological metaphors than previous chapters. After some more background investigation, it becomes possible to assay a coherent account of the soteriology expressed through the metaphors.

The cultic metaphors describe the death of Christ as a saving transaction. The beneficial *aftereffects* are depicted with *social* metaphors: justification (a judicial metaphor), redemption (an economic concept), reconciliation (summoning up the realms of personal and political relationships), and adoption (a legal procedure for designating a non-descendant an heir).

The judicial metaphor often implies a kind of penal substitution. Redemption involves not a penal but a monetary substitution; it can be a ransom payment, a purchase of slaves, or restitution. The latter is the significance of the אָשָׁם sacrifice, and of the restitutionary payment associated with it; God has been slighted, that is, temple property has been misappropriated, and the redemption-payment restores what is God's. The picture is further complicated by the metaphorical appropriation of these transactions. Penal substitution and the אָשָׁם both occur in the enigmatic chapter Isaiah 53 in the Hebrew, with the restitutionary sacrifice being changed to the purification sacrifice (περὶ ἁμαρτίας, v. 10) in the LXX. Paul seems to have blended penal and restitutionary substitution in his development of what we now call the doctrine of atonement.

In chapters one and two, I argued that various different kinds of substitution are present in sacrifice, but are not clearly spelled out in the texts. The main substitutionary theme in Hebrew sacrifice was economic and restitutionary. It will not do to be dogmatic and to insist that there were no penal ideas in Hebrew sacrifice, but it is true that the clear expressions of this idea are all late (rabbinic). More frequently the sacrificial animal was seen as a kind of gift or payment; after all, it is an item of significant economic value, as are the grain offerings. In the mind of a theologian, however, these two very different kinds of substitution (economic and penal) can be conflated, and we see this happening both in Paul's usage and in subsequent Christian atonement doctrines. Paul does it by adding the penal notion to either the sacrificial or the scapegoat image, as we will see.

I will begin with the key term for redemption in Paul, take a look at substitutionary themes in Romans 5 to 8, move on to substitutionary themes in Isaiah 53 and their usage by Paul, then assess an interpretation that understands Jesus to have "taken our place" in a cultic but non-substitutionary way.

4.1 The Usage of ἀπολύτρωσις in Romans 3

One of the crucial metaphors crammed into the dense passage in Rom 3:24–26 is "redemption," fundamentally an economic metaphor, but one that easily conflates with the sacrificial one.

4.1.1 Lexical Background

A key term in Rom 3:24 is ἀπολύτρωσις. Warfield's analysis of this word group is a good place to start. The various words from the λυτρο word group all indicate an idea of releasing. Λυτρόω in the active voice means to release upon payment of ransom, while in the middle voice it means to *secure* someone's release by making that payment.[1] The noun λύτρον denotes "means of deliverance," "ransom," or, occasionally, means of expiation. Λυτρόω became the specific term for ransoming,[2] and the particular form ἀπολύτρωσις in Jewish literature designates "ransoming a captive or prisoner of war from slavery."[3] But by Paul's time this term was more often used for the purchase or manumission of slaves.[4]

Confirming much of Warfield's research, Hill indicates that the middle voice verb (λύομαι) means to buy the freedom of a captive or slave; "ransom" or "release" is the consistent meaning of λύτρωσις throughout Greek literature; in the Bible, however, there is a change of emphasis away from the *means* of delivery and toward the *fact* of deliverance.[5] The Hebrew term ancestral to λύτρωσις (גָּאַל), underwent a development of meaning in Jewish thought. Although גָּאַל meant "ransoming" in the Pentateuch, in the prophets and Psalms "the idea of ransom falls into the background," and the term came

---

[1] B. Benjamin Warfield, "The New Testament Terminology of 'Redemption,'" *Princeton Theological Review* 15 (1917): 202–03.

[2] Warfield, "New Testament Terminology," 206, 208.

[3] Dunn, *Romans 1–8*, 169.

[4] Hill, *Greek Words*, 76.

[5] Hill, *Greek Words*, 49–52; cf. 58–59.

to mean a more general "deliverance, release."[6] This development is accelerated in the course of the Septuagint's composition, where λύτρον-words become soteriological terms for God's deliverance of the Jews from Egypt[7] or more generally, for rescuing the faithful.[8] Most instances of λυτρόω outside the Pentateuch refer to deliverance, with no notion of a payment; in 2 Macc 7:24; *4 Macc.* 8:4 and many Psalms, the focus is on "deliverance rather than on the particular method of gaining release."[9]

Hill stresses this point repeatedly, finding instances where "there is no suggestion of paying a ransom" (Ps 136:24; Lam 5:8); "there is no idea of a price" (Eph 4:30).[10] But he overstates his case, determined to distance the λύτρον words from their etymology, perhaps in reaction to Morris, who stresses: "Both inside and outside the New Testament writings the payment of a price is a necessary component of the redemption idea."[11] The truth is probably between the two positions: in the older period, the resonance of payment is preserved, even in figurative usages; with time, this specific meaning fades and the general idea of rescue grows, as often happens with nouns in any language (evolution from specific to general). Still, the *resonance* of λυτρόω includes the image of captive-ransoming or slave-releasing, just as the notion of payment is still part of the resonance of the English term "redemption."

The nouns of this word-group (including ἀπολύτρωσις) are commonly used in the NT epistles[12] to describe the saving death of Christ, but the only place they are used that way in the gospels is in the "ransom saying" (Mark 10:45). This Markan passage has parallels in the other Synoptics, but only in Matt 20:28 does the λύτρον clause occur: "to give his life a ransom for many"; this summarizing statement is not present in Luke, indicating it may be redacted. The intent of these passage is to state that the Son of Man came to serve others: "I am among you as one who serves" (Luke 22:27), an idea present in all three gospels. Mark (or a redactor), followed by Matthew, assimilates this idea to the concept of Jesus' death as redemption. Luke likely retains the earlier version of this saying, which emphasizes service but does not describe Jesus' death as a ransom payment. Ransom/redemption is a major NT theme only in the epistles and Revelation; it is out of place in the gospels.

---

[6] Hill, *Greek Words*, 55.
[7] Deut 7:8; Ps 136:24; Isa 43:1; 52:3.
[8] Ps 32:7; 130:7–8; Isa 41:14.
[9] Hill, *Greek Words*, 58–59.
[10] Hill, *Greek Words*, 63.
[11] Morris, *Apostolic Preaching*, 61.
[12] Rom 3:24; 1 Cor 1:30; Col 1:14; Eph 1:7, 14; 4:30; Tit 2:14; Heb 9:12, 15. In Luke 1:68; 2:38; 21:28; 24:21, however, λυτρ-words signify eschatological salvation, without reference to Jesus' death.

4.1.2 Paul's Usage

Since Paul uses ἀγοράζω purchase-words in soteriological metaphors four times (ἀγοράζω in 1 Cor 6:20; 7:23 and ἐξαγοράζω in Gal 3:13; 4:5), it is quite likely that ἀπολύτρωσις in Rom 3:24 has resonances of purchase. Fully consistent with these usages is Acts 20:28, where Paul is said to proclaim that Christ acquired or obtained (περιεποιήσατο) the church with his blood. Based on the OT usage of this word to refer to God delivering his people (Isa 31:5; 43:21), "my special possession" (Mal 3:17),[13] Lyonnet concedes that in 1 Cor 7:23 Paul "had the Greek notion in mind ... the price," although the main referent is the "purchase" of Israel through the covenant at Sinai.[14] He admits that ἀγοράζω "in itself has no connection with the O.T.," but he tries to create such a connection on the basis of the vicinity of remarks in Rev 5:9–10: a "purchased people"[15] (ἀγοράζω) in v. 9 and a quotation of Exod 19:6 in v. 10. This fails, however, to turn ἀγοράζω into a Septuagintal word.

Dale Martin argues: "*Agorazein* refers ... to the ordinary sale of a slave by one owner to another owner."[16] The slave gets a new and better owner in Christ. This would be a powerful rhetorical device in preaching to slaves or freedmen; to move up to Christ's house would be a tremendous advance. Martin shows how "slave of Christ .... could be understood as a positive metaphor for salvation as social mobility and power by association."[17] Martin has made a strong case for a Greco-Roman, rather than a biblical, background to ἀγοράζω. It seems sensible to award ἀγοράζω to Martin, and περιποιέω to Lyonnet, which gives us a non-biblical and a biblical word, respectively. Ἀπολύτρωσις, however, has strong backgrounds in both Jewish and Gentile texts.

Slave-purchase and manumission are the main meanings of ἀπολύτρωσις.[18] There may be ritual overtones to slave-purchase. Deissmann described a process in Hellenistic cultures of ritualized manumission of slaves who were able to come up with the price of their redemption. A priest oversaw the ritual whereby the slave was ritually sold to a god; "the slave in fact redeemed himself, and the deity only appeared as the fictitious purchaser."[19]

---

[13] Lyonnet, "Terminology," 111, 113.

[14] Lyonnet, "Terminology," 115.

[15] Lyonnet, "Terminology," 114.

[16] Dale Martin, *Slavery As Salvation: the Metaphor of Slavery in Pauline Christianity* (New Haven, Conn.: Yale University Press, 1990), 63.

[17] Martin, *Slavery*, 68. And to be a *freedperson* of Christ was even a higher status (67).

[18] Hooker, *Not Ashamed*, 26.

[19] Ridderbos, *Paul*, 193; summarizing Deissmann in *Licht vom Osten*, 322–34; cf. Campbell, *Rhetoric of Righteousness*, 104 n.2.

This view has frequently been challenged by those who say that Deissmann's examples are few and are distant from the biblical tradition.[20] But his evidence does show that sacred manumission is one of the known referents of ἀπολύτρωσις. Paul could be alluding to this ritual, or to the Jewish ritual whereby one redeemed oneself for owning an ox who gores someone to death.[21] The four main meanings of the term, then, are hostage-ransoming, slave-manumission, reparation for ox-goring, and rescue from slavery in Egypt.

Most of this is accepted by Hill, but he is so eager to deny that the NT teaches "the ransom theory" of atonement[22]—Christ's death as a ransom-payment—that he tries to sever the connection of ἀπολύτρωσις with its etymology and with its primary meaning in both biblical and nonbiblical Greek. Certainly the fully developed medieval ransom theory is not found in the NT, but the ideas that led to it *are* present in the repeated refrain "you have been bought with a price" (1 Cor 6:20; 7:23; cf. Acts 20:28). Even if we could rescue ἀπολύτρωσις from associations with purchase, how would we rescue the frankly economic terms ἀγοράζω and ἐξαγοράζω from those associations? Hill fails to sever completely these NT terms from the notion of purchase, and so fails to distance Paul utterly from the ransom idea of atonement.

Sanday and Headlam support Hill's remarks about the LXX but not about the NT. They say "there is no question of ransom" in the deliverance-passages in the Septuagint, but they see clear overtones of ransoming in Mark 10:45 and 1 Tim 2:6, "and in view also of the many passages in which Christians are said to be 'bought' or 'bought with a price' (1 Cor. vi.20, vii.23; Gal. iii.13; 2 Pet. ii.1; Rev. v.9 ... 1 Pet. i.18, 19), we can hardly resist the conclusion that the idea of the λύτρον retains its full force."[23] This is exegetically sound.

Balanced scholarship preserves both the ancient and the evolved meanings of ἀπολύτρωσις: Lightfoot wrote of "a price paid ... a deliverance thereby obtained."[24] Wright allows that "redemption ... evokes the slave-market [but] more fundamental by far, for a Jew, was the historical slave market of Egypt."[25]

However, for those Gentiles in Paul's audience who were literally slaves or ex-slaves, the association with manumission would be more evocative than the biblical association. The fact that Paul finds it necessary to instruct the Gentiles

---

[20] Lyonnet, "Terminology," 104–11.
[21] Ridderbos favors the latter (*Paul*, 194).
[22] *Greek Words*, 70–76, 81.
[23] Sanday and Headlam, *The Epistle to the Romans*, 86.
[24] J. B. Lightfoot, *Notes on Epistles of St. Paul from Unpublished Commentaries* (London: Macmillan, 1895), 271.
[25] N. T. Wright, "Romans and the Theology of Paul," in *Pauline Theology, vol. III: Romans*, eds. David M. Hay and E. Elizabeth Johnson (Minneapolis, Fortress, 1995), 38.

not to disrespect Jews[26] indicates the presence of both in the congregation. This image of "redemption," then, could be interpreted one way by Gentile and another way by Jewish believers. Again we find Paul using a term that can be understood in valuable—but different—ways by Gentile and Jewish Christians. Presumably some readers would understand both connotations.

By saying that the redemption is in Christ Jesus, who is put forward as ἱλαστήριον, Paul links these two metaphors, equating two different kinds of transaction (economic and sacrificial), and so rejoining ideas that were originally related in Hebrew. *Kipper* (atonement) is cognate with *kopher*, which means "payment for the redemption of forfeited life .... atonement by the payment of a sum of money."[27]

Breytenbach resists these conclusions, claiming that the relationship between *kipper* and *kopher* is unclear,[28] but many OT examples show that both words describe a type of exchange. Many scholars see a clear relationship between payment and *kippering*.[29] Milgrom says ransom is the "undisputed" meaning of *kofer*, and "there exists a strong possibility that all texts which assign to *kipper* the function of averting God's wrath have *kofer* in mind."[30] Purchase is present whether the main image behind ἀπολύτρωσις is Israel-redemption or Greco-Roman slave-purchase, or whether redemption is interpreted as a kind of sacrifice. But a purely biblical explanation is unable to account for the market word (ἐξ)ἀγοράζω. It is not possible to keep the Greco-Roman world out of Paul's letters.

It bears repeating that, for Paul, salvation is not free. Paul sometimes emphasizes the act of purchasing, and other times the new status of the redeemed people, but always there is this *transaction* at the heart of salvation. The transactional nature of captive-ransoming or slave-purchasing is easily conflated with the transactional nature of sacrifice, which resembles a tribute-payment to God.

The crucial ideas of justification, redemption, and atonement are chained together in Rom 3:24–25. We are justified *through* (διά) the redemption that is in the person who was put forward as the place of atonement. The economic model of redeeming is linked with the sacrificial model of *performing a ritual* to deal with the effects of sin. Both are transactions where something is done

---

[26] Rom 11:1, 28–31.

[27] Morris, *Apostolic Preaching*, 161–62; cf. Exod 32:30; Num 31:50.

[28] Cilliers Breytenbach, *Versöhnung: Eine Studie zur paulinischen Soteriologie* (WMANT 60; Düsseldorf: Neukirchener Verlag, 1989), 91–92.

[29] Gorman, *Ideology*, 184; Brichto, "On Slaughter," 34; Schenker, *Versöhnung und Sühne*, 55–59.

[30] Milgrom, "Kipper," 1040.

and something is expected in return from the deity. The person who "paid the price" in these arrangements is Christ,[31] not the believer. For the believer, justification is "by his grace as a gift" (Rom 3:24a). Because he paid nothing, the believer is deeply indebted to the one who did.

The notion of indebtedness to God and Christ supplies an essential part of the rhetorical force of redemption passages. Christ has not "died for nothing," but he obtained life for Paul when he "gave himself for me" (Gal 2:20). Paul owes his life to Christ. There is a serious price to pay if any believer does not appreciate what was done for him, does not "proclaim the Lord's death" in the Eucharist (1 Cor 11:26).

Substitutionary ideas underlie many of Paul's cultic and redemption metaphors. Different concepts of substitution, however, are involved. In redemption, *payment* is substituted for a life. The scapegoat is not a substitute, but it bears away an affliction that had belonged to others. Sacrifice has been interpreted numerous different ways both by participants and by scholars; it has been understood as a payment, a gift, a means of purification, and sometimes as a penal substitute, and one can detect signs of these in Paul.

However, it is misleading to speak of a common "substitutionary" meaning. Purchasing or ransoming involves an exchange of items or persons considered to be of equal worth; it is therefore substitution as trade. Sacrifice sometimes is seen this way, sometimes is exalted to the idea of a gift, and sometimes signifies substitution of one identity for a symbolically equivalent identity, which is *abstract* substitution, and can be called "penal" if the element of judicial penalty is present, as it is in Rom 8:3.

However, the wrath of God does not necessarily mean a judicial setting; death is threatened, but not necessarily a *judicial* death. A widespread theme in religions is the need to avert a deity's *personal* wrath, devoid of judicial implications, as seen in the occasional outbursts of Agni and Indra in the sacrificial Vedic texts, and in the story of God's attempt to kill Moses (Exod 4:24–26).

4.2 New Identity in Sonship

The result of being ransomed is that one becomes the property of the master who made the payment. In Paul's teaching, one even becomes an heir of the new master, being adopted as a son, thus becoming "Abraham's offspring" (Gal 3:29) and "heirs of God" (Rom 8:17). This sonship is not inherent, but is purchased for the believer. Paul would probably not have uttered the sentiment attributed to him in Acts 17:28, telling the Athenians that, "we too are his offspring," because this implies that all people are inherently the children of

---

[31] Cf. Marshall, "Development of the Concept," 163, 165.

God, but sonship, for Paul, is not the discovery of an inherited condition but comes with acceptance of a divine grant, and is conditional upon our believing in the divine Son who adopts us (Gal 3:26; Rom 8:14), and upon sharing in His sufferings (Rom 8:17). Thus does the Son become "the firstborn within a large family" (Rom 8:29).

All of this is a *new* identity, not the discovery of an existing identity; something had to happen to enable it to take place. In Hellenistic societies, υἱοθεσία is the term for legal adoption[32] of someone who is not a natural son: the perfect metaphor for Paul's concept of salvation as an event that legally changes one's status and identity. This change was necessary for Jews as well as Gentiles, although it can be conceded that adoption was particularly meaningful for Gentiles, who were being grafted into the prestigious line of Abraham. Parentage and lineage were crucial for status in the ancient world.[33]

Adoption can be linked with other metaphors. In Gal 4:5 redemption leads to adoption, and in Rom 8:23 adoption is identified with the (future) redemption of the body. It is likely that an Exodus image ties together adoption and redemption in Galatians 4, recalling God's redeeming Israel from Egypt, and adopting them as sons.[34]

The cultic, redemption, and adoption metaphors describe how God changed the status of humans from impure to pure, slave to free, and servant to son. Adoption is somewhat different than the other models because it is focused on the believer's experience, more than on the cross-event. The *change* experienced by the believer is crucial; *conversion* is central to the Pauline message. Christians have experienced and interpreted conversion largely under the tutelage of Paul.

4.3 Substitution and Aqedah Themes in Romans 5–8

The middle chapters of Romans are saturated with substitutionary and cultic themes. In chap. 5, the substitutionary death of Christ saves sinful humanity and propitiates God ("saved through him from the wrath"—v. 9) or reconciles us to God (v. 10). For Paul, these are the same transaction; he is not seeking rigid logical consistency, but metaphors with the most explanatory power. In these verses, he describes it two ways: in v. 9—having been acquitted by Christ's sacrificial death ("blood"), we will be delivered from the divine wrath; in v. 10—we were reconciled to God by this death, and we will

---

[32] James M. Scott, *Adoption As Sons of God: An Exegetical Investigation into the Background of ΥΙΟΘΕΣΙΑ in the Pauline Corpus*. WUNT 2, Reihe 48 (Tübingen: J. C. B. Mohr, 1992), 52–56.

[33] Stowers, *Rereading*, 229.

[34] Scott, *Adoption*, 172–73.

saved by—or *in*—Christ's life, ἐν τῇ ζωῇ αὐτοῦ. (Resurrected, he is alive *now*.) The logic in 5:9 is sacrificial, with an assist from the juridical. In v. 10 the logic is participatory, with his death bringing reconciliation (probably also a sacrificial image) and his life bringing life. The death seems to accomplish a kind of sacrificial payment, in that it averts God's wrath and accomplishes reconciliation.

In Rom 5:12–19 escape from condemnation is restated in terms of human participation in the two Adams: sin entered through the first Adam, death ruled over all, then the "gift" of Jesus' obedience overflowed with acquittal for all. There is a mystical participation of the whole race in the deeds of the Adam(s): as goes the "one," so go the "many" (5:16–19). The representative carries many in his wake.

Joining in the representative Second Adam continues in Romans 6, where Paul describes believers' participation in the death and resurrection of Christ (vv. 3–8). He twice (vv. 3–4) states that the Christian rite of baptism stands for dying with Christ, and then restates this as "dying" or being "crucified with him" in vv. 5–8. He had expressed the saving event with a cultic metaphor; now he inserts believers into the metaphor!—explaining that the Christian cult means participation in the life and resurrection of Christ.[35] The motif of ownership-transference occurs in vv. 11–23: believers are now owned by "righteousness" not "sin"; they are "slaves of God."

Ineffective and corrupted servitude is the theme of Romans 7: the law is spiritual, but sin and sensuality ("sinful passions . . . flesh sold into slavery . . . no good dwells in my flesh . . . at war . . . this body of death" vv. 5, 14, 18, 23, 24) prevented me from serving it properly. Servitude continues through chap. 8, even when the terminology of adoption predominates; adoption, in Roman society, means turning a servant into an heir. So sonship with God is not natural, but is legally conferred. And, once again, we note that salvation requires a transaction that brings about a change of status.

A judicial setting is implied by Paul's remarks in 8:27 that the Spirit *intercedes* for believers (so no charges can stick), and that the Son was "g[iven] up for all of us," and that *he* intercedes for us, so no one can "condemn" us any longer (8:32, 34). Some condemnation is still present, or at least potentially so, if intercession is necessary. So even when Paul is emphasizing the pardon from God, his judicial metaphor arouses the image of condemnation.

In sum, all of the soteriological images in these chapters of Romans entail either the aversion of judicial condemnation (mainly in chaps. 5 and 8), or the

---

[35] The idea of participation in the Savior's suffering distinguishes Paul's writings from his successors'. Stressing conformity and "sound doctrine" (1 Tim 1:10; 2:11; 4:6; 2 Tim 1:13; 2:23; 4:3; Tit 1:9; 2:1–9) is deutero-Pauline.

transfer from one owner's domain to another's, which involves *participation* in the new owner (chaps. 6–7). The lord-judge of a domain is implicit in the aversion of God's anger in Rom 5:9. It is now righteousness that shall "exercise dominion" (5:17); we lived with sin, but now we live with Christ (6:7–8); you are now under grace (6:14); "enslaved to God" (6:22); "in a new service, that of the spirit" (7:6 NJB).

The presumption of judicial condemnation and of substitution underlies chap. 8. Sinful flesh had to be condemned by God, for the flesh subverted the law, and "the mind that is set on the flesh is hostile to God" (8:3, 7). The Son was "given up" for humans, and intercedes for humans (8:32–34), which presumes that *someone* had to be given up for punishment, and that intercession is *still necessary* to avert punishment. The image in Rom 8:32 clearly uses the Aqedah as a model; God not sparing his son (τοῦ ἰδίου τοῦ υἱοῦ οὐκ ἐφείσατο) alludes to the Septuagint's οὐκ ἐφείσω τοῦ υἱοῦ σου τοῦ ἀγαπητοῦ (Gen 22:12b). This is not unprecedented. First- and second-century Jewish writings speak of "the sacrifice of Isaac" (one would expect "near-sacrifice"). Isaac was thought of by some Jews as the prototypical martyr, someone who dies or nearly dies in demonstration of his piety. The *Liber Antiquitatum Biblicarum* of Pseudo-Philo compares Isaac with the lamb that replaced him on the altar, and has God saying, "his sacrifice was well pleasing to me, and on the basis of his blood I chose these people."[36] The benefit effect of Isaac's self-sacrifice extends to all humanity.[37]

There are widely divergent positions on the possible presence of Aqedah themes in Paul. Schoeps goes so far as to say Paul's doctrine "cannot be fully understood apart from a tacit reference to the Aqedath."[38] He argued that "the atoning character of the Aqedath (Gen. 22:9; binding) of Isaac stood out clearly in the mind of the sometime Pharisee when he was preparing himself to develop the doctrine of the Messianic sacrificial death."[39] He finds the Aqedah in the sacrificial metaphors in 1 Cor 5:7 and Rom 5:9. However, the dating of many of Schoeps's Aqedah texts, particularly the Targums, is disputed.

Daly relies upon Schoeps in asserting that theologizing about the Aqedah (particularly in the Targums[40]) provided a basis for NT soteriology. Daly makes a dubious case when he draws up a long list of "certain," "probable," and

---

[36] *LAB* 18.5; translation by Hengel, *Atonement*, 62.
[37] Hayward, *Jewish Temple*, 185; *LAB* 32.3–4.
[38] Hans-Joachim Schoeps, *Paul: the Theology of the Apostle in the Light of Jewish Religious History* (London: Lutterworth, 1961), 148.
[39] Schoeps, *Paul*, 142; cherished in Jewish interpretations "at all periods" (147).
[40] Robert J. Daly, "The Soteriological Significance of the Sacrifice of Isaac," *CBQ* 39 (1977): 65.

"possible" allusions to the Aqedah, but many of them are little more than references to Abraham's faith[41] or to God's faithfulness. Daly is honest enough to admit (though with surprise) that the Aqedah does not "play a particularly prominent part in the NT."[42] Thus he is his own best critic: the Aqedah is not the "direct model . . . for Pauline soteriology [but] part of the background."[43]

I would share this moderate conclusion of Daly, but not his contradictory conclusion that Aqedah was the dominant soteriological metaphor in the NT. However, I wish to distance myself from the uncharitable and extreme critique of Davies and Chilton, who dogmatically reject all of Daly's points. For instance, they note that "*Barnabas* replies to Aqedah atonement with Christ atonement; not Isaac, but Jesus takes the place of sacrifice,"[44] but they seem not to notice that even such an oppositional comparison constitutes a re-usage of the Aqedah image. Their arguments against a pre-NT date for *any* interpretation of the Aqedah as atoning, are justly characterized as "poor" by Campbell.[45] Campbell sees Paul finding certain Aqedah themes useful: the *love* of the father for his son,[46] Isaac's "descent into suffering,"[47] "the death of the first-born son."[48] (Even though Isaac is not killed in Genesis 22, Jewish interpretation often treats the story as though Isaac had died.)

Still, the argument for the Aqedah as a *dominant* Pauline or Christian metaphor can hardly be sustained when one finds that it is clearly referred to in only three places in the NT—Rom 8:32; Heb 11:17; James 2:21. Rather, it is one among many substitutionary and sacrificial motifs used by Paul[49] (and others). Paul is not wedded to any one of these motifs, but is deeply committed to understanding the death of Christ as a cosmic transaction that can be compared to a ransoming, a curse-bearing, or a cultic death. The Aqedah was frequently interpreted under the latter category, and Paul was willing to use it,

---

[41] Such as Rom 4:16–25; Gal 3:13–14; Daly, "Soteriological," 72.

[42] Daly, "Soteriological," 66.

[43] Daly, "Soteriological," 74.

[44] P. R. Davies and B. D. Chilton, "The Aqedah: A Revised Tradition History," *CBQ* 40 (1978): 538.

[45] But the DSS show such an interpretation (Douglas A. Campbell, "The Story of Jesus in Romans and Galatians," in *Narrative Dynamics in Paul: A Critical Assessment*, ed. Bruce W. Longenecker [Louisville, Ky.: Westminster John Knox, 2002], 114 n.24).

[46] Campbell, "The Story," 115–16.

[47] Campbell, "The Story," 123.

[48] Campbell, "The Story," 117 n.34, referring to Levenson, *Death Beloved Son*.

[49] As says Nils Dahl, "The Atonement—an adequate reward for the Akedah? (Rom 8:32)," in *Neotestamentica et Semitica: Studies in Honour of Matthew Black*, eds. E. Ellis and Max Wilcox (Edinburgh: T&T Clark, 1969), 24–26.

probably (in his sermons) describing Isaac as a type of Christ, foretelling the Messiah's fate.

Paul is drawn to cultic metaphors, whether making a soteriological point, as in Rom 8:32, or a purely ecclesial point, as in 1 Cor 5:5. But it is also a fact that he is worried about some of the possible implications of his metaphors, and moves to correct potential misapprehension of God as cruel. After the judicial and sacrificial imagery of Rom 8:1–34, he gives a moving testimony to the certainty of God's loving care, where God sounds more like a loving parent than a judge. Paul's reach exceeds his grasp here; that is, his feeling for God's parental love exceeds the actual logic of substitution and atonement that informs his soteriology.

Like Second Isaiah, Paul is reaching to express a high concept of God's compassion, as exemplified by a particular individual (the Suffering Servant in Isaiah; Jesus in Paul), and like Second Isaiah, he expresses the idea of selfless surrender through a sacrificial or scapegoat metaphor, not in order to imply a capricious or sacrifice-demanding deity, but a loving one, who will go to any lengths to save wretched humanity.

Although Paul wants to emphasize the generosity and grace of God, he lets slip some remarks that envision God as either accuser or judge, entailed in the continuing need for the Son and Spirit to act as intercessors.

4.4 Notions of Representation and Substitution in Isaiah 53

There is a distinct possibility that some of Paul's notions of what Jesus underwent for others and accomplished by way of vicarious suffering, come from Isaiah 53. Many have noticed the occurrence three times in Isaiah 53 of παραδίδωμι (vv. 6, 12 bis), a word that is of paramount importance in the NT, meaning "handing over," either in the sense of "betrayal" or of "transmitting tradition" (Matt 11:27; John 13:11; Rom 1:24–28; 4:25; 8:32; 1 Cor 11:2 bis, 23; 15:3). Romans 4:25 (παρεδόθη διὰ τὰ παραπτώματα ἡμῶν) certainly looks like a quotation of Isa 53:12 (διὰ τὰς ἁμαρτίας αὐτῶν παρεδόθη).[50]

Some have seen Paul's remark that God "made him sin" in 2 Cor 5:21 relying on "the Lord has laid on him the iniquity of us all" (53:6).[51] The many being made righteous in Rom 5:19 is said to rely on the many being accounted righteous in Isa 53:11,[52] with some lexical parallels (Isaiah: δικαιῶσαι ... πολλοῖς; Romans: δίκαιοι ... οἱ πολλοί).

---

[50] Dunn, *Romans 1–8*, 241; Schoeps, *Paul*, 136.

[51] Victor Paul Furnish, *Second Corinthians*. AB 32A (New York: Doubleday, 1984), 351; Oscar Cullmann, *The Christology of the New Testament* (London: SCM, 1959), 76.

[52] Cullmann, *Christology*, 77.

Cullmann has astutely pointed out that the Suffering Servant idea seems to have been the basis of *Peter*'s teaching: only four times is Jesus called *pais*, and Peter is either the speaker or an auditor, each time; further, the theme occurs at 1 Pet 2:21–24.[53] Paul is more restrained in his usage of Isaiah. He never calls Jesus a Servant, and he spends more time applying Isaiah's prophecies to the *church* than to the Messiah.[54]

The Fourth Servant Song in Isaiah 52–53 has many conceptual links with early Christian (not just Pauline) teaching, including "good news" (52:7b), vindication of the just (52:13), and universalism ("all the ends of the earth shall see the salvation of our God," 52:10b; cf. v. 15). Chapter 53 has a heightened interpretation of suffering, from 1) vicarious suffering, that is, suffering *due to* the sin of others; to 2) penal substitution, actually *taking on* the punishment that is meant for someone else; to 3) suffering that has a healing effect on others, with this sometimes being expressed as 4) sin-bearing, carrying away. The Servant "has borne (נָשָׂא, φέρω) our infirmities" (53:4), and was wounded *for* or *on account of* (מִן) or *because of* (διά plus accus. and ἀπό plus genitive; vv. 5, 8) the transgressions of others. By themselves, these could indicate simply *result*, an accidental over-spilling of misfortune rather than a substitutionary punishment-bearing, were it not for the remarks of vv. 6 and 11 that the iniquity of others was laid on the Servant, and of v. 5 that "upon him was the punishment that made us whole." Thus, some sentences that otherwise might indicate chance suffering, take on the coloration of punishment-bearing.

The possibility that redemption (an economic substitution) is more to the fore than penal substitution must be considered, since he made himself an אָשָׁם (v. 10), a sacrifice that is paralleled with payment,[55] and even the "intercession" of v. 12c could be economic, but the repeated mentions of transgression-bearing and the one mention of punishment-bearing, definitely suggest a judicial/penal setting.

The Septuagint misidentifies the אָשָׁם as a sin-sacrifice, and changes to second person narrative: "if you give a sin sacrifice (περὶ ἁμαρτίας) your soul will see a long-lived seed." It is not clear what he intends to communicate by this half-verse, which is not clearly connected with the rest of the narrative. In any case, what is stressed in both Hebrew and Greek is the bearing of the burdens—and even the guilt—of others. The Servant does good to those who, apparently, are unappreciative and undeserving of it.

---

[53] Cullmann, *Christology*, 74. Of course, the notion is also present in Paul (Cullmann, 76–77).

[54] Hays, "Conversion of Imagination," 84–104.

[55] Milgrom, *Cult and Conscience*, 16; Levine, *Leviticus*, 18.

At the end of the chapter the element of sin-*bearing* is brought out, and Adela Collins insists that this "does not allude to the instructions for sacrifice but, rather, to . . . scapegoat."[56] However, a specific sacrifice is mentioned in v. 10, so a more sound conclusion is that the author of Isaiah 53 uses both sacrificial and scapegoat metaphors. In fact, Second Isaiah seems to conflate scapegoat and sacrificial themes: the Servant makes himself an אָשָׁם; he also bears away the punishment deserved by others.

What is the role of God in this Servant poem? Twice it is said that God caused the sufferings of the servant, and once (conversely) that we *thought* God caused them. I have listed these statements in italics in the right column below, and have used other typographic forms to set off other important themes:

verse	Text	themes
53:4	he has borne our infirmities . . . yet we accounted him stricken, struck down by God	vicarious suffering, *we thought God did it*
53:5	But he was wounded for our transgressions, crushed for our iniquities; upon him was the punishment that made us whole, and by his bruises we are healed.	vicarious suffering, PENAL SUBSTITUTION, healing effect
53:6b	the Lord has laid on him the iniquity of us all.	PENAL SUBSTITUTION/ sin-bearing, *God did it*
53:8–9	stricken for the transgression of my people. . . . made his grave with the wicked	Vicarious suffering, PENAL IMPLICATION
53:10	But the Lord was pleased to crush Him, putting *Him* to grief; If He would render Himself *as* a guilt offering, He will see *His* offspring, He will prolong *His* days. (NASB)[57]	*God did it*, PENAL IMPLICATION, guilt offering, vindication
53:11b	By His knowledge the Righteous One, My Servant, will justify many, As he will bear their iniquities. (NASB)	PENAL SUBSTITUTION/ sin-bearing, healing effect
53:12	he poured himself out to death, and . . . bore the sin of many, and made intercession for the transgressors.	PENAL SUBSTITUT./sin-bearing, healing effect

The theme of penal substitution is present in five or six of these verses. It probably serves a social and rhetorical function, rather than a dogmatic one: it is likely that Isaiah 53 was written by the followers of Second Isaiah after his death, and after they came to a chastened awareness of his suffering and of the significance of his life.[58]

---

[56] Collins, "Finding," 177.

[57] NAB and NRSV follow the Septuagint, but NASB follows the MT and thus, despite the distracting italics and capitalizations, is the most accurate.

[58] A viewpoint of H-J. Hermisson and B. Janowski, summarized by Daniel P. Bailey, "The Suffering Servant: Recent Tübingen Scholarship on Isaiah 53," in *Jesus and the Suffering Servant: Isaiah 53 and Christian Origins,* eds. William Bellinger Jr. and William Farmer (Harrisburg, Penn.: Trinity Press International, 1998), 254–55.

It would be equally difficult to argue that Paul based his teaching on this chapter (since only two passages, Rom 4:25; 5:19, seem to be clearly reliant on it), and to maintain that it had little or no effect on his teaching (when he may have taken important conceptual hints from it).

Isaiah 53 describes a man wounded and suffering for others, bringing healing to others (vv. 4–6), justification to many (v. 11). Paul's theology of suffering, if we can call it that, asks disciples to take a more active role. As they walk by faith, they must suffer with Christ. Only in such co-suffering is there salvation: "For while we live, we are always being given up to death for Jesus' sake, so that the life of Jesus may be made visible in our mortal flesh" (2 Cor 4:11). Suffering is a necessary aspect of choosing Christ and rejecting the present evil age.[59] This goes considerably further than Isaiah 53. There is active participation in the fate of the prophet/savior. The mark of genuine Pauline theology is this close bonding with the crucified savior, which makes one virtually an extension of Christ. Paul may get some of his ideas of heroic death from Isaiah, but his participationist notions cannot be found there.

"Penal substitution" does not quite do justice to this aspect of Paul's teaching, which might rather be denominated *redemptive co-suffering* with the Savior. This implies that believers somehow replicate what the Savior did in his redemptive death. This idea, apparently fraught with heretical or egotistical potentials, rapidly disappeared from Christian thought after Paul.

Further, the notion of a cultic solution is essential to Paul's message in a way that it is not to Isaiah's. Isaiah 53 turns a cultic image into a solution that is no longer cultic, but for Paul, the solution is fundamentally cultic. The אָשָׁם of Isaiah is a metaphor for a heroic life and death. The ἱλαστήριον or περὶ ἁμαρτίας or curse-bearer of Paul is God's *antitype* of the cult; it is the *new* cultic approach to God, and it is dramatized in the new cult. The pattern of expiation may operate in a new way, but it still obtains. Paul's gospel depends on cultic categories in a way that Isaiah's does not. One would not miss Isaiah's essential point if one did not know what an אָשָׁם was. One *would* miss Paul's point if one did not understand that salvation is brought about by a cultic act.

The idea of vicarious suffering became increasingly important in the centuries leading up to Paul's time, reflected in both *T. Benj.* 3:8; Wis 2:12–20; 5:1–7[60]; and in the Maccabean literature. Isaiah 53 was one of the sources drawn upon by these later writings; others will be mentioned in the next chapter.

---

[59] cf. Dunn, *Theology*, 487.
[60] Stuhlmacher, *Reconciliation, Law*, 24.

4.5 Kinds of Redemption

Although avoiding the term "penal substitution," Dunn argues that the penal theme underlies the ideology of sacrifice, and Paul's metaphorical appropriation thereof: "The wrath of God exhausted itself in the death of Jesus, and so is already exhausted for believers insofar as they identified themselves with Christ in his death—an implication probably already present in the theology of sacrifice."[61] However, OT scholarship now challenges the notion that Hebrew sacrifice was based on penal substitution, thus calling at least for a nuancing of Dunn's last clause, but Dunn is correct that Paul's *own* concept of sacrifice included penal substitution.

Penal substitution undoubtedly dominates some deutero-Pauline concepts of atonement, and it is definitely present in Paul, but I do not find it to be the *dominant* concept. Paul draws upon different elements within the cultic system that have metaphoric value: upon purity and boundary issues (as in 1 Cor 5:5–9); upon priestly roles (Rom 15:16; Phil 2:17); upon redemption/buy-out (1 Cor 7:23; Acts 20:28); upon sin-expiation (Rom 3:25); and on upon punishment-bearing (combining the scapegoat and judicial categories: Gal 3:13; Rom 8:3).

Redemption is substitutionary in an economic, not penal, sense. It is when Paul *conflates* it with a judicial image, that the notion of penal substitution appears. Sin-expiation involves more of purification than of substitution, more of magic than punishment, although it must be said that sacrifice does not easily yield up its underlying logic. For that very reason, Paul interprets sacrifice with the help of other categories: heroic death, expulsion ritual, judicial penalty. Christ died for us, bore away our sins, had sin condemned in his flesh. Paul explicates the sacrificial metaphor through these other metaphors.

Paul spins metaphors out of many different aspects of the cultic realm. In the metaphors themselves, he does not stress penal substitution any more highly than the themes of purification, magical sin-bearing, or costly payment. Metaphorically speaking, spiritual pollution and indebtedness can kill without any *sentence*. The danger from which salvation rescues people, is often, but not always, a judicial danger. By variously describing Christ as the typological fulfillment of the OT cult, he shows that Christ provides *all* the things the cult was thought to provide. "Take your choice," he seems to be saying, "Christ provides sin-riddance, purification, reconciliation." Of course, cultic symbolism does not preclude the presence of penal imagery (Rom 5:9; 8:33).

Substitution can be cultic, judicial, or economic, that is, it can be abstract, penal, or monetary.

---

[61] Dunn, *Romans 1–8*, 268.

4.6 Correcting the Atonement: Inclusive Place-Taking

The question of the representative or substitutionary role of the Messiah's death is related to the question of exactly what kind of role the Messiah was understood to be taking in his whole life. A very interesting attempt to explain away the difficulties with atonement is undertaken by Otfried Hofius. Dan Bailey summarizes the concept of two kinds of "place-taking" described by Hofius.[62] In *exclusive* place-taking, or substitution, one is "said to take another's place," to take that place *instead of* the other person. *Inclusive* place-taking means *sharing* the place of others, and "Christ always takes the place of others in a way that still *includes* them as persons, thus affecting their very being."[63] What kind of place-taking is described in Isaiah 53, and is that carried over into 2 Cor 5:21 and Rom 3:25; 4:25? Hooker sees *inclusive* place-taking in Isaiah 53, "*shared* rather than substitutionary suffering."[64] But Hofius insists that the substitution in Isaiah is exclusive, the Servant "has borne our infirmities" (53:4) *instead* of us—"one person has 'carried' the guilt of *others*."[65]

According to Hofius, inclusive place-taking "cannot be found in the ... fourth Servant Song ... but it can be found in the symbolism of the levitical sin-offering."[66] Here Hofius builds upon Gese's spiritualization of the cult (its supposed rectification of "damaged being"[67]), while rejecting Isaiah 53 as "theologically incomprehensible"[68] because a mere human accomplishes healing and salvation for others.

We have to consider several different kinds of assertions by Hofius: exegetical assertions about the differing notions of place-taking in Leviticus and in Isaiah; evaluations of the relative truth of these notions; assertions about the content of NT teachings and the extent of agreement among NT authors; and assertions about the actual nature of God. Some of his interpretations are stunningly brilliant, others simply fall flat.

---

[62] Daniel P. Bailey, "Concepts of *Stellvertretung* in the Interpretation of Isaiah 53," in *Jesus and the Suffering Servant*, 227, 241; and idem, "Recent Tübingen," in the same volume, 257. Cf. Hofius, *Paulusstudien*, 41–44.

[63] Bailey, "Recent Tübingen," 257.

[64] Bailey, "Concepts of *Stellvertretung*," 234.

[65] Bailey, "Concepts of *Stellvertretung*," 236.

[66] Bailey, "Concepts of *Stellvertretung*," 241–42.

[67] Gese, *Biblical Theology*, 110.

[68] The relevant passage is: "Befreiung von Sünde und Schuld durch *menschliche* Stellvertretung ist theologisch schlechterdings undenkbar!" (Otfried Hofius, "Das vierte Gottesknechtslied in den Briefen des Neuen Testaments," *NTS* 39 [1993]: 422).

Hofius eliminates every trace of superstition or bargaining from the Hebrew cult. The atoning rite is not a gift to God but a gift *from* God: "The OT expiatory cult is based not on the principle *do ut des* ('I [man] give so that you [God] may give,') but rather—as Bernd Janowski aptly formulates—on the concept of *do quia dedisti*: ('I [man] give because you [God] have already given')."[69] In the Old Testament, God is not the "annoyed [*zürnende*] recipient of atonement, but rather its salvation-creating donor."[70] Similarly, there is no trace, in the NT, of God being persuaded by a sacrifice: "God and Christ are *one* in the atoning and reconciling event of the crucifixion-death .... the Crucified was 'for us'—*not* for God!"[71] In fact, "Paul knows nothing of alteration in God, or of God changing his mind due to the crucifixion death of Jesus, and the reconciliation accomplished in the crucifixion event cannot be understood as the ending of the 'anger' of God nor as a gift to the till-then 'annoyed' God."[72] This makes it hard to make sense of the aversion of "the coming wrath" of 1 Thess 1:10 and Rom 5:9, or the "inflict[ed] wrath" of Rom 3:5.

Despite denials of penal substitution, Hofius describes the sacrificial cult thus: "The deadly charge of sin is transferred to the animal that stands in place of the sinner and vicariously dies for him.... The sinner himself evades the death he deserves due to his sin."[73] But *transfer, vicarious* victimage, and *evasion of* a *deserved* death are unavoidably *substitutionary*. And the adjective "penal" must certainly be added when he speaks (repeatedly) of a "deserved death": "For Paul, the 'righteousness of God' encompasses the redemptive acquittal by God, who has snatched godless Man from deserved death, set him in right relationship to God, and so opened up for him a new and healthy life."[74] Hofius wants to emphasize rescue, but his reasoning and his terminology entail a vicarious victim sustaining a punishment deserved by another.

Hofius does have an interesting concept of exactly what kind of representation took place in the Jesus' death. In Bailey's rephrasing, Hofius argues that "inclusive place-taking [i]s the only *divine* type of place-taking.... *Christ did not die in place of humanity, he died while he was in the place of humanity*."[75]

---

[69] Hofius, *Paulusstudien*, 40; the last internal quote is from Janowski, *Sühne*, 361.
[70] Hofius, *Paulusstudien*, 39–40.
[71] Hofius, *Paulusstudien*, 38.
[72] Hofius, *Paulusstudien*, 37–38.
[73] Hofius, *Paulusstudien*, 41.
[74] Hofius, *Paulusstudien*, 35.
[75] Bailey, "Concepts of *Stellvertretung*," 241.

This is one of the most insightful statements on the subject I have ever encountered. It states (to my understanding) the truth about God: God did not require a human sacrifice, but God suffered in the suffering of Jesus. In the life of Jesus, God occupied a *human place*. This affirms the central doctrine of Christianity, the Incarnation, without requiring any notion of Christ's death as a penal substitute, which many believers and theologians have recognized to be a distortion.

In fact, this insight should lead to an abandonment of vicarious atonement altogether, a concept that implies a vengeful Father and a compassionate Son, a scenario of "Christ appeasing God's wrath,"[76] where "the Father demands satisfaction, the Son pays it."[77] But instead Hofius uses his insight to attempt to rescue the atonement idea. His glorification of the Levitical cult as the model of "inclusive place-taking" is a Level Two spiritualization: attributing values to the cult that do not belong to it. Dying in the "human place" is a concept of divine incarnation, not of cultic gesticulation.

Hofius finds Isaiah 53 theologically useful only when it has been brought under the umbrella of Levitical thinking: "Isaiah 53 ... is integrated into a pattern of Christology that derives not so much from Isaiah ... as from the *levitical cult*"; actually from "the cultic *idea* more than" from Leviticus itself; Isaiah 53 is used at all only because "its language is adaptable to the New Testament's cultic, incorporative understanding of atonement."[78]

These statements require substantial correction. First of all, cultic atonement is not "the NT understanding" but a doctrine *found in the epistles and Revelation*; it cannot be said to be dominant throughout the NT, especially not in the Synoptic gospels, where it is found only in the institution passages. Indeed, the soteriology of the New Testament epistles (except James) centers upon substitutionary, cultic exchange. But the frequency of cultic language in the epistles stands in tension with the rarity of such language in the gospels. As M. Barth writes, "In the Synoptic Gospels the death of Jesus is extensively described, [but] only in the frame of the Last Supper does distinctly cultic terminology occur."[79]

---

[76] Timothy Gorringe, *God's Just Vengeance: Crime, Violence and the Rhetoric of Salvation* (Cambridge: Cambridge University Press, 1996), 115, summarizing the position of Hugh of St. Victor in *De Sacramentis* 1.8.7.

[77] Richard of St. Victor, *De Verbo Incarnato* (PG 196:1005), in Gorringe, *God's Just*, 116. Here, "satisfaction theory seems to pit the mercy and justice of God against each other" (Gorringe, 145), an implication that many contemporary theologians labor to avoid.

[78] Bailey, "Concepts of *Stellvertretung*," 244.

[79] Markus Barth, *Was Christ's Death a Sacrifice?*, Scottish Journal of Theology Occasional Papers No. 9 (1961), 6. Mark 10:45 has ransoming, but not cultic, language; the parallel passage in Luke 22:27 emphasizes service, without any ransom language.

And yet, Hofius does admit that, in Isaiah 53, Paul "saw the essence and center of his proclamation of Christ sketched out: in the atoning death of the sinless servant of God, who vicariously takes on himself the death sentence of sinners, God has given his peace to the guilty ones."[80] Hofius can say this in an article focused on the proclamation, for Israel and the human race, of reconciliation. It is only in another article, where he concentrates on the difference between the two kinds of place-taking, that he sees Isaiah 53 as embodying some kind of Arian tendency (my words, not his) that disqualifies this chapter as a basis for Paul.

Hofius's defense of the notion of atonement forces him to place an inordinately high value on *symbolic* place-taking (as in Leviticus), while devaluing the place-taking of one human actually bearing another's burdens (as in Isaiah). By Hofius's logic (although he never quite says this), the supreme act of grace in salvation history must be God's giving of the sacrificial cult. It is *cult* that rescues the sinner from a doomed fate: "cultic atonement is to be primarily and decisively understood as the separation of the sinner from his sin—that means, as an event of sin-removal, which includes the discharge of sin onto a substitutionary [*stellvertretenden*] sin-bearer and the negation of the sin through the negation of the sin-bearer."[81] Hofius understands sacrifice entirely through the expulsion metaphysics of scapegoat, and accepts this literally as the God-given method for removing sin.

For Hofius, the death of Christ is *Levitically* significant. One need not look outside the concept of "inclusive place-taking" he finds in the sacrificial cult. Forgiveness continues to be offered as it always has been: in a Levitical pattern.

Hofius's resistance to Isaiah 53 as an influence on Paul is probably based on anachronistic christological concerns. Because Isaiah's main character is "a mere human," everything this human is said to do is of limited use until it becomes assimilated to a Levitical/christological[82] pattern, at which point "does this text become theologically affirmable."[83] Apparently, only the operation of Levitical christology salvages Second Isaiah from a flavor of Arianism, from "a mere human" bearing others' sins. This is the reason Hofius does not allow that אשׁם is a cultic term![84] If it were a cultic term, he might have to allow Isaiah to

---

[80] Hofius, Otfried "Paulus—Missionar und Theologe," in *Evangelium—Schriftauslegung—Kirche; Festschrift für Peter Stuhlmacher*, eds., Jostein Ådna, et al (Göttingen: Vandenhoeck & Ruprecht, 1997), 235.

[81] Abridged excerpt from Hofius, *Paulusstudien*, 41.

[82] SBL standards require "Levitical" be capped, and "christological" lower case.

[83] Hofius, translated by Bailey, "Concepts of *Stellvertretung*," 245.

[84] Bailey, "Concepts of *Stellvertretung*," 244.

have more christological significance. But as it is, Isaiah 53 lacks the key salvific ingredient.

Hofius's mistake is to fail to see that the martyr model has more implications of genuine "inclusive place-taking" than does the Levitical model, where all place-taking is purely symbolic. In his drive to identify the origin of inclusive place-taking, Hofius has overlooked the courageous place-taking of the Hellenistic Jewish martyrological tradition (see next chapter).

A more well-rounded exegesis is that of Janowski, who allows the actions of the Servant in Isaiah 53 to be remarkable. He observes that the Servant's sufferings are both substitutionary and representative; "substitutionary because something is done for the 'we' that they could not do for themselves ... and representative because what the Servant suffered represented their fate and not his."[85]

Hofius finds inclusive place-taking where it does not exist (in the Levitical cult, and uniformly throughout the NT) and fails to see it where it *does* exist—in Second Isaiah: "When you pass through the waters, I will be with you .... Do not fear, for I am with you. ... he who vindicates me is near .... I dwell ... with those who are contrite and humble in spirit" (43:2, 5; 50:8; 57:15). *That* is shared place-taking!

Further, there is significant variance among the place-taking notions of various NT authors. In fact, Paul expresses both exclusive and inclusive place-taking. Christ is a substitute victim in Rom 4:25 and 8:3, but in Phil 2:7 he is "taking the form of a slave, being born in human likeness"—in the *human place*, and as a δοῦλος, not far from Isaiah's δουλεύοντα (53:11).

Hofius has applied his new insight like a *patch* to the old garment of atonement theology, but the patch will not stay; it will tear away. He subjugates his lively new analysis to a peculiar kind of dogmatic correctness that exalts the merely *symbolic* place-taking of sacrificial ritual over the *actual* and costly place-taking of heroic suffering described in Isaiah 53. He thinks it necessary to treat the ritual gesture of identification with the animal as authentically inclusive, while rejecting Isaiah's suffering and solidarity as theologically inferior. But is the ritual sacrificer wounded, crushed, sent to a grave, bearing the sin of many? Does he undergo anything for others (as does the Servant in 53:5–12)?

In the interests of defending a doctrine, Hofius has undervalued the prophetic viewpoint, and overvalued a ritual gesture. Nor is this as orthodox as Hofius seems to think. This promotion of Leviticus and denigration of Isaiah is quite out of step with church tradition. The church fathers, although believing

---

[85] Summary by Bailey, "Concepts of *Stellvertretung*," 248.

in the typological significance of the sacrificial cult,[86] did not link this with a denigration of the theology of the Servant Songs.[87] When they affirmed that the Levitical cult was a type of the Messiah's death, they did not make it the sole model for understanding atonement. In fact, they were more interested in the Isaianic servant songs as prophecies of Christ. They were unaware of a problem with the *humanity* of the Suffering Servant. Nor did they see any need to choose between Levitical and prophetic models, as though one excluded the other.

While the church fathers saw the OT cult having typological significance, they did not see the cult as *actually* repairing damaged being.[88] Their position was worlds away from that of Hofius, who affirms the literal efficacy of the cult, and sets it against the Isaianic model of compassionate burden-bearing. Hofius finds the precursor of Christ's suffering only in a ritual gesture, and not in the fellow-feeling and self-giving of the Isaiah record.

Is the Incarnation nothing more than a *gesture* of participation in human life? Is it important only if it fulfills a cultic pattern, and not if it demonstrates real co-suffering with humans? Hofius's insight (shared place-taking) should have led to a higher appreciation of the prophetic project instead of being forced onto a Procrustean bed of ritual correctness. He overlooks the artificiality in the sacrificial drama of identification with the victim. To say that blood is "the symbolic medium that 'brings people to God'"[89] is to rate symbolic gesture over moral content, and to undo the prophetic effort to make real interpersonal relations more important than ritual.

Hofius's attempt to spiritualize everything in the ancestry of the atonement doctrine is actually not orthodox; it fails to recognize the newness of what happened in Christ, which cannot be accounted for by old models and symbols. Hofius's revalorization of cult for its own sake takes cultic metaphors more literally than any NT author or orthodox father took them. A thoroughly

---

[86] "The two goats .... prefigure the two natures of Christ" (Tertullian, *Against Marcion* 3.7.7). The Passover lamb's blood "prefigures the Master's blood" (Chrysostom, *Baptismal Instructions* 3.14). These quotes are taken from *Exodus, Leviticus, Numbers, Deuteronomy*, ed. Joseph T. Lienhard. ACCS OT 3 (Downers Grove, Ill., InterVarsity, 2001), 185, 65.

[87] Christian reflection on sin often involved taking a look at Isaiah 53. The mention of sin in Num 5:6 causes Theodoret of Cyr to reflect on Isaiah 53:4 and 9 (Lienhard, *Exodus, Leviticus*, 209).

[88] "While the blood of the sacrificial victims ... was carried to the altars ... no one located within the vices of this world puts off sin nor is his blood accepted by God, unless he departs from the filth of this body"—Ambrose, Letter 14 extra collection (63).104, from Lienhard, *Exodus, Leviticus*, 147.

[89] Bailey, "Concepts of *Stellvertretung*," 242; apparently a passage from Gese.

priestly reading of the biblical tradition suffocates the prophetic voice. The mission of Jesus cannot be seen through a Sadducean lens. Hofius' effort is a spectacular and interesting failure.

4.7 Paul's Attitude Toward Cult

If Hofius is wrong about Paul's approach (and God's) being wholly cultic, what about two other alternatives, that Paul is completely indifferent to OT cult, or is anti-cultic?

We saw in chapter 1 that Paul's terms "living sacrifice (θυσίαν ζῶσαν)" and "spiritual worship (λογικὴν λατρείαν)" in Rom 12:1 resembled passages in the strongly anti-cultic *Corpus Hermeticum* 1.31; 12.23; 13.18–23. Räisänen says Paul's use of λογικὴ λατρεία may imply a negative attitude to cult.[90] Stuhlmacher says that Christ as new ἱλαστήριον "surpasses and renders obsolete all cultic atonement."[91] Stuhlmacher is not asserting that Paul is wholly anti-cultic, but that the Jewish cult is wholly surpassed.

Paul's treatment of the Jewish cult is thoroughly typologically; what matters is the *fulfillment* in Christ. Typological thinking is inherently supersessionist; if the old is superseded, it is, at least on the literal level, demoted. Paul does not need to say that; rather he focuses on fulfillment of the old in the new. Hübner goes so far as to say that he "radically ignores" the place of the cult in the OT itself; "the temple cult ... was without theological relevance" for him; in fact, "the atonement concept clearly occupies an extremely small place in Paul."[92] But that would cut the ground out from under typology altogether. It would render inexplicable his labeling of Christ as place of atonement, περὶ ἁμαρτίας, etc. Jewish cult has a *completely transformed* relevance in a supersessionist system.

More challenging is Breytenbach's suggestion. He insists that Paul's usage of cultic metaphors actually has an anti-cultic—especially an anti-temple—thrust. He acknowledges that Paul has a concept of substitutionary death, but insists that it is fundamentally "a temple-opposed understanding of atonement."[93] He argues that Paul "understands the death of Jesus not as a new, all-surpassing cultic event, but rather anti-typically, as the antithesis of the

---

[90] Heikki Räisänen, *Paul and the Law* (Philadelphia: Fortress, 1983), 77 n.180.

[91] Stuhlmacher, *Reconciliation, Law*, 174.

[92] Hans Hübner, "Sühne und Versöhnung: Anmerkungen zu einem umstrittenen Kapitel Biblischer Theologie," *Kerygma und Dogma* 29 (1983): 301.

[93] "*dem Tempel entgegengesetztes Sühneverständnis*" (Cilliers Breytenbach, "Versöhnung, Stellvertretung und Sühne: Semantische und traditionsgeschichtliche Bemerkungen am Beispiel der paulinischen Briefe," *NTS* 39 [1993]: 79).

cult."⁹⁴ Although Breytenbach is using a legitimate, secondary meaning of the term "antitype," I find his remark ironic, given that Paul's use of τύπος language shows the seriousness with which he takes the OT prophecies. His *types* are fulfilled in Christ (the second Adam) or the church. My point about typology is that it cannot be helpfully discussed unless one recognizes *both* continuity and discontinuity—more precisely, supersession. Where Hofius and Gese over-emphasize the continuity, Breytenbach over-emphasizes the discontinuity. Hübner stands for discontinuity by way of disinterest.

Still, Breytenbach's observations must be heard. He correctly points out that "the for us/for our sins-formula does not necessarily signal a connection with the Leviticus tradition, as 1 Cor 15:3b shows."⁹⁵ Wryly, he suggests that Paul "got along without the atonement concept up to the Epistle to the Romans," so it is hardly to be accepted that "a model that is first taken up in Romans can retroactively cover the dying-, surrender-, and sending-formulas"⁹⁶ that occur throughout his writings. And indeed, those formulas should not be automatically drawn within the orbit of sacrifice. Breytenbach makes a case that the sending formula (in Rom 8:3, for instance) goes back to the wisdom tradition,⁹⁷ but it seems more balanced to speak of Paul's "joining ... of priestly and wisdom traditions."⁹⁸

Further, we do find Paul using cultic metaphors outside Romans (in fact dozens of times, if we include non-soteriological usages). We have Jesus being "made sin," becoming a curse, or being "sacrificed" [ἐτύθη, from θύω, slaughter] as "our Passover"; Paul or his fellows are expulsion victims, serving at the altar, poured out as a libation; Gentiles are first fruits, an aroma, a sacrifice.⁹⁹ Large parts of the Corinthian and Philippian correspondence are saturated with cultic terminology.¹⁰⁰

Breytenbach begrudgingly allows evidence for a cultic connection only in the case of Rom 8:3, and even there, a cultic connection for "περὶ ἁμαρτίας is possible, but by no means necessary."¹⁰¹ Stuhlmacher's comment is appropriate: "Breytenbach works without consideration of the wholly essential

---

⁹⁴ Breytenbach, "Versöhnung, Stellvertretung," 78–79.
⁹⁵ Breytenbach, "Versöhnung, Stellvertretung," 72.
⁹⁶ Breytenbach, "Versöhnung, Stellvertretung," 79.
⁹⁷ Breytenbach, "Versöhnung, Stellvertretung," 73.
⁹⁸ Stuhlmacher, *Reconciliation, Law*, 162.
⁹⁹ 2 Cor 5:21; Gal 3:13; 1 Cor 5:7; 4:13; 9:13; Phil 2:17; 1 Cor 16:15; 2 Cor 2:15; Phil 2:17.
¹⁰⁰ Newton, *Concept of Purity*, 52–59, 62–67, 81–93, 110–14; Renwick, *Paul, the Temple*, 52–157.
¹⁰¹ Breytenbach, "Versöhnung, Stellvertretung," 72.

place of the OT and early Jewish tradition of atonement and reconciliation, and accordingly comes to a one-sided result."[102] Breytenbach boldly asserts that "it is more natural to ascribe to the word ἁμαρτίας overall the same sense, 'sin,' " than to let it change from sin to sin-offering.[103] But this bluff is exposed when he says, "A cultic reference is to be discerned only in the reception of the tradition in 1 John"[104]—an admission that the indisputably sacrificial ἱλασμός in 1 John 2:2 is part of the *same* tradition as περὶ ἁμαρτίας in Rom 8:3!

Breytenbach as much as admits that Rom 3:25 is cultic when he avoids discussing it because Paul *himself* does not refer back to the Levitical idea of atonement, and Rom 3:25 "comes via tradition."[105] But Paul does choose when to use any pre-existing tradition, how to re-shape it, and how to use it in an argument. In Romans, he uses cultic metaphors to answer how humanity is "reconciled to God through the death of his Son" (Rom 5:10), and this leads into his interpretation of the Christian cult as being "baptized into his death" (6:3). Indeed, this is hardly "Levitical," but it is certainly sacrificial. He caps his other reconciliation passage with God making Christ become sin so that we can become the righteousness of God, a classic summary of the cultic notion of exchange (2 Cor 5:15–21).

The question of the presence of Level Five spiritualizing (rejection of Jewish cult) in Paul, is complex and difficult. Paul never argues for or against the sacrificial cult. It is certainly not anti-Levitical to use Levitical metaphors for the salvation event. To say that Christ is the source of a new blood covenant is to affirm that God was previously working through such a covenant.

Further, the cultic metaphors imply that God still responds to some kind of cultic mechanism. Paul attributes literal power to the *Christian* cult: unworthy participation in the Lord's Supper can make one ill or even dead (1 Cor 11:29–30). Solemn piety is to be observed; believers are the new temple. These are cultic patterns.

4.8 Spiritualizing Strategies

Dodd has discussed how important was Paul's break with the old way of thinking about God. Dodd explains Paul's spiritualizations in Rom 3:24–25 while also heightening them: God's pity precludes any notion that "the law of

---

[102] Peter Stuhlmacher, "Cilliers Breytenbachs Sicht von Sühne und Versöhnung," in *Jahrbuch für Biblische Theologie, Band 6: Altes Testament und christlicher Glaube* (Neukirchen-Vluyn: Neukirchener Verlag, 1991), 349.

[103] "Versöhnung, Stellvertretung," 73.

[104] "Versöhnung, Stellvertretung," 71–72.

[105] "Versöhnung, Stellvertretung," 74.

retribution" dominates.[106] Paul accepts God's retribution, but believes that God's forgiveness does not allow retribution to have the last word.[107] The illustration in Romans 3, Dodd says, does not involve propitiation. God himself "set forth a means of expiation," so "the sacrifice of Christ" is not "a means of soothing an angry Deity."[108] This correctly represents Paul's argument, on the surface. However, the sacrificial metaphor has had the propitiatory implication for millions of readers, and other passages speak of the need to turn away God's wrath (1 Thess 1:10; Rom 3:10, 20; 5:9). Sacrificial metaphor inevitably implies that the Deity is *conciliated* by a cultic or economic transaction.

The redemption metaphor indicates that God did not offer salvation for free; there was a price to pay, and the Son of God paid it. Although spiritualizing can change such crude concepts (and Paul's certainly did), terms like *buying* and *offering* perpetuate the notion of *dealing* with the deity, of bargaining with God.

Paul does not say God was induced by a sacrifice, or that Jesus' blood had a magical quality. But those are popular assumptions about sacrifice that emerge from any sacrificial illustration, regardless of authorial intention. Before long, Christians were speaking of being "ransomed ... with the precious blood of Christ" (1 Pet 1:18–19).

Yet Paul forces Christians to rethink their stance before God. He holds up ideas of God that are incompatible with the ancient view. Paul's is a philosophy in movement, a continual rethinking of cultic and traditional concepts. Paul uses an old thing (the cult) to symbolize the new thing that God has done. But he does not attribute new values to the old cult. To assign spiritual and therapeutic qualities to the OT cult so as to give it the value that we imagine a soteriological symbol *should* have, is to give a distorted exegesis. There is a great difference between Paul's metaphorical appropriation of sacrifice to explain the new way of salvation (thus implicitly replacing the old way), and the revalorization of a sacrificial system that Paul was prepared to abandon. Attempts to sweeten the pill only confuse the palate.

The attempt to spiritualize the Jewish cult (Level Two) is an assertion of strong continuity between the old teaching and Paul's. This mutes the supersessionist aspects of Paul's teaching, seen in such remarks as "What once had glory has lost its glory because of the greater glory" (2 Cor 3:10); the Mosaic glory "was going to fade" (v. 11; NAB). Spiritualization Two attempts

---

[106] C. H. Dodd, *The Meaning of Paul for Today* (London: Fontana Books, 1920, 1958), 83.

[107] Dodd, *Meaning of Paul*, 90.

[108] Dodd, *Meaning of Paul*, 109.

to deny that there is any tension between the "law of retribution" and the desire to forgive.

Christian typological reinterpretation of Jewish traditions stands for a profound *discontinuity* with some aspects of the old, especially those things for which the national priesthood stood. Despite Paul's protestations that he did respect the law, one can truly speak, with Meyer, of "the reduction of the כפרה—and by implication, of the whole economy of ritual Torah and temple—to the role of 'type'."[109] Indeed, for Paul, the main function of the Torah was to point to the "offspring," Christ (Gal 3:16, 19).

Typological interpretation of sacrifice has outlived sacrifice. To understand Christianity it is necessary to appreciate this, and to recognize that both continuity and discontinuity are wrapped up in typology and in Spiritualization Four. The metaphor is mightier than the sword, that is, the sacrificial knife. The metaphor can bind as well as cut.

Paul is neither radical nor conservative, neither denying all validity to the cult (Level Five), nor defending and exalting it (Level Two). He respects and demotes the cult, just as he both respects and demotes the Torah. He will not gush with enthusiasm about cult and priesthood, as Philo and Sirach did; he knows that the cult is now to be replaced by that to which it was pointing. He thus raises the *symbolic* value of the old cult, while devaluing its *actual* practice.

One of the difficulties in assessing Paul's theology is to simultaneously recognize his perpetuation of cultic patterns and his articulation of a stunning vision of a transformed world (Rom 8:21–22), a renewed humanity, a restored amity between people and their Creator. He did not (usually) emphasize the retaliatory potential of God, but in his most comprehensive theological statement (Romans) it is prominent in the first three chapters, then relieved with the cultic solution of 3:21–29. In chapters 5 to 8 God is simultaneously generous and demands sacrifice and asceticism. Paul has blended what cannot really be blended, yet his mixture was overwhelmingly persuasive. It appealed both to primitive instincts about how God worked, and to the notion that God had done something new; it aroused loyalty and selflessness, while providing the individual with a vivid drama of salvation and participation in the sufferings of the Messiah.

Of course, Paul is not to blame for the primitive belief in a sacrifice-demanding God, which has existed for untold generations. However, because of the success of Paul's sacrificial metaphors, the fate of the notion of a sacrifice-demanding God is now permanently bound to the question of the

---

[109] Meyer, "The Pre-Pauline Formula," 206.

analysis and understanding of Pauline teaching. Scholarship can help to unfold the complex and contradictory ideas upon which Paul drew.

Paul certainly does not emphasize propitiation and expiation, but he does seem to accept them. The sacrificial themes that are emphasized are victim as *payment*, as *pioneer* ("first fruits of those who have died," 1 Cor 15:20), and (when blended with a judicial or reconciliation metaphor) as *mediator* (Rom 8:32–34; 5:8–11).

I asked in the first chapter whether Paul's metaphors imply any of the three or four ideas we found in Hebrew and Gentile sacrificial practice: spirit-mediumship, ritual as something required by God, or substitute (penal or economic). I conclude that the notion of spirit-mediumship in Paul is communicated not through OT metaphors but through his doctrine of the Spirit and through the intensely participatory understanding of *Christian* cult practice: sharing in the body of Christ (1 Cor 10:16), being buried with Christ and raised with him (Rom 6:4). The Christian cult provides access to God, but so does faithful daily living, preaching, and bearing "one another's burdens" (Gal 6:2). Cult is not the *only* method of access to God, for Paul.

As for the idea of ritual as something required by God, I think this is strongly implied by Paul's repeated return to cultic metaphors to summarize his soteriology at key moments in all the *Hauptbriefe*; the Son had to be sent as a περὶ ἁμαρτίας so that sin could be judged at *that* moment, a *ritual* moment. Salvation is a reversal of status, and this is best communicated through cultic metaphor.

Finally, Paul's frequent linking of judicial and redemption ideas with the cultic metaphors constitutes the cultic victim both a penal and economic substitute (see next chapter). Penal substitution is certainly implied by some of the "dying formula" passages, and any of the blended metaphors where either the Mosaic law or an implied eschatological judgment are present (Rom 4:25; 8:3, 32; Gal 3:13).

4.9 Conclusion

In Paul's soteriology, the *mechanism* of salvation is Christ's death functioning as a payment or a ritual action, being *handed over* for our transgressions, being *made sin* for us, and so on.

There seem to be four main kinds of substitution upon which Paul could draw: economic (either a ransom-payment or a sacrifice as gift), penal, abstract (the parade example being the imaginative "confusion of identities"[110] in the Vedic/Hindu system), and the heroic substitution of a martyr. Hebrew sacrifice has been understood as embodying any of the first three of these. The rabbis

---

[110] Smith and Doniger, "Sacrifice," 207.

and many Christians articulated a notion of the animal as a penal substitute. The notion of payment is well-attested. Abstract substitution was absorbed into the other two. Paul introduces new concepts of substitution when he blends any two or three of the following: payment, punishment, heroic substitution, and a non-substitutionary cultic event: the scapegoat. The scapegoat takes on penal substitutionary meaning when it is blended with the judicial and sacrificial images (Rom 8:3). Payment takes on both a sacred and a penal character in Gal 3:13 when it is blended with the scapegoat image, and rescues one from the law's condemnation; there seems to be both a literal sin-carrying and a legal penalty-bearing. Recognition of this blending of metaphors helps make sense of some otherwise baffling expressions that mix a crude literalism with a judicial image: "you have died to the law through the body of Christ" (Rom 7:4). The punished *body* is a scapegoat-legal blended image.

Paul's mixed metaphors create new meanings, combining elements from the metaphoric terms. In that Jesus died because of our transgressions (Rom 4:25), there is heroic and penal substitution. In that our trespasses were "not counted," while Christ was "made sin" (2 Cor 5:19, 21) there is penal substitution and animistic sin-dumping. In that he became our redemption and the new place of atonement (Rom 3:24–25), his blood is a payment and a purification. In that the new covenant is in his blood, his death is a covenant sacrifice that creates a new community.

Spiritualization and abstraction have been going on for so long in Christian thought, that "sacrifice" now means a fusion of cultic, redemptive, and heroic categories. Before very long, the Christian understanding of "sacrifice" came not from Leviticus, but from a combination of three substitutionary notions: beneficial and heroic death, redemption payment, and bearing a judicial penalty incurred by others. This means Christ endured the penalty that was deserved by others, he paid the debt that was owed by others, and he died as a martyr. That he carried away sins, like a scapegoat, lies in the background, somewhat muted, while the heroic and sacred connotations are highlighted.

The soteriology of Romans entails both the transfer from one owner's domain to another's as a result of being purchased, and the aversion of judicial condemnation as a result of someone being handed over for us. Change of ownership entails a change of status, from slave of sin to adopted son of God (and of Abraham). Penalty-aversion also means a new status: justified (in the sense of *acquitted*). The Son and Spirit will *intercede* for us judicially (Rom 8:27, 34).

Paul tries to forestall some of the unpleasant possible implications of his metaphors, as when he describes God as a loving parent rather than a judge at the end of the extended judicial metaphor in Romans 8. Denying the implications of metaphors became a Christian growth industry, reaching a kind of peak with Hofius denying that the elements of payment and substitution are present at all, even while claiming that only the priestly gesture over the animal (surely either a payment or a substitute) adequately symbolizes the kind of *place-taking* that Jesus performed. By suppressing the payment and penal options and depicting salvation as a purely ritual operation, Hofius unconsciously heightens the option that it was a magical substitution.

For Paul, God acted compassionately to save humanity through the death of Christ, who died as a martyr (see next chapter). The significance of this death is best conveyed through a variety of transactional metaphors, three that describe the saving transaction itself (sacrifice, scapegoat, or redemption payment), and three that describe the beneficial after-effect for believers (reconciliation, justification, adoption).

I define metaphor as the usage of terms and ideas from one realm to describe an event in another realm or category of existence. Since the thing being described is a human death, and martyrdom, *by definition*, describes a human death, martyrdom is not metaphoric; it does not transfer terminology from another realm, a realm *besides* human dying.

I refer here to the Jewish Hellenistic notion of noble death. Literally speaking, "martyrdom" does transfer terminology from the judicial realm (a μάρτυς is a *witness*), but the English word has now taken on another meaning as primary: the noble death theme. Paul speaks of Jesus "dying for us" without using any μαρτυ-words. I simply use the term "martyrdom" because it now refers to the noble death tradition, and has lost the judicial implications that it still shows in numerous NT passages. However, I am not referring to passages that use μαρτυ-words, but to passages where Paul speaks of Jesus "dying for us," "for me," "for the ungodly." It is the battlefield, not the courtroom, that provides the conceptual background to Maccabean martyrology, which martyrology seems to be the general background for Paul's dying-for motif. Upon a background of widely recognized (but simple) martyrological notions, Paul then composes his (considerably more complex) cultic metaphors.

I refer to martyrdom as a *model* for interpretation of the death of Christ, but not as a *metaphor*. Even in the some of the pre-Pauline Jewish martyrdom texts, the *meaning* of the martyrdom is expressed through one or another metaphor imported from the courtroom, the cult, or the agora.

5.
Martyrology and Metaphor

Paul's usage of cultic metaphors is complicated by the fact that he also seems to understand the death of Christ in terms of a martyrological model. The important Hellenistic category of "noble death" must be examined, and the nature and degree of its effect upon Jewish literature and upon Paul. Lastly, we will see how martyrology relates to Paul's usage of cultic and social metaphors.

5.1 Martyrological Soteriology

In some ways, martyrdom may be the most fundamental of Paul's models for interpreting the death of Christ. But it is hardly a separate image for Paul, since its meaning is conveyed *through* the sacrificial, scapegoat, and redemption metaphors. It seems to have been absorbed into these other metaphors, to be interpreted *by* them; it may be the most fundamental of Paul's concepts, but its *meaning* requires the usage of metaphors from the cultic and social realms.

Dying for others was a major theme of Greek literature, and was adapted by Jewish religious ideology and by Roman political thought and literature. The principle martyrological formula in Greek literature was "so and so died for X," with X being the city-state, Greece, or some religious principle (as in the case of Antigone). Paul gives us numerous examples of the noble death theme in his "dying formulae": "Christ died for us" (Rom 5:8; 1 Thess 5:10); "Christ died for the ungodly" (Rom 5:6); "weak believers for whom Christ died" (1 Cor 8:11). These are "to be understood against a background of wide distribution of the substitutionary death in the Hellenistic world."[1]

If Christ is a martyr, in fact the martyred Messiah, how can Paul find words to express this monumental tragedy and triumph, the sublime reversal of fortunes whereby God reached out to humanity during humanity's darkest

---

[1] Breytenbach, "Versöhnung, Stellvertretung," 78.

hour?—by describing Christ as the new Passover, as the new sin offering through which sin is condemned in the flesh, as the sin-bearer who causes us to take on the righteousness of God at the exact moment that he takes on our sin.

Paul prefers to embody the martyrological notion in these cultic and social metaphors, probably to avoid the nationalism that both Jewish and pagan martyrology entailed. Martyrology affirms loyalty to a Greek city-state, or to Greece against barbarians, or to Rome, or to "the ancestral law" (*4 Macc.* 4:23; 5:33; 16:16; cf. 8:7; 9:1). In *Fourth Maccabees*, the conflict is expressed "as a contest between the Greek king and the Jewish people," with the king seeking "to destroy by force the way of life of the Hebrews"; instead the martyrs "vindicated their people," in 17:10.[2] And so, "in both 2 and 4 Maccabees, the martyrdoms end in the restoration of the Jewish polity," and the authors have endeavored to show "that the Jewish way of life is unique."[3] In their battle with the tyrant, they "are called to bear witness for the nation. Fight zealously for our ancestral law" (*4 Macc.* 16:16). In *Fourth Maccabees* this happens even without military battle, the tyrant is defeated in a spiritual war.[4]

Fourth Maccabees is more interested in abstract ideas than in specific institutions such as the temple cult. Its "political views ... have become spiritualized"; the Jewish way of life is defended, but "specific Jewish institutions are no longer central."[5] Unlike the author of 2 Maccabees, the author of *4 Maccabees* "did not have detailed knowledge of his own about Jerusalem."[6] But even when its conceptuality has been partly spiritualized, martyrology still has a political subtext.

5.1.1 The "Dying Formula"

The "effective" or "beneficial" death was a central theme of Greek and Roman literature and political rhetoric. Euripides is the greatest of the early literary representatives; many of his heroes die for the sake of Thebes or Athens. *Iphigenia at Aulis* may contain "the most elaborate political motivation for self-sacrifice" in his work.[7] The heroine says, "All these things I shall achieve by my death ... as the liberator of Hellas .... I give my body to

---

[2] Jan Willem Van Henten, *The Maccabean Martyrs as Saviours of the Jewish People: A Study of 2 and 4 Maccabees*. JSJ Sup 57 (Leiden: Brill, 1997), 121.

[3] Van Henten, *Maccabean Martyrs*, 300. The enemy is also an *ethnic* entity (236).

[4] Van Henten, *Maccabean Martyrs*, 300.

[5] Van Henten, *Maccabean Martyrs*, 150.

[6] Van Henten, *Maccabean Martyrs*, 269.

[7] Jan Willem Van Henten and Friedrich Avemarie, eds., *Martyrdom and Noble Death: Selected Texts from Graeco-Roman, Jewish and Christian Antiquity* (London: Routledge, 2002), 31.

Hellas. Sacrifice [θύετ'] me, sack Troy."[8] Her death is "on behalf of all the land of Hellas. Lead me to the altar to sacrifice"[9] [θῦσαι]. This is a major theme in many of his other plays: *The Phoenician Women* "repeats time and again that Monoeceus' almost ceremonial self-sacrifice benefited the land of Thebes (*Phoen*. 913–14; 997–98; 1090)."[10]

The theme is partly depoliticized, turned into principled loyalty to *right*[11] and to *law*,[12] by Plato in his description of the heroic death of Socrates, who regards not "death and danger," but only what is right.[13] Socrates embodied the individual who would never betray his convictions.[14]

Hengel shows the importance of the noble death theme in his astounding chain of quotes from Greek literature that goes on for twenty-three pages.[15] He describes "the legendary last king of Athens," who let himself be killed to save the city. This is "the classical Greek concept of ὑπεραποθνῄσκειν," which Clement then applied to the death of Jesus.[16] A cultic metaphor is prominent in some of the Euripidean stories of "voluntary sacrifice," even involving "cutting the throat in ritual fashion."[17] Even the murder of her children by Medea is depicted in vase paintings as taking place on an altar.[18]

These self-sacrificial deaths can atone for past crimes, can soothe an angry goddess, or avert a god's wrath.[19] The point that is strongly established in the first half of Hengel's book is that dying-for-others was a dominant theme of Hellenistic literature and a major social value; Hengel's attempt in the second half of his book, to show that Paul's "dying-for" formula is purely Jewish, fails to overcome the evidence of the first half of the book, showing that it was a Hellenistic theme before it became a Jewish theme. Hengel is correct that, in its biblical form, it is a Hellenistic-*Jewish* theme, but he argues against his own evidence when he tries to minimize the Hellenistic side of that label. More correct would be the opinion of Adela Collins, who says the Maccabean

---

[8] *Iph. aul.* 1379, 1397; from Hadas and McLean, *Ten Plays*, 348.
[9] *Iph. aul.* 1553–55; from Hadas and McLean, *Ten Plays*, 352.
[10] Van Henten and Avemarie, *Noble Death*, 16.
[11] *Crito* 49C–50A.
[12] *Crito* 50B–51E, 52D; it flows directly from the argument for *doing right*.
[13] *Apol.* 28B–D, 29B.
[14] Van Henten and Avemarie, *Noble Death*, 14.
[15] Hengel, *Atonement*, 9–31.
[16] Hengel, *Atonement*, 12–15.
[17] Hengel, *Atonement*, 20.
[18] Walter Burkert, "Greek Tragedy and Sacrificial Ritual," *GRBS* 7 (1966): 118.
[19] Hengel, *Atonement*, 19.

martyrdom motifs "are clearly modeled on the death of Socrates."[20] Socrates also died for *principles*, not just for the nation.

The political motivation of "noble death" became a prominent theme for the Romans. Just one of many examples is that of the General P. Decius Mus in 340 B.C.E. who "devoted" himself and the enemy to underworld deities, and hurled himself into the enemy's ranks, seeking death, believing that it would gain victory for the Roman side,[21] dying "on behalf of the army . . . and the Roman people."[22] The Romans had other favorite stories of heroic devotion, and "such self-sacrifices were considered a means of atonement (*piaculum*)."[23]

Expanding on the work of Martin Hengel, Jeffrey Gibson has investigated the "dying formula" in Hellenistic literature, some version of the expression " 'X died/gave himself for Y' and which conveys the idea that the death of X is salvific for Y."[24] Using only the TLG database, leaving out scholia of unknown date, and leaving out a large number of inscriptions, Gibson finds 111 instances of the dying formula, including "at least twenty seven times in Euripides . . . at least five times in 4 Macc (6:22, 27, 30; 11:14; 13:9), five times in Josephus."[25]

Some of the people give their lives for their friends or for a religious idea (such as Antigone), but the overwhelming majority give their lives for their city or fatherland; this action can be described as a "noble struggle" (Homer) or as a "holy sacrifice"[26] (as in Pindar *Frag.* 78). *Never* do these people die for an enemy, Gibson observes (except for one instance where it is done for a *former* enemy); it is always for someone or something that has nurtured them.[27] Hellenistic cultures frequently gave utterance to the dying formula in connection with the civic cult, in political deliberations, courtroom arguments,[28] at funerary rites or in speeches before or by soldiers.[29]

Gibson's research indicates that the purpose of the dying formula is to affirm a society's way of life, and more: to affirm "that violence is a constructive force in the building of civilization," that values must be defended

---

[20] Collins, "Finding," 181.
[21] Van Henten, *Maccabean Martyrs*, 147.
[22] Van Henten, *Maccabean Martyrs*, 159.
[23] Van Henten, *Maccabean Martyrs*, 149.
[24] Jeffrey Gibson, "Paul's 'Dying Formula': Prolegomena to an Understanding of Its Import and Significance" (paper presented at the Annual Meeting of the SBL, Toronto, Ontario, 25 November, 2002), 1.
[25] Gibson, "Dying Formula," 4.
[26] Gibson, "Dying Formula," 7.
[27] Gibson, "Dying Formula," 7–8.
[28] Gibson, "Dying Formula," 11–16.
[29] Gibson, "Dying Formula," 16–20.

with force, and so, "to underscore the warrior ideal," to defend "the idea that ... peace and security ultimately comes through readiness for war."³⁰ This has quite a Girardian sound to it, although there are no Girardian terms in Gibson's paper. But he does note that "Paul was engaged in a profound polemic against the prevailing values of his day .... Instead of ... grasping δοξη [sic], he shuns it (Philip. 2:6–8)"; this, then, constitutes "a major challenge to the validity of the ideology of the imperial cult."³¹

Paul uses the dying formula in two principal ways, to say Christ died "for us" (Rom 5:6–8; 8:32; 1 Cor 8:11; 2 Cor 5:14–15; Gal 2:20; 3:13; 1 Thess 5:10) or to say he died "for our sins" (1 Cor 15:3; Rom 4:25; Gal 1:4). These passages distinctly echo the "noble death" theme in Greek literature. We now use the word "martyrdom" for this, and when I use that English term, I am referring to the noble death theme, and not to the meaning of μάρτυς, "witness," that is ancestral to our word.

Themes occurring in several of Paul's passages are: rescue or liberation; admonitions to be grateful and not selfish; Christ taking on sin or curse for the benefit of sinners; and the fact that Christ was offered by God. If the Hellenistic dying formula motivated people to defend civic values, Paul's dying formula admonishes people to be loyal to Christ and God. Gratitude is the natural response to being rescued; this gratitude is partly driven by shame at realizing that one's sinfulness caused Christ to have to take on sin, to die "for our trespasses" (Rom 4:25).

Universalism characterizes Paul's teaching. *His* martyr is more than a nationalistic martyr; *his* Messiah is more than a "Jewish Messiah,"³² he is the world savior and even "part of the meaning of the word *God*."³³ The Messiah of Paul's teaching opens up a new era for all descendants of Adam.

5.1.2 The Effective Death Motif in Maccabean Literature

Moore comments that Second Maccabees, "though written in Greek, is in general accord with Palestinian thinking."³⁴ by which he means that God punishes for rebellion ("We suffer on account of our own sins" 7:32), but is ready to forgive and restore the nation. What is unusual about Second

---

³⁰ Gibson, "Dying Formula," 20.
³¹ Gibson, "Dying Formula," 21.
³² Repeatedly in N. T. Wright, "Paul's Gospel and Caesar's Empire," in *Paul and Politics: Ekklesia, Israel, Imperium, Interpretation. Essays in Honor of Krister Stendahl*, ed. Richard A. Horsley (Harrisburg, Penn.: Trinity, 2000), 165–69.
³³ Wright, "Paul's Gospel," 169; cf. 166, 183.
³⁴ George Foot Moore, *Judaism in the First Centuries of the Christian Era* (Cambridge, Mass.: Harvard University Press, 1927, 1955), 1:548.

Maccabees, then, is that God's wrath is exhausted in the deaths of the martyrs. The martyrdoms, then, are part and parcel of God's tutoring of the people Israel: "these punishments were designed not to destroy but to discipline our people" (2 Macc 6:12). God does not wait for Israel's sins to reach their height, but punishes them immediately. He does this so that he will *not* have to exact vengeance when they have built up to a large amount (6:14–15). This notion of punishment as discipline is very close conceptually to Deuteronomy, but expressed in terms of martyrdom. On the other hand, "the author of 4 Maccabees hardly pays attention to the notion of disciplinary suffering."[35] Second Maccabees is closer to Deuteronomy than *Fourth Maccabees* is.

Second Maccabees blends Jewish scriptural loyalties with Hellenistic concepts of civic loyalty. At one point, the lead character (Eleazar) even makes a very Hellenistic distinction between body and soul, speaking of "terrible sufferings *in my body* . . . but *in my soul* I am glad to suffer these things."[36]

The deaths of the martyrs are a momentary disciplining of the nation, but "he will again be reconciled with his own servants" (2 Macc 7:33). The deaths are instructional, and will be imitated by the next generation; Eleazar is leaving "to the young a noble [γενναῖον] example of how to die a good death willingly and nobly for the revered and holy laws" (6:28). The seventh son sees his self-surrender as a way of "appealing to God to show mercy soon (ταχὺ) to our nation" (7:37), and their deaths are *effective*: "through me and my brothers to bring to an end the wrath (ὀργὴν) of the Almighty" (7:38).[37] The plea for deliverance "soon" is answered. God responds to the "intercessory prayer" of the martyrs to "show mercy,"[38] and he shortens the afflictions of the nation. The martyrs' deaths actually made the atonement possible, so they can be described as propitiatory deaths. God *became conciliated*—the literal meaning of ἵλεως γενέσθαι, translated as "show mercy" in 7:37.

Van Henten thinks the author of the central chapters of 2 Maccabees "may have combined Greek and possibly Roman views about sacrificial death with biblical traditions about Moses and Phinehas or other mediators who stopped the Lord's wrath."[39] This is not inconsistent with other Biblical usages, such as Moses' "standing in the breach" in Ps. 106:23.[40] The main example of non-cultic

---

[35] Van Henten, *Maccabean Martyrs*, 140; cf. 185.
[36] 2 Macc 6:30; Van Henten, *Maccabean Martyrs*, 128.
[37] On the last point, cf. Van Henten, *Maccabean Martyrs*, 185.
[38] According to Kellermann, this prayer is the key event that brings about reconciliation; Ulrich Kellermann, *Auferstanden in den Himmel: 2 Makkabäer 7 und die Auferstehung der Märtyrer* (Stuttgart: Verlag Katholisches Bibelwerk, 1979), 54–55.
[39] Van Henten, *Maccabean Martyrs*, 185.
[40] Van Henten, *Maccabean Martyrs*, 163.

atonement is the act of Phinehas, who kills an Israelite and his Midianite woman, ingratiating himself to the Lord who explicitly says that this act "turned back my wrath from the Israelites"; because Phinehas "made atonement" (ἐξιλάσατο) by this act (Num 25:11, 13).

Ironically, this non-cultic atonement is considerably more problematic than is animal sacrifice, since it entails killing people! Here a cultic concept is utilized to articulate strict nationalistic boundary-marking. National boundaries are strongly affirmed in the Maccabean literature, but the only violence is violence *received* ... and violence *expected* from God, who will vindicate the martyrs. Second Maccabees and *Fourth Maccabees* are very much focused on the martyrs and God.

Before I move to the crucial book *Fourth Maccabees*, some other possible predecessors of Pauline thought may be mentioned. Hill finds an instance of "vicarious atoning power"[41] in the intertestamental work *Ps Sol* 10:2: "The one who prepares his back for the whip shall be purified." A more important example would be the death of Taxo and his seven sons in the work that R. Charles called *The Assumption of Moses* but which *OTP* calls *The Testament of Moses*. The narrative is meant to be a foretelling, by Moses, of large stretches of Jewish history; in Taxo's time, Jews are pressured to follow pagan rituals. Taxo and his sons decide to commit suicide rather than submit, recalling both Eleazar and Razis (who committed suicide in 2 Macc 14:37ff). Taxo resolves to do this action, knowing that "our blood will be avenged before the Lord" (9:7; *OTP* 1:931).

As Priest says, the author "perhaps, has hinted at the idea of vicarious propitiation, although this is not clear."[42] God's vindicating the persecuted, is undoubtedly intended, whether or not this means that their deaths performed a vicarious function.

God's vengeance on behalf of the murdered righteous ones becomes a widespread theme in Jewish thought: "The blood of the righteous from the earth [ascends] before the Lord of Spirits" (*1 En* 47:1). The earth will "testify" (μαρτυρεῖ) that the Jews were killed unjustly (1 Macc 2:37).

This may be the moment to make a point about the noble death theme. Martyrdom needs to be recognized as a category in its own right, not just drawn into the sacrificial orbit as though it were simply a subset of sacrificial metaphor. Its primary orbit is martial and patriotic.

Sacrifice and martyrdom are independent realms of concept, neither one a subset of the other. A martyr is *sometimes* described with a sacrificial metaphor, but he or she may also called an athlete, guardian of the law, fortifier

---

[41] Hill, *Greek Words*, 44.
[42] J. Priest, "Testament of Moses, Introduction," in *OTP*, 1:923.

of harbors, a holy chorus, fiercer than fire,[43] and so on. Christian interpretation has tended to make sacrifice the all-dominating interpretive category.

5.1.3 The Usage of ἱλαστήριον in Fourth Maccabees

The discussion of martyrdom now intersects with the consideration of ἱλαστήριον, occurring in a martyrological passage, *4 Macc.* 17:22. Bailey claims that this occurrence represents the common pagan meaning of ἱλαστήριον, "propitiatory votive offering," and not the biblical mercy seat—"We cannot translate τὸ ἱλαστήριον τοῦ θανάτου αὐτῶν by 'the atoning *victim* of their death.' "[44] To equate this ἱλαστήριον with a sacrificial victim "is a category mistake."[45] If one tries to translate *4 Macc.* 17:22 with "act of sacrifice," one is going against all known usages of ἱλαστήριον, which never denote an action. In fact, all the -τήριον words are concrete rather than denoting actions,[46] or abstract notions like "expiation."[47] Usually, -τήριον endings signify places. The LXX has four "neologisms in -τήριον. Each of them signifies a place: θυσιαστήριον, ἱλαστήριον, φυγαδευτήριον, ἁγιαστήριον—*place of sacrifice, place of atonement, place for fleeing . . . holy place.*"[48]

Bailey's lexical work is excellent, but he then allows himself to make rigid categorizations. Ancient and modern writers *do* make "category mistakes," they *do* allow meanings to be stretched beyond "proper" usage whenever they create metaphors. Calling Christ a "mercy seat" in Rom 3:25 is also a category mistake, strictly speaking, since a person is being compared to a thing. And *4 Macc.* 17:22 would be making the same mistake if it is comparing human deaths to a statue or monument. If we required every metaphor to be rigidly proper and logical, there is no metaphor that would escape whipping. But metaphors work because the reader or listener immediately perceives the one or two key features that the metaphor is highlighting,[49] and both *Fourth Maccabees* and Paul are drawing out the appeasement/reconciliation for which a ἱλαστήριον stands.

---

[43] *4 Macc.* 17:16; 15:32; 13:6–7; 13:8; 7:10, for instance.

[44] Bailey, "Jesus," 1 §4, 10, 12.

[45] Daniel P. Bailey, "Greek Heroes Who Happen to be Jewish: The Meaning of ἱλαστήριον in 4 Maccabees 17:22," paper at 2002 SBL Annual Meeting, page 6.

[46] Bailey, "Jesus," 1 §4, 12.

[47] Bailey, "Greek Heroes," 7.

[48] Bailey, "Jesus," Appendix B, Note A, 237–38; cf. "the role of the suffix -τήριον in forming *place nouns*" (64).

[49] This choosing of some qualities and dropping of others is mentioned by Eco, *Semiotics*, 100–101.

Even if pagan and biblical ἱλαστήρια have independent origins, they originated from the same *linguistic* logic: both mean the *place* where the action of ἱλάσκομαι is accomplished, either in a votive offering or memorial, or at the divinely appointed object in the Most Holy Place. Etymology partly undermines the strict wall of separation that Bailey wants to maintain between the biblical and Hellenistic meanings of ἱλαστήριον. It does not mean he is wrong about independent lexical origins for ἱλαστήριον in *Fourth Maccabees* and in Rom 3:25; it just means that we need to allow ancient authors to do what is always done with metaphor: to extend the meaning of a term.

Recognizable cultic themes are too frequent in *Fourth Maccabees* 17 to dismiss cult simply on the basis of lexical origins; and the same can be said about the frequency of martyrological formulas in Paul. The origin of a word sometimes has little do with the complex ways it is used. The meanings of different words "infect" each other through usage, as we see in the current confusion about usage of "comprise" and "compose," of "affect" and "effect," and so on. Of vastly more importance than lexical origin is the fact that, in both Paul and in the Maccabean literature, martyrdom has a vicarious saving effect.

Bailey is certainly correct that, in its *non-metaphorical* usages, ἱλαστήριον cannot be extended to cover the *act* of sacrifice, sacrificial *victim*, and *result* of sacrifice (atonement),[50] but it is also true that the biblical ἱλαστήριον is the geographic center of the whole sacrificial cult, and that metaphorical usage of ἱλαστήριον in connection with other clues to a cultic setting, signifies a sacrificial metaphor. Even if the author of *Fourth Maccabees* was mostly familiar with Hellenistic terms, and therefore with ἱλαστήριον as votive offering, there is no reason he could not have encountered the identically-spelled term for the temple's place of atonement. The term "blood" is out of place if only a votive offering is envisioned, but it is precisely the right feature to signal a metaphoric parallel between martyrs' deaths and sacrificial cult. The literal purity of the temple was a crucial theme for Second Maccabees, the predecessor text to *Fourth Maccabees*.

If Bailey is correct about independent origins for ἱλαστήριον in *Fourth Maccabees* and in Romans, then he is right, strictly in terms of *lexical origin*, to reject the assertion that the two passages "are parallel extensions of the same cultic language,"[51] yet that does negate Dunn's point that the passages involve the same *usage* of the term. The term could have a different origin, but the same *usage*, in the two texts, thus constituting the "same sacrificial metaphor."[52] Bailey may be winning a minor lexical battle and losing the

---

[50] Bailey, "Jesus," 1 §4, 11–12.
[51] Dunn, *Romans 1–8*, 180.
[52] Dunn, *Theology*, 215.

semantic war, here. Clearly, we must examine the context more before we can proceed.

Fourth Maccabees amplifies the propitiatory theme that was already present in Second Maccabees by using three metaphors to describe the significance of the martyrs' deaths: purification, ransoming, and some kind of atonement accomplished by means of "blood":

> The tyrant was punished, and the homeland purified (καθαρισθῆναι)—they having become, as it were, a ransom (ἀντίψυχον) for the sin of our nation. And through the blood of these devout ones and their death as an atoning sacrifice (τοῦ ἱλαστηρίου τοῦ θανάτου αὐτῶν), divine Providence preserved Israel that previously had been mistreated. 4 Macc. 17:21–22

This is the only occurrence of ἱλαστήριον in a soteriological metaphor, before Rom 3:25. It is also one of only two occurrences of ἀντίψυχον[53] in the LXX, the other instance being in *4 Macc.* 6:29, where Eleazar prays "make my blood their purification (καθάρσιον), and take my life in exchange (ἀντίψυχον) for theirs." This pairing of purity and payment, accomplishing atonement by means of "blood," amounts to *sacrificial* atonement.

The martyrs fill the role formerly taken up by the temple sacrifices, before the temple was defiled.[54] Metaphorical atonement is performed when cultic atonement, temporarily, cannot be.

There are four sacrificial elements here: there is a *cleansing* of sin, a *payment*, *atonement* with God expressed through a ἱλασ-word, and the designation of *blood* as the instrument. If one had just one of these ideas, one could argue against a sacrificial image, but with the presence of all four of these ideas in both 6:28–29 and in 17:21–22, sacrificial atonement is unavoidable. God is persuaded *to be merciful* (ἵλεως) by the *blood* of the martyrs acting as the people's *purification* and an *exchange* for their lives (6:28–29). The homeland is *purified* and the sin *ransomed* through *blood* and death functioning as a ἱλαστήριον (17:21–22). I do not know of anything but sacrifice that is said to accomplish purification and reconciliation in connection with blood, and therefore Bailey's anti-sacrificial reading does not convince.

Bailey demonstrates that NRSV's translation of τοῦ ἱλαστηρίου τοῦ θανάτου αὐτῶν as "their death as an atoning sacrifice" is untenable, but does not show why "their death as a place of atonement" cannot be accepted, with

---

[53] This becomes a favorite term of the Christian martyr Ignatius of Antioch (*Eph.* 21:1; *Smyrn.* 10:2; *Pol.* 2:3). See David A. deSilva, *4 Maccabees* (Sheffield: Sheffield Academic, 1998), 150 for further points of contact with Ignatius. All early usages of this rare word are martyrological (Lohse, *Märtyrer*, 70 n.6).

[54] Van Henten, *Maccabean Martyrs*, 142.

"atonement" occurring in a connection with sacrificial ideas: purification of people or land (1:11; 6:29; 17:21); redemption-payment for sin (6:29; 17:21); God being appeased (ἴλεως γενοῦ) by means of "our punishment" (6:28); a ἱλαστήριον "through the blood" (17:22). These are things that would not be said of an inanimate votive offering.

The metaphorical accomplishment of atonement means a *transformation*, not necessarily a diminution, of the cultic concept. For instance, we see that purification of the literal temple is a major theme in 2 Macc 1:18; 2:16–19; 10:3–7; 14:36. However, purification becomes purely metaphorical in *Fourth Maccabees*, no longer linked to the temple. An originally temple-linked purification is accomplished by the deaths of the martyrs. Yet *Fourth Maccabees* makes the purifying/atoning role of the martyrs even clearer than Second Maccabees does.

The relationship between these two Maccabean books, with one genuinely interested in the temple and the other only interested in metaphorical usage of temple phenomena, is like the relationship between temple-interested Leviticus and metaphor-interested Paul. Second Maccabees and Leviticus are Israel-centered in their thinking. *Fourth Maccabees* and Paul use Hellenistic categories of thinking to argue against pagan Hellenism.

Fourth Maccabees has considerable relevance for Paul studies. That it utilizes Hellenistic terms and conceives of biblical realities in a somewhat abstract manner, does more to *indicate* than to *eliminate* relevance for Paul studies, especially when one encounters two passages that draw together sin-repair, purification, blood, and saving (σώζεσθαι, *4 Macc.* 6:27; διασώζω, 17:22). Paul uses δικαι-words rather than σωζ-words in Rom 3:21–30, but rescue/salvation is clearly present.[55] The connections are so suggestive that it is tempting to exaggerate the relevance of this book for Paul studies.

There is even an intriguing foreshadowing of Pauline teaching in the after-effects of the martyrdoms in *Fourth Maccabees*. "Devout reason is master of all emotions" (18:2). "By their right reasoning [the martyrs] nullified his tyranny" (8:15); "your tyranny being defeated by our endurance for the sake of religion" (9:30). So also do Christ and his followers conquer, despite, or perhaps because of, their acceptance of violence against themselves.

The martyrs' deaths led to God's preserving Israel. It is "because of them the nation gained peace" (*4 Macc.* 18:4); their deaths have a vicarious saving effect upon the whole nation. God is *moved* to act because of the heroic deaths of the martyrs, that is, he is persuaded. Even Van Henten, who resists all implications of "propitiation," observes that "the passive καταλλαγήσεται" in 2 Macc 7:33 "may suggest that the Lord is not the one who takes the initiative

---

[55] He does use σωζ-words in Rom 10:1–10; cf. Sanders, *Paul, the Law*, 46.

in the reconciliation."⁵⁶ The martyrs themselves get God's attention and persuade him to ἵλεως γενέσθαι, a common phrase of pleading in Greek and Jewish texts. The martyrs' deaths are propitiatory in that they get God to show mercy.

5.1.4 Paul's Martyrology

It is on this theme of propitiation that Paul clearly departs from the Maccabean theology, at least as regards its overt expression. Paul does not want to describe God as being persuaded or appeased in any way. He specifically indicates in Rom 5:5 that God took the initiative, and in the next verse he has Christ taking the initiative, implying complete unity of purpose between the two. This, of course, is not derived from Maccabean theology. But there are other passages that do say that Christ rescues us from God's wrath, such as "we will be saved through him from the wrath of God"; "Jesus, who rescues us from the wrath that is coming" (Rom 5:9 and 1 Thess 1:10). At least in those verses, Christ's death averts a looming wrath.

Thus, it will not do, to play down the propitiatory implications in Paul as well as in these Maccabean passages. As deSilva argues, "Within the Deuteronomistic world-view ... God's wrath indeed had to be averted before the divine punishment could be lifted."⁵⁷ Paul himself wanted to avoid speaking of God as needing persuasion, otherwise he would not have emphasized generosity; but Paul is somewhat constrained by the popular belief in stern and sure divine judgment, any escape from which must involve persuading God to change his attitude.

The key factor that gives reconciling power to the deaths is the *obedience* of Jesus or of the martyrs, deSilva says.⁵⁸ Obedience amounts to "a perfect sacrifice," and God responds to it as Deuteronomy indicates God would respond to national repentance, by restoring the blessings.⁵⁹ The martyr accomplishes what (in Deuteronomy) the whole people were supposed to accomplish, so one can call the martyr a "mediator ... who restores the relationship between the wayward clients and the offended Patron."⁶⁰

Indeed, this is the effect that Christ's obedience has for Paul; in Rom 5:19 "one man's obedience" overflows and makes "the many ... righteous," much as "the blood of those devout ones and τοῦ ἱλαστηρίου τοῦ θανάτου αὐτῶν" (*4 Macc.* 17:22) preserves Israel. And in Rom 5:9 the obedient one saves others

---

⁵⁶ Van Henten, *Maccabean Martyrs*, 142.
⁵⁷ deSilva, *4 Maccabees*, 139.
⁵⁸ deSilva, *4 Maccabees*, 144.
⁵⁹ deSilva, *4 Maccabees*, 140.
⁶⁰ deSilva, *4 Maccabees*, 138.

from wrath, just as the "devout ones" moved God to "let our punishment suffice for them" (*4 Macc.* 6:28). The obedience of a few (or of one) can avert punishment for the many. There is something *persuasive* about a martyr's death.

What is lacking in deSilva's observations are the similar cultic implications in Second Maccabees, and some connections between Paul and Isaiah 53. The effect of Isaiah 53 is also downplayed by Sam Williams (subsection 5.1.6).

5.1.5 A Standardized Martyrological Formula in Romans?

Van Henten argues that Rom 3:25 fits a standard and recognized pattern of phraseology in martyrological texts that places words related to ἱλαστήριον alongside πίστις-words and αἷμα. In 2 Macc 7:37, the martyrs petition God to be *merciful* (ἵλεως); in v. 40 they die *faithful* (πεποιθώς, a perfect participle related to the noun πίστις); in 8:3 their *blood* cries out to God. In *4 Macc.* 17:21–22, salvation comes through the *blood* of pious martyrs, through the *atonement* that is their death, and back in v. 2 this showed the courage of their *faith* (πίστεως). This shows, says Van Henten,

> that the triad of ἱλαστήριον, αἷμα and πίστις is traditional in a martyrological context, and that therefore πίστις probably refers to the faithfulness of the martyr until death.[61]

This means that it is precisely the collocation of "faith," "blood," and ἱλαστήριον in Rom 3:25 that causes readers to recognize it as a martyrological statement. Changing his terms considerably, Van Henten concludes, "the combination of faithfulness, effective death, and vindication ... was traditional indeed" by the time Paul used it.[62] But in order to make these claims, Van Henten requires a range of nine verses in the earlier book, and twenty-one in the later one, and must draw in different word-forms (adverbial, participial, adjectival, and nominal) in order to find his three word-groups. Further, he has only two predecessor passages upon which to base his assertion about Romans. He may be right, but the evidence is insufficient to assert some formal martyrological code language on the basis of these texts.

Martyrology is a major theme in the Maccabean works and in Romans, with or without Van Henten's formula. All he has shown is that we have three texts where different forms of ἱλασ-words, πιστ-words, and αἷμα occur within

---

[61] Jan Willem Van Henten, "The Tradition-Historical Background of Rom 3:25: A Search for Pagan and Jewish Parallels," in *From Jesus to John: Essays on Jesus and New Testament Christology in Honour of Marinus de Jonge*, ed. Martinus C. De Boer. JSNT Sup 84 (Sheffield: JSOT Press, 1993), 126.

[62] Van Henten, "Tradition-Historical," 127.

spans of one to 21 verses. He tries to enlist Daniel in this series, but there he has to stretch across several chapters to find the desired word-forms, thus showing the paucity of evidence for his thesis.

The connection between Maccabean and Pauline martyrology need not hang on a strained linguistic argument. There are common *ideas*: the purifying significance of the martyrs' deaths (*4 Macc.* 6:30 "my blood their purification"); ideas of ransom or substitution (cf. Rom 3:24; 2 Cor 5:21 with *4 Macc.* 17:22), and, of course, the recurrence of phrases like "who died for us."

Once again, it is important to stress that the martyrdom metaphor is not to be swept into the all-consuming category of "sacrificial theology." The realms in which it originates are martial and political. Only by secondary interpretation does it receive sacrificial metaphorical interpretation. But it receives other metaphors as well. *Fourth Maccabees* likes to return to the athletic one (6:10; 14:5; 17:11–16). But it also chooses the sacrificial one, as we have seen. *Fourth Maccabees* and Paul (especially in Romans) *choose* to interpret martyrdom through sacrificial images. They are under no compulsion to do so; martyrdom can remain fairly free of metaphoric interpretation, affirming only the fundamental values of patriotism, from which it originates.

Even in Paul, we see that he does not always interpret his noble death theme with a metaphor, and that he may use other metaphors than sacrifice. A brief sampling of passages with a dying formula will reveal whether they are always promptly interpreted with a metaphor:

1 Thess 5:10—no metaphor follows;
Gal 1:4—no;
Gal 2:20—yes, justification in next verse;
1 Cor 8:11—no;
1 Cor 15:3—no;
2 Cor 5:14—not promptly, but new creation in v.17, reconciliation in v. 18, ambassadorship in v. 20, and scapegoat in v. 21;
Rom 4:25—yes, juridical words in same verse;
Rom 5:6—yes, with mixed metaphor in v. 9 (juridical and cultic);
Rom 8:32—yes, with juridical metaphor in following verses.

Paul does not always feel obligated to interpret his martyrological comments, although he usually does so in Romans. Unlike the Roman one, he founded the other three congregations addressed above, and they would have heard his metaphors in his preaching.

It is evidence such as this that leads some scholars to argue that cultic imagery plays a minor role in Pauline soteriology. One such is Sam Williams, who sees the martyrology of *Fourth Maccabees* as the only significant influence on Paul's soteriology.

5.1.6 Williams: The Dominance of Fourth Maccabees

Sam Williams claims that the theme of noble death, and *not* sacrifice, motivates Paul's metaphors. He argues that the atonement in *4 Macc.* 17:22 is "the 'answer' to Eleazar's plea at 6:29 ... that God will *make* his blood their purification."[63] And just as God had accepted the martyrs' deaths, so God regards Christ's death as a means of expiation.

Williams says that *4 Maccabees* was written in Antioch around 35 to 40 C.E.[64] He presents strong evidence for its influence on the Epistle to the Hebrews and on Ignatius; and weaker evidence for alleged influence upon Paul.[65]

Williams delineates four possible "models for event interpretation," but for some reason he underestimates the first three:

> 1. ... Jesus himself interpreted his death as a saving event. ... 2. ... The concept of Jesus' death as saving event was a more or less natural outgrowth of familiar OT ideas and current practices: sacrifice, substitution, satisfaction for blood guilt, ransom. ... 3. conceptual parallels ... are sought deliberately. ... The conscious search for the meaning of the crucifixion in scripture. ... 4 ... Similarity of that event to events already interpreted. ... a current tradition of effective and beneficial human death.[66]

Williams thinks that the fourth model excludes the others. The fourth takes place before conscious reflection on the event.[67] He sees the Maccabean martyr model suddenly becoming the dominant interpretation upon its first acceptance by a Christian, without, apparently, building upon previous Christian interpretations. I think it makes more sense to see Christian interpretation as *developmental*, with the more detailed ideas growing out of the simpler ones, that is, to see Williams's models two through four as all operating simultaneously.

Those who had been closest to Jesus surely reflected on his death. According to Acts, it was with Peter's first speech that "this Jesus, delivered up according to the definite plan and foreknowledge of God" (2:23) became a central feature of the proclamation. Three facts are important to note: the death is a *central* part of the message, but there are no "dying for our sins" or

---

[63] Williams, *Jesus' Death*, 41.
[64] Williams, *Jesus' Death*, 248–53.
[65] Williams, *Jesus' Death*, 236–41; on Paul, the strongest of which is on Phil 1:12–30: see 242, 245–47.
[66] Williams, *Jesus' Death*, 57–58.
[67] Williams, *Jesus' Death*, 58.

sacrificial formulas, yet this death was intended and planned by God. As soon as the latter point is made, the door is open for further interpretations along scriptural lines. Before long, Philip is interpreting Isaiah 53 as prophetic (Acts 8:30–35). There are "slaughter" and "humiliation" in Acts 8, but no ἱλασ- words in Acts 8 and no mention of reconciliation through sacrifice. Reflection on the basis of the Suffering Servant precedes the emergence of the atonement metaphors. Jesus' followers found it necessary to interpret his death right from the start, although the notion of his death as cultically-effective did not occur at first. As Horvath says, "The sacrificial interpretation of Jesus' achievement is rather a late development"[68]—late *within earliest Christianity*, that is.

Peter and others reflected on Jesus as rejected Messiah and Suffering Servant, but the explicit interpretation of the death as a cultic event and the centerpiece of soteriology is a further development, to which Paul is our earliest witness, and also the earliest of whom Acts testifies (20:28, expressed in a ransoming metaphor). For Williams, there may have been earlier interpretations than the martyrological metaphor, but they are not worth investigating. He seems not to appreciate the dialogic dimension, the emergence of Christian interpretation in an environment of debate and interpretation.

Seifrid says Williams fails to note vicarious expiation in Isaiah 53 and 2 Macc 7:37, and also overlooks the possibility of atoning ideas emerging among Palestinian believers.[69] I would say that, as the OT's principal example of Level Four spiritualization, Isaiah 53 may be the grandfather of NT spiritualizing strategies. It paved the way by picturing heroic suffering through the metaphors of sacrifice and scapegoat (the latter being present in the bearing-away image).[70] Williams rejects this understanding,[71] arguing for a single metaphor and a single dominant source for Paul, yet one that was written between 35 and 40—probably a number of years after Paul's conversion![72]

Fourth Maccabees is not the only place where Paul and others would have encountered martyrological ideas; that book is part of an already existing

---

[68] Horvath, *Sacrificial Interpretation*, 85; cf. Stuhlmacher's view that the sacrificial death idea comes from "the Stephen circle" (*Reconciliation, Law*, 67, n.20; or possibly from Jerusalem, 99, 175).

[69] *Justification*, 169 n.132. Seifrid, on the other hand, seems not to notice that the Maccabean literature develops the idea much further than Isaiah.

[70] Collins, "Finding," 177, 184.

[71] Williams, *Jesus' Death*, 225–29.

[72] The Damascus road experience is dated at 33 by Martin Hengel and Anna Maria Schwemer (*Paul between Damascus and Antioch: The Unknown Years* [Louisville, Ky.: Westminster John Knox, 1997], xi), and at either 34 or 37 by Knox (*Chapters in a Life*, 85).

martyrological tradition. The notion that the sufferings of Christ took place "in accordance with the scriptures" (1 Cor 15:3) may allude to OT passages about the rejection of prophets (Zech 1:2–6; 7:4–14), the "smiting" of an unnamed prophet or leader (Zech 12:10; 13:7), the sin-bearing "Suffering Servant" of Isaiah 53 (even attributed to Jesus himself in Luke 22:37), and to references to being raised or rescued on the third day (Hos 6:2; Jonah 2:1).

Hengel notes that Isaianic phraseology was attached to the Jewish Hellenistic martyr theologies,[73] but, of course, making a cultic death the *centerpiece* of salvation goes beyond Hellenistic martyrology. The martyr theme could, at best, only account for a portion of Christology. There is nothing in the martyr tradition to indicate that terms such as "Lord" or he "through whom are all things" (1 Cor 8:6) could be applied to a human martyr.

The remarkable deeds and sayings of Jesus had already commanded adulation from his disciples while he yet lived, and his death and resurrection compelled reflection in terms more exalted than "martyr." The real reason why the death of Jesus mattered is because of who Jesus was *before* he was martyred. He taught with authority (Mark 1:22), performed unheard-of healings, sometimes allowed himself to be called Messiah and at other times treated that title with contempt.[74] The death mattered because it was *his* death. It was appropriate—but certainly not sufficient—to apply to him the terms of heroic martyrdom.

Williams ought to have given more credence to models 2 and 3 of his "event interpretation": the need of the followers of Jesus to interpret his death in the light of scripture. He does helpfully draw attention to Hellenistic influence upon Christian thought, but unconvincingly tries to narrow it down to the influence of one Jewish Hellenistic book.

In fact, as Adela Collins argues, the Maccabean fusion of Jewish covenant-loyalty with the Greek idea of an "effective death" is itself *particularly Hellenistic*; it is "typically Hellenistic in that it is created through the fusion of Greek cultural traditions and traditions of a . . . non-Greek culture, " the Jewish culture.[75] I would restate her point by saying: the philosophic[76] and literary identification of values of nobility and loyalty from local cultures with those from the (perceived) "universal" Greek culture was a characteristic of Hellenistic philosophy. It was a way of simultaneously promoting Middle Platonic values and honoring local beliefs; the Maccabean literature

---

[73] Hengel, *Atonement*, 64.
[74] The likely purport of Matt 27:11b; Luke 22:70; 23:3; John 18:36.
[75] Collins, "Finding," 180–81.
[76] By "philosophy" I refer to an activity in which any reader of Greek could participate. It was not just an activity for aristocratic elites, as in Plato's Athens.

emphasizes the latter, but it is trading in Hellenistic currency when it presents loyalty to the Law as the secret of *self-control* (ἐγκράτεια; cf. Gal 5:23). This strategy enables a local culture to claim the badge of universalism for its particularism! Paul's soteriological images also resonate with Hellenistic overtones: the noble death, participation in the fate of a resurrected savior,[77] the atoning effect of expulsion rituals.

As scholars are wont to do, Williams has overstated his case, especially when he claims that his thesis disproves the presence of sacrificial metaphors for the death of Jesus. Sacrificial thinking is already present in *Fourth Maccabees*, as it was in Second Isaiah centuries earlier. Pitting the martyr model against the sacrifice model is a false opposition. It is precisely the conflation of models that makes Paul's arguments compelling, piling illustration upon illustration, each one confirming the other.

I have argued against the one-sidedness of Williams's thesis, but I think it is quite possible that ideas of Maccabean martyrology, as Christianized in Antioch, were a major factor in shaping Paul's gospel. It is likely that, in Paul's time, the Maccabean martyrs were the objects of hero veneration by the Jews of Antioch, something that was Christianized early in that city's congregational history.[78] It is possible that Paul's atonement ideas owe much to Antiochene Christianity.[79] Stuhlmacher doth protest too much, however, on behalf of this idea. Bousset is better: "The full import is first given to the idea by Paul. But the images are at hand."[80]

---

[77] Paul's μυστήρια (1 Cor 4:1) may have triggered associations with the popular "mysteries" such as those of Osiris and Orpheus, with their participatory and resurrection motifs; Günther Bornkamm, *Early Christian Experience* (London: SCM Press, 1969), 190; Bultmann, *Theology 1*, 130, 148–52; W. G. Kümmel, *The Theology of the New Testament According to Its Major Witnesses: Jesus-Paul-John* (tr. John E. Steely; Nashville: Abingdon, 1973), 213.

Even those scholars who argue most vehemently against any possible connection, have grudgingly admitted that Paul borrowed their terminology (Arthur Darby Nock, "Early Gentile Christianity and Its Hellenistic Background," in *Essays on Religion and the Ancient World I* [Cambridge, Mass.: Harvard University Press, 1972], 100–101; A. J. M. Wedderburn, *Baptism and Resurrection: Studies in Pauline Theology against Its Graeco-Roman Background* [WUNT 44; Tübingen: J. C. B. Mohr, 1987], 160–61). This is not to deny that some "History of Religions" scholars went overboard in drawing connections.

[78] Stephen Anthony Cummins, *Paul and the Crucified Christ in Antioch: Maccabean Martyrdom and Galatians 1 and 2*. SNTSMS 114 (Cambridge: Cambridge University Press, 2001), 83–85.

[79] Stuhlmacher, *Paul's Letter*, 59; Idem, *Reconciliation, Law*, 67, 99, 104, 124, 175.

[80] Bousset, *Kyrios Christos*, 116.

5.2 Six Soteriological Metaphors and A Literal Model

Martyrdom is one of Paul's models for understanding salvation, but it is not, strictly speaking, a metaphor. Martyrdom is literal, not metaphoric, since martyrdom, *by definition*, concerns heroic death for others or for a principle, while metaphors utilize imagery from one realm (courtroom, slave-market, the cultic arena, etc.) to describe events in another (an execution). "The metaphor selects, emphasizes, suppresses, and organizes features of the principal subject by" making statements that apply to some other object.[81]

Effective metaphors have deep roots in human experience. Ricoeur says "certain fundamental human experiences make up an immediate symbolism that presides over the most primitive metaphoric order";[82] effective metaphors have their roots in such experiential symbols.[83]

To say that martyrdom is a model for understanding, but not a metaphor, is not to say that there is no interpretation involved. On the contrary, the concept of martyrdom tends to trigger metaphors that will give explanatory power. The martyr model is a first level of interpretation: it only says that someone died for the benefit of others. It is a recognized *category* of deaths, not a metaphoric illustration. To explain the *logic* of the martyr death requires a second level of interpretation, expressed (by Paul) with a cultic or redemptive metaphor. Only when the martyr model is interpreted with the help of a metaphor, does one get an idea of *why* martyrdom had saving power.

I see Paul using this literal model and six metaphors to picture salvation and its beneficial aftereffect. He uses two cultic metaphors, and four "social" metaphors (juridical, reconciliation, adoption, and redemption). Three metaphors picture the actual saving *transaction*: a martyr's death that is interpreted in terms of sacrificial ritual, scapegoat rite, or redemption. The other three metaphors describe the resultant new status of believers: humans are acquitted in the divine assize, they are reconciled to God, they are adopted as sons of God and heirs of Christ.

Paul's soteriological tropes fall into two types of literary usage: models and metaphors. Further, they describe two different things: either the saving event itself, or the resultant status of believers. The following is an attempt to graph this:

---

[81] Max Black, *Models and Metaphors: Studies in Language and Philosophy* (Ithaca, N.Y.: Cornell University Press, 1962), 44–45.

[82] Paul Ricoeur, *Interpretation Theory: Discourse and the Surplus of Meaning* (Fort Worth, Tex.: TCU Press, 1976), 65.

[83] Ricoeur, *Interpretation*, 69.

Kind of literary trope	Realm	Those describing the saving event	Describing believers' resultant status
literal model:	MARTIAL:	martyrdom	
metaphors:	CULTIC:	sacrifice	
		scapegoat	
	ECONOMIC:	redemption	redemption
	SOCIAL:		adoption
			reconciliation
	JURIDICAL:		justification

Is it correct to label the juridical element as "metaphoric"? Since Paul believed in the literal reality of a coming judgment of every person, was the juridical trope metaphorical at all? I think his *usage* of it, at least, is metaphoric, because he repeatedly mixes this image with metaphors from other realms (justification is *by faith*, it is *in his blood*; it is *through the redemption* [Rom 5:1, 9; 3:24]). He is willing to let justification be expressed through and blended with various metaphors. Who ever heard of a ritual substance determining the verdict in a trial? A ransom payment is comprehensible—but also reprehensible—in this connection, suggesting a corrupt judge.

Paul clearly wants his hearers to exercise some imaginative power, not to take metaphors with absolute literalness, but to picture a certain *kind* of transaction, one in which an intercessor obtains mercy for a defendant who was expecting a harsh sentence.

The graph is helpful in several ways. It shows that two of the three metaphors that Paul uses to describe the death of Christ are cultic, while the other (redemption) is often linked to a cultic one. Further, we see that Paul uses the social metaphors to describe the happy aftermath of the saving event. Martyrdom underlies the cultic metaphors, but its *significance* is explained via the metaphors, and Paul is quite comfortable using several. No *single* metaphor has dominating interpretive power.

There is a suggestion of payment in some of the cultic metaphors, but not all of them. Scapegoat has nothing to do with paying anyone, and sacrifice is only sometimes conceived as being a kind of payment. The idea of Christ "paying for your sins" over-emphasizes one of Paul's conceptual models. It makes sense of some passages ("you were bought with a price") but not of others, 2 Cor 5:21, for instance, which involves no payment, but a scapegoat-type of exchange, a magical change of status between righteous Christ and sinful mortals). It is perilous to attempt to reduce Paul's metaphorical repertoire to one image, as McLean and Williams do.

Can Paul's soteriology be sketched out? Roughly speaking, there is an implied 3-step sequence. First there is the martyr-death of Christ, describable either as a ritual or a payment. Then there is a recognition of new status, expressible as redemption or justification; and the final, restored condition is best described with the adoption or reconciliation metaphor, or with the idea of new creation (2 Cor 5:17; Gal 6:15).

Evidently, redemption or ransoming is the one metaphor that underwent a change over time, for Paul. In First Corinthians it could be used for the actual saving event (6:20; 7:23), but in Romans, it only describes the change-of-status result. Believers are justified *through* the redemption that is in Christ Jesus, whom God first had to put forward as the place of atonement (3:24–25). The ritual death of Christ is the foundational event.

5.3 Cultic Thinking

5.3.1 Primacy of the Cultic Metaphor

Noticing that Paul spends more time in Romans explaining the middle steps of the salvation sequence (redemption and justification, or rescue and rightwising) than the first step (the sacrificial or scapegoat death) or the final transformative result, some scholars conclude that justification is the most important element.[84] But in fact the cultic death underlies and precedes justification, and the sacrificial and scapegoat formulas occur at key moments, summarizing or climaxing an argument (3:25; 4:25; 7:4; 8:34; 2 Cor 5:21; Gal 3:13), or providing the foundation upon which an argument is based (Rom 5:9; 6:4–6; 8:3).

The foundation stone of Paul's theology is that the martyr-death of Jesus the Messiah was a great sacrifice or redemption that cleansed or rescued the whole human race, or as many choose to believe.

Despite Paul's extended discussion of justification and his affirmation of new creation, Christ's death as sacrifice or curse-bearer is presupposed. The cultic act precedes both the juridical and transformative outcome.

As regards the sequence of salvation, justification is merely an end-product. The saving act itself—the death of Christ—was not juridical but cultic, with Christ becoming the place where purificatory blood was splashed.

The act of atonement precedes believers' change of status, as cause precedes effect. In Rom 5:9–10, "blood" is the means for the change-of-status, a change described juridically ("justified"), personally ("saved from the wrath"), and diplomatically ("reconciled to God"), but in every case made secondary to the cultic death: "justified *by* his blood," "saved *through* him,"

---

[84] Käsemann, *Romans*, 99–101.

"reconciled ... *through* the death." Justification does not occur by a judicial process, nor reconciliation by normal diplomatic means; rather, a *cultic* substance (blood) somehow wins acquittal and achieves reconciliation. Sacrificial blood has gained juridical, personal, and diplomatic currency!

Paul is deliberately mixing these metaphors, making the cultic metaphor fundamental to the others. The judicial and the ritual models bleed into each other, so to speak. But the ritual act had to precede the legal or transformative result (justification/rightwising) and the interpersonal and diplomatic results (saved, reconciled).

A quick look at how the cultic metaphor underlies the other three is in order:

5:9	Justified by his blood...saved by him from the wrath of God	=	*Sacrificial blood provides a basis for acquittal before God and avoidance of his anger; cultic remedy underlies juridical and personal*
5:10	While we were enemies we were reconciled to God by the death of his Son	=	*Death of the Son is the bargaining chip that negotiates reconciliation, so cultic act precedes diplomatic result*

Participation in the life and, finally, the *resurrection* of the Savior is brought in at the end of 5:10 ("saved by his life").

In Rom 3:24–25, justification and redemption are "in his blood." Even in Acts 20:28, blood is the legal tender that "acquired" the church. The cultic substance has purchasing-power. Luke has a different understanding, but he is aware of Paul's teaching about blood-acquired salvation. He correctly attributes it to Paul in Acts 20:28, the only *indisputably* Lukan passage that makes salvation dependent on blood-redemption. The "body ... blood" passage in Luke 22:19b–20, missing from many important manuscripts, is not likely from Luke's hand. The addition of these words represents "a partial assimilation to the familiar institution narrative reflected in Paul."[85]

In fact, blood atonement occurs in the gospels *only* in the institution passages, which, because of their liturgical significance, early came under the influence of textual correction, most visible in the Lukan textual tradition.[86]

---

[85] Bart D. Ehrman, "The Cup, The Bread, and the Salvific Effect of Jesus' Death in Luke-Acts," *SBLSP* 1991, ed.Eugene H. Lovering, Jr.(Atlanta: Scholars Press), 577–78, 591.

[86] Extensive disagreement among Luke manuscripts (Joseph A. Fitzmyer, *The Gospel According to Luke [X–XXIV]*, AB 28A [Garden City, N.Y.: Doubleday, 1985], 1387) shows that it was a highly contested text. The verses are absent from the oldest Western manuscript (D), the oldest Latin versions (it$^{a\ d\ ff2\ i\ l\ b\ e}$), and the Old Syriac (Curetonianus), but are present in most Greek manuscripts, although with significant variance in verse ordering. REB drops these verses altogether.

Luke is the only gospel that gives us explicit textual evidence of this "correction" of the text by early tradents, but it is likely that in all the NT versions of the institution, "sacrificial concepts ... are historically secondary" and "have overlaid"[87] the story of this event. The original meaning of the Eucharist can be glimpsed in the farewell saying in Luke 22:16–18 and in the Messianic but non-sacrificial version in *Didache* 9–10.

I have noted that Paul used the redemption metaphor for the saving event in First Corinthians, and for the after-result in Romans. Still, even in 1 Cor 7:23, the objective act comes first ("you were bought with a price"), and subjective piety follows ("remain with God," v. 24). This logic never changes. The foundational atoning act brings about the change-of-status for believers, and the ritual killing has to precede any celebration: the (human) paschal lamb was sacrificed before Christians could "celebrate the festival" (1 Cor 5:7–8). In Rom 3:24, Paul separates redemption more fully from the cultic salvation event that preceded it: redemption describes the believer's resultant status. In both epistles, as in Acts 20, salvation is purchased with blood.

Similarly, the curse-transmission also precedes any change of status for the believer, whether the latter is seen as a transformation or a rescue. Christ was "made sin" before we could "become righteousness" (2 Cor 5:21). It is by becoming a curse that Christ redeems us, and only after that do the Gentiles receive a blessing (3:13–14). Rescue (Galatians) and renewal (2 Corinthians) follow the ritual deed.

In all these various descriptions, Christ *does* something (dies, becomes sin), and humans *get* something (righteousness, life, blessing). To speak colloquially, a *deal* was made for us, resulting in release from captivity or condemnation.

Bultmann says that, as Jewish sacrifice was the product of "juristic thinking," so one can say that the notion of Christ as a ritual victim reflects "cultic-juristic thinking."[88] But we do need to note the sequence of salvation: the cultic self-sacrifice of "the one" precedes the juridical rescue of "the many" (Rom 5:15–18). Ritual concepts are never far from Paul's thinking. Not surprisingly, Paul often describes himself and his congregations in cultic terms, especially at the end of his major letter (Romans 15) and throughout his last letter (Philippians).

Dunn says the justification "metaphor is partly cultic"; being rightwised as to legal standing means "unhindered 'access' to God," which is the main function of the cult.[89] Being under legal condemnation would prevent one from

---

[87] McGuckin, "Sacrifice and Atonement," 656.
[88] Bultmann, *Theology* 1:296, 295.
[89] Dunn, *Theology*, 387.

getting the full benefit of the cult. If Dunn is correct this would make justification merely a prerequisite to cultic repair. Dunn's remark implies that the *supreme* end is unhindered access to the cult, and justification is merely a means toward that end. This insight affirms that, despite Paul's lengthy judicial metaphors, he thinks of access to God in cultic terms, as is seen in his vividly participationist interpretations of the eucharistic and baptismal cults.

Paul's lengthy justification discussions are set within a cultic frame of thinking. Justification is merely the middle-piece of a longer discussion that begins and ends in cultic categories. The initial problem is a breakage in cultic access to God, and the final stance of the justified believer is renewed cultic access. If Dunn and Bultmann are on the right track, then Paul's concern with justification is motivated by a perceived need for restored cultic access to God. The old cult has metaphoric relevance, and the new cult is intensely participationist. Access to God still has a *cultic pattern*. When sin interrupts communion with God, expiation must take place, and this requires a successful cultic transaction, winning "access to this grace" (Rom 4:25–5:2). In this process, "Christ" is virtually a cultic event that restores access to God.

Despite the different metaphors Paul uses, a consistent soteriology emerges: salvation results from the death of Jesus, which functions as a cultic event, even a cultic *transaction* that obtained salvation for "the many." Except for Rom 4:25, there is no mention of resurrection in the soteriological formulas, but it would be a mistake to think that resurrection is ever far from Paul's consciousness when he speaks of the death of Christ, as is seen in his repeated mention of it in the participatory remarks in Romans 6. Once Christ did the hard work of taking away sin, his resurrection followed. Likewise, once believers confess Christ and participate in his passion, they too will be resurrected and delivered "from this body of death" (Rom 7:24).

5.3.2 Is Paul's Thinking "Fundamentally Cultic"?

So, does all this mean that "Paul functions within a framework that is fundamentally cultic in orientation"[90]? Did he take purity and impurity literally, believing that cultic purity was now transferred to the church? Was "purity," then, not a metaphorical but a literal notion in Paul's own mind? This is the view of Renwick: "Holiness and purity were ... *essential* qualities of those who could gain valid access to and who were allowed to live within the church, which, to Paul, was the 'temple of God'. . . . 1 Cor 3:16–17."[91] Renwick does not mention that each individual Christian is also the temple of God (1 Cor 6:19),

---

[90] Renwick, *Paul, the Temple*, 74.
[91] Renwick, *Paul, the Temple*, 66.

which suggests a certain fluidity in Paul's expression. Renwick's approach does not allow much room for flexibility in Paul's thinking.

Renwick does not take account of Paul's use of organic images like sowing and reaping, growing by stages, and being transformed. Nor does he do justice to Paul in saying that "the covenantal change instituted by Christ was not first of all a moral one (leading to a change in behavior) but a legal one (leading to a change in covenantal rules)."[92] Surely Paul saw Christ's work as doing both. "Loving" and "bearing one another's burdens" would not have been such central notions in Paul if the moral element were of secondary importance.

Renwick is too literal when he says "In 1 Cor 5:1–8 Paul discusses morality from a cultic perspective."[93] Rather, Paul is *using* cultic metaphors. He is not concerned with a literal problem of "old leaven" in the community, but with improper sexual relationships (5:6–7). And when he culminates this passage by calling for the "unleavened bread of sincerity and truth" (v. 8, *all* the translations at which I looked), this means sincerity is of prime importance, yet Renwick claims "sincerity . . . is clearly not central."[94]

Similarly, Newton opposes understanding Paul as giving an ethical message with cultic metaphors, rather, "such a division between the realm of cult and that of morality would never have occurred to the semitic mind."[95] Newton's view is skewed by extreme hostility to a "liberal" emphasis on ethics. He claims that "ancient Judaism failed to perceive any difference between the ethical and the ritual," sin was a ritual, not a moral, conception.[96] Micah and Jeremiah might wish to demur. Paul certainly knew the difference. He used ritual metaphors as ways to express both ethics and soteriology, but he was not under the spell of a purely ritual paradigm; he could say, "real circumcision is a matter of the heart—it is spiritual and not literal (οὐ γράμματι)" (Rom 2:29). Paul's ritual metaphors carried such rhetorical weight both because ritual concepts were taken seriously *and* because his audience could comprehend an emphasis upon inwardness, on πνεῦμα and καρδία.

A different view is Käsemann's, who argues that cultic metaphor does not mean that the gospel is fundamentally cultic. Paul can use military images (2 Cor 10:4), but we do not conclude that he really conceives of the church as an army, Käsemann argues;[97] and he goes further: he argues for a non-cultic content to Rom 12:1–2, even though cultic imagery is utilized:

---

[92] Renwick, *Paul, the Temple*, 128.
[93] Renwick, *Paul, the Temple*, 79.
[94] Renwick, *Paul, the Temple*, 64.
[95] Newton, *Concept of Purity*, 92.
[96] Newton, *Concept of Purity*, 3.
[97] Käsemann, *Romans*, 393.

Paradoxically the cultic vocabulary which he uses here serves a decidedly anti-cultic thrust.... Christian worship does not consist of what is practiced at sacred sites, at sacred times, and with sacred acts.[98]

This means the replacement of any cultic thinking.... Either the whole of Christian life is worship ... or [worship] gatherings and acts lead in fact to absurdity.[99]

Seifrid also sees "a devaluing of cultic observances," even that "Christian obedience stands in the place of the Temple cult."[100]

But cultic metaphor *does* perpetuate cultic thinking, though in an altered form. Paul's concepts of Christ as a new place of atonement or a new paschal lamb are not anti-cultic, but testify to the development of new cultic forms, with borrowing from the conceptual matrix of the old cult. Such a conceptual form ensured that sacred times and sacred professionals would eventually make their appearance in Christianity. Sacred times are certainly hinted at in the paschal lamb metaphor: "Therefore let us celebrate the festival" (1 Cor 5:8).

It is hardly adequate to say that Paul is "fundamentally cultic," and it is misleading to say he is "decidedly anti-cultic." The one overrates and the other underrates the centrality of cultic events for Paul. It is necessary to study the *metaphoric* transformation of cult in his teaching, in order to properly assess the extent to which Paul's thinking may be "cultic."

The valid insights of Renwick, Newton, and Käsemann need to be synthesized, and shorn of their one-sidedness. Paul *does* think cultically, but cult has been spiritualized, that is, transformed into metaphor, which Newton does not appreciate, sharing a common perception that "spiritualized" means "unreal."[101]

The ethical and the cultic are linked in Paul's thinking,[102] but he can also speak about ethics without mentioning cultic categories (1 Thess 2:12–16; 2 Cor 5:10–12; Rom 7:5–11); they are not inseparable or indistinguishable for him. In 1 Corinthians, however, Paul does speak of ethical wrong as creating pollution that threatens to drive God away from the community, just as Israel's

---

[98] Käsemann, *Romans*, 329.

[99] Käsemann, *Romans*, 327.

[100] Mark A. Seifrid, *Justification by Faith: The Origin and Development of a Central Pauline Theme*. NovTSup 68 (Leiden: Brill, 1992), 191, including n.38.

[101] Newton, *Concept of Purity*, 8–9, 120. Renwick and Käsemann also have difficulties understanding spiritualization.

[102] As they were for some in Qumran: "working justice and suffering affliction" atone for sin; people who live that way will become "a Holy of Holies for Aaron" (1QS 8:3–6).

sin could pollute the temple and drive God out. Here, when the unity of the church is threatened, Paul's "high-group" side comes out, and he shapes his ethical arguments in Jewish cultic categories: sin creates a stain that infects and endangers the community. This side of Paul's thought also appears in his advice to the Philippians to be without grumbling and without blemish, so that he does not regret "being poured out as a libation" (2:14–17). Cultic metaphors are used to encourage subjugation to the group. There is almost no trace of this in Romans, Galatians, or Second Corinthians, where cultic metaphors describe the salvation event and believers' changed status.

When Paul interprets the *Christian* cult, he emphasizes participation in Christ (1 Cor 10:1–21; Rom 6:3–19), which was probably an important point of emphasis in Pauline congregations. *Cult* designates *group* religious practice, and cultic metaphor contributes to the self-consciousness of the group, but that does not mean that Paul's entire thinking is group dominated, that he is unacquainted with the notions of individual moral responsibility or personal faith-experience. The fact is, Paul demonstrates both high-group and low-group thinking; there is some coercive pressure on individuals, but there also is an emphasis on individual confession and salvation (Rom 10:9–10; 1 Cor 4:5).

To say that Paul thinks cultically is to make only the most elementary of observations. The same can be said about the Qumran sectarians, and Newton does say this. What Newton does not observe are the extraordinary differences between the two, the social narrowness of a secessionist sect that disappeared not long after the Jewish War, as compared to the world-embracing vision of Paul and its greater effect.

Unless we take seriously the transformations in theology wrapped up in Paul's metaphors, it is superficial to say that he thinks cultically, for he also thinks *universally*, including the Gentiles in salvation history. One can emphasize this social side, as Dunn and Sanders do, or the connection between hermeneutical method and sociological vision, as Boyarin does, and these are ways of noticing that Paul's metaphors significantly transform cultic thinking. Unless we see that, it is misleading to say that he "thinks cultically" because cult usually reinforces ethnic boundaries, while Paul spiritualizes and transforms it so that the opposite happens:

> "True Jewishness" ends up having nothing to do with family connection . . . but paradoxically consists of participating in universalism.[103]

Paul does not dwell on any metaphor; he will use cultic, economic, and judicial ones, frequently in the same clause. It is important to note the

---

[103] Boyarin, *A Radical Jew*, 94–95.

eagerness with which he mixes them so that the *underlying* point is not overshadowed by any one metaphor. And he can use one metaphor to interpret another.

Paul wants his readers not to forget that Christ fulfills both the promises and the cultic actions of scripture, that his death accomplishes atonement, that his resurrection is the first-fruits of the resurrection of the dead, that Christ and God send the Spirit as a foretaste of the future consummation of our salvation, and that Christ will return in power and judgment. He was the first and will be the first in all these ways, and he will show that he is humanity's leader when he returns in power. Paul does not provide details about most of this, just as he does not provide details about Jesus' life, but he repeatedly restates his main points in different ways. God acts in Christ to fulfill scripture (including providing a new method of cultic atonement), to bestow the Spirit, and to open up a new creation.

Eschatological hope informs every step in this process. I have been obliged to leave most of that aside in this study, but can say at word at this point. Examination of the last sentences in Paul's longer soteriological passages shows that eschatological conviction brings joy: at the end of Romans 5, grace abounds and will exercise dominion; at the end of Romans 8, believers are glorified, and nothing can separate them from the love of God and Christ; capping 1 Corinthians 2, believers have the mind of Christ; culminating 2 Corinthians 5, believers are ambassadors of Christ; and at the end of Galatians 3, they are children of God and Abraham's heirs. By the ends of these soteriological chapters, sorrow and fear are nowhere in sight.

Since rituals are believed to be established by God, there is an aura of solemnity about them, and this carries over into the cultic metaphors. The death of Jesus ceases to be solely a sordid human affair and becomes an expression of God's mysterious way of carrying off human guilt. More than that, the metaphors convey the idea of God coming into human life and suffering as a human. Most of what Paul has to say about the Incarnation (Jesus' obedience unto death, his being born under the law and then taking on the curse of the law, his being sent to deal with sin) is communicated through these metaphors.

Paul did what no one else was able to do: effect a powerful merging of the political/heroic theme of substitutionary death with the mystery theme of representative death, and attach them to sturdy Jewish monotheism. Thus were blended the heroic, mystical, and moral elements into an ethos, a pathos, and an ethic of unparalleled intensity. Ethics now had the depth of self-giving heroism, while heroism had the vivid spirituality of mysticism, and mysticism had the dignity of ethics. This is why discussion of "participationism" must delve into spirituality and into the ethos of noble death, while discussions of "Pauline ethics" have often been found returning to the principal "participationist" passages.

5.4 Formulas of Salvation

Paul wants his readers to get a mental picture of the salvation transaction he proclaims. His *formulas* of salvation often express both an objective atonement (Jesus' death) and a subjective atonement (the new life for believers). Each different version of the formula takes account of some, but not all, of the following elements: sin, sacrifice, martyrdom, sin bearing, penal substitution, interchange, reconciliation, God's love, propitiation, captive-purchase, adoption, justification, vindication, participation, and resurrection. Romans 3:21–26 presents justification and rescue from sin occurring through God's generosity and Jesus' sacrifice. Romans 4:25 articulates penal substitution, resurrection, and justification. Romans 5:8–11 proceeds from love, sin, and substitutionary sacrifice to propitiation ("saved from the wrath") and reconciliation. Romans 5:18–19 hits upon sin, interchange, participation, justification.

Although it must be expressed with more than one metaphor, readers are expected to get a grasp on the kind of transaction being described. *Believing* is essential to benefiting from the righteousness of God (Rom 3:22). In Rom 6:17b, obedience means adhering "to the form of teaching to which you were entrusted." Paul would seem to be equating *obedience* with *belief* here.[104] One is entrusted to a *teaching*. Of course it is far more than *just* a teaching; it is the fundamental orientation and loyalty of a person, serving God rather than sin, becoming "slaves to righteousness" (Rom 6:18).

"Faith" for Paul is trust in, and experience with, God, but it is also essentially the belief in a certain kind of transaction that God has accomplished in Christ's death and resurrection. It is essential to have a conceptual grasp of the salvation transaction, expressible in terms of soteriological formulas. Paul's formulas often allude to Jewish cultic concepts, but with enough generality that Gentiles could understand the images (and that some scholars can still argue against the presence of any cultic allusions). Paul also used economic and political terms (ἀγοράζω, υἱοθεσία, καταλλάγη, δικαίωσις) common among Gentiles.

Paul leaves us guessing as to precisely how and why the sacrificial mechanism works. There is more emphasis on the "righteousness of God" (asserted three times in Rom 3:21–26) than on the details of the sacrificial transaction, more focus on God's generosity than on the nature of the transaction that achieves acquittal for the guilty. The *effect* of atonement for

---

[104] Johnson, "Romans 3:21–26," 85.

Christians is expiation of guilt, aversion of God's anger, reconciliation between God and man—three ways to interpret the same transaction. Paul tends to emphasize expiation and reconciliation, but appeasement is also implied in "rescue from the wrath that is coming" (1 Thess 1:10).

Since *deliverance* is highlighted, is Paul gravitating toward the apotropaic image—causing the wrath of God to pass over? No; apotropaism is an impersonal charm that averts spirit-peril, and Paul is not describing an impersonal event. In many places he makes it clear that it is God's personal attitude that makes him withhold inflicting punishment (Rom 2:8; 3:5; 9:22–24). Paul prefers to emphasize God's generosity and Christ's self-giving, thus partly obscuring the propitiatory and purificatory implications of his metaphors.

Paul affirmed values from both the Jewish scriptures and the best of Gentile philosophy. He described the saving event primarily in ritual terms, while describing its beneficial results in terms of the most pleasant outcomes available in the Hellenistic society of his day: acquittal, reconciliation, and adoption. He linked the martyrdom theme, which had compelling power for Greeks and Romans, to the clear monotheism of the Jewish tradition. Jewish piety and Gentile martyr-phraseology are linked in the statement that "Christ died for the ungodly" (Rom 5:6).

Those apostles and evangelists who were best able to explain the divine irony of the surprising "obedience of faith among all the Gentiles" (Rom 1:5), namely Paul, John, and Luke, became the most influential voices in Christian scripture. Each of them had a typological way of describing Christ and the church as fulfillments of scriptural promise. One of them (Luke) stayed fairly close to the message of the historical Jesus, while positioning Jesus within salvation history; one (John) interpreted Christ as the fulfillment of Jewish holy days and Gentile hopes of illumination; while Paul focused particularly on Christ's death as a saving event, a kind of cosmic transaction that averted the looming divine punishment, but only for those who would obey "the form of teaching to which you were entrusted" (Rom 6:17). This made it especially urgent for Paul (and even moreso for his successors) to articulate brief summaries of the significance of that soteriological transaction.

It is often baffling to account for the emergence of so much superstition and religious extremism in Christian history, given that people like Paul were clearly aware of the dangers of imbalance. The dark under-currents of Christianity were conveyed by the soteriological metaphors. Transactional metaphors of soteriology—adoptive, manumissive, juristic, or cultic—are more than just *pictorial vehicles* for the salvation event, they provide *conceptual content* as well. Each of them utilizes a recognized public transaction that changes a person's legal status or purity condition.

Subsequent generations of Christians developed their understanding of salvation by elaborating Paul's metaphors. These models, then, helped to *shape* the meaning, not just passively to *convey* it. Metaphors carry their primordial baggage with them. Sacrificial metaphors carry ancient ideas of gods who can be conciliated with gifts. The adoption metaphor means humans are not children of God to start with. Scapegoat rituals are based on a primitive notion of manipulation of invisible qualities. It is not surprising, then, that many subsequently developed atonement concepts communicate "a morally monstrous saga."[105]

Paul's message is both part of the problem and part of the solution here. By embodying problematic ideas about God in his *metaphors*, but offering the basis for a solution to such problems in his *arguments*, Paul is at the beginning and the end of all Christian conversation about God. Paul can even be used against Paul, in order to get at the truth about God. To some degree, this means pitting his arguments against his metaphors. I have chosen in this thesis to focus on that aspect which I consider to be more problematic: his metaphors.

There is a heated interaction between scholars who identify sacrificial theology as problematic, and those who see that critique as distasteful. Hanna Wolff identifies with scholars who identify "sacrificial religion" as "quite simply regressive.... one does not at all take responsibility, but transfers it ... onto another who then has to carry my guilt and its consequences."[106] Janowski says this concept of a "cruel" and "unrelenting Judge-God" is not biblical, but comes from the "psychological critique of sacrifice" itself; however, he does admit that the critics point out scholarship's failure effectively to explain how the ancients comprehended cult.[107] What Janowski does not mention is that there is a strong incentive to avoid clear-headed interpretation of cult, since that would uncover ancient assumptions about violent and temperamental gods. Further, there are biblical texts that assume a fairly "unrelenting Judge-God."[108]

Paul is beyond that level, but he utilizes olden ideas in shaping his message. Many of his expressions are strategically designed to appeal to people of his time, but embody implications that can no longer be accepted at face

---

[105] S. W. Sykes, "Sacrifice in the New Testament and Christian Theology," in *Sacrifice*, ed. M. Bourdillon (London: Academic Press, 1980), 74.

[106] Hanna Wolff, *Neuer Wein—alte Schläuche. Das Identitätsproblem des Christentums im Lichte der Tiefenpsychologie* (Stuttgart: Radius-V., 1981), 82.

[107] Bernd Janowski, "'Hingabe' oder 'Opfer'? Zur gegenwärtigen Kontroverse um die Deutung des Todes Jesu," in *Das Kreuz Jesu: Gewalt—Opfer—Sühne*, ed. R. Weth (Neukirchen-Vluyn: Neukirchener Verlag, 2001), 22.

[108] Judg 5:23; 1 Sam 15:18; 28:18–19; Ps 7:11; Hos 14:1.

value (and against which he himself argued: God is not appeased [2 Cor 5:21], justification is a gift [Rom 3:24], God has no intention of condemning [Rom 8:33]).

Many Christian thinkers have felt obliged to find some way of retaining and restating the atonement, and so they have engaged in Herculean efforts at spiritualizing the doctrine, modernizing and altering the primitive notions, so that propitiation gets redefined as reconciliation, penal substitution as co-suffering, and redemption as rescue. Some, but not all, of this redefinition finds roots in the biblical text. Sometimes the spiritualizing effort leads to an assertion that the old notions of appeasement or purchase were never present in the first place.

The problem with all this spiritualizing is that, when its practitioners do not understand their own motives, they distort Paul in order to rescue him. Believers and scholars need instead to uncover and honestly examine their own spiritualizing strategies, their patterns of rationalization, and to scrutinize the value basis underlying the strategies. Only a breakthrough in understanding of our own spiritualizing rationalizations can help us develop a philosophy of spiritual progress, a legitimate goal of Level Six spiritualizing, and the only type of religious philosophy that has any hope of providing common ground between Level Two conservatives and Level Five radicals.

Some differences of interpretation and social vision can actually be resolved through analysis that has explanatory power comprehensive enough to unite conservatives and liberals, which is a pressing need in our time of polarization.

Spiritualization involves a dual commitment, philosophically speaking: one to sincerity of motivation and to ethics, and another to perpetuating the ancient symbol. But eventually the primitive assumptions of sacrificial thinking reemerge in the form of morbid doctrines and psychological distortions. What have been the historical consequences of the recurrent Christian belief that the Jews were the human agents for carrying out a ritual murder, performed upon the body of God? It becomes necessary, eventually, to recognize that certain sacrificial ideas "did not enter my mind" (Jer 32:35).

Conclusion

The soteriology of Paul is found in his interpretation of the death of Jesus, the Messiah. The numerous occurrences of the "dying formula" in Paul are very close to phrases that abound in Greek literature explicating the theme of "noble death" or "beneficial death." With these Greek authors, the significance of the martyrdom comes from the given background of the noble death motif: martial heroism and political loyalty. But with Paul, the meaning of the martyrdom is pictured with a series of cultic and redemption metaphors. The death of Jesus amounted to a kind of transaction that obtained freedom for others, like a redemption payment, or that cleansed them from sin, like a cultic event.

Paul describes the saving event itself (the death of Jesus) with cultic and redemption metaphors, and its beneficial *aftereffects* with social metaphors. Thus, Christ died as a purification offering (Rom 8:3), as a covenant-establishing sacrifice (1 Cor 11:25), as our redemption and place of atonement (Rom 3:24–25), as a sin-bearer (2 Cor 5:21; Gal 3:13), or as the Paschal lamb (1 Cor 5:7). The result for believers is that they are justified, adopted, or reconciled.

The cultic metaphors (sacrifice and scapegoat) convey the impression of a God-appointed method for purification and sin-removal. The social metaphors (redemption, reconciliation, adoption, and justification) indicate a change of social status or standing. When one is justified, adopted, or reconciled, one's social status changes from condemned to acquitted, from servant to adopted son, and from alienated to restored, respectively. With redemption, one is changed from slave to free; this is the one metaphor that Paul uses both to describe the saving transaction and its beneficial aftereffects. Even the cultic metaphors imply a change of spiritual status from sinful to blameless, or from impure to pure.

Cultic metaphors imply that God chooses to *recognize* the crucifixion as an effective ritual and to respond to it. As in Greek and Hebrew cultic practice, what is *done* in ritual evokes a desired response from the god, and the person for whom the ritual is performed experiences an improved status before the god.

Explicating *how* Paul understands the soteriological transaction to work, requires attention to the metaphysical logic of the cultic metaphors, and of redemption. The scapegoat, but not the sacrificial animal, is a sin-bearer. The scapegoat is made loathsome, is abused and driven out to a wilderness demon, while the sacrificial victim is a pure creature carefully offered up to Yahweh at the central sanctuary. The metaphysical logic of these rituals is directly opposite to each other's. Yet Paul uses both as metaphors, even conflating the two in Rom 8:3. Clearly, Paul is less concerned with the whole logic of the ancient rites than with the one aspect—a death for the benefit of others—that suggested these metaphors in the first place. Cultic metaphors confer an aura of solemnity or sacredness on what otherwise was an ugly affair, and enable triumph to be discerned in tragedy.

Levitical sacrifice combines two metaphysical notions: purification (of temple and, correlatively, of people), and tribute-payment to a sovereign. Paul does not remove these meanings of sacrifice, but adds to them. The element of *payment* in what Jesus did is communicated through the market terms ἀγοράζω and ἐξαγοράζω, used four times to describe salvation as purchase or redemption (1 Cor 6:20; 7:23; Gal 3:13; 4:5). Acts 20:28 has Paul describe the church being purchased with blood. The term commonly used for the purchase or manumission of slaves, ἀπολύτρωσις, describes salvation in Rom 3:24; 1 Cor 1:30; and Col 1:14. Redemption is easily conflated with sacrifice, since payment is one of the notions underlying Hebrew sacrifice: the word for sacrificial cleansing (כִּפֶּר) is cognate with the word for payment (כֹּפֶר). However, sacrifice is only sometimes conceived as being a kind of payment; it has a purifying function, with the implied correlate of forgiveness.

Scapegoat has nothing to do with payment, it is purely a transporter. But the sin-riddance and the victimization entailed by scapegoat can be combined with martyrdom to heighten the sacredness of a heroic death for the sins of others.

The atoning death is prior to the acquittal that will happen in the eschatological judgment. Justification is *through* (διά) the redemption, and redemption is *in* (ἐν) the person who was first put forward as ἱλαστήριον (Rom 3:24–25). Ἱλαστήριον means literally "the place of atonement," but *biblically* the most common referent is the mercy seat, the lid of the ark of the covenant. This occupies the holiest location in the temple's sacred space, and the holiest moment in the calendar is the Yom Kippur sprinkling of blood on the ἱλαστήριον. This is truly an awesome and sacred moment, when the temple is cleansed of accumulated impurity resulting from sin.

Paul is describing Jesus as a new ἱλαστήριον, in fact a ἱλαστήριον of faith. This blood-sprinkling is logically prior to the redemption and justification of believers. The same implication is wrapped up in the sequence of events in several other cultic metaphors. Justification is *in* the blood (Rom 5:9); righteousness for believers follows Christ's being made sin (2 Cor 5:21); blessing for the Gentiles follows Christ's becoming a curse (Gal 3:13). The cultic event precedes the beneficial afterresults.

Paul is not tied to any one of these metaphors, but wants the reader to understand that salvation had to be *obtained* for believers by Christ's martyr-sacrificial death. Sonship had to be *secured*: people are not naturally the children of God. People had to be redeemed: they are not naturally free from the enslaving power of sin. A transaction was necessary to secure salvation for alienated, corrupted humanity (Jew and Gentile alike), but to describe the transaction requires the blending of several concepts.

Cultic formulas are the doctrinal bedrock upon which the rest of Paul's argument rests, and are often uttered in passing, in brief clauses. His discussion of spirit and flesh in Romans 8 is surrounded by a sending formula that blends sacrifice and scapegoat (v. 3), and a surrender formula that combines the Aqedah and judicial images (vv. 32–34). Christ died to save us, and Christ will continue to intercede for us. The asceticism of Romans 8 is nailed down at beginning and end by soteriological formulas. Even if Paul is drawing on earlier Christian tradition, the formulas are his own and contain the ingredients he considers crucial. His unique contribution appears to be an emphasis on participation in the fate of the savior: sharing his sufferings and his resurrection (Phil 3:10–11; Rom 8:17), and being liberated from the body's passions by "crucif[ying] the body of sin" (Rom 6:6).

Paul alludes to different aspects of cult in his metaphors: expiation, purity, priestly service. Expiation involves more of purification than of substitution, more of magic than punishment. But in his mixed metaphor in Rom 8:3, sacrifice and punishment are juxtaposed; the Son is sent as a sin offering (περὶ ἁμαρτίας) and sin is punished in the flesh. Mixed metaphors such as this one do entail the notion of penal substitution, even though this is not the idea behind Levitical sacrifice, whose substitutionary theme is mainly economic, functioning like a payment to a sovereign. Penal substitution has undoubtedly been exaggerated by many interpreters of Paul, but the idea is indeed present in his metaphors. And when Paul blends a non-substitutionary cultic event (the scapegoat) with connotations of judgment, he makes the scapegoat take on substitutionary meaning ("for our sake," 2 Cor 5:21). When Christ "dies for us," he is a heroic and a cultic victim; he is victimized by people, but the meaning is turned around by God so as to accrue to people's benefit, when God acknowledges this event as a *cultic* event.

Paul gives his most extended soteriological message in Romans 3–10, and there is no denying that the judicial image recurs frequently in these chapters. Jesus takes on the condemnation that the flesh deserves (8:3), "justifies" believers (both averts the wrath of God [5:9] and makes believers righteous [5:19]), and continues to intercede for believers (8:34). There is undeniably a theme of penal substitution here, along with other themes: magical sin-bearer, heroic death of a sinless martyr, liberator who enables slaves of sin (and law) to become adopted children of God, servants of the passions to become servants of the Spirit (6:4–6, 11–14; 7:4–6, 24–25; 8:3). Jesus is the new ἱλαστήριον, purifying from sin. Believers have only to believe in the Messiah's death and resurrection and to confess them to be saved, and this requirement is the same for Jew and Greek (3:29–30; 4:16, 24; 9:24; 10:9–12). Justification is by faith (3:26, 28; 5:1; 10:10) and righteousness is for those who believe (3:22; 9:30; 10:4).

The key moment in the history of salvation is when, "while we were enemies, we were reconciled to God through the death of his Son" (5:10). This reconciliation is through blood (5:9), which recalls other passages where martyrdom is interpreted through sacrificial images like "mercy seat," "sin sacrifice," "paschal lamb," and "covenant in my blood" (Rom 3:25; 8:3; 1 Cor 5:7; 11:25). Redemption is also blended with cultic images. No one image communicated everything Paul wanted to say about the death of Jesus; from martyrology he draws heroic suffering for others; by blending this with the judicial image, he gets the idea of a penal substitute; by adding the cultic, this penal victim can carry away curse and sin, as though they had never existed.

The logic entailed in these metaphors sometimes goes against the God-concept for which Paul wants to argue. The redemption metaphor indicates that salvation was "purchased," but Paul wants it to be recognized "as a gift" (Rom 3:24). In successive verses, Paul can say that God initiated the saving event, and that the spilt blood averted God's wrath (Rom 5:8–9). Thus, God acts freely, *and also* extends salvation in response to the death of his Son functioning as both a cultic act and a payment.

Paul's insistence on the generosity of God stands in some tension with the implications wrapped up in his soteriological metaphors, which convey the idea of wrath needing to be averted, accusations requiring intercession, curse needing to be borne away, sinful flesh needing to be condemned. Only ritual has such power of reversal.

Paul's metaphors imply both transformation and acquittal, both an inner change, and an outward change of status. He speaks of being filled with the Spirit and becoming children of God, but the same passages (Gal 3 and Rom 8) envision an eschatological court scene. Both judgment and new creation are expressed. His metaphors draw together different and even *competing* concepts of God into one vivid and sustained argument. The concepts are perfectly and consistently balanced, in his own mind. God will punish sinners ... *and* will rescue sinners. Christ had to die so that salvation could be made available ... *and* God offers salvation as a gift. People's wretched sinfulness provokes both the judgment and the interventionist saving activity of God. Some Christians have thought that Paul was indicating that justice was the Father's province, and mercy the Son's, and his metaphors sometimes do imply this, but he never says this overtly. Rather he argues for complete unity of purpose between Father and Son. He also argues that all of this was foretold in the scriptures.

Paul expresses his soteriology through a metaphorical spiritualization of OT events and cult. He interprets the OT typologically, both the narratives and the cult practices; these things were "written for our sake" (1 Cor 9:10) and "our instruction" (Rom 15:4), they were "examples for us" to indicate the church's rituals (1 Cor 10:6). There is an implied rejection or demotion of the old cult, when every benefit formerly thought to come from the cult is now ascribed to Jesus' death. Thus, his stance is completely different from that of scholars who ascribe the powers of soul repair to the sacrificial cult, and find the essence of Jesus' incarnation in it. This Level Two spiritualizing strategy differs completely from that of Paul and the early church fathers, who saw the cult's real function as presaging the saving event, but did not ascribe new values to the old cult, which is a hyper-conservative strategy.

Paul's typology involves setting the new and spiritual way in opposition to the old and material way. This is implied in Paul calling Jesus a "mercy-seat *of faith*" (ἱλαστήριον διὰ πίστεως, Rom 3:25), which recalls his other spiritualized terms: circumcision of the heart, a living sacrifice, the Jerusalem above, in spirit not in letter, all of which speak of a certain break with the old covenant community. Paul's typology provides support and meaning for *Christian* cult, but implies at least some degree of opposition to the Jewish cult, although he never openly expresses rejection of cult. His restraint on this point enables him to claim continuity with the old covenant, and to keep the Jewish scriptures for the church.

Now that the new glory has come, the old is "set aside" (2 Cor 3:11). The new covenant in the Messiah's blood creates the new cult, and leaves for the old one only *typological* significance. Yet it is the type that shapes the antitype. The "feast" that Christians keep was founded by the Messiah being "sacrificed" (ἐτύθη, 1 Cor 5:7). The "new covenant" is established by a covenant *sacrifice*. The significance of the Messiah's martyrdom is interpreted through cultic metaphors; even justification and reconciliation emanate from the place of sacrifice. Jesus was killed before he could be raised, and so believers must be (Rom 6:6–8). Fortunately, the one who functions as the new mercy seat also has transcended death. The story begins, but does not end, at the mercy seat.

Bibliography

PRIMARY SOURCES (AND FOR WHICH LANGUAGE):
BARNABAS (English): James A. Kleist, translator. *The Didache, the Epistle of Barnabas, the Epistles and Martyrdom of St. Polycarp, the Fragments of Papias, the Epistle to Diognetus.* Ancient Christian Writers: the Works of the Fathers in Translation 6. New York and Mahwah: Paulist, 1948.
BARNABAS (Greek): *Épître de Barnabé.* Edited by R. A. Kraft. Sources chrétiennes 172. Paris: Cerf, 1971.
THE BIBLE (English): New Revised Standard Version (NRSV): unless otherwise indicated. (See "Greek New Testament" and "Hebrew Bible," below.)
THE CYNIC EPISTLES (English): Abraham J. Malherbe, editor. *The Cynic Epistles: A Study Edition.* SBLSBS 12. Missoula, Mont.: Scholars Press, 1979.
THE DEAD SEA SCROLLS (English): *The Dead Sea Scrolls: A New Translation.* Michael Wise, Martin Abegg, Jr. and Edward Cook. New York: HarperCollins, 1996.
DIDACHE (English): James A. Kleist, translator. *The Didache, the Epistle of Barnabas, the Epistles and Martyrdom of St. Polycarp, the Fragments of Papias, the Epistle to Diognetus.* Ancient Christian Writers: the Works of the Fathers in Translation 6. New York and Mahwah: Paulist, 1948.
DIO CHRYSOSTOM (English and Greek): *Dio Chrysostom,* Volume 1: Orations 1–11. Translated by J. Cohoon. LCL. London: Heinemann, 1932.
EURIPIDES (English): *Ten Plays by Euripides.* Translated by Moses Hadas and John McLean. New York: Bantam Books, 1960.
EURIPIDES (Greek): *Euripidis Tragoediae,* volume 2. Edited by August Nauck. Leipzig: B. G. Teubneri, 1901.
GREEK NEW TESTAMENT: *Novum Testamentum Graece.* Nestle-Aland[27]. Edited by Barbara and Kurt Aland, Johannes Karavidopoulos, Carlo M. Martini, and Bruce M. Metzger. Stuttgart: Deutsche Bibelgesellschaft, 1993.
HEBREW BIBLE: *Biblia Hebraica Stuttgartensia.* Edited by K. Elliger and W. Rudolph. Stuttgart: Württembergische Bibelanstalt Stuttgart, 1976.
JOSEPHUS (English): *The Works of Josephus: Complete and Unabridged.* Translated by William Whiston. New Updated Edition. Peabody, Mass.: Hendrickson, 1987.
PHILO (English): *The Works of Philo.* Translated by C. D. Yonge. Peabody, Mass.: Hendrickson, 1993.

PLATO (English and Greek):
  Alcibiades. Translated by W. R. M. Lamb, Loeb Classical Library, Plato vol. 8. London: Wm. Heinemann and New York: G. P. Putnam's Sons, 1927.
  Laws. Translated by Robert Gregg Bury, Loeb Classical Library, Plato vol. 10. London: Wm. Heinemann and New York: G. P. Putnam's Sons, 1926.
PROTEVANGELIUM OF JAMES (Greek): TLG electronic database, document 1637.001. © Silver Mountain Software, 1999.
PSEUDEPIGRAPHA (English): *The Old Testament Pseudepigrapha*, 2 vols. Edited by James H. Charlesworth. New York: Doubleday, 1983, 1985.
RASHI (English and Hebrew): *Rashi: Commentary on the Torah; vol. 3: Vayikra/Leviticus*. The Sapirstein Edition. Translated by Rabbi Yisrael Isser Zvi Herczeg. Jerusalem: Mesorah Heritage Foundation, 1999.
SATAPATHA-BRÂHMANA (English): *The Satapatha-Brâhmana According to the Text of the Mâdhyandina School, Part II*. Translated by Julius Eggling. Oxford: Clarendon, 1885.
SEPTUAGINT (Greek): *Septuaginta: Id est Vetus Testamentum Graece iuxta LXX interpres*. Edited by Alfred Rahlfs. Stuttgart: Deutsche Bibelgesellschaft, 1979 [1935].
TESTAMENTS OF THE TWELVE PATRIARCHS (Greek): *The Greek Versions of the Testaments of the Twelve Patriarchs*. Edited by R. H. Charles. Oxford: Oxford University Press, 1908, 1966.
TESTAMENTS OF THE TWELVE PATRIARCHS (English): *The Old Testament Pseudepigrapha*, vol. 1. Edited by James H. Charlesworth. New York: Doubleday, 1983.

SECONDARY SOURCES:
Anderson, Gary. "The Interpretation of the Purification Offering (החטאת) in the *Temple Scroll* (11QTemple) and Rabbinic Literature." *Journal of Biblical Literature* 111 (1992): 17–35.
———. "Sacrifice and Sacrificial Offerings (OT)." Pages 870–86 in *Anchor Bible Dictionary* V. New York: Doubleday, 1994.
Anderson, Jeff. "The Social Function of Curses in the Hebrew Bible. *Zeitschrift für die Alttestamentliche Wissenschaft* 110 (1998): 223–37.
Anderson, Megory and Philip Culbertson. "The Inadequacy of the Christian Doctrine of Atonement in Light of Levitical Sin Offering." *Anglican Theological Review* 68 (1986): 303–28.
Attridge, Harold W. "Philosophical Critique of Religion Under the Early Empire." *ANRW* 16.1:45–78. Part 2, *Principat* 16.1. Edited by W. Haase. New York: de Gruyter, 1978.
———. Review of Robert J. Daly, *Christian Sacrifice: The Judaeo-Christian Background before Origen*. *Journal of Biblical Literature* 100 (1981): 145–47.
Aune, David E. *Revelation 1–5*. Word Biblical Commentary 52a. Dallas: Word, 1997.
Bailey, Daniel P. "Concepts of *Stellvertretung* in the Interpretation of Isaiah 53." Pages 223–50 in *Jesus and the Suffering Servant: Isaiah 53 and Christian Origins*. Edited by William H. Bellinger Jr. and William R. Farmer. Harrisburg, Penn.: Trinity Press International, 1998.

———. "Greek Heroes Who Happen to be Jewish: The Meaning of ἱλαστήριον in 4 Maccabees 17:22." Talk and printed paper given at 2002 Annual Meeting of the Society of Biblical Literature.

———. "Jesus as the Mercy Seat: The Semantics and Theology of Paul's Use of *Hilasterion* in Romans 3:25." *Tyndale Bulletin* 51 (2000): 155–58.

———. "Jesus as the Mercy Seat: The Semantics and Theology of Paul's Use of *Hilasterion* in Romans 3:25." Ph.D. dissertation, Cambridge University, 1999.

———. "The Suffering Servant: Recent Tübingen Scholarship on Isaiah 53." Pages 251–59 in *Jesus and the Suffering Servant: Isaiah 53 and Christian Origins*. Edited by William H. Bellinger Jr. and William R. Farmer. Harrisburg, Penn.: Trinity Press International, 1998.

Barker, Margaret. *The Gate of Heaven: The History and Symbolism of the Temple in Jerusalem*. London: SPCK, 1991.

———. *The Revelation of Jesus Christ Which God Gave to Him to Show to His Servants What Must Soon Take Place (Revelation 1:1)*. Edinburgh: T&T Clark, 2000.

Barrett, C. K. *A Commentary on the Epistle to the Romans*. London: Adam and Charles Black, 1962.

———. "The Background of Mark 10:45." Pages 1–18 in *New Testament Essays: Studies in Memory of Thomas Walter Manson*. Edited by A. J. B. Higgins (Manchester: Manchester University, 1959).

Barth, Karl. *The Epistle to the Romans*. Oxford: Oxford University Press, 1933.

Barth, Markus. *Was Christ's Death a Sacrifice? Scottish Journal of Theology* Occasional Papers No. 9. Edinburgh: Oliver & Boyd, 1961.

Barton, Edwin J. and Glenda A. Hudson. *A Contemporary Guide to Literary Terms with Strategies for Writing Essays about Literature*. Boston: Houghton Mifflin, 1997.

Bary, Wm. Theodore de, editor. *Sources of Indian Tradition*, volume 1. Introduction to Oriental Civilizations. New York: Columbia University Press, 1958.

Bauer, Walter. *A Greek-English Lexicon of the New Testament and Other Early Christian Literature*. Translated and adapted by William F. Arndt and F. Wilbur Gingrich. Second edition. Chicago: University of Chicago Press, 1979.

Beattie, J. H. M. "On Understanding Sacrifice." Pages 29–44 in *Sacrifice*. Edited by M. Bourdillon. London: Academic Press, 1980.

Beers, William. *Women and Sacrifice: Male Narcissism and the Psychology of Religion*. Detroit, Mich.: Wayne State University Press, 1992.

Black, Matthew. *Romans*. New Century Bible. London: Marshall, Morgan & Scott, 1973.

Black, Max. *Models and Metaphors: Studies in Language and Philosophy*. Ithaca, N.Y.: Cornell University Press, 1962.

Blissett, William. "The Scapegoat in Art." Paper presented at the University College Symposium on Post-Modernism, University of Toronto, January 20, 1987.

Bloch, Maurice. *Prey into Hunter: The Politics of Religious Experience*. Cambridge: Cambridge University Press, 1992.

Bockmuehl, Markus. *Revelation and Mystery in Ancient Judaism and Pauline Christianity*. Grand Rapids: Eerdmans, 1997; originally Tübingen: J. C. B. Mohr, 1990.

Borgen, Peder. *Philo, John and Paul: New Perspectives on Judaism and Early Christianity*. BJS 131. Atlanta: Scholars Press, 1987.

Bornkamm, Günther. *Early Christian Experience*. London: SCM Press, 1969.

Botterweck, G. Johannes, Helmer Ringgren, and Heinz-Josef Fabry, eds. *Theological Dictionary of the Old Testament*. Translated by David E. Green. 13 vols. Grand Rapids: Eerdmans, 1980–2004.

Bousset, Wilhelm. *Kyrios Christos*. Translated by John E. Steely. Nashville: Abingdon, 1970; originally published 1913.

Boyarin, Daniel. *A Radical Jew: Paul and the Politics of Identity*. Berkeley: University of California Press: 1994.

Breytenbach, Cilliers. *Versöhnung: Eine Studie zur paulinischen Soteriologie*. Wissenschaftliche Monographien zum Alten und Neuen Testament 60. Düsseldorf: Neukirchener Verlag, 1989.

———. "Versöhnung, Stellvertretung und Sühne: Semantische und traditionseschichtliche Bemerkungen am Beispiel der paulinischen Briefe." *New Testament Studies* 39 (1993): 59–79.

Brichto, Herbert Chanan. "On Slaughter and Sacrifice, Blood and Atonement." *Hebrew Union College Annual* 47 (1976): 19–55.

Brondos, David. "The Cross and the Curse: Galatians 3:13 and Paul's Doctrine of Redemption." *Journal for the Study of the New Testament* 81 (2001): 2–32.

Brown, John Pairman. "The Sacrificial Cult and Its Critique in Greek and Hebrew (I)." *Journal of Semitic Studies* 24 (1979): 159–73.

Bultmann, Rudolf. *Theology of the New Testament*, volume 1. New York: Charles Scribner's Sons, 1951.

Burkert, Walter. "Greek Tragedy and Sacrificial Ritual." *Greek, Roman, and Byzantine Studies* 7 (1966): 87–121.

———. *Structure and History in Greek Mythology and Ritual*. Sather Classical Lectures 47. Berkeley: University of California Press, 1979.

Byrne, Brendan. *Romans*. Sacra Pagina 6. Collegeville, Minn.: Liturgical, 1996.

Campbell, Douglas A. *The Rhetoric of Righteousness in Romans 3.21–26*. JSNT Sup 65. Sheffield: JSOT Press, 1992.

———. "The Story of Jesus in Romans and Galatians." Pages 97–124 in *Narrative Dynamics in Paul: A Critical Assessment*. Edited by Bruce W. Longenecker. Louisville, Ky.: Westminster John Knox, 2002.

Carroll, John T. and Joel B. Green with Robert E. Van Voorst, Joel Marcus, and Donald Senior. *The Death of Jesus in Early Christianity*. Peabody, Mass.: Hendrickson, 1995.

Chilton, Bruce. "The Hungry Knife: Toward a Sense of Sacrifice." Pages 122–38 in *The Bible in Human Society: Essays in Honour of John Rogerson*. Edited by M. Daniel Carroll R., David J. A. Clines, and Philip R. Davies. JSOT Sup 200. Sheffield: Sheffield Academic, 1995.

———. *The Temple of Jesus: His Sacrificial Program within a Cultural History of Sacrifice*. University Park: Pennsylvania State University Press, 1992.

Ciholas, Paul. "Knowledge and Faith: Pauline Platonisms and the Spiritualization of Reality." *Perspectives in Religious Studies* 3 (1976): 188–201.

Cohen, Shaye J. D. *From the Maccabees to the Mishnah*. LEC. Philadelphia: Westminster, 1987.

Collins, Adela Yarbro. "Finding Meaning in the Death of Jesus." *Journal of Religion* 78 (1998): 175–96.

Collins, John J. "The Place of the Fourth Sibyl in the Development of the Jewish Sibyllina." *Journal of Jewish Studies* 25 (1974): 365–80.

Clooney, Francis X. "Sacrifice and Its Spiritualization in Christian and Hindu Traditions: A Study in Comparative Theology [Jaimin, Ramanuja, Srivaisnava]." *Harvard Theological Review* 78 (1985): 361–80.

Cranfield, C. E. B. *A Critical and Exegetical Commentary on the Epistle to the Romans*, volume 1. ICC. Edinburgh: T&T Clark Ltd., 1975.

Cullmann, Oscar. *The Christology of the New Testament*. London: SCM, 1959.

Cummins, Stephen Anthony. *Paul and the Crucified Christ in Antioch: Maccabean Martyrdom and Galatians 1 and 2*. SNTSMS 114. Cambridge: Cambridge University Press, 2001.

Cumont, Franz. *The Oriental Religions in Roman Paganism*. New York: Dover, 1956 (original English: 1911).

Dahl, Nils. "The Atonement—an adequate reward for the Akedah? (Rom 8:32)." Pages 15–29 in *Neotestamentica et Semitica: Studies in Honour of Matthew Black*. Edited by E. Earle Ellis and Max Wilcox. Edinburgh: T&T Clark, 1969.

Dalferth, I. U. "Christ Died For Us: Reflections on the Sacrificial Language of Salvation." Pages 299–325 in *Sacrifice and Redemption: Durham Essays in Theology*. Edited by S. W. Sykes. Cambridge: Cambridge University Press, 1991.

Daly, Robert J., S.J. *Christian Sacrifice: The Judaeo-Christian Background before Origen*. Catholic University of America Studies in Christian Antiquity 18. Washington: Catholic University of America Press, 1978.

———. "Is Christianity Sacrificial or Antisacrificial?" *Religion* 27 (1997): 231–43.

———. *The Origins of the Christian Doctrine of Sacrifice*. Philadelphia: Fortress, 1978.

———. "The Soteriological Significance of the Sacrifice of Isaac." *Catholic Biblical Quarterly* 39 (1977): 45–75.

Daube, David. *The New Testament and Rabbinic Judaism*. London: University of London, 1973; originally published 1956.

Davies, P. R. and B. D. Chilton. "The Aqedah: A Revised Tradition History." *Catholic Biblical Quarterly* 40 (1978): 514–46.

Davies, W. D. *The Gospel and the Land: Early Christianity and Jewish Territorial Doctrine*. Berkeley: University of California Press, 1974.

———. *Paul and Rabbinic Judaism: Some Rabbinic Elements in Pauline Theology*. Revised edition. New York: Harper, 1948.

Deissmann, G. Adolf. *Bible Studies: Contributions Chiefly from Papyri and Inscriptions to the History of the Language, the Literature, and the Religion of Hellenistic Judaism and Primitive Christianity.* Translated by Alexander Grieve. Edinburgh: T&T Clark, 1901.

Dennis, John. "The Function of the חטאת Sacrifice in the Priestly Literature." *Ephemerides theologicae lovanienses* 78,1 (2002): 108–29.

deSilva, David A. *4 Maccabees.* Guides to Apocrypha and Pseudepigrapha. Sheffield: Sheffield Academic, 1998.

Detienne, Marcel. "The Violence of Wellborn Ladies: Women in the Thesmophoria." Pages 129–47 in *The Cuisine of Sacrifice among the Greeks.* Edited by Marcel Detienne and Jean-Pierre Vernant. Chicago: University of Chicago Press, 1989.

Dodd, C. H. *The Bible and the Greeks.* London: Hodder & Stoughton, 1935.

———. *The Meaning of Paul for Today.* London: Fontana Books, 1920, 1958.

Douglas, Mary. *In the Active Voice.* London: Routledge & Kegan Paul, 1982.

———. "Justice as the Cornerstone: An Interpretation of Leviticus 18–20." *Interpretation* 53 (1999): 341–50.

———. *Natural Symbols: Explorations in Cosmology.* New York: Pantheon, 1982.

———. *Purity and Danger: An Analysis of Concepts of Pollution and Taboo.* New York: Frederick A. Praeger, 1966.

Draper, Jonathan Alfred. "The Jesus Tradition in the *Didache.*" Pages 72–91 in *The Didache in Modern Research.* Edited by Jonathan A. Draper. AGJU 37. Leiden: E. J. Brill, 1996.

Dunn, James D. G. *Jesus, Paul, and the Law: Studies in Mark and Galatians.* Louisville, Ky.: Westminster SPCK, 1990.

———. "Once More: ΠΙΣΤΙΣ ΧΡΙΣΤΟΥ." Pages 730–44 in *SBLSP* 1991. Edited by Eugene H. Lovering, Jr. Atlanta: Scholars Press, 1991.

———. "Paul: Apostate or Apostle of Israel?" *Zeitschrift für die Neutestamentliche Wissenschaft* 89 (1998): 256–71.

———. "Paul's Understanding of the Death of Jesus." Pages 35–56 in *Sacrifice and Redemption: Durham Essays in Theology.* Edited by S. W. Sykes. Cambridge: Cambridge University Press, 1991.

———. *Romans 1–8.* Word Biblical Commentary 38A. Dallas: Word, 1988.

———. *The Theology of Paul the Apostle.* Grand Rapids: Eerdmans, 1998.

———. *Unity and Diversity in the New Testament: An Inquiry into the Character of Earliest Christianity.* London: SCM, 1977.

Durand, Jean-Louis. "Greek Animals: Toward a Topology of Edible Bodies." Pages 87–118 in *The Cuisine of Sacrifice among the Greeks.* Edited by Marcel Detienne and Jean-Pierre Vernant. Chicago: University of Chicago Press, 1989.

Durkheim, Emile. *The Elementary Forms of the Religious Life.* Translated by Joseph Ward Swain. London: Allen & Unwin, 1915.

Eco, Umberto. *Semiotics and the Philosophy of Language.* Advances in Semiotics. Bloomington: Indiana University Press, 1984.

Edersheim, Alfred. *The Life and Times of Jesus the Messiah.* Peabody, Mass.: Hendrickson, 1993.

Ehrman, Bart D. "The Cup, The Bread, and the Salvific Effect of Jesus' Death in Luke-Acts," *SBLSP* 1991. Edited by Eugene H. Lovering, Jr. Atlanta: Scholars Press, 1991.

Elliott, Susan Margaret. "Choose Your Mother, Choose Your Master: Galatians 4:21–5:21 in the Shadow of the Anatolian Mother of the Gods." *Journal of Biblical Literature* 118 (1999): 661–83.

———. "The Rhetorical Strategy of Paul's Letter to the Galatians in Its Anatolian Cultic Context: Circumcision and the Castration of the *Galli* of the Mother of the Gods." Ph.D. dissertation, Loyola University Chicago, 1997.

Engberg-Pedersen, Troels. *Paul and the Stoics*. Louisville, Ky.: Westminster John Knox, 2000.

Enslin, Morton Scott. *The Ethics of Paul*. New York: Abingdon, 1957.

Evans, Christopher. "Romans 12.1–2: The True Worship." Pages 7–49 in *Dimensions de la Vie Chrétienne (Rm 12–13)*. Edited by Lorenzo De Lorenzi. Série Monographique de "Benedictina." Rome: Abbaye de S. Paul, 1979.

Evans-Pritchard, E. E. *Theories of Primitive Religion*. Oxford: Clarendon, 1965.

Everett, Charles Carroll. *The Gospel of Paul*. Boston: Houghton Mifflin & Co., 1893.

Farnell, Lewis Richard. *The Cults of the Greek States*, in five volumes. New Rochelle, N.Y.: Caratzas Brothers, 1977.

Ferguson, Everett. "Spiritual Sacrifice in Early Christianity and Its Environment." *ANRW* 23.2:1151–89. Part 2, *Principat* 23.2. Edited by W. Haase. New York: de Gruyter, 1980.

Fitzmyer, Joseph A. *The Gospel According to Luke (X–XXIV)*. Anchor Bible 28A. Garden City, N.Y.: Doubleday, 1985.

———. *Romans: A New Translation with Introduction and Commentary*. Anchor Bible 33. New York: Doubleday, 1993.

———. "The Targum of Leviticus from Qumran Cave 4." *Maarav* 1 (1978): 5–23.

Fitzpatrick, P. J. "On Eucharistic Sacrifice in the Middle Ages." Pages 129–56 in *Sacrifice and Redemption: Durham Essays in Theology*. Edited by S. W. Sykes. Cambridge: Cambridge University Press, 1991.

Freedman, David Noel, editor-in-chief. *Anchor Bible Dictionary*. New York: Doubleday, 1987–1994.

Fryer, Nico S. L. "The Meaning and Translation of *Hilasterion* in Romans 3:25." *Evangelical Quarterly* 59 (1987): 99–116.

Füglister, Notker. "Sühne durch Blut—zur Bedeutung von Leviticus 17,11." Pages 143–64 in *Studien zum Pentateuch: Walter Kornfeld zum 60*. Edited by Georg Braulik. Vienna: Herder, 1977.

Furnish, Victor Paul. *Second Corinthians*. Anchor Bible 32A. New York: Doubleday, 1984.

Gaster, T. H. "Sacrifices and Offerings, OT." Pages 147–59 in vol. 4 of *The Interpreter's Dictionary of the Bible*. Edited by George Arthur Buttrick. 4 vols. New York: Abingdon, 1962.

Gese, Hartmut. *Essays on Biblical Theology*. Minneapolis: Augsburg, 1981.

Gibson, Jeffrey. "Paul's 'Dying Formula': Prolegomena to an Understanding of Its Import and Significance." Paper presented at the Annual Meeting of the SBL. Toronto, Ontario, November 25, 2002. 22 pages.

Girard, René. *Things Hidden Since the Foundation of the World*. London: Athlone, 1987.

———. *Violence and the Sacred*. Translated by Patrick Gregory. Baltimore: Johns Hopkins University Press, 1977.

Glasson, T. Francis. "Ensign of the Son of Man (Matt 24:30)." *Journal of Theological Studies* n.s. 15 (1964): 299–300.

Goldingay, John. "Old Testament Sacrifice and the Death of Christ." Pages 3–20 in *Atonement Today*. Edited by John Goldingay. London: SPCK, 1995.

Goodenough, Erwin R. *Goodenough on the History of Religion and on Judaism*. Edited by Ernest S. Frerichs and Jacob Neusner. BJS 121. Atlanta: Scholars Press, 1986.

Goodspeed, Edgar J. "Some Greek Notes." *Journal of Biblical Literature* 73 (1954): 84–92.

Goppelt, Leonhard. *Typos: The Typological Interpretation of the Old Testament in the New*. Grand Rapids: Eerdmans, 1982.

Gorman, Frank H. Jr. *The Ideology of Ritual: Space, Time and Status in the Priestly Theology*. JSOT Sup91. Sheffield: Sheffield Academic, 1990.

Gorringe, Timothy. *God's Just Vengeance: Crime, Violence and the Rhetoric of Salvation*. Cambridge Studies in Ideology and Religion 9. Cambridge: Cambridge University Press, 1996.

Grabbe, Lester L. "The Scapegoat Tradition: A Study in Early Jewish Interpretation." *Journal for the Study of Judaism* 18 (1987): 152–67.

Gray, George Buchanan. *Sacrifice in the Old Testament: Its Theory and Practice*. Oxford: Clarendon, 1925.

Greenberg, Moshe. "The Design and Themes of Ezekiel's Program of Restoration." *Interpretation* 38 (1984): 181–208.

Grenfell, Bernard P. and Arthur S. Hunt. *Fayûm Towns and Their Papyri*. London: Egypt Exploration Fund, 1900.

Gundry-Volf, J. M. "Expiation, Propitiation, Mercy Seat." Pages 279–84 in *Dictionary of Paul and His Letters*. Edited by Gerald F. Hawthorne, Ralph P. Martin, associate editor Daniel G. Reid. Downers Grove, Ill.: InterVarsity, 1993.

Gunther, John J. *St. Paul's Opponents and Their Background: A Study of Apocalyptic and Jewish Sectarian Teachings*. NovTSup 35. Leiden: E. J. Brill, 1973.

Gunton, Colin E. *The Actuality of Atonement: A Study of Metaphor, Rationality and the Christian Tradition*. Grand Rapids: Eerdmans, 1989.

Hamerton-Kelly, Robert G. "Sacred Violence and Sinful Desire: Paul's Interpretation of Adam's Sin." Pages 35–54 in *The Conversation Continues: Studies in Paul and John in Honor of J. Louis Martyn*. Edited by Robert T. Fortna and Beverly R. Gaventa. Nashville: Abingdon, 1990.

———. *Sacred Violence: Paul's Hermeneutic of the Cross*. Minneapolis: Augsburg Fortress, 1992.

Hanson, Anthony Tyrrell. *The Paradox of the Cross in the Thought of St. Paul*. JSNT Sup 17. Sheffield: JSOT Press, 1987.

Harrison, Jane Ellen. *Prolegomena to the Study of Greek Religion*. Cambridge: Cambridge University Press, 1903.
Hartley, John E. *Leviticus*. Word Biblical Commentary 4. Dallas: Word Books, 1992.
Hays, Richard B. "The Conversion of the Imagination: Scripture and Eschatology in 1 Corinthians." *New Testament Studies* 45 (1999): 391–412.
———. *Echoes of Scripture in the Letters of Paul*. New Haven, Conn.: Yale University Press, 1989.
———. "Three Dramatic Roles: The Law in Romans 3–4." Pages 151–64 in *Paul and the Mosaic Law*. Edited by James D. G. Dunn. Wissenschaftliche Untersuchungen zum Neuen Testament 89. Tübingen: J. C. B. Mohr, 1996.
Hayward, C. T. R. *The Jewish Temple: a Non-biblical Sourcebook*. London: Routledge, 1996.
Heesterman, J. C. *The Inner Conflict of Tradition: Essays in Indian Ritual, Kingship, and Society*. Chicago: University of Chicago Press, 1985.
Hendel, Ronald S. "Prophets, Priests, and the Efficacy of Ritual." Pages 185–98 in *Pomegranates and Golden Bells: Studies in Biblical, Jewish, and Near Eastern Ritual, Law, and Literature in Honor of Jacob Milgrom*. Edited by David P. Wright, David Noel Freedman and Avi Hurvitz. Winona Lake, Ind.: Eisenbrauns, 1995.
Hengel, Martin. *The Atonement: The Origins of the Doctrine in the New Testament*. London: SCM, 1981.
Hengel, Martin and Anna Maria Schwemer. *Paul between Damascus and Antioch: The Unknown Years*. Louisville, Ky.: Westminster John Knox, 1997.
Hermisson, Hans-Jürgen. *Sprache und Ritus im Altisraelitischen Kult: zur "Spiritualisierung" der Kultebegriffe im Alten Testament*. Neukirchen-Vluyn: Neukirchener Verlag, 1965.
Hill, David. *Greek Words and Hebrew Meanings: Studies in the Semantics of Soteriological Terms*. Cambridge: Cambridge University Press, 1967.
Hofius, Otfried. "Paulus—Missionar und Theologe." Pages 224–37 in *Evangelium—Schriftauslegung—Kirche; Festschrift für Peter Stuhlmacher zum 65. Geburtstag*. Edited by Jostein Ådna, Scott J. Hafemann, and Otfried Hofius, in Zusammenarbeit mit Gerlinde Feine. Göttingen: Vandenhoeck & Ruprecht, 1997.
———. *Paulusstudien*. Wissenschaftliche Untersuchungen zum Neuen Testament 51. Tübingen: J. C. B. Mohr, 1989.
———. "Das vierte Gottesknechtslied in den Briefen des Neuen Testaments." *New Testament Studies* 39 (1993): 414–37.
Hooke, S. H. "The Theory and Practice of Substitution." *Vetus Testamentum* 2 (1952): 2–17.
Hooker, Morna D. "Interchange in Christ." *Journal of Theological Studies* n.s. 22 (1971): 349–61.
———. "Interchange and Atonement." *Bulletin of the John Rylands Library* 60 (1978): 462–81.
———. *Not Ashamed of the Gospel: New Testament Interpretations of the Death of Christ*. Grand Rapids: Eerdmans, 1994.

Horbury, William. "Land, Sanctuary and Worship." Pages 207–24 in *Early Christian Thought in Its Jewish Context*. Edited by John Barclay and John Sweet. Cambridge: Cambridge University Press, 1996.

———. "New Wine in Old Wine-Skins: IX. The Temple." *Expository Times* 86 (1974–75): 36–42.

———. "Septuagintal and New Testament Conceptions of the Church." Pages 1–17 in *A Vision for the Church: Studies in Early Christian Ecclesiology in Honour of J. P. M. Sweet*. Edited by Markus Bockmuehl and Michael B. Thompson. Edinburgh: T&T Clark, 1997.

Horvath, Tibor. *The Sacrificial Interpretation of Jesus' Achievement in the New Testament: Historical Development and Its Reasons*. New York: Philosophical Library, 1979.

Hubert, Henri and Marcel Mauss. *Sacrifice: Its Nature and Function*. Translated by W. D. Halls. 1898. Repr. Chicago: University of Chicago Press, 1964.

Hübner, Hans. "Sühne und Versöhnung: Anmerkungen zu einem umstrittenen Kapitel Biblischer Theologie." *Kerygma und Dogma* 29 (1983): 284–305.

Hughes, Dennis D. *Human Sacrifice in Ancient Greece*. London: Routledge, 1991.

Hultgren, Arland J. *Paul's Gospel and Mission: The Outlook from His Letter to the Romans*. Philadelphia: Fortress, 1985.

Hunter, A. M. *The Epistle to the Romans: Introduction and Commentary*. London: SCM, 1955.

Janowski, Bernd. "'Hingabe' oder 'Opfer'? Zur gegenwärtigen Kontroverse um die Deutung des Todes Jesu." Pages 13–43 in *Das Kreuz Jesu: Gewalt—Opfer—Sühne*. Edited by Rudolf Weth. Neukirchen-Vluyn: Neukirchener Verlag, 2001.

———. *Sühne als Heilsgeschehen: Studien zur Sühnetheologie der Priesterschrift und zur Wurzel KPR im Alten Orient und im Alten Testament*. Wissenschaftliche Monographien zum Alten und Neuen Testament 55. Düsseldorf: Neukirchener Verlag, 1982.

Jervis, L. Ann. "Becoming Like God through Christ: Discipleship in Romans." Pages 143–62 in *Patterns of Discipleship in the New Testament*. Edited by Richard N. Longenecker. Grand Rapids: Eerdmans, 1996.

Johnson, Luke Timothy. *Reading Romans: A Literary and Theological Commentary*. New York: The Crossroad Publ. Co., 1997.

———. "Romans 3:21–26 and the Faith of Jesus." *Catholic Biblical Quarterly* 44 (1982): 77–90.

Judisch, Douglas McC. L. "Propitiation in the Language and Typology of the OT." *Concordia Theological Quarterly* 48 (1984): 221–43.

Käsemann, Ernst. *Commentary on Romans*. Translated by Geoffrey W. Bromiley. Grand Rapids: Eerdmans, 1980; originally Tübingen: J. C. B. Mohr, 1973.

———. *Perspectives on Paul*. London: SCM, 1971.

———. "Zum Verständnis von Römer 3 24–26." *Zeitschrift für die Neutestamentliche Wissenschaft* 43 (1950–51): 150–54.

Kaylor, R. David. *Paul's Covenant Community: Jew and Gentile in Romans*. Atlanta: John Knox Press, 1988.

Keck, Leander E. "'Jesus' in Romans." *Journal of Biblical Literature* 108 (1989): 443–60.

Kellermann, Ulrich. *Auferstanden in den Himmel: 2 Makkabäer 7 und die Auferstehung der Märtyrer*. Stuttgart: Verlag Katholisches Bibelwerk, 1979.

Kittel, G., and G. Friedrich, eds. *Theological Dictionary of the New Testament*. Translated by G. W. Bromiley. 10 vols. Grand Rapids: Eerdmans, 1964–1976.

Kiuchi, N. *The Purification Offering in the Priestly Literature: Its Meaning and Function*. JSOT Sup 56. Sheffield: Sheffield Academic, 1987.

Knohl, Israel. "The Sin Offering Law in the 'Holiness School.'" Pages 192–203 in *Priesthood and Cult in Ancient Israel*. Edited by Gary A. Anderson and Saul M. Olyan. JSOT Sup 125. Sheffield: Sheffield Academic, 1991.

Knox, John. *Chapters in a Life of Paul*. Nashville: Abingdon, 1950.

Koch, Klaus. "The Translation of *kapporet* in the Septuagint." Pages 65–75 in *Pomegranates and Golden Bells: Studies in Biblical, Jewish, and Near Eastern Ritual, Law, and Literature in Honor of Jacob Milgrom*. Edited by David P. Wright, David Noel Freedman and Avi Hurvitz. Winona Lake, Ind.: Eisenbrauns, 1995.

Kraus, Wolfgang. *Der Tod Jesu als Heiligtumsweihe: Eine Untersuchung zum Umfeld der Sühnevorstellung in Römer 3,25–26a*. Wissenschaftliche Monographien zum Alten und Neuen Testament 66. Düsseldorf: Neukirchener Verlag, 1991.

Kümmel, W. G. *The Theology of the New Testament According to Its Major Witnesses: Jesus-Paul-John*. Translated by John E. Steely. 1973.

Lercaro, Giacomo Cardinal, et al. *Instruction on Worship of the Eucharistic Mystery*. Boston: Daughters of St. Paul, 1967.

Levine, Baruch A. *In the Presence of the Lord: A Study of Cult and Some Cultic Terms in Ancient Israel*. Leiden: E. J. Brill, 1974.

———. *Leviticus: The Traditional Hebrew Text with the New JPS Translation*. The JPS Torah Commentary. Philadelphia: Jewish Publication Society, 1989.

Levenson, Jon D. *The Death and Resurrection of the Beloved Son: The Transformation of Child Sacrifice in Judaism and Christianity*. New Haven, Conn.: Yale University Press, 1993.

Liddell, H. G. and R. Scott, revised by H. S. Jones. *A Greek-English Lexicon*. Oxford: Clarendon, 1940.

Liebeschuetz, J. H. W. G. "Religion." Pages 984–1008 in *The Cambridge Ancient History, Vol. XI: The High Empire, A.D. 70–192*, Second edition. Edited by Alan K. Bowman, Peter Garnsey, and Dominic Rathbone. Cambridge: Cambridge University Press, 2000.

Lienhard, Joseph T., S.J. Editor, *Exodus, Leviticus, Numbers, Deuteronomy*. ACCS Old Testament 3. Downers Grove, Ill., InterVarsity, 2001.

Lightfoot, J. B. *Notes on Epistles of St. Paul from Unpublished Commentaries*. London: Macmillan, 1895.

———. *St. Paul's Epistle to the Galatians*. Revised Third Edition. London: Macmillan, 1869.

Lincoln, Bruce. *Death, War, and Sacrifice: Studies in Ideology and Practice*. Chicago: University of Chicago Press, 1991.

Longenecker, Bruce W. "ΠΙΣΤΙΣ in Romans 3:25: Neglected Evidence for the 'Faithfulness of Christ'?" *New Testament Studies* 39 (1993): 478–80.

Lohse, Eduard. *Märtyrer und Gottesknecht: Untersuchungen zur urchristlichen Verkündigung vom Sühntod Jesu Christi.* Göttingen: Vandenhoeck & Ruprecht, 1963.

Lyonnet, Stanislas. "The Terminology of Redemption." Pages 61–184 in *Sin, Redemption and Sacrifice: A Biblical and Patristic Study*, by Stanislas Lyonnet and Léopold Sabourin. Analecta Biblica 48. Rome: Biblical Institute, 1970.

Maccoby, Hyam. *Paul and Hellenism.* Philadelphia: Trinity Press International, 1991.

Malherbe, Abraham J. *Paul and the Popular Philosophers.* Minneapolis: Fortress, 1989.

———. *Paul and the Thessalonians: The Philosophic Tradition of Pastoral Care.* Philadelphia: Fortress, 1989.

Malina, Bruce J. "Mediterranean Sacrifice: Dimensions of Domestic and Political Religion." *Biblical Theology Bulletin* 26 (1996): 26–44.

Manson, T. W. " 'ΙΛΑCΤΗΡΙΟΝ." *Journal of Theological Studies* o.s. 46 (1945): 1–10.

Marshall, I. Howard. "The Development of the Concept of Redemption in the New Testament." Pages 153–69 in *Reconciliation and Hope: Essays on Atonement and Eschatology Presented to L. L. Morris on His 60th Birthday.* Edited by Robert Banks. Grand Rapids: Eerdmans, 1974.

Martin, Dale. *Slavery As Salvation: The Metaphor of Slavery in Pauline Christianity.* New Haven, Conn.: Yale University Press, 1990.

Martin, Ralph. *Second Corinthians.* Word Biblical Commentary 40. Dallas: Word, 1986.

Mathews, Shailer, and Gerald Birney Smith. *A Dictionary of Religion and Ethics.* New York: Macmillan, 1921.

McGuckin, J. A. "Sacrifice and Atonement: An Investigation into the Attitude of Jesus of Nazareth towards Cultic Sacrifice." Pages 648–661 in *Remembering for the Future: Working Papers and Addenda; Volume 1: Jews and Christians During and After the Holocaust.* Oxford: Pergamon, 1989.

McKane, William. "Prophet and Institution." *Zeitschrift für die Alttestamentliche Wissenschaft* 94 (1982): 251–66.

McKelvey, R. J. *The New Temple: The Church in the New Testament.* Oxford Theological Monographs. Oxford: Oxford University Press, 1969.

McLean, Bradley Hudson. "A Christian Sculpture in Old Corinth." *Orientalia Christiana Periodica* 56 (1990): 199–205.

———. *The Cursed Christ: Mediterranean Expulsion Rituals and Pauline Soteriology.* JSNT Sup 126. Sheffield: Sheffield Academic, 1996.

———. "The Interpretation of the Levitical Sin Offering and the Scapegoat." *Studies in Religion/Sciences Religieuses* 20 (1991): 345–56.

———. "On the Revision of Scapegoat Terminology." *Numen* 37 (1990): 168–73.

Merkel, H. "Καταλλάσσω, κτλ." Pages 261–63 in *Exegetical Dictionary of the New Testament*, volume 2. Edited by Horst Balz and Gerhard Schneider. Grand Rapids: Eerdmans, 1991.

Meyer, Ben F. "The Pre-Pauline Formula in Rom. 3:25–26a." *New Testament Studies* 29 (1983): 198–208.

Milavec, Aaron. "The Saving Efficacy of the Burning Process in *Didache* 16.5." Pages 131–55 in *The Didache in Context: Essays on Its Text, History, and Transmission*. Edited by Clayton N. Jefford. NovTSup 77. Leiden: E. J. Brill, 1995.

Milgrom, Jacob. *Cult and Conscience: The Asham and the Priestly Doctrine of Repentance*. Leiden: E. J. Brill, 1976.

———. "Further on the Expiatory Sacrifices." *Journal of Biblical Literature* 115 (1996): 511–14.

———. "Kipper." Pages 1039–44 in *Encyclopaedia Judaica*, volume 10. New York: Macmillan, 1971.

———. *Leviticus 1–16*. Anchor Bible 3. Garden City, N.Y.: Doubleday, 1991.

———. *Leviticus 17–22*. Anchor Bible 3A. Garden City, N.Y.: Doubleday, 2000.

———. "The Priestly Laws of Sancta Contamination." *"Sha'arei Talmon": Studies in the Bible, Qumran, and the Ancient Near East Presented to Shemaryahu Talmon*." Edited by Michael Fishbane and Emanuel Tov, 137–46. Winona Lake, Ind.: Eisenbrauns, 1992.

———. "Rationale for Cultic Law: The Case of Impurity." *Semeia* 45 (1989): 103–09.

———. *Studies in Cultic Theology and Terminology*. SJLA 36. Leiden: E. J. Brill, 1983.

Moore, George Foot. *Judaism in the First Centuries of the Christian Era*. 2 volumes. Cambridge, Mass.: Harvard University Press, 1927, 1955.

Morland, Kjell Arne. *The Rhetoric of Curse in Galatians: Paul Confronts Another Gospel*. Emory Studies in Early Christianity 5. Atlanta: Scholars Press, 1995.

Morris, Leon. *The Apostolic Preaching of the Cross*. 3d ed., rev. Grand Rapids: Eerdmans, 1965.

———. "Atonement." Pages 102–04 in *New Bible Dictionary*. 3d ed. Edited by D. R. Wood. Downers Grove, Ill.: InterVarsity, 1996.

———. *The Atonement: Its Meaning and Significance*. Downers Grove, Ill.: InterVarsity, 1983.

Moule, C. F. D. "Preaching the Atonement." *Epworth Review* 10, no. 2 (1983): 70–78.

———. "Sanctuary and Sacrifice in the Church of the New Testament." *Journal of Theological Studies* n.s. 1 (1950): 29–41.

Moulton, James H. and George Milligan. *The Vocabulary of the Greek New Testament Illustrated from the Papyri and Other Non-Literary Sources*. London: Hodder & Stoughton, 1929.

Newton, Michael. *The Concept of Purity at Qumran and in the Letters of Paul*. SNTSMS 53. Cambridge: Cambridge University Press, 1985.

Neyrey, Jerome H. *Paul, in Other Words: A Cultural Reading of His Letters*. Louisville, Ky.: Westminster John Knox, 1990.

Nikiprowetzky, Valentin. "La Spiritualisation des sacrifices et le culte sacrificiel au Temple de Jérusalem chez Philon d'Alexandrie." *Semitica* 17 (1967): 97–116.

Nock, Arthur Darby. "Early Gentile Christianity and Its Hellenistic Background." Pages 49–133 in *Essays on Religion and the Ancient World I*. Cambridge, Mass.: Harvard University Press, 1972.

Olford, David Lindsay. "Paul's Use of Cultic Language in Romans: An Exegetical Study of Major Texts in Romans Which Employ Cultic Language in a Non-literal Way." Ph.D. thesis, Sheffield, 1985.

Pancino, Antonio. "An Aspect of Sacrifice in the Avesta." *East and West* n.s. 36 (1986): 271–74.

Pardee, Nancy. "The Curse that Saves (*Didache* 16.5)." Pages 156–76 in *The Didache in Context: Essays on Its Text, History, and Transmission*. Edited by Clayton N. Jefford. NovTSup 77. Leiden: E. J. Brill, 1995.

Parker, Robert. *Miasma: Pollution and Purification in Early Greek Religion*. Oxford: Clarendon, 1983.

Patrologia graeca. Edited by J.-P. Migne. 162 vols. Paris, 1857–1886.

Peters, Ted. "Atonement and the Final Scapegoat." *Perspectives in Religious Studies* 19 (1992): 151–81.

Pfluger, Carl. "Progress, Irony, and Human Sacrifice." *The Hudson Review* 48 (1995): 67–92.

Priest, J. "Testament of Moses, Introduction." Pages 919–26 in *OTP*, volume 1. Edited by James H. Charlesworth. New York: Doubleday, 1983.

Prince, J. Dyneley. "Scapegoat (Semitic)." Pages 221–23 in *Encyclopaedia of Religion and Ethics*, volume 11. Edited by James Hastings. Edinburgh: T&T Clark, 1920.

Propp, William H. C., translator and editor. *Exodus 1–18: A New Translation with Introduction and Commentary*. Anchor Bible 2. New York: Doubleday, 1999.

Pruyser, Paul W. "Anxiety, Guilt, and Shame in the Atonement." *Theology Today* 21 (1964): 15–33.

Räisänen, Heikki. *Paul and the Law*. Philadelphia: Fortress, 1983.

———. *The Torah and Christ: Essays in German and English on the Problem of the Law in Early Christianity*. Publications of the Finnish Exegetical Society 45. Helsinki: Kirjapaino Raamattutalo, 1986.

Reich, Tamar C. "Sacrificial Violence and Textual Battles: Inner Textual Interpretation in the Sanskrit Mahabharata." *History of Religions* 41 (2001): 142–69.

Rentdorff, Rolf. "Another Prolegomenon to Leviticus 17:11." Pages 23–28 in *Pomegranates and Golden Bells: Studies in Biblical, Jewish, and Near Eastern Ritual, Law, and Literature in Honor of Jacob Milgrom*. Edited by David P. Wright, David Noel Freedman and Avi Hurvitz. Winona Lake, Ind.: Eisenbrauns, 1995.

———. *Studien zur Geschichte des Opfers im Alten Israel*. Wissenschaftliche Monographien zum Alten und Neuen Testament 24. Düsseldorf: Neukirchener Verlag, 1967.

Renwick, David A. *Paul, the Temple, and the Presence of God*. BJS 224. Atlanta: Scholars Press: 1991.

Reumann, John. "The Gospel of the Righteousness of God: Pauline Interpretation in Romans 3:21–31." *Interpretation* 20 (1966): 432–52.

Ricoeur, Paul. *Interpretation Theory: Discourse and the Surplus of Meaning*. Fort Worth, Tex.: TCU Press, 1976.

Ridderbos, Herman N. *Paul: An Outline of His Theology*. London: SPCK, 1997.

Rives, J. "Human Sacrifice Among Pagans and Christians." *Journal of Roman Studies* 85 (1995): 65–85.

Rodriguez, Angel G. *Substitution in the Hebrew Cultus*. Berrien Springs, Mich.: Andrews University Press, 1979.

Roetzel, Calvin J. *Paul: The Man and the Myth*. Columbia: University of South Carolina Press, 1998.

Rogerson, J. W. *Anthropology and the Old Testament*. Oxford: Blackwell, 1978.

Sanday, W. and A. C. Headlam. *The Epistle to the Romans*. ICC. Edinburgh: T&T Clark, 1900.

Sanders, E. P. *Jesus and Judaism*. Philadelphia: Fortress, 1985.

———. *Paul and Palestinian Judaism*. Philadelphia: Fortress, 1977.

———. *Paul, the Law, and the Jewish People*. Minneapolis: Fortress, 1983.

Sansom, M. C. "Laying on of Hands in the Old Testament." *Expository Times* 94 (1982–83): 323–26.

Schenker, Adrian. *Versöhnung und Sühne: Wege gewaltfreier Konfliktlösung im Alten Testament mit einem Ausblick auf das Neue Testament*. Biblische Beiträge 15. Freiberg: Verlag Schweizerisches Katholisches Bibelwerk, 1981.

Schoeps, Hans-Joachim. *Paulus: Die Theologie des Apostels im Lichte der Jüdischen Religionsgeschichte*. Tübingen: J. C. B. Mohr, 1959. (E.T. below)

———. *Paul: the Theology of the Apostle in the Light of Jewish Religious History*. London: Lutterworth, 1961. (German original above)

Schwartz, Baruch J. "The Bearing of Sin in the Priestly Literature." Pages 3–21 in *Pomegranates and Golden Bells: Studies in Biblical, Jewish, and Near Eastern Ritual, Law, and Literature in Honor of Jacob Milgrom*. Edited by David P. Wright, David Noel Freedman and Avi Hurvitz. Winona Lake, Ind.: Eisenbrauns, 1995.

———. "The Prohibitions Concerning the 'Eating' of Blood in Leviticus 17." Pages 34–66 in *Priesthood and Cult in Ancient Israel*. Edited by Gary A. Anderson and Saul M. Olyan. JSOT Sup 125. Sheffield: Sheffield Academic, 1991.

Schwartz, Daniel R. "Two Pauline Allusions to the Redemptive Mechanism of the Crucifixion." *Journal of Biblical Literature* 102 (1983): 259–68.

Scott, James M. *Adoption As Sons of God: An Exegetical Investigation into the Background of ΥΙΟΘΕΣΙΑ in the Pauline Corpus*. Wissenschaftliche Untersuchungen zum Neuen Testament 2, Reihe 48. Tübingen: J. C. B. Mohr, 1992.

Seifrid, Mark A. *Justification by Faith: The Origin and Development of a Central Pauline Theme*. NovTSup 68. Leiden: E. J. Brill, 1992.

Smith, Brian K. *Reflections on Resemblance, Ritual, and Religion*. Delhi: Motilal Banarsidass, 1989.

Smith, Brian K. and Wendy Doniger. "Sacrifice and Substitution: Ritual Mystification and Mythical Demystification." *Numen* 36 (1989): 189–224.

Smith, Morton. "Pauline Worship as Seen by Pagans." *Harvard Theological Review* 73 (1980): 241–49.

Smith, William Robertson. *Lectures on the Religion of the Semites: The Fundamental Institutions*. 3d ed. New York: Macmillan, 1927.

Smyth, Herbert Weir. *Greek Grammar*. Revised by Gordon M. Messing. Cambridge, Mass.: Harvard University Press, 1920.

Snaith, Norman H. *Mercy and Sacrifice: A Study of the Book of Hosea*. London: SCM, 1953.

Solovyov, Vladimir (here spelled Solovyev). *God, Man and the Church: The Spiritual Foundations of Life*. Translated by Donald Attwater. London: James Clarke, 1938.

———. *Lectures on Divine Humanity*. Translated by Peter Zouboff, revised by Boris Jakim. Hudson, New York: Lindisfarne, 1995.

Stökl Ben Ezra, Daniel. *The Impact of Yom Kippur on Early Christianity: The Day of Atonement from Second Temple Judaism to the Fifth Century*. Wissenschaftliche Untersuchungen zum Neuen Testament 163. Tübingen: J. C. B. Mohr, 2003.

Stowers, Stanley K. "Greeks Who Sacrifice and Those Who Do Not: Toward an Anthropology of Greek Religion." Pages 293–333 in *The Social World of the First Christians: Essays in Honor of Wayne A Meeks*. Edited by L. Michael White and O. Larry Yarbrough. Minneapolis: Fortress, 1995.

———. *A Rereading of Romans: Justice, Jews, and Gentiles*. New Haven, Conn.: Yale University Press, 1994.

———. Review of Troels Engberg-Pedersen, *Paul and the Stoics*. *Review of Biblical Literature* 3 (2001): 24–31.

Strenski, Ivan. "The Social and Intellectual Origins of Hubert and Mauss's Theory of Ritual Practice." Pages 511–37 in *India and Beyond: Aspects of Literature, Meaning, Ritual and Thought; Essays in Honour of Frits Staal*. Edited by Dick van der Meij. Studies from the International Institute for Asian Studies. London: Kegan Paul International, 1997.

Stuhlmacher, Peter. "Cilliers Breytenbachs Sicht von Sühne und Versöhnung." Pages 339–54 in *Jahrbuch für Biblische Theologie, Band 6: Altes Testament und christlicher Glaube*. Neukirchen-Vluyn: Neukirchener Verlag, 1991.

———. *Paul's Letter to the Romans: A Commentary*. Louisville, Ky.: Westminster John Knox, 1994.

———. *Reconciliation, Law and Righteousness: Essays in Biblical Theology*. Philadelphia: Fortress, 1986. [Translation of *Versöhnung*, below.]

———. *Versöhnung, Gesetz und Gerechtigkeit: Aufsätze zur biblischen Theologie*. Göttingen: Vandenhoeck & Ruprecht, 1981.

Swain, C. William. "'For our Sins': The Image of Sacrifice in the Thought of the Apostle Paul." *Interpretation* 17 (1963): 131–39.

Sykes, S. W. "Sacrifice in the New Testament and Christian Theology." Pages 61–83 in *Sacrifice*. Edited by M. Bourdillon. London: Academic Press, 1980.

Symington, William. *On the Atonement and Intercession of Jesus Christ*. New York: R. Carter, 1868.

Talbott, Rick Franklin. *Sacred Sacrifice: Ritual Paradigms in Vedic Religion and Early Christianity*. New York: Peter Lang, 1995.

Tannehill, Robert C. *Dying and Rising with Christ: A Study in Pauline Theology*. Berlin: Verlag Alfred Töpelmann, 1967.

Thayer, Joseph Henry (translated and enlarged by): from Grimm. *A Greek-English Lexicon of the New Testament*, Fourth edition. Edinburgh: T&T Clark, 1901.

Theissen, Gerd. *Social Reality and the Early Christians: Theology, Ethics, and the World of the New Testament.* Minneapolis: Fortress, 1992.

Thielman, Frank. *Paul and the Law: A Contextual Approach.* Downers Grove, Ill.: InterVarsity, 1994.

Thompson, James W. "Hebrews 9 and Hellenistic Concepts of Sacrifice." *Journal of Biblical Literature* 98 (1979): 567–78.

Tomson, Peter J. *Paul and the Jewish Law: Halakha in the Letters of the Apostle to the Gentiles.* Minneapolis, Fortress Press, 1990.

Travis, Stephen H. "Christ as Bearer of Divine Judgment in Paul's Thought about the Atonement." Pages 332–45 in *Jesus of Nazareth: Lord and Christ.* Edited by Joel B. Green and Max Turner. Grand Rapids: Eerdmans, 1994.

Tylor, Edward Burnett. *Religion in Primitive Culture,* volume 2 of *Primitive Culture.* London: John Murray, 1874. Reprinted New York: Harper & Bros., 1958.

Valeri, Valerio. *Kingship and Sacrifice: Ritual and Society in Ancient Hawaii.* Chicago: University of Chicago Press, 1985.

Van Gemeren, William A., general editor. *New International Dictionary of Old Testament Theology and Exegesis,* 4 vols. and Indexes. Carlisle, U.K.: Paternoster Press, 1997.

Van Henten, Jan Willem and Friedrich Avemarie, editors. *Martyrdom and Noble Death: Selected Texts from Graeco-Roman, Jewish and Christian Antiquity.* London: Routledge, 2002.

Van Henten, Jan Willem. *The Maccabean Martyrs as Saviours of the Jewish People: A Study of 2 and 4 Maccabees.* JSJ Sup 57. Leiden: Brill, 1997.

———. "The Tradition-Historical Background of Rom 3:25: A Search for Pagan and Jewish Parallels." Pages 101–28 in *From Jesus to John: Essays on Jesus and New Testament Christology in Honour of Marinus de Jonge.* Edited by Martinus C. De Boer. JSNT Sup 84. Sheffield: JSOT Press, 1993.

Vaux, Roland de. *Ancient Israel: Its Life and Institutions; Volume 2: Religious Institutions.* Translated by J. McHugh. New York: McGraw-Hill, 1961.

Vernant, Jean-Pierre. *Mortals and Immortals: Collected Essays.* Edited by Froma I. Zeitlin. Princeton, N.J.: Princeton University Press, 1991.

Warfield, B. Benjamin. "The New Testament Terminology of 'Redemption.'" *Princeton Theological Review* 15 (1917): 201–49.

Watson, Frances. *Paul, Judaism and the Gentiles: A Sociological Approach.* Cambridge: Cambridge University Press, 1986.

Wedderburn, A. J. M. *Baptism and Resurrection: Studies in Pauline Theology against Its Graeco-Roman Background.* Wissenschaftliche Untersuchungen zum Neuen Testament 44. Tübingen: J. C. B. Mohr, 1987.

Wenham, Gordon J. "The Theology of Old Testament Sacrifice." Pages 75–87 in *Sacrifice in the Bible.* Edited by Roger T. Beckwith and Martin J. Selman. Carlisle, U.K.: Paternoster, 1995.

Wenschkewitz, Hans. *Die Spiritualisierung der Kultusbegriffe: Tempel, Priester und Opfer im Neuen Testament. Angelos-Beiheft* 4 (1932). Leipzig: Verlag von Eduard Pfeiffer.

Whale, J. S. *Victor and Victim: The Christian Doctrine of Redemption.* Cambridge: Cambridge University Press, 1960.

White, John L. *The Apostle of God: Paul and the Promise of Abraham.* Peabody, Mass.: Hendrickson, 1999.

Williams, James G. *The Bible, Violence, and the Sacred: Liberation from the Myth of Sanctioned Violence.* San Francisco: Harper San Francisco, 1991.

———. "Introduction: 'Christianity: a Sacrificial or Nonsacrificial Religion?'" *Religion* 27 (1997): 219–24.

———. "Steadfast Love and Not Sacrifice." Pages 71–99 in *Curing Violence.* Edited by Mark I. Wallace and Theophilus H. Smith. Forum Facsimiles 3. Sonoma, Calif.: Polebridge Press, 1994.

Williams, Sam K. *Jesus' Death as Saving Event: The Background and Origin of a Concept.* Harvard Dissertations in Religion 2. Missoula, Mont.: Scholars Press, 1975.

Willi-Plein, Ina. *Opfer und Kult im alttestamentlichen Israel: Textbefragungen und Zwischenergebnisse.* Stuttgart: Verlag Katholisches Bibelwerk, 1993.

Wilson, Thomas A. "Sacrifice and the Imperial Cult of Confucius." Pages 251–87 in *History of Religions* 41 (2002).

Winter, Michael. *The Atonement.* Problems in Theology. Collegeville, Minn.: Liturgical, 1995.

Wolff, Hanna. *Neuer Wein—alte Schläuche. Das Identitätsproblem des Christentums im Lichte der Tiefenpsychologie.* Stuttgart: Radius-V., 1981.

Wright, David P. "Day of Atonement." Pages 70–76 in *Anchor Bible Dictionary* II. New York: Doubleday, 1987.

———. *The Disposal of Impurity: Elimination Rites in the Bible and in Hittite and Mesopotamian Literature.* SBLDS 101. Atlanta: Scholars Press, 1987.

———. "The Gesture of Hand Placement in the Hebrew Bible and in Hittite Literature." *Journal of the American Oriental Society* 106 (1986): 433–46.

Wright, N. T. *The Climax of the Covenant: Christ and the Law in Pauline Theology.* Edinburgh: T&T Clark, 1991.

———. *The New Testament and the People of God,* volume 1 of *Christian Origins and the Question of God.* Minneapolis: Fortress, 1992.

———. "On Becoming the Righteousness of God: 2 Corinthians 5:21." Pages 200–208 in *Pauline Theology, volume II: 1 & 2 Corinthians.* Edited by David M. Hay. Minneapolis: Fortress, 1993.

———. "Paul's Gospel and Caesar's Empire." Pages 160–83 in *Paul and Politics: Ekklesia, Israel, Imperium, Interpretation. Essays in Honor of Krister Stendahl.* Edited by Richard A. Horsley. Harrisburg, Penn.: Trinity, 2000.

———. "Romans and the Theology of Paul." Pages 30–67 in *Pauline Theology, volume III: Romans.* Edited by David M. Hay and E. Elizabeth Johnson. Minneapolis, Fortress, 1995.

Yoder, J. Howard. *The Politics of Jesus.* Grand Rapids: Eerdmans, 1972.

Young, Frances M. *Sacrifice and the Death of Christ.* Cambridge: Cambridge University Press, 1975.

———. "Temple Cult and Law in Early Christianity: A Study in the Relationship between Jews and Christians in the Early Centuries." *New Testament Studies* 19 (1972–73): 325–38.

———. *The Use of Sacrificial Ideas in Greek Christian Writers from the New Testament to John Chrysostom*. Patristic Monograph 5. Cambridge, Mass.: The Philadelphia Patristic Foundation, 1979.

Zatelli, Ida. "The Origin of the Biblical Scapegoat Ritual: The Evidence of Two Eblaite Texts." *Vetus Testamentum* 48 (1998): 254–63.

Index of Modern Authors

Anderson, Gary, 31, 32, 35, 40, 55
Anderson, Jeff, 108
Anderson, Megory, 141
Attridge, Harold W., 58, 63
Aune, David E., 44
Avemarie, Friedrich, 194–95
Bailey, Daniel P., 9, 124–35, 140–43, 147, 149–54, 156, 176, 179–84, 200–202
Barker, Margaret, 149
Barrett, C. K., 159
Barth, Karl, 141
Barth, Markus, 181
Barton, Edwin J., 155
Bary, Wm. Theodore de, 51
Bauer, W., 128
Beattie, J. H. M., 84
Beers, William, 16, 18
Black, Matthew, 142–43
Black, Max, 211
Blissett, William, 83
Bloch, Maurice, 17, 19–21, 28, 46
Bockmuehl, Markus, 50
Borgen, Peder, 113
Bornkamm, Günther, 210
Bousset, Wilhelm, 72, 210
Boyarin, Daniel, 3, 62, 112–13, 219
Breytenbach, Cilliers, 168, 185–87, 193
Brichto, Herbert Chanan, 39, 43, 168
Brondos, David, 107
Büchsel, Friedrich, 127, 136, 141
Brondos, David, 107
Bultmann, Rudolf, 4, 100, 149, 159, 210, 215–16

Burkert, Walter, 78–80, 195
Burrowes, Bret, 112
Byrne, Brendan, 155
Campbell, Douglas A., 133, 145, 155–56, 166, 173
Carroll, John T., 95
Charles, R. H., 59, 199
Chilton, Bruce, 16, 61, 173
Ciholas, Paul, 60–61
Clooney, Francis X., 50
Cohen, Shaye J. D., 46
Collins, Adela Yarbro, 79, 176, 195–96, 208–9
Collins, John J., 59
Cranfield, C. E. B., 138, 141
Culbertson, Philip, 141
Cullmann, Oscar, 174–75
Cummins, Stephen Anthony, 210
Cumont, Franz, 108
Dahl, Nils, 173
Dalferth, I. U., 61
Daly, Robert J., S.J., 49, 63, 87, 92, 162, 172–73
Daube, David, 88
Davies, P. R., 173
Davies, W. D., 12, 151
Deissmann, G. Adolf, 127–28, 133, 156, 166
Dennis, John, 33–35
deSilva, David A., 202, 204–5
Detienne, Marcel, 23, 28
Dodd, C. H., 136–39, 141, 187–88
Doniger, Wendy, 18–19, 25–26, 51, 60, 65, 190

Douglas, Mary, 21–22, 28, 42, 48, 56, 133
Draper, Jonathan Alfred, 120
Dunn, James D. G., 3, 38, 88–95, 98, 101, 105, 139–40, 142, 146, 148, 161, 164, 174, 177–78, 201, 215–16, 219
Durand, Jean-Louis, 27
Durkheim, Emile, 12, 16
Eco, Umberto, 156, 200
Edersheim, Alfred, 37
Eggling, Julius, 14
Ehrman, Bart D., 214
Elliott, Susan Margaret, 108–9
Engberg-Pedersen, Troels, 110
Evans, Christopher, 58
Farnell, Lewis Richard, 83
Ferguson, Everett, 51, 58
Fitzmyer, Joseph A., 142, 146, 214
Friedrich, G., 132
Fryer, Nico S. L., 145
Füglister, Notker, 89
Furnish, Victor Paul, 174
Gaster, T. H., 82, 102
Gese, Hartmut, 48, 66–68, 88–89, 179, 184, 186
Gibson, Jeffrey, 196–97
Girard, René, 23–28, 81, 197
Glasson, T. Francis, 120
Goodenough, Erwin R., 58
Goodspeed, Edgar J., 159
Goppelt, Leonhard, 70
Gorman, Frank H. Jr., 8, 22, 43, 82, 168
Gorringe, Timothy, 181
Grabbe, Lester L., 24, 83, 91
Gray, George Buchanan, 49
Green, Joel B., 93, 95
Greenberg, Moshe, 33
Gundry-Volf, J. M., 137, 142
Gunther, John J., 59
Gunton, Colin E., 22
Hamerton-Kelly, Robert G., 23–24
Hanson, Anthony Tyrrell, 97
Harrison, Jane Ellen, 83
Hartley, John E., 35, 38
Hays, Richard B., 3, 69, 175
Hayward, C. T. R., 49, 76, 172

Headlam, A. C., 127, 141, 167
Heesterman, J. C., 25–26, 49–51
Hendel, Ronald S., 22, 53, 55
Hengel, Martin, 79, 142, 172, 195–96, 208–9
Hermisson, Hans-Jürgen, 54–56, 176
Hill, David, 1, 86, 164–65, 167, 199
Hofius, Otfried, 101, 179–86, 192
Hooke, S. H., 48, 75
Hooker, Morna D., 99, 117, 166, 179
Horbury, William, 12, 59, 149–53
Horvath, Tibor, 208
Hubert, Henri, 16–19, 28, 46, 80, 84
Hübner, Hans, 185–86
Hudson, Glenda A., 155
Hughes, Dennis D., 47, 65, 80
Hultgren, Arland J., 133, 140, 142, 149
Hunter, A. M., 145
Jackson, Shirley, 81
Janowski, Bernd, 79, 84, 87–89, 176, 180, 183, 223
Johnson, Luke Timothy, 147, 221
Judisch, Douglas McC. L., 29, 137
Käsemann, Ernst, 62–63, 141, 213, 217–18
Keck, Leander E., 147–48
Kellermann, Ulrich, 198
Kiuchi, N., 34–35, 82, 85, 90
Knohl, Israel, 40
Knox, John, 159, 208
Koch, Klaus, 38, 89, 91, 138
Kraus, Wolfgang, 89, 149–50, 152, 153, 156
Kümmel, W. G., 210
Lang, B., 90
Lercaro, Giacomo Cardinal, 7
Levenson, Jon D., 47, 66, 173
Levine, Baruch A., 13, 30, 32, 35–36, 75–77, 83, 175
Liebeschuetz, J. H. W. G., 52
Lienhard, Joseph T., S.J., 184
Lightfoot, J. B., 99, 167
Lincoln, Bruce, 14
Lohse, Eduard, 129–30, 202
Longenecker, Bruce W., 142
Lyonnet, Stanislas, 38, 137, 142, 166–67

Malherbe, Abraham J., 109, 111
Malina, Bruce J., 13, 18
Manson, T. W., 126
Marcus, Joel, 95
Marshall, I. Howard, 149, 169
Martin, Dale, 166
Martin, Ralph, 4
Mathews, Shailer, 75
Mauss, Marcel, 16–19, 28, 46, 80, 84
McGuckin, J. A., 57, 215
McKane, William, 55–56
McKelvey, R. J., 52, 59
McLean, Bradley Hudson, 5–6, 9, 36–37, 48, 73–76, 78–81, 83–84, 86, 88–89, 96, 98–99, 102–3, 106, 115, 119, 123, 140, 142, 212
Merkel, H., 101
Meyer, Ben F., 69–70, 142, 189
Meyer, H. A. W., 131
Milavec, Aaron, 120
Milgrom, Jacob, 13–15, 29–35, 37–40, 43, 48, 75, 77, 83, 85–86, 89, 92–93, 144, 168, 175
Milligan, George, 97, 98, 127
Moore, George Foot, 197
Morland, Kjell Arne, 104
Morris, Leon, 13, 38, 136–39, 141, 156, 165, 168
Moule, C. F. D., 58, 61
Moulton, James H., 97, 98, 127
Newton, Michael, 144, 162, 186, 217–19
Neyrey, Jerome H., 109, 162
Nikiprowetzky, Valentin, 51
Nock, Arthur Darby, 210
Olford, David Lindsay, 50, 70
Pancino, Antonio, 13
Pardee, Nancy, 119–20
Parker, Robert, 82, 97, 106
Peters, Ted, 27
Pfluger, Carl, 48
Priest, J., 199
Prince, J. Dyneley, 5
Propp, William H. C., 75
Pruyser, Paul W., 118
Räisänen, Heikki, 62, 185

Reich, Tamar C., 26
Rentdorff, Rolf, 41, 85
Renwick, David A., 2, 72, 162, 186, 216–18
Reumann, John, 4
Ricoeur, Paul, 211
Ridderbos, Herman N., 141, 166–67
Rives, J., 65
Rodriguez, Angel G., 33–34, 43, 85, 90
Roetzel, Calvin J., 62, 113, 116
Rogerson, J. W., 16, 74
Sanday, W., 127, 141, 167
Sanders, E. P., 50, 117, 160, 203, 219
Sansom, M. C., 83, 88
Schenker, Adrian, 39–40, 79, 87, 89, 168
Schoeps, Hans-Joachim, 43, 172, 174
Schwartz, Baruch J., 40–41, 85–86, 90
Schwartz, Daniel R., 106
Schwemer, Anna Maria, 208
Scott, James M., 170
Seeley, D., 132
Seifrid, Mark A., 208, 218
Senior, Donald, 95
Smith, Brian K., 18–19, 25–26, 49, 51, 60, 65, 190
Smith, Gerald Birney, 75
Smith, William Robertson, 15–16, 28
Smyth, Herbert Weir, 132–33
Snaith, Norman H., 74
Solovyov, Vladimir, 60
Stählin, Gustav, 97–98
Stökl Ben Ezra, Daniel, 83, 119
Stowers, Stanley K., 6, 23, 28, 37–38, 123, 142, 170
Strenski, Ivan, 61–62
Stuhlmacher, Peter, 128, 140, 142, 149, 177, 185–87, 208, 210
Swain, C. William, 12
Sykes, S. W., 141, 223
Talbott, Rick Franklin, 12, 16
Thayer, Joseph Henry, 97
Theissen, Gerd, 105, 158
Thielman, Frank, 140
Thompson, James W., 52, 58
Tomson, Peter J., 110

Tylor, Edward Burnett, 12, 28
Valeri, Valerio, 18
Van Henten, Jan Willem, 194–96, 198, 202–5
Van Voorst, Robert E., 95
Vaux, Roland de, 86, 134
Vernant, Jean-Pierre, 64–65
Warfield, B. Benjamin, 164
Watson, Frances, 113
Wedderburn, A. J. M., 210
Wenham, Gordon J., 29, 91
Wenschkewitz, Hans, 11, 57–58
White, John L., 3, 23
Willi-Plein, Ina, 7, 89
Williams, James G., 23, 55
Williams, Sam K., 141, 149, 205–10, 212
Wilson, Thomas A., 14, 49
Wolff, Hanna, 223
Wright, David P., 35, 76, 78, 86–87, 90, 92
Wright, N. T., 11, 100–101, 107–8, 114–15, 167, 197
Young, Frances M., 57–58, 162
Zatelli, Ida, 82

Index of Ancient Texts

Hebrew Bible
*('MT' or 'LXX' given only
when versification differs
from NRSV)*

Genesis
4:3–5	13
8:20	40
8:21	15, 29
15:9–21	71
22	173
22:9	172
22:12b	172
22:13	64
22:17	20
32:20–21	39
50:17	86

Exodus
4:24–26	19, 169
6:6	151
10:17	86
12–13	66
12:23	74
13:2	47
13:13	47
14:31–15:1	150
15	150–51
15:1	151
15:13	151
15:13–17	151
19:6	166
21:30	43
22:7–9	44
22:29	47
24:6–8	71
24:7–8	140
24:8	71
25:17	125, 150
25:18–22	125
25:21	125
25:22	125, 153
29:1	162
29:23	140
29:36	32
29:42	162
30:16	39
32:7	138
32:10–14	38
32:11	138
32:12	138
32:14	136, 138
32:30	168
34:20	47
40:23	140

Leviticus
1:9	18
1:17	29
3:11	14
4	32, 34, 37
4:1–5:13	34
4:6	34
4:20	34
4:26	34
4:31	34
4:35	34
5	37
5:1	85
5:1–3	34
5:2	85
5:6	32
5:10	34
5:13	34
5:18	34
5:24 MT	43
6:5	43
6:17ff MT	32
6:25ff	32
7:1–7	32
7:7	32
7:8	161
9:24	31, 45
10:2	46
10:17	84–85
13:2	162
14	106
14:1–7	76
14:7	106
14:48–54	76
14:53	106
16	106, 154
16:2	125, 153
16:5–15	32
16:6	36
16:7–10	36
16:8–9	76
16:9–10	76
16:10	36, 77, 88, 106
16:11–14	36
16:15	36
16:16	33
16:16–17	36
16:17	36
16:18–19	36
16:20	36
16:21	86, 88–89
16:21–22	36, 75, 88, 106

255

Leviticus (cont'd)		17:5	31	2 Kings	
16:22	76, 88	18:23	39	24:4	139
16:23–24a	36	25:11	39, 199		
16:24	34, 36	25:13	39, 199	1 Chronicles	
16:24b	36	26:10	46	21:26	31, 45, 154
16:25	36	27:18	88	28:18	125
16:26	36, 75–76	27:23	88		
16:27	36	28:2	14, 29	2 Chronicles	
16:27–28	36	28:24	14	6:21	138
16:29–34	36	31:50	39, 168	6:25	138
16:30	36, 137			7:1	31, 45, 154
16:32–34	36	Deuteronomy		26:16–21	46
16:33	34, 36	7:8	135, 165		
17	40, 67	12:23	41	Psalms	
17:3–5	67	16	65	4:5	53
17:7	66	16:2	75	7:11	223
17:10	67	16:16	13	22	8
17:11	41–43, 67	21:8	138	32:7	165
17:12–13	67	24:16	18	40	56
17:14	41	26:18	105	40:6	54
17:15	67	30:1–3	105	40:8	54
21:6	14	30:19	105	50	56
21:8	14	32	150	50:9	53
21:17	14	34:9	86	50:12–13	53
21:21	14			51	56
22:25	29	Judges		51:1–2	137
24:14	88	5:23	223	51:10	49
		6:18	13	51:14	53
Numbers		6:21	31	51:16	53
1:53	39	9:20	108	51:17	49
3:4	31, 46	15:18	223	68:30	13
3:6	31, 45			69	8
3:10	11, 31	1 Samuel		77:54 LXX	150
3:12	162	15:22	54	78:38	38
3:13	98	26:19	40	98:2	150
5:7	43	28:18–19	223	106:23	198
5:20–27	108			106:30	139
6:11	33	2 Samuel		106:31	39
7:89	125, 153–54	6:6–7	30, 46	106:37–42	48
8:10	88	21:6–6	39	119:154–165	151
8:17	162	24:24	93	130:7–8	165
8:17–19	43			136:24	165
8:19	39	1 Kings		141:2	49
12:10	46	6:23–28	125		
15	37	8:30	138	Proverbs	
15:7	31	8:44	30	15:8	53
15:9	31	8:48	30	16:14	39
15:25	13	16:34	47	21:3	54
16:35–38	31, 46	18:38	31	30:10	108

Isaiah		7:4–5	56	6:5	55
1	56–57	7:9–11	55	6:6	54–55, 57
1:13	54	7:11	57	6:8–10	55
1:18	88	7:22	57	6:10	56
18:3	120	7:22–23	54	7:13	151
18:7	13	7:31	48	8:11	55
19:21	54	19:5	48	8:11–14	56
21:18	97	26:6	104	8:12	55
30:27	49	29:18	104	8:13	56
31:5	166	31	71	10:1	55
41:14	165	31:29–30	18	10:2	55
43:1	165	31:31	71	11:1	55
43:2	183	32:35	48, 224	12:7	151
43:5	183	34:18–20	71	13:14	151
43:21	166	38:31 LXX	71	14:1	223
50:8	183				
52-53	175	*Ezekiel*		*Amos*	
52:3	165	4	48	5	57
52:7b	175	6:13	29	5:12	43
52:10b	175	16:21	74	5:21	54
52:13	175	18	18	5:21–25	54
52:15	175	37:28	162	5:23	57
53	8, 48, 96,	41:22	29	7:2	138
	107, 163–64,	43	133, 149–50	7:10	56
	174–77, 179,	43:14	134	9:1	133–34
	181–84, 205,	43:18	149		
	208–9	43:20	33, 134, 150		
53:4	175–76, 179	43:20–23	134	*Jonah*	
53:4–6	176	43:21	32	2:1	209
53:5	175–76	43:22	127, 134		
53:5–12	183	43:26	33, 127	*Micah*	
53:6	174–75	43:26–27	150	6	55
53:6b	176	43:27	127	6:6	57
53:8	175	44:16	29	6:7	53
53:8–9	176			6:8	53, 57
53:10	32, 163,	*Lamentations*			
	175–76	5:8	165	*Zechariah*	
53:11	174–75, 177,			1:2–6	209
	183	*Daniel*		5	76
53:11b	176	9:16–19	138	7:2	136, 139
53:12	174, 176			7:4–14	209
53:12c	175	*Hosea*		8:22	137, 139
56:1	150	2:14–15	55	9	71
57:15	183	4:1–2	56	9:11	71
66	56	4:6	55–56	9:11a	71
66:3	54	4:8	55	11	8
		4:10–18	55	12:10	209
Jeremiah		5:3	56	13	8
2:8	55	5:4	56	13:7	209
7:4	55	6:2	209		

Malachi		*Acts*		3:24–25	5, 100, 124, 144, 151–53, 158, 168, 187, 191, 213–14, 225–26
1-2	53	2:23	207		
1:7	29, 53	8:30–35	208		
1:7–8	45	17:28	169		
1:8	53	20	215		
1:9	136, 139	20:28	162, 166–67, 178, 208, 214, 226	3:24–26	149, 164
1:12	29			3:24–31	152
1:13–14	53			3:24a	169
2:6–7	45, 53	*Romans*		3:25	8, 51, 70, 116, 123, 126–29, 131–35, 141, 145–49, 152–53, 157, 178–79, 187, 200–202, 205, 213, 228–29
3:3	48	1–3	123, 137		
3:5	48	1-10	117		
3:17	166	1:1–3:20	140		
		1:4	146		
New Testament		1:5	222		
		1:18	137		
Matthew		1:24–28	174	3:25a	146
5:45	159	1:32	137	3:25b	124, 154
9:13	57	2:5	137	3:26	146–48
11:27	174	2:5–8	94	3:26–28	153
12:7	57	2:6	118	3:26–30	148
20:28	165	2:8	222	3:26a	154
21:13	57	2:26–29	51	3:29	2, 145
23:23	57	2:29	146, 217	3:29–30	152, 228
24	120	3	121, 125, 140, 144, 149, 164	3:29–31	153
24:30	120			3:30–31	146
27:11b	209	3:5	180, 222	4	148, 153, 160
		3:10	188	4:4	144
Mark		3:12	144	4:5	148
1:22	209	3:19	144–45	4:7	144
10:45	165, 181	3:20	188	4:9	148
12:33	57	3:20–22	148	4:12	148
		3:21	143, 145, 150, 154, 157	4:14–18	117
Luke				4:16	147, 228
1:68	165	3:21–25	150	4:16–25	173
2:38	165	3:21–26	145, 152, 123, 157, 160, 221	4:21	140
6:35	159			4:24	140, 160, 228
18:13	136	3:21–29	140, 189	4:25	95, 103, 140, 160–61, 174, 177, 179, 183, 191, 197, 206, 213, 216, 221
21:28	165	3:21–30	203		
22:16–18	215	3:22	140, 147–48, 221, 228		
22:19b–20	214				
22:27	165, 181	3:22–23	157		
22:37	209	3:22–chap. 4	140		
22:70	209	3:23	144, 152	4:25–5:2	216
23:3	209	3:23–25	148	5	117, 151, 153, 170–71, 220
24:21	165	3:24	1, 135, 140, 151–52, 156, 164–65, 206, 212, 215, 224, 226, 228		
				5-8	164, 170, 189
John				5:1	144, 159, 161, 212
13:11	174				
14:26	133				
18:36	209			5:1-2	161

Index of Ancient Texts

5:2	140	6:13	118	8:16	115, 117
5:5	204	6:13a	113	8:17	169–70, 227
5:6	161, 193, 206, 222	6:14	113–14, 172	8:21–22	189
		6:17	222	8:23	6, 162, 170
5:6–8	161, 197	6:17b	221	8:24	159
5:8	4, 193	6:18	221	8:26	159
5:8–9	228	6:22	172	8:26–27	159
5:8–11	101, 190, 221	7	171	8:26–29	117
5:9	4, 159, 161, 170–72, 178, 180, 188, 204, 206, 212–14, 227–28	7–8	153	8:27	171, 191
		7:4	103, 112, 114, 117, 120, 191, 213	8:29	170
				8:32	159, 161, 171–74, 190, 197, 206
		7:4–6	228		
5:9–10	117, 213	7:5	113–14, 171	8:32–34	172, 190, 227
5:10	170–71, 187, 214, 228	7:5–11	218	8:33	178, 224
		7:6	112, 114, 172	8:33–34	159–60
5:12–19	171	7:14	171	8:34	103, 171, 191, 213, 228
5:15–18	215	7:18	111, 171		
5:15–21	117	7:23	171	8:39	159
5:16–19	171	7:24	112, 114, 171, 216	9:4	70, 153
5:17	172			9:8	151
5:18	160	7:24–25	228	9:17	153
5:18–19	140, 221	8	114, 117, 161, 171–72, 191, 220, 227–28	9:22–24	222
5:19	160, 174, 177, 204, 228			9:24	228
				9:25–26	151
5:20	144	8:1	114–15, 159	9:30	228
6	114, 117, 153, 171, 216	8:1–34	174	10:1–10	203
		8:2	117	10:2–3	151
6-7	172	8:2–4	115	10:4	68, 116, 228
6:3	187	8:3	4, 6, 70, 95–96, 111–12, 114–16, 120–21, 157, 161, 169, 172, 178, 183, 186–87, 190–91, 213, 225–28	10:9	148, 161
6:3–4	171			10:9–10	219
6:3–6	117			10:9–12	228
6:3–8	171			10:10	150–51
6:3–19	219			10:12	152
6:4	160, 190			11–14	117
6:4–5	115			11:1	168
6:4–6	213, 228			11:18	117
6:5	112, 117	8:3–4	121	11:23	117
6:5–8	171	8:3–11	115	11:26	151
6:6	72, 111–12, 114, 116, 120–21, 227	8:4	116, 160	11:28–31	168
		8:5–10	115	12	117
		8:7	111, 172	12:1	59, 62, 70, 118, 144, 146, 185
6:6–8	229	8:10	114, 116		
6:6b	111	8:10–11	111, 115, 117	12:1–2	217
6:7-8	172	8:11	115, 159	12:2	146
6:11	117	8:12–14	115	12:4–9	117
6:11–14	228	8:13	112, 114, 116	13:14	117
6:11–23	171	8:13–17	6	14:20	110
6:12	114	8:14	115, 159, 170	14:23	112

Romans (cont'd)

15	215
15:4	69, 229
15:16	51, 161–62, 178
15:31	162

1 Corinthians

1:17	98
1:25	98
1:27	98
1:30	165, 226
2	220
3:13	118
3:16	143
3:16–17	154, 216
4:1	210
4:4	159
4:5	219
4:13	60, 97–98, 120, 186
5:1	116
5:1–8	217
5:1–13	111
5:5	98, 116, 121, 174
5:5–8	98
5:5–9	178
5:6–7	217
5:7	4, 70, 75, 116, 162, 172, 186, 225, 228–29
5:7–8	215
5:8	217–18
6:9–13	112
6:11	162
6:15–19	98
6:15–20	162
6:18–19	112
6:19	51, 154, 216
6:20	5, 94, 98, 102, 166–67, 213, 226
7:14	98, 162
7:23	5, 94, 98, 166–67, 178, 213, 215, 226
7:24	215
8:6	151, 209
8:11	98, 193, 197, 206
9:10	229
9:13	186
10	151
10:1–21	219
10:2	3
10:4	3, 116
10:6	3, 229
10:11	68
10:16	72, 190
11:2	174
11:23	174
11:25	8, 71, 225, 228
11:25b	71
11:26	169
11:29–30	187
15	151
15:3	98, 174, 197, 206, 209
15:3b	186
15:4	103
15:20	162, 190
16:15	162, 186

2 Corinthians

2:15	162, 186
3:3	146
3:6	101, 146
3:6–9	63
3:7–11	69
3:10	2, 188
3:11	188, 229
3:14	69
4:4–11	27
4:11	177
5	220
5:10–12	218
5:12	146
5:14	98, 101, 206
5:14–15	98–99, 197
5:15	103
5:15–21	187
5:17	4, 9, 160, 206, 213
5:17–18	99
5:18	100, 206
5:18–20	100
5:19	99–100, 191
5:20	99, 206
5:21	4–5, 91, 95, 98, 100, 111, 116, 120, 157, 159–60, 174, 179, 186, 191, 206, 212–13, 215, 224–25, 227
6:16	143, 154
7:1	162
9:8	160
10:4	217

Galatians

1:4	27, 107, 197, 206
2:20	169, 197, 206
3	104–5, 111, 220, 228
3:1	109, 141
3:5	148
3:7	103
3:10	103–5
3:11	159
3:11–14	95
3:13	4–5, 98, 100–105, 107–8, 111, 116, 119–21, 166–67, 178, 186, 190–91, 197, 213, 225–27
3:13–14	103, 173, 215
3:13a	119
3:13b	104–5, 119
3:13c	119
3:14	71, 110
3:16	103, 116, 189
3:19	189
3:21	159
3:25	9
3:26	159, 170
3:27	159
3:29	103, 169
4	170
4:4	106–7
4:5	103, 166, 170, 226
4:6	106

Index of Ancient Texts

4:24	69
4:25	70, 152
4:26	70, 146
4:27	151
4:29	70
5:16	112
5:17	111
5:21	109
5:23	210
5:24	112
6:2	190
6:15	213

Ephesians

1:7	165
1:14	165
2:13–15	71
4:30	165

Philippians

1:12–30	207
2:6–8	197
2:7	183
2:14–17	219
2:15	162
2:17	50, 60, 162, 178, 186
3:3	51
3:9	146
3:10	112
3:10–11	227
4:18	162

Colossians

1:14	165, 226

1 Thessalonians

1:5	146
1:10	180, 188, 204, 222
2:1–8	109
2:2–4	27
2:12–16	218
2:14–18	27
3:4	27
5:10	193, 197, 206
5:23	162

1 Timothy

1:10	171
2:11	171
4:6	171

2 Timothy

1:13	171
2:23	171
3:15	146
4:3	171

Titus

1:9	171
2:1–9	171
2:14	165

Hebrews

1:7	133
9:12	165
9:15	165
11:17	173

James

2:21	173

1 Peter

1:18–19	167, 188
2:21–24	175

2 Peter

2:1	167

1 John

2:2	187

Revelation

4:11	15
5:9	166–67
5:9–10	166
5:10	166

Apocrypha

Tobit

5:19	97

Judith

16:16	58
16:19–20	58

1 Maccabees

1:18	203
2:37	199

2 Maccabees

2:10	31
2:16–19	203
6–7	96
6:12	198
6:14–15	198
6:18–7:41	8
6:28	198
6:30	198
7:9	8
7:14	8
7:24	165
7:32	197
7:33	198, 203
7:36	8
7:37	198, 205, 208
7:38	198
7:40	205
8:3	205
10:3–7	203
14:36	203
14:37ff	199

Wisdom

1:15–3:10	8
2	8
2:12–20	177
5:1–7	177

Sirach

7:9	58
34:20	161
35:1–2	50
35:7 [=35:5 RSV]	12
45:15–24	51

Pseudepigrapha

Aristeas

234	53

1 Enoch

47:1	199

2 Enoch

45:3	49

Jubilees		Psalms of Solomon		Her.	
1:27–29	149	1:8	57	166	126
4:24–26	149	3:8	57		
		8:12	57	Leg.	
Liber Antiq. Biblicarum		9:6	57	3.135	161
(Pseudo-Philo)		10:2	199		
18.5	172			Migr.	
32.3–4	172	Sibylline Oracles		2.7	68
		4:27-30	57	2.10	68
4 Maccabees				16.92	113
1:11	50, 203	Testament of Benjamin			
4:23	194	3:8	177	Mos. (= Vit. Mos.)	
5:33	194			2.94	126
6:10	206	Testament of Levi		2.95	126
6:22	196	3:6	59	2.97	126
6:27	196, 203	30:14	49	2.108	58
6:27–29	8	31:14	49		
6:28	138, 205			Spec. Leg.	
6:28–29	202	Testament of Moses		1.96	49
6:29	50, 202–3, 207	9:7	199	1.166ff	58
6:30	196, 206			1.188	76
7:10	200	**Dead Sea Scrolls**			
8:4	165			Virt.	
8:7	194	*1QS*		74	161
8:15	203	3.10–11	59		
9:1	194	8.3–6	218	**Josephus**	
9:30	203	8.10	59		
11:14	196	9.3–6	59	Ag. Ap.	
13:6–7	200			2.193–98	11
13:8	200	*11Q19 (=Temple Scroll)*			
13:9	196	26–27	89	Ant.	
14:5	206	29.8-10	149	3.135	127
15:32	200	29.9	149	3.137	127
16:16	194			3.180	49
17	201	*CD (=Damascus*		3.202	45
17:2	205	*Document)*		3.203	45
17:10	194	4.1–3	59	3.207	45
17:11–16	206			3.209–10	45
17:16	200	**Philo**		3.215	45
17:20–22	8			20.166	45
17:21	203	Cher.			
17:21–22	50, 202, 205	25	126	J.W.	
17:22	131, 200,	100	49	5.459	45
	203–4, 206–7			6.99	13
18:2	203	Det.			
18:3–4	8	21	58	**Rabbinic Literature**	
18:4	203				
		Fug.		'Abot de Rabbi Nathan	
		100	133	9b	50
		100–101	126		

Num. Rabbah
19   12

Pesiq. Rab. Kah.
4,7   12

m. Yoma
3:8   89
4:2   89
6:1–8   89
6:4   83, 103
6:4ff   88
6:8   88

m. Shebuoth
1:6   89
1:7   89

Sifra
181.2.9   89

Tg. Isa.
53:5   149

Christian Literature

AMBROSE
Letter 14,
extra collection
(63).104 185

BARNABAS
7   91
7:3   119
7:7   103, 119
7:7–9   24, 83
7:7–10   119
7:9   103
16:2   59

DIDACHE
9–10   215
16:5   120
16:6   120

HELLADIOS
5   74

HUGH OF ST. VICTOR
De Sacramentis
1.8.7   181

IGNATIUS OF ANTIOCH
Ephesians
21:1   202

To Polycarp
2:3   202

Smyrnaeans
10:2   202

JOHN CHYSOSTOM
Baptismal Instructions
3.14   184

JOHN TZETZES
Chiliades
729–31   96

JUSTIN MARTYR
Dial. Try.
111.2   119

PHOTIUS
Bibliotheque
534a   74, 80–81

PROTEVANGELION OF JAMES
6   106

PSEUDO-CLEMENT
Recognitions
1:37   59

RICHARD OF ST. VICTOR
De Verbo Incarnato
(PG 1005) 181

TERTULLIAN
Adv. Jud.
14.9   83

Adv. Marc.
3.7.7   83, 120, 184

TESTAMENT OF OUR LORD JESUS IN GALILEE
7   59
8   59

Greek Papyri and Inscriptions

Cos 81   130
Cos 347   130
Fayûm 337 129

Cynic Epistles

CRATES
29.10–11 109

HERACLITUS
9.32–35   109

Greek Literature

AESCHYLUS
Ag.
236   106

APOLLODORUS
Bibliotheca
1.9.1   65

ARISTOTLE
Rhetoric
1401b   156

CORPUS HERMETICUM
1.3.1   58, 185
12.23   58, 185
13.18   58
13.18–23 185
13.19   58
13.21ff   58

DIO CHRYSOSTOM
Or. 11 (Troj.)
121–24   130

EURIPIDES
Herc. fur.
1345 51

Iph. aul.
1379 195
1397 195
1553–55 195

Iph. taur.
389–99 48

Med.
608 106

Phoen.
913–14 195
997–98 195
1090 195

HIPPONAX
fr. 4 81

HOMER
Iliad
IX.497–500 15

LUCIAN
Sacr.
1–2 13

PAUSANIAS
3.16.10–17 65
9.8.2 47

PINDAR
Frag.
78 196

PLATO
Apology
28B–D 195
29B 195

Alcibiades
II 149E 52

Crito
49C–50A 195

50B–51E 195
52D 195

Laws
10.885C 13, 52
10.862C 136
10.909B 52
10.910D 52
10.948C 52
12.955E 52

SOPHOCLES
Oed. tyr.
246–54 106
1290–93 102
1291 106

Vedic and Hindu Scriptures

Aitareya Brâhmaṇa
2.8–9 65

Bṛhad-Araṇyaka Upanishad
1.4.17 49

Mahabharata
Parvan section 26

Mandaka Upanishad
1.2.2 51

Manusmṛti
6.25 49
6.38 49

Rg veda
1:64:50 14
10:90:16 14

Satapatha Brâhmaṇa
3.9.1.8 14
6.2.1.1 65

Chinese Scriptures

Li Ki (Book of Rites)
22.1 49

www.ingramcontent.com/pod-product-compliance
Lightning Source LLC
Chambersburg PA
CBHW020644300426
44112CB00007B/231